THE SELECTED POETRY OF ROBINSON JEFFERS

Robinson and Una Jeffers. Photograph by Horace Lyon, 1937. Courtesy of Peter Lyon.

THE SELECTED POETRY OF
Robinson Jeffers

Edited by Tim Hunt

STANFORD UNIVERSITY PRESS 2001
Stanford, California

Printed in the United States of America
Library of Congress Cataloging-in-Publication Data
    Jeffers, Robinson, 1887–1962.
    [Poems. Selections]
    The selected poetry of Robinson Jeffers / edited by Tim Hunt.
        p.   cm.
    Includes index.
    ISBN 0-8047-3890-4 (acid-free paper) — ISBN 0-8047-4108-5 (pbk. : acid-free paper)
        I. Hunt, Tim, 1949–   II. Title.
    PS3519.E27 A6 2001
    811'.52—dc21   00-048490

This book is printed on acid-free, archival-quality paper.
Original printing 2001
Last figure below indicates the year of this printing:
10   09   08   07   06   05   04   03   02   01

CONTENTS

Introduction   1

TAMAR
1917-23

To His Father   15
Suicide's Stone   16
Divinely Superfluous Beauty   17
The Excesses of God   17
To the Stone-Cutters   18
To the House   18
Salmon Fishing   19
Natural Music   19
Wise Men in Their Bad Hours   20
To the Rock That Will Be a Cornerstone of the House   21
The Cycle   22
Shine, Perishing Republic   23
Continent's End   24
Tamar   26
Point Joe   98
Gale in April   99
The Treasure   100

ROAN STALLION
1924-25

Birds   103

Fog   104

Boats in a Fog   105

People and a Heron   106

Night   107

Autumn Evening   110

Joy   110

Phenomena   111

from The Tower Beyond Tragedy (final scene)   112

Roan Stallion   115

THE WOMEN AT POINT SUR
1925-26

Post Mortem   137

Clouds at Evening   139

Pelicans   140

Apology for Bad Dreams   141

Love-Children   145

Credo   147

Prelude   148

CAWDOR
1926-28

Birth-Dues   159
The Broken Balance   160
Hurt Hawks   165
Bixby's Landing   167
An Artist   168
The Machine   171
Meditation on Saviors   172
A Redeemer   178
Tor House   181
Cawdor   182

DEAR JUDAS
1928-29

Hooded Night   297
Evening Ebb   298
Hands   298
The Loving Shepherdess   299
from Descent to the Dead   361
    Shane O'Neill's Cairn   361
    Ossian's Grave   362
    The Broadstone   365

In the Hill at Newgrange   366
Ghosts in England   370
Inscription for a Gravestone   372
Subjected Earth   373
Notes to "Descent to the Dead"   375
The Bed by the Window   376
Winged Rock   376

THURSO'S LANDING
1930-31

The Place for No Story   379
New Mexican Mountain   380
November Surf   381
Margrave   382
Fire on the Hills   394

GIVE YOUR HEART TO THE HAWKS
1931-33

A Little Scraping   397
Triad   398
Still the Mind Smiles   399
Give Your Heart to the Hawks   400

SOLSTICE
1933-35

Return   499
Love the Wild Swan   500
The Cruel Falcon   501
Distant Rainfall   501
Rock and Hawk   502
Shine, Republic   503
Sign-Post   504
Flight of Swans   505
from At the Birth of an Age (vision of the self-hanged God)   506
Gray Weather   508
Red Mountain   509

SUCH COUNSELS YOU GAVE TO ME
1935-38

Rearmament   513
The Purse-Seine   514
The Wind-Struck Music   516
Memoir   518
Nova   520
The Answer   522
The Beaks of Eagles   523

All the Little Hoof-Prints   524
Contemplation of the Sword   527
Oh Lovely Rock   529
October Week-End   531
Steelhead, Wild Pig, The Fungus   532
Night without Sleep   541
Self-Criticism in February   543
Shiva   544
Now Returned Home   545
Theory of Truth   547

BE ANGRY AT THE SUN
1938-41

Faith   553
Come Little Birds   554
The House-Dog's Grave   559
Prescription of Painful Ends   561
The Day Is a Poem   562
The Bloody Sire   563
The Stars Go over the Lonely Ocean   564
For Una   565
Drunken Charlie   568

THE DOUBLE AXE
1942-47

Pearl Harbor   577
Advice to Pilgrims   579
Cassandra   579
Historical Choice   580
Calm and Full the Ocean   581
The Blood-Guilt   582
Invasion   583
Original Sin   585
Orca   587
The Inquisitors   589
Quia Absurdum   591
The Inhumanist (Part II of *The Double Axe*)   592

HUNGERFIELD
1948-53

Animals   651
The Beauty of Things   652
Hungerfield   653
Carmel Point   676
De Rerum Virtute   677
The Deer Lay Down Their Bones   680

LAST POEMS
1953-62

The Shears   685
Patronymic   686
Birds and Fishes   687
Let Them Alone   688
"The unformed volcanic earth"   689
The Ocean's Tribute   694
On an Anthology of Chinese Poems   695
"The mathematicians and physics men"   696
Vulture   697
Granddaughter   698
The Epic Stars   699
"Goethe, they say, was a great poet"   700
Hand   701
Oysters   702
"It nearly cancels my fear of death"   704

PROSE

Preface, *Tamar* (1923)   707
Introduction, *Roan Stallion, Tamar and Other Poems* (1935)   710
Foreword, *The Selected Poetry of Robinson Jeffers* (1938)   713

Preface, *The Double Axe and Other Poems* (original version, 1947)   719
Poetry, Gongorism, and a Thousand Years (1948)   723

UNPUBLISHED POEMS

Aesthetics (1910)   731
The Palace (1914)   733
May 5, 1915 (1915)   735
Oblation/Testament (1918)   737
The Shore of Dreams (1919?)   738
The Hills Beyond the River (1919)   739
Doors to Peace (mid-1920s)   740
Forecast (1925)   742
Not a Laurel on the Place (1926)   743
Ninth Anniversary (1928)   744
Oct. 27 Lunar Eclipse — 98% (On the Calendar) (1939)   745
Tragedy Has Obligations (1943)   746
Rhythm and Rhyme (1949)   747

Index of Titles   749
Index of First Lines   752

THE SELECTED POETRY OF ROBINSON JEFFERS

INTRODUCTION

In 1938 Random House published *The Selected Poetry of Robinson Jeffers*, a six-hundred-page volume that would remain in print for more than fifty years. Over time, it lost some of its grandeur: the publisher dropped the frontispiece photograph, reduced the trim size, and shifted to cheaper materials; the type began to show the wear of the many reprintings. Yet until it finally went out of print, it stood as a broad-spined presence among the slimmer poetic reeds on library and bookstore shelves and drew enough poets, students, and general readers to keep Jeffers a force in American poetry, in spite of the almost total academic neglect that followed his fame in the 1920's and 1930's. Now scholars are at last beginning to recognize that he created a significant alternative to the High Modernism of Pound, Eliot, and Stevens. Similarly, contemporary poets who have returned to the narrative poem acknowledge Jeffers, along with Frost and E. A. Robinson, as a major poet, while those exploring California and the American West as literary regions have discovered in him a foundational figure. Moreover, Jeffers stands as a crucial precursor to contemporary attempts to rethink our practical, ethical, and spiritual obligations to the natural world and the environment.

These developments underscore the need for a new selected edition that would, like the 1938 volume, include the long narratives that Jeffers considered his major work along with the more easily anthologized shorter poems. This new selected poetry differs from its predecessor in several ways. When Jeffers shaped the 1938 *Selected Poetry*, he drew from his most productive period (1917–37), but his career was not yet over. In the quarter century that followed, he wrote *Be Angry at the Sun* (1941), *The Double Axe* (1948), *Hungerfield* (1954), and the poems included in the posthumous collection *The Beginning and the End* (1963). This new selected edition draws from these later volumes and includes as well a sampling of the poems Jeffers left unpublished, along with several prose pieces in which he reflects on his poetry and poetics.

This edition adopts the texts of the recently completed *The Collected Poetry of Robinson Jeffers* (5 vols., Stanford University Press). When the poems were originally published, copy editors and typesetters frequently adjusted Jeffers' idiosyncratic punctuation to make his lines more conventionally "correct." This added layer of punctuation often obscures the rhythm and pacing of what Jeffers actually wrote, and at points even obscures meaning and nuance. (Volume 5 of *The Collected Poetry* includes a fuller discussion of these issues, with illustrative examples.)

This new selected edition, then, is meant to be a broader, more accurate representation of Jeffers' career than the 1938 *Selected Poetry*. It is a somewhat less comprehensive record of the period covered by the original selected edition, however, since several of the longer poems included there (*Thurso's Landing*, for instance) had to be set aside to make room for the later poems (among them the narratives *The Inhumanist* and *Hungerfield*) and other work.

◆ ◆ ◆

Jeffers' early years were dominated by his father, a Presbyterian minister and professor of Old Testament literature. Dr. William Hamilton Jeffers was a 46-year-old widower when he married Annie Robinson Tuttle, a church organist 22 years his junior. John Robinson Jeffers was born in Pittsburgh a year and a half later, on January 10, 1887. His only sibling, Hamilton, who became a research astronomer, was born in 1894. Jeffers' father introduced him to Latin, Greek, and the Bible early on, and his first ten years were a succession of houses and schools as the elder Jeffers searched for the right combination of seclusion for himself and intellectual rigor for his son. In 1898 Jeffers entered the first of five Swiss boarding schools he would attend, and four years later, when he entered the University of Pittsburgh, he already had a command of French, German, Greek, and Latin to go with his newest enthusiasms — poetry and Dante Gabriel Rossetti. After his first year at Pittsburgh the family moved to Los Angeles. From 1903 to 1910 Jeffers completed his formal education: earning his B.A. from Occidental College, continuing his studies in literature and languages at the University of Southern California and the University of Zurich, trying out medicine at the University of Southern California and forestry at the University of Washington.

These years were also complicated by Jeffers' relationship with Una Call Kuster, the wife of a prominent Los Angeles lawyer. She and Jeffers met at the University of Southern California, where she was also a student, in 1905. Their friendship evolved into a romantic liaison, eventual scandal, and Una's decision to divorce her husband and marry Jeffers. They were married on August 2, 1913, and settled first in the Los Angeles area. Their daughter, Maeve, was born May 5, 1914, but survived only a day. The Jefferses had been planning to move to England after the birth of their child, but the war in Europe led them to rethink their plans. In September 1914 they moved instead to Carmel, California, already something of an artists' colony, where they lived the rest of their lives. Una Jeffers died on September 1, 1950; and Robinson Jeffers on January 20, 1962.

Jeffers matured somewhat late as a poet. When he moved to Carmel in 1914, he had only the minor work gathered in the privately published *Flagons and Apples* (1912) and two dozen poems from his college years to show for his efforts, while such near contemporaries as Pound and Eliot were already writing important pieces. In the Introduction to the Modern Library reissue of *Roan Stallion, Tamar and Other Poems* (1935), Jeffers recalls that he was then still "imitating Shelley and Milton" and lacked the "originality, without which a writer of verses is only a verse-writer." Worse, he recognized that the early Modernists were already doing original work, but he believed they "had turned off the road into a narrowing lane" that would eventually reduce poetry to a kind of virtuoso triviality. He could not, he decided, accept their assumptions or adopt their innovations. He could not, as he put it, become a "modern." It took him until the early 1920's to develop his own voice, measure, and understanding of poetry. The impact of the Big Sur coast was one element, as he noted in the Foreword to the 1938 *Selected Poetry*, and the landscape's epic scale and the isolated lives of its ranching folk became his distinctive material. His transformations of this material were shaped variously by his scientific training, his Calvinist heritage, the initial explorations of Freud and Jung into the mechanisms of consciousness and dreams, the work of Sir James Frazer and the Cambridge anthropologists on myth and ritual, and a conviction (influenced by both the Egyptologist Flinders Petrie and the deep cultural and historical tragedy of the First World War) that history was cyclical and that Western civilization was poised for an inevitable slide into decadence and barbarism. Jeffers first attempted to express the Big Sur region in the narrative poems gathered in the transitional collection *Californians* (Macmillan, 1916).

Wordsworth's *Lyrical Ballads* was probably one model for these first narratives, as were, perhaps, E. A. Robinson's treatment of region and contemporary life in his brief narratives and Edgar Lee Masters' *Spoon River Anthology*. By the time Jeffers published *Tamar and Other Poems* in 1924, his approach in both shorter poems and narratives had been transformed by the trauma of the war. It had also been steadied by a deeper commitment to place. Shortly after the Armistice the Jefferses purchased a headland on the south edge of Carmel and in 1919 built a low stone cottage from the granite about the site. Working with the masons, Jeffers discovered his other lifework — building with stone. Soon after he and Una settled in Tor House with their twin sons (born in 1916), Jeffers began a two-and-a-half-story stone tower, a six-year project. Typically, he wrote in the mornings and devoted the afternoons to work with stone and to caring for the groves of trees he soon planted.

It took reviewers nearly a year to discover the privately printed *Tamar*, but when they did, they likened the sweep and intensity of Jeffers' narrative vision to Shakespeare and the Greek tragedians, and they found his voice in the shorter meditations and lyrics both timeless and contemporary. When Boni & Liveright reissued *Tamar* in an expanded edition as *Roan Stallion, Tamar and Other Poems* in November 1925, Jeffers quickly became a major figure in the poetic landscape, a peer to Frost and Eliot. Enthusiastic reviews, helped along by the narratives' use of incest and other sexually taboo themes, made Jeffers a popular success as well. His reputation remained high throughout the 1920's and 1930's (even though his most ambitious work, *The Women at Point Sur*, published in 1927, elicited dismay and bewilderment) and was capped by a *Time* cover story in 1932 and *The Selected Poetry* in 1938.

The crisis of the First World War was an important factor in developing Jeffers' voice as a poet and an impetus for much of his work in the 1920's, even though it was seldom invoked explicitly. (See the discussions of the poems of this period in Volume 5 of *The Collected Poetry*.) The Second World War was similarly an imaginative crisis for Jeffers, one that threatened the aesthetic and the views he had advanced and explored through the mid-1930's. The poems in *Be Angry at the Sun* (1941) reflect his concern with history and a growing dismay at national and international affairs, while the poems written during the war — collected in *The Double Axe* (1948) — show this dismay deepening to the point of despair. At one point Jeffers labeled the short poems in *The Double Axe* "Mornings in Hell," and the first of the book's two narratives — *The Love and the Hate* — has a young soldier will his decomposing body back to life to seek revenge on his father for involving him in the war. Both of the narratives underscore the intensity of Jeffers' reaction to the war

The Double Axe was one factor in the eclipse of Jeffers' reputation. His isolationist politics and criticisms of Roosevelt (who he thought had let personal ambition cloud his judgment) were unacceptable to an America that had won the war against Germany and Japan, only to be thrust into the Cold War. That in *The Inhumanist*, the second *Double Axe* narrative, Jeffers moves beyond his despair, engages the nuclear threat, and reconfirms the perspective he now termed "Inhumanism" made little difference, nor did the critical and commercial success of the New York production of Jeffers' adaptation of *Medea*, produced in fall 1947 and starring Judith Anderson as Medea. Even though *Hungerfield* (1954) featured Jeffers at his most personal and elegiac and won several awards, it did little to reverse the decline of his reputation, in part because the poetic canon was increasingly defined and enforced by the academy, where the critical sons and daughters of the New Critics were establishing norms for poetry that privileged compressed, complex, short poems — well-wrought urns in which the poet maintains an ironic distance from both the text and reader. This perspective offered little room to appreciate Jeffers' reinvention of the poetic narrative as a modern form, his discursive poetic meditations, or his intentionally nonironic celebrations of a redemptively beautiful nature. In "The Ocean's Tribute," a late poem included in this selection, Jeffers seems quite aware of New Critical fashion and as determined to go his own way as he was in 1914 "not to become a 'modern.'"

· · ·

Jeffers based his approach to poetry on a few basic principles. He explained these variously in the introductory notes he wrote for some of the collections, perhaps most directly in the Preface he wrote (but did not use) for *Tamar*. There he asserts that "poetry's function" is "the passionate presentment of beauty." It is to be an "intensification" of life, not a "refuge" from it. To do this it must, he believed, "be rhythmic, and must deal with permanent things, and must avoid affectation." Where the Modernists valued the imagination's power to transform (and transcend) perception, Jeffers sought to intensify perception and thereby deepen our awareness of and participation in the natural world.

The revisions to "Salmon Fishing," a lyric Jeffers wrote soon after first developing his mature aesthetic, illustrate his approach. The poem exists in three drafts: two preliminary typescripts and the version published in *Tamar*. In the earlier of the typescripts the fishermen are "anglers / On the rocks," who "torture" the fish. Framed against the "Red ash" of the solstice "sundown," they intrude violence and death into an otherwise beautiful and energized nature (a nature that even speaks: "The southwind shouts to the rivers"). As Jeffers revised the poem, he shifted to a more complex equation. In the second typescript the anglers are "Like dark herons, like priestlings / Of a most patient mystery, at the river mouth." Recasting the fishermen as "herons" integrates them into the natural scene. They are of nature, not outside and in opposition to it, and in ritualizing them as "priestlings" within nature, Jeffers projects a world where salmon and anglers are both enmeshed in a sacrificial landscape of fire and blood. This sacrificial unfolding is itself nature and a feature of its transformative beauty, with the "Red of the dark solstice" now fully a figure for this and not simply a backdrop. For publication in *Tamar* Jeffers further refined the shifts he introduced in the second typescript. (The entry for "Salmon Fishing" in Volume 5 of *The Collected Poetry* provides a complete record of the drafts and revisions.)

The various revisions to "Salmon Fishing" point to Jeffers' determination to engage the world as it is in its physicality and to represent it in clear, accessible language. Yet the revisions also point — linguistically, perceptually, and conceptually — to the subtlety and resonance in what might seem at a casual glance to be simply scene painting. They reflect the approach to nature and consciousness that threads throughout his mature work, which he was developing in the early 1920's as he wrote and revised such pieces as "Salmon Fishing" and "Natural Music." For Jeffers the pain of nature is its flux, yet this constant alternation of death and renewal — nature's sacrificial essence — is also its beauty: the beauty of the whole, in which anglers, spawning salmon, and contemplating poets are participating parts. The challenge is to see and identify with the whole. Human consciousness allows this, as the speaker in "Salmon Fishing" demonstrates. Yet consciousness can also alienate us from the whole and its processes. In "Salmon Fishing" the anglers seem oblivious to the scene's ritual dynamic and its beauty, while the speaker appears to recognize these things because he stands apart from the ritual that anglers, fish, river, and sundown enact without consciousness. To Jeffers this is both the value of consciousness and its danger or dilemma. It enables transcendent awareness, yet this awareness can easily decay into an evasion of nature's full reality — its intertwined dynamic of painful change and redemptive beauty — if, whether as speaker or reader, one simply contemplates nature's flux rather than identifying with it and recognizing one's final and inevitable participation in it.

Poems like "Salmon Fishing" can be read as celebrations of, and meditations on, consciousness and its relationship to nature. The shorter poems are also often meditations on the problematic relationship of consciousness to culture and society — constructions that consciousness supports but that often obscure our relationship to nature's fundamental dynamic (including our individual and collective mortality) and that can place us in a destructive relationship to it, to ourselves, and to each other. The call to personal integrity in the face of cultural decadence in "Shine, Perishing Republic" is a clear instance of this. "Invasion," a Second World War poem, is another, perhaps less obvious example. In it Jeffers attempts to make sense of (and accept) the war's violence by projecting it and the social and historical patterns that generate it as natural forces: if history is a form of nature and nature is a process that can be read historically, then history and politics, like the scene of ritual sacrifice in "Salmon Fishing," might also become realms of experience and transcendence, and occasions for consciousness. In a quite different way, the late poem "Granddaughter" participates in this project, covertly contrasting the way the poet relates to the portrait of his granddaughter with the way the duke relates to the portrait of his last duchess in the most famous of Browning's dramatic monologues, in order to underscore the generative vitality of the granddaughter's relationship to nature and life in contrast to the duke's elegant, morbid rejection of vitality and spontaneity.

Perhaps most importantly the revisions to "Salmon Fishing" can help us see that Jeffers was, at root, a visionary poet. This is explicit in "Doors to Peace," which may be why Jeffers never published it. The early, unpublished lyric "The Hills Beyond the River" points to the basis of the visionary impulse (though presenting it more optimistically than he would probably have expressed it). But moments of heightened awareness of the natural world and our place in it are found throughout his work. The complex participation in, yet transcendence of time that closes "Oh Lovely Rock" is such a moment, and the anticipated "enskyment" in "Vulture" is perhaps the wish for such a moment. This visionary dynamic is even present in such poems as "Invasion," where the sometimes didactic wrestlings with history and politics alternately follow from and reach toward transformational moments of consciousness. Above all, the visionary dynamic is to be found in the narratives that Jeffers wrote following the formulation of his mature voice in the early

1920's. In them he sought—through the violations enacted by the characters he projected—to create poems that both participate in the flux of nature and reach moments of intense, redemptive consciousness. We see this at its most apocalyptic in the first mature narrative, *Tamar*. The short narrative *Prelude*, used to introduce *The Women at Point Sur*, underscores Jeffers' immersion in his narrative creations. *Roan Stallion* is narrative Jeffers at his most austere; *The Inhumanist*, at his most philosophical; and *Hungerfield*, at his most lyric and elegiac.

What needs most simply to be stressed is that—for all his lyric flights, narrative probings, historical pronouncements, and excoriations of human solipsism in all its individual and collective forms—Jeffers believed poetry should bring us to reality rather than transform or replace it. Poetry's task, he said, was to engage "permanent things" and reveal the permanence beyond the poem. This may be why his work continues to speak to readers who sense that our technological environment places us in a false relationship to space, time, and the physical world and why it continues to speak to those who sense that the social and cultural "reality" the mass media offers is, finally, insufficient and alienating.

◆　◆　◆

I would like to thank the readers of Jeffers who offered advice on which poems to include. In all some thirty friends and colleagues, both academic readers and general readers, shared their ideas on what should constitute the Jeffers canon. I have used these recommendations and Jeffers' own choices in the 1938 *Selected Poetry* as guides in shaping this volume. Although a few pieces—"Boats in a Fog" and *Roan Stallion*, for instance—were on every list, using all the poems nominated would have required a volume twice this size, and some suggestions had to be set aside. Thus, every veteran Jeffers reader will find a poem or two she or he would have dropped to make room for a missing favorite. My own regret is the omission of *Thurso's Landing*. There was room for it or *Give Your Heart to the Hawks*, not both. Several colleagues argued that *Thurso's Landing* resembles *Cawdor* and that including *Give Your Heart* would broaden the portrait of the career more than *Thurso's Landing* would.

Others may lament the absence of *The Women at Point Sur*. In the Foreword to the 1938 *Selected Poetry* Jeffers commented: "*The Women at Point Sur* seems to me — in spite of grave faults — the most inclusive, and poetically the most intense of any of my poems; it is omitted from this selection because it is the least understood and the least liked, and because it is the longest." It is omitted from the current selection for the same reasons. It is, I would argue, Jeffers' most ambitious, complex, and difficult narrative. For readers who become serious students of his work, *Point Sur* is the daunting peak that has to be climbed. But including it in this collection would have required setting aside too many other poems that most people would choose to read and study first. Similarly, Part I of *The Double Axe*, *The Love and the Hate*, is not included. This most despairing and horrific of the narratives is an important part of the record of Jeffers' response to the Second World War, but it, too, is perhaps mostly for readers whose interests extend beyond the inevitable limitations of the present volume. Part II of *The Double Axe*, *The Inhumanist*, is included, however; these reflections of the old caretaker offer both Jeffers' most sustained meditation on his Inhumanist perspective and his reflections on the emerging Cold War. The verse dramas *The Tower Beyond Tragedy* and *At the Birth of an Age* are each represented by excerpts. Jeffers included the entire texts in the 1938 *Selected Poetry*, but for reasons of space the excerpts he used in the script for his 1941 reading tour (printed in 1954 as the pamphlet *Themes in My Poems*) have been chosen for this edition. Space was also a factor in the decision to excerpt *Descent to the Dead* rather than present the sequence in its entirety.

In choosing the poems for this volume, then, the goal has been to select not only the best work (although because of their length it was not possible to include all of the best narratives) but also to choose the most representative poems and those that can add significantly to an understanding of Jeffers (such as "Credo," which Jeffers did not include in the 1938 *Selected Poetry*, as well as the baker's dozen of unpublished poems I have included). In a few cases, academic and general readers have different views of certain poems. General readers, for instance, often admire "The House-Dog's Grave," while academic readers tend to find it a weaker piece. This selection will, I hope, serve both of these audiences. I should probably confess that I have also allowed myself an idiosyncratic choice or two, perhaps most obviously the mid-1930's lyric "Memoir," which offers a glimpse of the Jeffers behind the austere, at times aloof voice of his most famous short poems and can thereby (I suggest) complicate and deepen our appreciation of these better-known poems. Still, in spite of an instance or two of such special pleading, the goal has been to shape a selection that will offer new readers of Jeffers a balanced portrait of the career and convenient access to his most appealing and compelling work, while also providing students and researchers with a broad and deep enough selection to support serious investigation.

◆   ◆   ◆

In closing I would like to express my appreciation for the support, cooperation, and many courtesies extended to me in my work by the late Mrs. Donnan Jeffers and the late Garth Jeffers. And I would like to acknowledge the debt that readers of Jeffers owe to Stanford University Press, especially to Helen Tartar, who has guided the press's various Jeffers projects and helped make it possible for Jeffers' work — his voice, vision, meditations, and indictments — to provoke and sometimes comfort readers of this new millennium.

Tamar

1917-23

TO HIS FATHER

Christ was your lord and captain all your life,
He fails the world but you he did not fail,
He led you through all forms of grief and strife
Intact, a man full-armed, he let prevail
Nor outward malice nor the worse-fanged snake
That coils in one's own brain against your calm,
That great rich jewel well guarded for his sake
With coronal age and death like quieting balm.
I Father having followed other guides
And oftener to my hurt no leader at all,
Through years nailed up like dripping panther hides
For trophies on a savage temple wall
Hardly anticipate that reverend stage
Of life, the snow-wreathed honor of extreme age.

SUICIDE'S STONE

Peace is the heir of dead desire,
Whether abundance killed the cormorant
In a happy hour, or sleep or death
Drowned him deep in dreamy waters,
Peace is the ashes of that fire,
The heir of that king, the inn of that journey.

This last and best and goal: we dead
Hold it so tight you are envious of us
And fear under sunk lids contempt.
Death-day greetings are the sweetest.
Let trumpets roar when a man dies
And rockets fly up, he has found his fortune.

Yet hungering long and pitiably
That way, you shall not reach a finger
To pluck it unripe and before dark
Creep to cover: life broke ten whipstocks
Over my back, broke faith, stole hope,
Before I denounced the covenant of courage.

DIVINELY SUPERFLUOUS BEAUTY

The storm-dances of gulls, the barking game of seals,
Over and under the ocean . . .
Divinely superfluous beauty
Rules the games, presides over destinies, makes trees grow
And hills tower, waves fall.
The incredible beauty of joy
Stars with fire the joining of lips, O let our loves too
Be joined, there is not a maiden
Burns and thirsts for love
More than my blood for you, by the shore of seals while the wings
Weave like a web in the air
Divinely superfluous beauty.

THE EXCESSES OF GOD

Is it not by his high superfluousness we know
Our God? For to equal a need
Is natural, animal, mineral: but to fling
Rainbows over the rain
And beauty above the moon, and secret rainbows
On the domes of deep sea-shells,
And make the necessary embrace of breeding
Beautiful also as fire,
Not even the weeds to multiply without blossom
Nor the birds without music:
There is the great humaneness at the heart of things,
The extravagant kindness, the fountain
Humanity can understand, and would flow likewise
If power and desire were perch-mates.

TO THE STONE-CUTTERS

Stone-cutters fighting time with marble, you foredefeated
Challengers of oblivion
Eat cynical earnings, knowing rock splits, records fall down,
The square-limbed Roman letters
Scale in the thaws, wear in the rain. The poet as well
Builds his monument mockingly;
For man will be blotted out, the blithe earth die, the brave sun
Die blind and blacken to the heart:
Yet stones have stood for a thousand years, and pained thoughts found
The honey of peace in old poems.

TO THE HOUSE

I am heaping the bones of the old mother
To build us a hold against the host of the air;
Granite the blood-heat of her youth
Held molten in hot darkness against the heart
Hardened to temper under the feet
Of the ocean cavalry that are maned with snow
And march from the remotest west.
This is the primitive rock, here in the wet
Quarry under the shadow of waves
Whose hollows mouthed the dawn; little house each stone
Baptized from that abysmal font
The sea and the secret earth gave bonds to affirm you.

SALMON FISHING

The days shorten, the south blows wide for showers now,
The south wind shouts to the rivers,
The rivers open their mouths and the salt salmon
Race up into the freshet.
In Christmas month against the smoulder and menace
Of a long angry sundown,
Red ash of the dark solstice, you see the anglers,
Pitiful, cruel, primeval,
Like the priests of the people that built Stonehenge,
Dark silent forms, performing
Remote solemnities in the red shallows
Of the river's mouth at the year's turn,
Drawing landward their live bullion, the bloody mouths
And scales full of the sunset
Twitch on the rocks, no more to wander at will
The wild Pacific pasture nor wanton and spawning
Race up into fresh water.

NATURAL MUSIC

The old voice of the ocean, the bird-chatter of little rivers,
(Winter has given them gold for silver
To stain their water and bladed green for brown to line their banks)
From different throats intone one language.
So I believe if we were strong enough to listen without
Divisions of desire and terror
To the storm of the sick nations, the rage of the hunger-smitten cities,
Those voices also would be found
Clean as a child's; or like some girl's breathing who dances alone
By the ocean-shore, dreaming of lovers.

WISE MEN IN THEIR BAD HOURS

Wise men in their bad hours have envied
The little people making merry like grasshoppers
In spots of sunlight, hardly thinking
Backward but never forward, and if they somehow
Take hold upon the future they do it
Half asleep, with the tools of generation
Foolishly reduplicating
Folly in thirty-year periods; they eat and laugh too,
Groan against labors, wars and partings,
Dance, talk, dress and undress; wise men have pretended
The summer insects enviable;
One must indulge the wise in moments of mockery.
Strength and desire possess the future,
The breed of the grasshopper shrills, "What does the future
Matter, we shall be dead?" Ah grasshoppers,
Death's a fierce meadowlark: but to die having made
Something more equal to the centuries
Than muscle and bone, is mostly to shed weakness.
The mountains are dead stone, the people
Admire or hate their stature, their insolent quietness,
The mountains are not softened nor troubled
And a few dead men's thoughts have the same temper.

TO THE ROCK THAT WILL BE
A CORNERSTONE OF THE HOUSE

Old garden of grayish and ochre lichen,
How long a time since the brown people who have vanished from here
Built fires beside you and nestled by you
Out of the ranging sea-wind? A hundred years, two hundred,
You have been dissevered from humanity
And only known the stubble squirrels and the headland rabbits,
Or the long-fetlocked plowhorses
Breaking the hilltop in December, sea-gulls following,
Screaming in the black furrow; no one
Touched you with love, the gray hawk and the red hawk touched you
Where now my hand lies. So I have brought you
Wine and white milk and honey for the hundred years of famine
And the hundred cold ages of sea-wind.

I did not dream the taste of wine could bind with granite,
Nor honey and milk please you; but sweetly
They mingle down the storm-worn cracks among the mosses,
Interpenetrating the silent
Wing-prints of ancient weathers long at peace, and the older
Scars of primal fire, and the stone
Endurance that is waiting millions of years to carry
A corner of the house, this also destined.
Lend me the stone strength of the past and I will lend you
The wings of the future, for I have them.
How dear you will be to me when I too grow old, old comrade.

THE CYCLE

The clapping blackness of the wings of pointed cormorants, the great indolent planes
Of autumn pelicans nine or a dozen strung shorelong,
But chiefly the gulls, the cloud-calligraphers of windy spirals before a storm,
Cruise north and south over the sea-rocks and over
That bluish enormous opal; very lately these alone, these and the clouds
And westering lights of heaven, crossed it; but then
A hull with standing canvas crept about Point Lobos . . . now all day long the steamers
Smudge the opal's rim; often a seaplane troubles
The sea-wind with its throbbing heart. These will increase, the others diminish; and later
These will diminish; our Pacific have pastured
The Mediterranean torch and passed it west across the fountains of the morning;
And the following desolation that feeds on Crete
Feed here; the clapping blackness of the wings of pointed cormorants, the great sails
Of autumn pelicans, the gray sea-going gulls,
Alone will streak the enormous opal, the earth have peace like the broad water, our blood's
Unrest have doubled to Asia and be peopling
Europe again, or dropping colonies at the morning star: what moody traveller
Wanders back here, watches the sea-fowl circle
The old sea-granite and cemented granite with one regard, and greets my ghost,
One temper with the granite, bulking about here?

SHINE, PERISHING REPUBLIC

While this America settles in the mould of its vulgarity, heavily
    thickening to empire,
And protest, only a bubble in the molten mass, pops and sighs out, and the
    mass hardens,

I sadly smiling remember that the flower fades to make fruit, the fruit rots
    to make earth.
Out of the mother; and through the spring exultances, ripeness and
    decadence; and home to the mother.

You making haste haste on decay: not blameworthy; life is good, be it
    stubbornly long or suddenly
A mortal splendor: meteors are not needed less than mountains: shine,
    perishing republic.

But for my children, I would have them keep their distance from the
    thickening center; corruption
Never has been compulsory, when the cities lie at the monster's feet there
    are left the mountains.

And boys, be in nothing so moderate as in love of man, a clever servant,
    insufferable master.
There is the trap that catches noblest spirits, that caught — they say — God,
    when he walked on earth.

CONTINENT'S END

At the equinox when the earth was veiled in a late rain, wreathed with
    wet poppies, waiting spring,
The ocean swelled for a far storm and beat its boundary, the ground-swell
    shook the beds of granite.

I gazing at the boundaries of granite and spray, the established sea-marks,
    felt behind me
Mountain and plain, the immense breadth of the continent, before me the
    mass and doubled stretch of water.

I said: You yoke the Aleutian seal-rocks with the lava and coral sowings that
    flower the south,
Over your flood the life that sought the sunrise faces ours that has followed
    the evening star.

The long migrations meet across you and it is nothing to you, you have
    forgotten us, mother.
You were much younger when we crawled out of the womb and lay in the
    sun's eye on the tideline.

It was long and long ago; we have grown proud since then and you have
    grown bitter; life retains
Your mobile soft unquiet strength; and envies hardness, the insolent
    quietness of stone.

The tides are in our veins, we still mirror the stars, life is your child, but
    there is in me
Older and harder than life and more impartial, the eye that watched before
    there was an ocean.

That watched you fill your beds out of the condensation of thin vapor and
  watched you change them,
That saw you soft and violent wear your boundaries down, eat rock, shift
  places with the continents.

Mother, though my song's measure is like your surf-beat's ancient rhythm I
  never learned it of you.
Before there was any water there were tides of fire, both our tones flow
  from the older fountain.

TAMAR

I

A night the half-moon was like a dancing-girl,
No, like a drunkard's last half dollar
Shoved on the polished bar of the eastern hill-range,
Young Cauldwell rode his pony along the sea-cliff;
When she stopped, spurred; when she trembled, drove
The teeth of the little jagged wheels so deep
They tasted blood; the mare with four slim hooves
On a foot of ground pivoted like a top,
Jumped from the crumble of sod, went down, caught, slipped;
Then, the quick frenzy finished, stiffening herself
Slid with her drunken rider down the ledges,
Shot from sheer rock and broke
Her life out on the rounded tidal boulders.

The night you know accepted with no show of emotion the little accident;
    grave Orion
Moved northwest from the naked shore, the moon moved to meridian, the
    slow pulse of the ocean
Beat, the slow tide came in across the slippery stones; it drowned the dead
    mare's muzzle and sluggishly
Felt for the rider; Cauldwell's sleepy soul came back from the blind course
    curious to know
What sea-cold fingers tapped the walls of its deserted ruin. Pain, pain and
    faintness, crushing
Weights, and a vain desire to vomit, and soon again
The icy fingers, they had crept over the loose hand and lay in the hair now.
    He rolled sidewise
Against mountains of weight and for another half hour lay still. With a
    gush of liquid noises

The wave covered him head and all, his body

Crawled without consciousness and like a creature with no bones, a seaworm, lifted its face

Above the sea-wrack of a stone; then a white twilight grew about the moon, and above

The ancient water, the everlasting repetition of the dawn. You shipwrecked horseman

So many and still so many and now for you the last. But when it grew daylight

He grew quite conscious; broken ends of bone ground on each other among the working fibres

While by half inches he was drawing himself out of the sea-wrack up to sandy granite,

Out of the tide's path. Where the thin ledge tailed into flat cliff he fell asleep. . . .

        Far seaward

The daylight moon hung like a slip of cloud against the horizon. The tide was ebbing

From the dead horse and the black belt of sea-growth. Cauldwell seemed to have felt her crying beside him,

His mother, who was dead. He thought "If I had a month or two of life yet

I would remember to be decent, only it's now too late, I'm finished, mother, mother,

I'm sorry." After that he thought only of pain and raging thirst until the sundown

Reddened the sea, and hands were reaching for him and drawing him up the cliff.

      His sister Tamar

Nursed him in the big westward bedroom

Of the old house on Point Lobos. After fever

A wonderful day of peace and pleasant weakness

Brought home to his heart the beauty of things. "O Tamar
I've thrown away years like rubbish. Listen, Tamar,
It would be better for me to be a cripple,
Sit on the steps and watch the forest grow up the hill
Or a new speck of moss on some old rock
That takes ten years agrowing, than waste
Shame and my spirit on Monterey rye whiskey,
And worse, and worse. I shan't be a cripple, Tamar.
We'll walk along the blessed old gray sea,
And up in the hills and watch the spring come home."

Youth is a troublesome but a magical thing,
There is little more to say for it when you've said
Young bones knit easily; he that fell in December
Walked in the February fields. His sister Tamar
Was with him, and his mind ran on her name,
But she was saying, "We laugh at poor Aunt Stella
With her spirit visitors: Lee, something told her truth.
Last August you were hunting deer, you had been gone
Ten days or twelve, we heard her scream at night,
I went to the room, she told me
She'd seen you lying all bloody on the sea-beach
By a dead deer, its blood dabbling the black weeds of the ebb."
"I was up Tassajara way," he answered,
"Far from the sea." "We were glad when you rode home
Safe, with the two bucks on the packhorse. But listen,
She said she watched the stars flying over you
In her vision, Orion she said, and made me look
Out of her window southward, where I saw
The stars they call the Scorpion, the red bead
With the curling tail. 'Then it will be in winter,'
She whispered to me, 'Orion is winter.'" "Tamar, Tamar,

Winter is over, visions are over and vanished,
The fields are winking full of poppies,
In a week or two I'll fill your arms with shining irises."

The winter sun went under and all that night there came a roaring from the
    south; Lee Cauldwell
Lay awake and heard the tough old house creak all her timbers; he was
    miserably lonely and vacant,
He'd put away the boyish jets of wickedness, loves with dark eyes in
    Monterey back-streets, liquor
And all its fellowship, what was left to live for but the farm-work, rain
    would come and hinder?
He heard the cypress trees that seemed to scream in the wind, and felt the
    ocean pounding granite.
His father and Tamar's, the old man David Cauldwell, lay in the eastern
    chamber; when the storm
Wakened him from the heartless fugitive slumber of age he rose and made
    a light, and lighted
The lamp not cold yet; night and day were nearly equal to him, he had seen
    too many; he dressed
Slowly and opened his Bible. In the neighboring rooms he heard on one
    side Stella Moreland,
His dead wife's sister, quieting his own sister, the idiot Jinny Cauldwell,
    who laughed and chuckled
Often for half the night long, an old woman with a child's mind and mostly
    sleepless; in the other
Chamber Tamar was moaning, for it seemed that nightmare
Within the house answered to storm without.
To Tamar it seemed that she was walking by the seaside
With her dear brother, who said "Here's where I fell,
A bad girl that I knew in Monterey pushed me over the cliff,
You can see blood still on the boulders." Where he vanished to

She could not tell, nor why she was crying "Lee. No.
No dearest brother, dearest brother no." But she cried vainly,
Lee was not there to help her, a wild white horse
Came out of the wave and trampled her with his hooves,
The horror that she had dreaded through her dreaming
With mystical foreknowledge. When it wakened her,
She like her father heard old Jinny chuckling
And Stella sighing and soothing her, and the southwind
Raging around the gables of the house and through the forest of the
    cypresses.
"When it rains it will be quieter," Tamar thought. She slept again, all night
    not a drop fell.
Old Cauldwell from his window saw the cloudy light seep up the sky from
    the overhanging
Hilltops, the dawn was dammed behind the hills but overflowed at last and
    ran down on the sea.

II

Lee Cauldwell rode across the roaring southwind to the winter pasture up
    in the hills.
A hundred times he wanted Tamar, to show her some new beauty of
    canyon wildflowers, water
Dashing its ferns, or oaktrees thrusting elbows at the wind, black-oaks
    smouldering with foliage
And the streaked beauty of white-oak trunks, and redwood glens; he rode
    up higher across the rainwind
And found his father's cattle in a quiet hollow among the hills, their horns
    to the wind,
Quietly grazing. He returned another way, from the headland over Wildcat
    Canyon,
Saw the immense water possessing all the west and saw Point Lobos

Gemmed in it, and the barn-roofs and the house-roof
Like ships' keels in the cypress tops, and thought of Tamar.
Toward sundown he approached the house; Will Andrews
Was leaving it and young Cauldwell said, "Listen, Bill Andrews,
We've had gay times together and ridden at night.
I've quit it, I don't want my old friends to visit my sister.
Better keep off the place." "I will," said the other,
"When Tamar tells me to." "You think my bones
Aren't mended yet, better keep off." Lee Cauldwell
Rode by to the stable wondering why his lips
Twitched with such bitter anger; Tamar wondered
Why he went up-stairs without a word or smile
Of pleasure in her. The old man David Cauldwell,
When Lee had told him news of the herd and that Ramon
Seemed faithful, and the calves flourished, the old man answered:
"I hear that there's a dance at Notley's Landing Saturday. You'll be riding
Down the coast, Lee. Don't kill the horse, have a good time." "No, I've
    had all I want, I'm staying
At home now, evenings." "Don't do it; better dance your pony down the
    cliffs again than close
Young life into a little box; you've been too wild; now I'm worn out, but I
    remember
Hell's in the box." Lee answered nothing, his father's lamp of thought was
    hidden awhile in words,
An old man's words, like the dry evening moths that choke a candle. A
    space, and he was saying,
"Come summer we'll be mixed into the bloody squabble out there, and
    you'll be going headforemost
Unless you make your life so pleasant you'd rather live it. I mayn't be living
To see you home or hear you're killed." Lee, smiling at him,
"A soldier's what I won't be, father." That night
He dreamed himself a soldier, an aviator

Duelling with a German above a battle
That looked like waves, he fired his gun and mounted
In steady rhythm; he must have been winged, he suddenly
Plunged and went through the soft and deadly surface
Of the deep sea, wakening in terror.
He heard his old Aunt Jinny chuckling,
Aunt Stella sighing and soothing her, and the southwind
Raging around the gables of the house and through the forest of the
    cypresses.

III

They two had unbridled the horses
And tied them with long halters near the thicket
Under Mal Paso bridge and wandered east
Into the narrow cleft, they had climbed the summit
On the right and looked across the sea.
The steep path down, "What are we for?" said Tamar wearily, "to want and
    want and not dare know it."
"Because I dropped the faded irises," Lee answered, "you're unhappy. They
    were all withered, Tamar.
We have grown up in the same house." "The withered house
Of an old man and a withered woman and an idiot woman. No wonder if
    we go mad, no wonder."
They came to the hid stream and Tamar said, "Sweet, green and cool,
After the mad white April sun: you wouldn't mind, Lee?
Here where it makes a pool: you mustn't look; but you're my brother. And
    then
I will stand guard for you." The murmur and splash of water made his fever
    fierier; something
Unfelt before kept his eyes seaward: why should he dread to see the round
    arm and clear throat

Flash from the hollow stream? He trembled, thinking "O we are beasts, a
      beast, what am I for?
Was the old man right, I must be drunk and a dancer and feed on the
      cheap pleasures or it's dangerous?
Lovely and thoughtless, if she knew me how she'd loathe and avoid me.
      Her brother, brother. My sister.
Better the life with the bones, and all at once have broken." Meanwhile
      Tamar
Uneasily dipped her wrists, and crouching in the leaf-grown bank
Saw her breasts in the dark mirror, she trembled backward
From a long ripple and timidly wading entered
The quiet translucence to the thighs. White-shining
Slender and virgin pillar, desire in water
Unhidden and half reflected among the inter-branching ripples,
Arched with alder, over-woven with willow.
Ah Tamar, stricken with strange fever and feeling
Her own desirableness, half innocent Tamar
Thought, "If I saw a snake in the water he would come now
And kill the snake, he is keen and fearless but he fears
Me I believe." Was it the wild rock coast
Of her breeding, and the reckless wind
In the beaten trees and the gaunt booming crashes
Of breakers under the rocks, or rather the amplitude
And wing-subduing immense earth-ending water
That moves all the west taught her this freedom? Ah Tamar,
It was not good, not wise, not safe, not provident,
Not even, for custom creates nature, natural,
Though all other license were; and surely her face
Grew lean and whitened like a mask, the lips
Thinned their rose to a split thread, the little breasts
Erected sharp bright buds but the white belly
Shuddered, sucked in. The lips writhed and no voice

Formed, and again, and a faint cry. "Tamar?"
He answered, and she answered, "Nothing. A snake in the water
Frightened me." And again she called his name.
"What is it, Tamar?" "Nothing. It is cold in the water.
Come, Lee, I have hidden myself all but the head.
Bathe, if you mean to bathe, and keep me company.
I won't look till you're in." He came, trembling.
He unclothed himself in a green depth and dared not
Enter the pool, but stared at the drawn scars
Of the old wound on his leg. "Come, Lee, I'm freezing.
Come, I won't look." He saw the clear-skinned shoulders
And the hollow of her back, he drowned his body
In the watery floor under the cave of foliage,
And heard her sobbing. When she turned, the great blue eyes
Under the auburn hair, streamed. "Lee.
We have stopped being children; I would have drowned myself;
If you hadn't taught me swimming — long ago — long ago, Lee —
When we were children." "Tamar, what is it, what is it?"
"Only that I want . . . death. You lie if you think
Another thing." She slipped face down and lay
In the harmless water, the auburn hair trailed forward
Darkened like weeds, the double arc of the shoulders
Floated, and when he had dragged her to the bank both arms
Clung to him, the white body in a sobbing spasm
Clutched him, he could not disentangle the white desire,
So they were joined (like drowning folk brought back
By force to bitter life) painfully, without joy.
The spasm fulfilled, poor Tamar, like one drowned indeed, lay pale and
    quiet
And careless of her nakedness. He, gulfs opening
Between the shapes of his thought, desired to rise and leave her and was
    ashamed to.

He lay by her side, the cheek he kissed was cold like a smooth stone, the
    blue eyes were half open,
The bright smooth body seemed to have suffered pain, not love. One of
    her arms crushed both her breasts,
The other lay in the grass, the fingers clutching toward the roots of the soft
    grass. "Tamar,"
He whispered, then she breathed shudderingly and answered, "We have it,
    we have it. Now I know.
It was my fault. I never shall be ashamed again." He said, "What shall I do?
    Go away?
Kill myself, Tamar?" She contracted all her body and crouched in the long
    grass, shivering.
"It hurts, there is blood here, I am too cold to bathe myself again. O
    brother, brother,
Mine and twice mine. You knew already, a girl has got to learn. I love you,
    I chose my teacher.
Mine, it was my doing." She flung herself upon him, cold white and
    smooth, with sobbing kisses.
"I am so cold, dearest, dearest." The horses at the canyon mouth tugged at
    their halters,
Dug pits under the restless forehooves, shivered in the hill-wind
At sundown, were not ridden till dark, it was near midnight
They came to the old house.

IV

When Jinny Cauldwell slept, the old woman with a child's mind, then Stella
    Moreland
Invoked her childish-minded dead, or lying blank-eyed in the dark egged
    on her dreams to vision,
Suffering for lack of audience, tasting the ecstasy of vision. This was the
    vaporous portion

She endured her life in the strength of, in the sea-shaken loneliness, little
    loved, nursing an idiot,
Growing bitterly old among the wind-torn Lobos cypress trunks. (O
    torture of needled branches
Doubled and gnarled, never a moment of quiet, the northwind or the
    southwind or the northwest.
For up and down the coast they are tall and terrible horsemen on patrol,
    alternate giants
Guarding the granite and sand frontiers of the last ocean; but here at Lobos
    the winds are torturers,
The old trees endure them. They blew always thwart the old woman's
    dreams and sometimes by her bedside
Stood, the south in russety black, the north in white, but the northwest
    wave-green, sea-brilliant,
Scaled like a fish. She had also the sun and moon and mightier presences in
    her visions.) Tamar
Entered the room toward morning and stood ghost-like among the old
    woman's ghosts. The rolled-up eyes,
Dull white, with little spindles of iris touching the upper lids, played back
    the girl's blown candle
Sightlessly, but the spirit of sight that the eyes are tools of and it made
    them, saw her. "Ah Helen,"
Cried out the entranced lips, "We thought you were tired of the wind, we
    thought you never came now.
My sister's husband lies in the next room, go waken him, show him your
    beauty, call him with kisses.
He is old and the spittle when he dreams runs into his beard, but he is your
    lover and your brother."
"I am not Helen," she said, "what Helen, what Helen?" "Who was not the
    wife but the sister of her man,
Mine was his wife." "My mother?" "And now he is an old hulk battered
    ashore. Show him your beauty,

Strip for him, Helen, as when he made you a seaweed bed in the cave.
　　What if the beard is slimy
And the eyes run, men are not always young and fresh like you dead
　　women." But Tamar clutching
The plump hand on the coverlet scratched it with her nails, the old woman
　　groaned but would not waken,
And Tamar held the candle flame against the hand, the soot striped it, then
　　with a scream
The old woman awoke, sat up, and fell back rigid on the bed. Tamar found
　　place for the candle
On a little table at the bedside, her freed hands could not awaken a second
　　answer
In the flesh that now for all its fatness felt like a warmed stone. But the
　　idiot waked and chuckled,
Waved both hands at the candle saying, "My little star, my little star, come
　　little star."
And to these three old Cauldwell sighing with sleeplessness
Entered, not noticed, and he stood in the open door. Tamar was bending
Over the bed, loose hair like burnished metal
Concealed her face and sharply cut across one rounded shoulder
The thin nightdress had slipped from. The old man her father
Feared, for a ghost of law-contemptuous youth
Slid through the chilly vaults of the stiff arteries,
And he said, "What is it, Tamar?" "She was screaming in a dream,
I came to quiet her, now she has gone stiff like iron.
Who is this woman Helen she was dreaming about?"
"Helen? Helen?" he answered slowly and Tamar
Believed she saw the beard and the hands tremble.
"It's too cold for you, Tamar, go back to bed
And I'll take care of her. A common name for women."
Old Jinny clapped her hands, "Little star, little star,
Twinkle all night!" and the stiff form on the bed began to speak,

In a changed voice and from another mode of being
And spirit of thought: "I cannot think that you have forgotten.
I was walking on the far side of the moon,
Whence everything is seen but the earth, and never forgot.
This girl's desire drew me home, we also had wanted
Too near our blood,
And to tangle the interbranching net of generations
With a knot sideways. Desire's the arrow-sprayer
And shoots into the stars. Poor little Tamar
He gave you a luckless name in memory of me
And now he is old forgets mine." "You are that Helen,"
Said Tamar leaning over the fat shape
The quiet and fleshless voice seemed issuing from,
A sound of youth from the old puffed lips, "What Helen? This man's . . .
Sister, this body was saying?" "By as much more
As you are of your brother." "Why," laughed Tamar trembling,
"Hundreds of nasty children do it, and we
Nothing but children." Then the old man: "Lies, lies, lies.
No ghost, a lying old woman. Your Aunt Helen
Died white as snow. She died before your mother died.
Your mother and this old woman always hated her,
This liar, as they hated me. I was too hard a nature
To die of it. Lily and Stella." "It makes me nothing,
My darling sin a shadow and me a doll on wires,"
Thought Tamar with one half her spirit; and the other half said,
"Poor lies, words without meaning. Poor Aunt Stella,
The voices in her have no minds." "Poor little Tamar,"
Murmured the young voice from the swollen cavern,
"Though you are that woman's daughter, if we dead
Could be sorrowful for anyone but ourselves
I would be sorrowful for you, a trap so baited
Was laid to catch you when the world began,"

Before the granite foundation. I too have tasted the sweet bait.

But you are the luckier, no one came home to me

To say there are no whips beyond death — but only memory,

And that can be endured." The room was quiet a moment,

And Tamar heard the wind moving out-doors. Then the idiot Jinny
    Cauldwell

Whose mind had been from birth a crippled bird but when she was twelve
    years old her mind's cage

Was covered utterly, like a bird-cage covered with its evening cloth when
    lamps are lighted,

And her memory skipped the more than forty years between but caught
    stray gleams of the sun of childhood,

She in her crumpled voice: "I'd rather play with Helen, go away Stella.
    Stella pinches me,

Lily laughs at me, Lily and Stella are not my sisters." "Jinny, Jinny,"

Said the old man shaking like a thin brick house-wall in an earthquake, "do
    you remember, Jinny?"

"Jinny don't like the old man," she answered, "give me the star, give me my
    star,"

She whined, stretching from bed to reach the candle, "why have they taken
    my little star?

Helen would give it to Jinny." Then Stella waking from the trance sighed
    and arose to quiet her

According to her night's habit. Tamar said, "You were screaming in your
    sleep." "I had great visions.

And I have forgotten them. There Jinny, there, there. It'll have the candle,
    will it? Pretty Jinny.

Will have candle to-morrow. Little Jinny let Aunt Stella sleep now." Old
    Cauldwell tottering

Went to his room; then Tamar said, "You were talking about his sister
    Helen, my aunt Helen,

You never told me about her." "She has been dead for forty years, what should we tell you about her?

Now little Jinny, pretty sister." And laying her hands upon the mattress of the bed

The old woman cradled it up and down, humming a weary song. Tamar stood vainly waiting

The sleep of the monstrous babe; at length because it would not sleep went to her room and heard it

Gurgle and whimper an hour; and the tired litanies of the lullabies; not quiet till daylight.

V

O swiftness of the swallow and strength
Of the stone shore, brave beauty of falcons,
Beauty of the blue heron that flies
Opposite the color of evening
From the Carmel River's reed-grown mouth
To her nest in the deep wood of the deer
Cliffs of peninsular granite engirdle,
O beauty of the fountains of the sun
I pray you enter a little chamber,
I have given you bodies, I have made you puppets,
I have made idols for God to enter
And tiny cells to hold your honey.
I have given you a dotard and an idiot,
An old woman puffed with vanity, youth but botched with incest,
O blower of music through the crooked bugles,
You that make signs of sins and choose the lame for angels,
Enter and possess. Being light you have chosen the dark lamps,
A hawk the sluggish bodies: therefore God you chose

Me; and therefore I have made you idols like these idols
To enter and possess.

                    Tamar, finding no hope,
Slid back on passion, she had sought counsel of the dead
And found half scornful pity and found her sin
Fore-dated; there was honey at least in shame
And secrecy in silence, and her lover
Could meet her afield or slip to her room at night
In serviceable safety. They learned, these two,
Not to look back nor forward; and but for the hint
Of vague and possible wreck every transgression
Paints on the storm-edge of the sky, their blue
Though it dulled a shade with custom shone serene
To the fifth moon, when the moon's mark on women
Died out of Tamar. She kept secret the warning,
How could she color such love with perplexed fear?
Her soul walked back and forth like a new prisoner
Feeling the plant of unescapable fate
Root in her body. There was death; who had entered water
To compass love might enter again to escape
Love's fruit; "But O, but O," she thought, "not to die now.
It is less than half a year
Since life turned sweet. If I knew one of the girls
My lover has known
She'd tell me what to do, how to be fruitless,
How to be . . . happy? They do it, they do it, all sin
Grew nothing to us that day in Mal Paso water.
A love sterile and sacred as the stars.
I will tell my lover, he will make me safe,
He will find means . . .

Sterile and sacred, and more than any woman
... Unhappy. Miserable," she sobbed, "miserable,
The rough and bitter water about the cliff's foot
Better to breathe."

            When Lee was not by her side
She walked the cliffs to tempt them. The calm and large
Pacific surge heavy with summer rolling southeast from a far origin
Battered to foam among the stumps of granite below.
Tamar watched it swing up the little fjords and fountain
Not angrily in the blowholes; a gray vapor
Breathed up among the buttressed writhings of the cypress trunks
And branches swollen with blood-red lichen. She went home
And her night was full of foolish dreams, two layers of dream, unrelative in
    emotion
Or substance to the pain of her thoughts. One, the undercurrent layer that
    seemed all night continuous,
Concerned the dead (and rather a vision than a dream, for visions gathered
    on that house
Like corposant fire on the hoar mastheads of a ship wandering strange
    waters), brown-skinned families
Came down the river and straggled through the wood to the sea, they
    kindled fires by knobs of granite
And ate the sea-food that the plow still turns up rotting shells of, not only
    around Point Lobos
But north and south wherever the earth breaks off to sea-rock; Tamar saw
    the huddled bodies
Squat by the fires and sleep; but when the dawn came there was throbbing
    music meant for daylight
And that weak people went where it led them and were nothing; then
    Spaniards, priests and horseback soldiers,

Came down the river and wandered through the wood to the sea, and
    hearing the universal music
Went where it led them and were nothing; and the English-speakers
Came down the river and wandered through the wood to the sea, among
    them Tamar saw her mother
Walking beside a nameless woman with no face nor breasts; and the
    universal music
Led them away and they were nothing; but Tamar led her father from that
    flood and saved him,
For someone named a church built on a rock, it was beautiful and white,
    not fallen to ruin
Like the ruin by Carmel River; she led him to it and made him enter the
    door, when he had entered
A new race came from the door and wandered down the river to the sea
    and to Point Lobos.
This was the undertow of the dream, obscured by a brighter surface layer
    but seeming senseless.
The tides of the sea were quiet and someone said "because the moon is
    lost." Tamar looked up
And the moon dwindled, rocketing off through lonely space, and the people
    in the moon would perish
Of cold or of a star's fire: then Will Andrews curiously wounded in the face
    came saying
"Tamar, don't cry. What do you care? I will take care of you." Wakening,
    Tamar thought about him
And how he had stopped coming to see her. Perhaps it was another man
    came through her dream,
The wound in the face disguised him, but that morning Lee having ridden
    to Mill Creek
To bargain about some fields of winter pasture
Now that the advancing year withered the hill-grass,

Tamar went down and saddled her own pony,
A four-year-old, as white as foam, and cantered
Past San Jose creek-mouth and the Carrows' farm
(Where David Carrow and his fanatical blue eyes,
That afterward saw Christ on the hill, smiled at her passing)
And three miles up the Carmel Valley came
To the Andrews place where the orchards ran to the river
And all the air was rich with ripening apples.
She would not go to the house; she did not find
Whom she was seeking; at length sadly she turned
Homeward, for Lee might be home within two hours,
And on the Carmel bridge above the water
(Shrunken with summer and shot with water lichen,
The surface scaled with minute scarlet leaves,
The borders green with slimy threads) met whom she sought.
"Tamar," he said, "I've been to see you." "You hadn't
For a long time." "I had some trouble with Lee,
I thought you didn't want me." While they talked
Her eyes tasted his face: was it endurable?
Though it lacked the curious gash her dream had given him . . .
"I didn't want you, you thought?" "Lee said so." "You might have waited
Till Tamar said so." "Well," he answered, "I've been,
And neither of you was home but now I've met you."
— Well-looking enough; freckles, light hair, light eyes;
Not tall, but with a chest and hard wide shoulders,
And sitting the horse well — "O I can do it, I can do it,
Help me God," murmured Tamar in her mind,
"How else — what else can I do?" and said, "Luck, isn't it?
What did you want to see me about?" "I wanted . . .
Because I . . . like you, Tamar." — "Why should I be careful,"
She thought, "if I frighten him off what does it matter,
I have got a little beyond caring." "Let's go down

Into the willow," she said, "we needn't be seen
Talking and someone tell him and make trouble
Here on the bridge." They went to the hidden bank
Under the deep green willows, colored water
Stagnated on its moss up to the stems,
Coarse herbage hid the stirrups, Tamar slid from the saddle
As quietly as the long unwhitening wave
Moulds a sunk rock, and while he tethered the horses,
"I have been lonely," she said. "Not for me, Tamar."
"You think not? Will, now that all's over
And likely we'll not see each other again
Often, nor by ourselves, why shouldn't I tell you . . ."
"What, Tamar?" "There've been moments . . . hours then . . .
When anything you might have asked me for
Would have been given, I'd have done anything
You asked me to, you never asked anything, Will.
I'm telling you this so that you may remember me
As one who had courage to speak truth, you'll meet
So many others." "But now" — he meant to ask,
"Now it's too late, Tamar?" and hadn't courage,
And Tamar thought "Must I go farther and say more?
Let him despise me as I despise myself.
I have got a little beyond caring." "Now?" she said.
"Do you think I am changed? You have changed, Will, you have grown
Older, and stronger I think, your face is firmer;
And carefuller: I have not changed, I am still reckless
To my own injury, and as trustful as a child.
Would I be with you here in the green thicket
If I weren't trustful? If you should harm me, Will,
I'd think it was no harm." She had laid her hand
On the round sunburnt throat and felt it throbbing,
And while she spoke the thought ran through her mind,

"He is only a little boy but if he turns pale
I have won perhaps, for white's the wanting color.
If he reddens I've lost and it's no matter." He did not move
And seemed not to change color and Tamar said,
"Now I must go. Lee will be home soon.
How soft the ground is in the willow shadow.
I have ended with you honestly, Will; remember me
Not afraid to speak truth and not ashamed
To have stripped my soul naked. You have seen all of me.
Good-bye." But when she turned he caught her by the arm,
She sickened inward, thinking, "Now it has come.
I have called and called it and I can't endure it.
Ah. A dumb beast." But he had found words now and said,
"How would you feel, Tamar, if all of a sudden
The bird or star you'd broken your heart to have
Flew into your hands, then flew away. O Tamar, Tamar,
You can't go now, you can't." She unresisting
Took the hot kisses on her neck and hair
And hung loose in his arms the while he carried her
To a clean bank of grass in the deep shadow.
He laid her there and kneeling by her: "You said you trusted me.
You are wise, Tamar; I love you so much too well
I would cut my hands off not to harm you." But she,
Driven by the inward spark of life and dreading
Its premature maturity, could not rest
On harmless love, there were no hands to help
In the innocence of love, and like a vision
Came to her the memory of that other lover
And how he had fallen a farther depth
From firmer innocence at Mal Paso, but the stagnant
Autumn water of Carmel stood too far
From the April freshet in the hills. Tamar pushed off

His kisses and stood up weeping and cried
"It's no use, why will you love me till I cry?
Lee hates you and my father is old and old, we can't
Sour the three years he has before he dies."
"I'll wait for you," said the boy, "wait years, Tamar." Then Tamar
Hiding her face against his throat
So that he felt the tears whispered, "But I . . ."
She sobbed, "Have no patience . . . I can't wait. Will . . .
When I made my soul naked for you
There was one spot . . . a fault . . . a shame
I was ashamed to uncover." She pressed her mouth
Between the muscles of his breast: "I want you and want you.
You didn't know that a clean girl could want a man.
Now you will take me and use me and throw me away
And I've . . . earned it." "Tamar, I swear by God
Never to let you be sorry, but protect you
With all my life." "This is our marriage," Tamar answered.
"But God would have been good to me to have killed me
Before I told you." The boy feeling her body
Vibrant and soft and sweet in its weeping surrender
Went blind and could not feel how she hated him
That moment; when he awakened she was lying
With the auburn hair muddied and the white face
Turned up to the willow leaves, her teeth were bared
And sunk in the under lip, a smear of blood
Reddening the corner of the lips. One of her arms
Crushed both her breasts, the other lay in the grass,
The fingers clutching toward the roots of the soft grass. "O Tamar,"
Murmured the boy, "I love you, I love you. What shall I do? Go away?
Kill myself, Tamar?" She contracted all her body and crouched in the long
    grass, thinking

"That Helen of my old father's never fooled him at least," and said, "There
   is nothing to do, nothing.
It is horribly finished. Keep it secret, keep it secret, Will. I too was to
   blame a little.
But I didn't mean . . . this." "I know," he said, "it was my fault, I would
   kill myself, Tamar,
To undo it but I loved you so, Tamar." "Loved? You have hurt me and
   broken me, the house is broken
And any thief can enter it." "O Tamar!" "You have broken our crystal
   innocence, we can never
Look at each other freely again." "What can I do, Tamar?" "Nothing. I
   don't know. Nothing.
Never come to the farm to see me." "Where can I see you, Tamar?" "Lee is
   always watching me,
And I believe he'd kill us. Listen, Will. To-morrow night I'll put a lamp in
   my window,
When all the house is quiet, and if you see it you can climb up by the
   cypress. I must go home,
Lee will be home. Will, though you've done to me worse than I ever
   dreamed, I love you, you have my soul,
I am your tame bird now."

VI

This was the high plateau of summer and August waning; white vapors
Breathed up no more from the brown fields nor hung in the hills; daily the
   insufferable sun
Rose, naked light, and flaming naked through the pale transparent ways of
   the air drained gray
The strengths of nature; all night the eastwind streamed out of the valley
   seaward, and the stars blazed.

The year went up to its annual mountain of death, gilded with hateful
  sunlight, waiting rain.
Stagnant waters decayed, the trickling springs that all the misty-hooded
  summer had fed
Pendulous green under the granite ocean-cliffs dried and turned foul, the
  rock-flowers faded,
And Tamar felt in her blood the filth and fever of the season. Walking
  beside the house-wall
Under her window, she resented sickeningly the wounds in the cypress
  bark, where Andrews
Climbed to his tryst, disgust at herself choked her, and as a fire by water
Under the fog-bank of the night lines all the sea and sky with fire, so her
  self-hatred
Reflecting itself abroad burned back against her, all the world growing
  hateful, both her lovers
Hateful, but the intolerably masculine sun hatefullest of all. The heat of
  the season
Multiplied centipedes, the black worms that breed under loose rock, they
  call them thousand-leggers,
They invaded the house, their phalloid bodies cracking underfoot with a
  bad odor, and dropped
Ceiling to pillow at night, a vile plague though not poisonous. Also the
  sweet and female sea
Was weak with calm, one heard too clearly a mounting cormorant's
  wing-claps half a mile off shore;
The hard and dry and masculine tyrannized for a season. Rain in October
  or November
Yearly avenges the balance; Tamar's spirit rebelled too soon, the female fury
  abiding
In so beautiful a house of flesh. She came to her aunt the ghost-seer.
  "Listen to me, Aunt Stella.

I think I am going mad, I must talk to the dead, Aunt Stella will you help
    me?" That old woman
Was happy and proud, no one for years had sought her for her talent.
    "Dear Tamar, I will help you.
We must go down into the darkness, Tamar, it is hard and painful for me."
    "I am in the darkness
Already, a fiery darkness." "The good spirits will guide you, it is easy for
    you; for me, death.
Death Tamar, I have to die to reach them." "Death's no bad thing," she
    answered, "each hour of the day
Has more teeth." "Are you so unhappy, Tamar, the good spirits will help
    you and teach you." "Aunt Stella,
To-night, to-night?" "I groan when I go down to death, your father and
    brother will come and spoil it."
"In the evening we will go under the rocks by the sea." "Well, in the
    evening." "If they talk to us
I'll buy you black silk and white lace."

                                      In and out of the little fjord swam
    the weak waves
Moving their foam in the twilight. Tamar at one flank, old Stella at the
    other, upheld poor Jinny
Among the jags of shattered granite, so they came to the shingle. Rich,
    damp and dark the sea's breath
Folding them made amend for days of sun-sickness, but Jinny among the
    rubble granite
(They had no choice but take her along with them, who else would care for
    the idiot?) slipped, and falling
Gashed knees and forehead, and she whimpered quietly in the darkness.
    "Here," said Tamar, "I made you
A bed of seaweed under the nose of this old rock, let Jinny lie beside you
    Aunt Stella,

I'll lay the rug over you both." They lay on the odorous kelp, Tamar
    squatted beside them,
The weak sea wavered in her rocks and Venus hung over the west between
    the cliff-butts
Like the last angel of the world, the crystal night deepening. The sea and
    the three women
Kept silence, only Tamar moved herself continually on the fret of her taut
    nerves,
And the sea moved, on the obscure bed of her eternity, but both were
    voiceless. Tamar
Felt her pulse bolt like a scared horse and stumble and stop, for it seemed
    to her a wandering power
Essayed her body, something hard and rounded and invisible pressed itself
    for entrance
Between the breasts, over the diaphragm. When she was forced backward
    and lay panting, the assault
Failed, the presence withdrew, and in that clearance she heard her old Aunt
    Stella monotonously muttering
Words with no meaning in them; but the tidal night under the cliff seemed
    full of persons
With eyes, although there was no light but the evening planet's and her trail
    in the long water.
Then came a man's voice from the woman, saying "Que quieres pobrecita?"
    and Tamar, "Morir,"
Trembling, and marvelling that she lied for no reason, and said, "Es porque
    no entiendo,
Anything but ingles." To which he answered, "Ah pobrecita," and was
    silent. And Tamar
Cried, "I will talk to that Helen." But instead another male throat spoke
    out of the woman's
Unintelligible gutturals, and it ceased, and the woman changing voice, yet
    not to her own:

"An Indian. He says his people feasted here and sang to their Gods and the
  tall Gods came walking
Between the tide-marks on the rocks; he says to strip and dance and he will
  sing, and his Gods
Come walking." Tamar answered crying, "I will not, I will not, tell him to
  go away and let me
Talk to that Helen." But old Stella after a silence: "He says No, no, the
  pregnant women
Would always dance here and the shore belongs to his people's ghosts nor
  will they endure another
Unless they are pleased." And Tamar said, "I cannot dance, drive him
  away," but while she said it
Her hands accepting alien life and a strange will undid the fastenings of her
  garments.
She panted to control them, tears ran down her cheeks, the male voice
  chanted
Hoarse discords from the old woman's body, Tamar drew her beauty
Out of its husks; dwellers on eastern shores
Watch moonrises as white as hers
When the half moon about midnight
Steps out of her husk of water to dance in heaven:
So Tamar weeping
Slipped every sheath down to her feet, the spirit of the place
Ruling her, she and the evening star sharing the darkness,
And danced on the naked shore
Where a pale couch of sand covered the rocks,
Danced with slow steps and streaming hair,
Dark and slender
Against the pallid sea-gleam, slender and maidenly
Dancing and weeping...
It seemed to her that all her body
Was touched and troubled with polluting presences

Invisible, and whatever had happened to her from her two lovers
She had been until that hour inviolately a virgin,
Whom now the desires of dead men and dead Gods and a dead tribe
Used for their common prey . . . dancing and weeping,
Slender and maidenly . . . The chant was changed,
And Tamar's body responded to the change, her spirit
Wailing within her. She heard the brutal voice
And hated it, she heard old Jinny mimic it
In the cracked childish quaver, but all her body
Obeyed it, wakening into wantonness,
Kindling with lust and wilder
Coarseness of insolent gestures,
The senses cold and averse but the frantic too-governable flesh
Inviting the assaults of whatever desired it, of dead men
Or Gods walking the tide-marks,
The beautiful girlish body as gracile as a maiden's
Gone beastlike, crouching and widening,
Agape to be entered, as the earth
Gapes with harsh heat-cracks, the inland adobe of sun-worn valleys
At the end of summer
Opening sick mouths for its hope of the rain,
So her body gone mad
Invited the spirits of the night, her belly and her breasts
Twisting, her feet dashed with blood where the granite had bruised them,
And she fell, and lay gasping on the sand, on the tide-line. Darkness
Possessed the shore when the evening star was down; old Stella
Was quiet in her trance; old Jinny the idiot clucked and parroted to herself,
    there was none but the idiot
Saw whether a God or a troop of Gods came swaggering along the
    tide-marks unto Tamar, to use her
Shamefully and return from her, gross and replete shadows, swaggering
    along the tide-marks

Against the sea-gleam. After a little the life came back to that fallen flower; for fear or feebleness
She crept on hands and knees, returning so to the old medium of this infamy. Only
The new tide moved in the night now; Tamar with her back bent like a bow and the hair fallen forward
Crouched naked at old Stella's feet, and shortly heard the voice she had cried for. "I am your Helen.
I would have wished you choose another place to meet me and milder ceremonies to summon me.
We dead have traded power for wisdom yet it is hard for us to wait on the maniac living
Patiently, the desires of you wild beasts. You have the power." And Tamar murmured, "I had nothing,
Desire nor power." And Helen, "Humbler than you were. She has been humbled, my little Tamar.
And not so clean as the first lover left you, Tamar. Another, and half a dozen savages,
Dead, and dressed up for Gods." "I have endured it," she answered. Then the sweet disdainful voice
In the throat of the old woman: "As for me, I chose rather to die." "How can I kill
A dead woman," said Tamar in her heart, not moving the lips, but the other listened to thought
And answered "O, we are safe, we shan't fear murder. But, Tamar, the child will die, and all for nothing
You were submissive by the river, and lived, and endured fouling. I have heard the wiser flights
Of better spirits, that beat up to the breast and shoulders of our Father above the star-fire,
Say, 'Sin never buys anything.' " Tamar, kneeling, drew the thickness of her draggled hair

Over her face and wept till it seemed heavy with blood; and like a snake lifting its head

Out of a fire, she lifted up her face after a little and said, "It will live, and my father's

Bitch be proved a liar." And the voice answered, and the tone of the voice smiled, "Her words

Rhyme with her dancing. Tamar, did you know there were many of us to watch the dance you danced there,

And the end of the dance? We on the cliff; your mother, who used to hate me, was among us, Tamar.

But she and I loved each only one man, though it were the same. We two shared one? You, Tamar,

Are shared by many." And Tamar: "This is your help, I dug down to you secret dead people

To help me and so I am helped now. What shall I ask more? How it feels when the last liquid morsel

Slides from the bone? Or whether you see the worm that burrows up through the eye-socket, or thrill

To the maggot's music in the tube of a dead ear? You stinking dead. That you have no shame

Is nothing: I have no shame: see I am naked, and if my thighs were wet with dead beasts' drippings

I have suffered no pollution like the worms in yours; and if I cannot touch you I tell you

There are those I can touch. I have smelled fire and tasted fire,

And all these days of horrible sunlight, fire

Hummed in my ears, I have worn fire about me like a cloak and burning for clothing. It is God

Who is tired of the house that thousand-leggers crawl about in, where an idiot sleeps beside a ghost-seer,

A doting old man sleeps with dead women and does not know it,

And pointed bones are at the doors

Or climb up trees to the window. I say He has gathered
Fire all about the walls and no one sees it
But I, the old roof is ripe and the rafters
Rotten for burning, and all the woods are nests of horrible things, nothing
    would ever clean them
But fire, but I will go to a clean home by the good river." "You danced,
    Tamar," replied
The sweet disdainful voice in the mouth of the old woman, "and now your
    song is like your dance,
Modest and sweet. Only you have not said it was you,
Before you came down by the sea to dance,
That lit a candle in your closet and laid
Paper at the foot of the candle. We were watching.
And now the wick is nearly down to the heap,
It's God will have fired the house? But Tamar,
It will not burn. You will have fired it, your brother
Will quench it, I think that God would hardly touch
Anything in that house." "If you know everything,"
Cried Tamar, "tell me where to go.
Now life won't do me and death is shut against me
Because I hate you. O believe me I hate you dead people
More than you dead hate me. Listen to me, Helen.
There is no voice as horrible to me as yours,
And the breasts the worms have worked in. A vicious berry
Grown up out of the graveyard for my poison.
But there is no one in the world as lonely as I,
Betrayed by life and death." Like rain breaking a storm
Sobs broke her voice. Holding by a jag of the cliff
She drew herself full height. God who makes beauty
Disdains no creature, nor despised that wounded
Tired and betrayed body. She in the starlight
And little noises of the rising tide

Naked and not ashamed bore a third part
With the ocean and keen stars in the consistence
And dignity of the world. She was white stone,
Passion and despair and grief had stripped away
Whatever is rounded and approachable
In the body of woman, hers looked hard, long lines
Narrowing down from the shoulder-bones, no appeal,
A weapon and no sheath, fire without fuel,
Saying, "Have you anything more inside you
Old fat and sleepy sepulchre, any more voices?
You can do better than my father's by-play
And the dirty tricks of savages, decenter people
Have died surely. I have so passed nature
That God himself, who's dead or all these devils
Would never have broken hell, might speak out of you
Last season thunder and not scare me." Old Stella
Groaned but not spoke, old Jinny lying beside her
Wakened at the word thunder and suddenly chuckling
Began to mimic a storm, "whoo-whoo" for wind
And "boom-boom-boom" for thunder. Other voices
Wakened far off above the cliff, and suddenly
The farm-bell ringing fire; and on the rock-islets
Sleepy cormorants cried at it. "Why, now He speaks
Another way than out of the fat throat,"
Cried Tamar, and prayed, "O strong and clean and terrible
Spirit and not father punish the hateful house.
Fire eat the walls and roofs, drive the red beast
Through every wormhole of the rotting timbers
And into the woods and into the stable, show them,
These liars, that you are alive." Across her voice
The bell sounded and old Jinny mimicking it,
And shouts above the cliff. "Look, Jinny, look,"

Cried Tamar, "the sky'll be red soon, come and we'll dress
And watch the bonfire." Yet she glanced no thought
At her own mermaid nakedness but gathering
The long black serpents of beached seaweed wove
Wreaths for old Jinny and crowned and wound her. Meanwhile
The bell ceased ringing and Stella ceased her moan,
And in the sudden quietness, "Tamar," she said
In the known voice of Helen so many years
Dead, "though you hate me utterly, Tamar, I
Have nothing to give back, I was quite emptied
Of hate and love and the other fires of the flesh
Before your mother gave the clay to my lover
To mould you a vessel to hold them." Tamar, winding
Her mindless puppet in the sea-slough mesh
Said over her shoulder, hardly turning, "Why then
Do you trouble whom you don't hate?" "Because we hunger
And hunger for life," she answered. "Did I come uncalled?
You called me, you have more hot and blind, wild-blooded
And passionate life than any other creature.
How could I ever leave you while the life lasts?
God pity us both, a cataract life
Dashing itself to pieces in an instant.
You are my happiness, you are my happiness and death eats you.
I'll leave you when you are empty and cold and join us.
Then pity me, then Tamar, me flitting
The chilly and brittle pumice-tips of the moon,
While the second death
Corrodes this shell of me, till it makes my end."
But Tamar would not listen to her, too busily
Decking old Jinny for the festival fire,
And sighing that thin and envious ghost forsook

Her instrument, and about that time harsh pain
Wrung Tamar's loins and belly, and pain and terror
Expelled her passionate fancies, she cried anxiously,
"Stella, Aunt Stella, help me, will you?" and thinking,
"She hears when Jinny whimpers," twistingly pinched
Her puppet's arm until it screamed. Old Stella
Sat up on the seaweed bed and turned white eyes
No pupils broke the diffused star-gleam in
Upon her sixty-year-old babe, that now
Crouched whimpering, huddled under the slippery leaves
And black whips of the beach; and by it stood gleaming
Tamar, anguished, all white as the blank balls
That swept her with no sight but vision: old Stella
Did not awake yet but a voice blew through her,
Not personal like the other, and shook her body
And shook her hands: "It was no good to do too soon, your fire's out, you'd
    been patient for me
It might have saved two fires." But Tamar: "Stella.
I'm dying: or it is dying: wake up Aunt Stella.
O pain, pain, help me." And the voice: "She is mine while I use her.
    Scream, no one will hear but this one
Who has no mind, who has not more help than July rain." And Tamar,
    "What are you, what are you, mocking me?
More dirt and another dead man? O," she moaned, pressing her flanks with
    both her hands, and bending
So that her hair across her knees lay on the rock. It answered, "Not a voice
    from carrion.
Breaker of trees and father of grass, shepherd of clouds and waters, if you
    had waited for me
You'd be the luckier." "What shall I give you," Tamar cried, "I have given
    away —" Pain stopped her, and then

Blood ran, and she fell down on the round stones, and felt nor saw nothing.
    A little later
Old Stella Moreland woke out of her vision, sick and shaking.

                                                          Tamar's
    mind and suffering
Returned to her neither on the sea-rocks of the midnight nor in her own
    room; but she was lying
Where Lee her brother had lain, nine months before, after his fall, in the
    big westward bedroom.
She lay on the bed, and in one corner was a cot for Stella who nursed her,
    and in the other
A cot for the idiot, whom none else would care for but old Stella. After the
    ache of awakening
And blank dismay of the spirit come home to a spoiled house, she lay
    thinking with vacant wonder
That life is always an old story, repeating itself always like the leaves of a
    tree
Or the lips of an idiot; that herself like Lee her brother
Was picked up bleeding from the sea-boulders under the sea-cliff and
    carried up to be laid
In the big westward bedroom ... was he also fouled with ghosts before
    they found him, a gang
Of dead men beating him with rotten bones, mouthing his body, piercing
    him? "Stella," she whispered,
"Have I been sick long?" "There, sweetheart, lie still; three or four days."
    "Has Lee been in to see me?"
"Indeed he has, hours every day." "He'll come, then," and she closed her
    eyes and seemed to sleep.
Someone tapped at the door after an hour and Tamar said, "Come, Lee."
    But her old father

Came in, and he said nothing but sat down by the bed; Tamar had closed
  her eyes. In a little
Lee entered, and he brought a chair across the room and sat by the bed.
  "Why don't you speak,
Lee?" And he said, "What can I say except I love you, sister?" "Why do
  you call me sister,
Not Tamar?" And he answered, "I love you, Tamar." Then old Aunt Stella
  said, "See, she's much better.
But you must let her rest. She'll be well in a few days; now kiss her, Lee,
  and let her rest."
Lee bent above the white pure cameo-face on the white pillow, meaning to
  kiss the forehead.
But Tamar's hands caught him, her lips reached up for his: while Jinny the
  idiot clapped and chuckled
And made a clucking noise of kisses; then, while Lee sought to untwine the
  arms that yoked his neck,
The old man, rising: "I opened the Book last night thinking about the
  sorrows of this house,
And it said, 'If a man find her in the field and force her and lie with her,
  nevertheless the damsel
Has not earned death, for she cried out and there was none to save her.' Be
  glad, Tamar, my sins
Are only visited on my son, for you there is mercy." "David, David
Will you be gone and let her rest now," cried old Stella, "do you mean to
  kill her with a bible?"
"Woman," he answered, "has God anything to do with you? She will not
  die, the Book
Opened and said it." Tamar, panting, leaned against the pillow and said,
  "Go, go. To-morrow
Say all you please; what does it matter?" And the old man said, "Come,
  Lee, in the morning she will hear us."

Tamar stretched out her trembling hand, Lee did not touch it, but went
    out ahead of his father.
So they were heard in the hall, and then their foot-steps on the stair. Tamar
    lay quiet and rigid,
With open eyes and tightening fists, with anger like a coiled steel spring in
    her throat but weakness
And pain for the lead weights. After an hour she said, "What does he mean
    to do? Go away?
Kill himself, Stella?" Stella answered, "Nothing, nothing, they talk, it's to
    keep David quiet.
Your father is off his head a little, you know. Now rest you, little Tamar,
    smile and be sleepy,
Scold them to-morrow." "Shut the sun out of my eyes then," Tamar said,
    but the idiot Jinny
Made such a moaning when the windows were all curtained they needed to
    let in one beam
For dust to dance in; then the idiot and the sick girl slept. About the hour
    of sundown
Tamar was dreaming trivially — an axeman chopping down a tree and
    field-mice scampering
Out of the roots — when suddenly like a shift of wind the dream
Changed and grew awful, she watched dark horsemen coming out of the
    south, squadrons of hurrying horsemen
Between the hills and the dark sea, helmeted like the soldiers of the war in
    France,
Carrying torches. When they passed Mal Paso Creek the columns
Veered, one of the riders said, "Here it began," but another answered, "No.
    Before the granite
Was bedded to build the world on." So they formed and galloped north
    again, hurrying squadrons,

And Tamar thought, "When they come to the Carmel River then it will happen. They have passed Mal Paso."

Meanwhile —

Who has ever guessed to what odd ports, what sea buoying the keels, a passion blows its bulkless

Navies of vision? High up in the hills

Ramon Ramirez, who was herdsman of the Cauldwell herds, stood in his cabin doorway

Rolling a cigarette a half hour after sundown, and he felt puffs from the south

Come down the slope of stunted redwoods, so he thought the year was turning at last, and shortly

There would come showers; he walked therefore a hundred yards to westward, where a point of the hill

Stood over Wildcat Canyon and the sea was visible; he saw Point Lobos gemmed in the darkening

Pale yellow sea; and on the point the barn-roofs and the house-roof breaking up through the blackness

Of twilight cypress tops, and over the sea a cloud forming. The evening darkened. Southwestward

A half mile loop of the coast-road could be seen, this side Mal Paso. Suddenly a nebular company

Of lights rounded the hill, Ramirez thought the headlights of a car sweeping the road,

But in a moment saw that it was horsemen, each carrying a light, hurrying northward,

Moving in squads he judged of twenty or twenty-five, he counted twelve or thirteen companies

When the brush broke behind him and a horseman rode the headlong ridge like level ground,

Helmeted, carrying a torch. Followed a squad of twelve, helmeted,
    cantering the headlong ridge
Like level ground. He thought in the nervous innocence of the early war,
    they must be Germans.

Tamar awoke out of her dream and heard old Jinny saying, "Dear sister
    Helen, kiss me
As you kiss David. I was watching under a rock, he took your clothes off
    and you kissed him
So hard and hard, I love you too, Helen; you hardly ever kiss me." Tamar
    lay rigid,
Breathless to listen to her; it was well known in the house that under the
    shell of imbecility
Speech and a spirit however subdued existed still; there were waking flashes,
    and more often
She talked in sleep and proved her dreams were made out of clear
    memories, childhood sights and girlhood
Fancies, before the shadow had fallen; so Tamar craving food for passion
    listened to her,
And heard: "Why are you cross, Helen? I won't peek if you'd rather I
    didn't. Darling Helen,
I love him, too; I'd let him play with me the way he does with you if he
    wanted to.
And Lily and Stella hate me as much as they hate you." All she said after
    was so mumbled
That Tamar could not hear it, could only hear the mumble, and old Aunt
    Stella's nasal sleep
And the sea murmuring. When the mumbled voice was quiet it seemed to
    Tamar
A strange thing was preparing, an inward pressure
Grew in her throat and seemed to swell her arms and hands
And join itself with a fluid power

Streaming from somewhere in the room — from Jinny?
From Stella? — and in a moment the heavy chair
That Lee had sat in, tipped up, rose from the floor,
And floated to the place he had brought it from
Five hours ago. The power was then relaxed,
And Tamar could breathe and speak. She awaked old Stella
And trembling told her what she had seen; who laughed
And answered vaguely so that Tamar wondered
Whether she was still asleep, and let her burrow
In her bed again and sleep. Later that night
Tamar too slept, but shudderingly, in snatches,
For fear of dreaming. A night like years. In the gray of morning
A horse screamed from the stableyard and Tamar
Heard the thud of hoofs lashing out and timbers
Splintering, and two or three horses broken loose
Galloped about the grounds of the house. She heard men calling,
And down-stairs Lee in a loud angry tone
Saying "Someone's pitched the saw-buck and the woodpile
Into the horse-corral." Then Tamar thought
"The same power moved his chair in the room, my hatred, my hatred,
Disturbing the house because I failed to burn it.
I must be quiet and quiet and quiet and keep
The serving spirits of my hid hatred quiet
Until my time serves too. Helen you shadow
Were never served so handily." Stella had awakened,
And Tamar asking for a drink of water
She waddled to fetch it and met Lee at the door.
"O Lee," she said, "that noise — whatever has happened?"
He: "I don't know. Some fool has pitched the whole woodpile
Into the horse-corral. Is Tamar awake?
I want to see Tamar." He entered the room
As Stella left it. Old withered Aunt Jinny

Sat up in her bed saying "David, David," but Lee
Kneeling at Tamar's bedside, "O Tamar, Tamar.
The old man's out-doors tottering after the horses
So I can see you a minute. O why, why, why,
Didn't you tell me Tamar? I'd have taken you up
In my arms and carried you to the end of the world."
"How it's turned sour," she thought, "I'd have been glad of this
Yesterday," and she clinched her finger-nails
Into her palms under the bed-covers,
Saying, "Tell you — what? What have they told you," she asked
With a white sidelong smile, "people are always lying?"
"Tamar, that you — that we . . . O I've lived hell
Four or five days now." "You look well enough,"
She answered, "put yours by mine," laying her white, lean,
And somewhat twitching hand on the counterpane,
"Mine used to manage a bridle as well as yours
And now look at them. I don't suppose you want me
Now, but it doesn't matter. You used to come to my bed
With something else than pity, convenient, wasn't it?
Not having to ride to Monterey?" He answered frowning,
"However much you hurt me I am very glad too
That all the joys and memories of a love
As great and as forbidden as ours are nothing to you
Or worse than nothing, because I have to go away,
Two days from now, and stay till the war's over
And you are married and father is dead. I've promised him
Never to see him again, never to see his face.
He didn't ask it because he thinks his Book
Told him I'm to be killed. That's foolishness,
But makes your peace with him and thank God for that.
What his Book told him." "So here's the secret
I wasn't strong enough yesterday to hear.

I thought maybe you meant to kill yourself."
"Thanks, Tamar. The old man thinks I don't need to." "O,
You beast," she said, "you runaway dog.
I wish you joy of your dirty Frenchwomen
You want instead of me. Take it, take it.
Old people in their dotage gabble the truth,
You won't live long." "What can I say, Tamar?
I'm sorry, I'm sorry, I'm sorry." "But go away,"
She said, "and if you'll come again to-night
Maybe I'll tell you mine, my secret."

                            That morning
Ramon Ramirez who watched the Cauldwell cattle
Up in the hills kept thinking of his vision
Of helmets carrying torches; he looked for tracks
On the ridge where he had seen the riders cantering,
And not a bush was broken, not a hoof-mark
Scarred the sear grass. At noon he thought he'd ride
To Vogel's place taking his lunch in the saddle
And tell someone about it. At the gap in the hill
Where storm-killed redwoods line both sides he met
Johnny Cabrera with a flaming bundle
Of dead twigs and dry grass tied with brown cord.
He smelled the smoke and saw the flame sag over
On a little wind from the east, and said in Spanish
"Eh Johnny, are you out of matches?" who answered flashing
His white teeth in a smile, "I'm carrying fire to Lobos
If God is willing," and walked swinging ahead,
Singing to himself the fool south-border couplet
"No tengo tabaco, no tengo papel,
No tengo dinero, God damn it to hell,"
And Ramon called "Hey Johnny," but he would not stop

Nor answer, and thinking life goes wild at times
Ramon came to the hill-slope under Vogel's
And smelled new smoke and saw the clouds go up
And this same Johnny with two other men
Firing the brush to make spring pasture. Ramon
Felt the scalp tighten on his temples and thought best
Not to speak word of either one of his visions,
Though he talked with the men, they told him Tamar Cauldwell
Was sick, and Lee had enlisted.

                              The afternoon
Was feverish for so temperate a sea-coast
And terribly full of light, the sea like a hard mirror
Reverberated the straight and shining serpents
That fell from heaven and Tamar dreamed in a doze
She was hung naked by that tight cloth bandage
Half way between sea and sky, beaten on by both,
Burning with light; wakening she found she had tumbled
The bed-clothes to the floor and torn her night-gown
To rags, and was alone in the room, and blinded
By the great glare of sun in the western windows.
She rose and shut the curtains though they had told her
She mustn't get out of bed, and finding herself
Able to walk she stood by the little window
That looked southeast from the south bay of the room
And saw the smoke of burning brushwood slopes
Tower up out of the hills in the windless weather
Like an enormous pinetree, "Everybody
But me has luck with fire," she thought to herself,
"But I can walk now," and returned to bed
And drew the sheets over her flanks, but leaving

The breasts and shoulders bare. In half an hour
Stella and old Jinny came into the room
With the old man David Cauldwell. Stella hastily
Drew up the sheet to Tamar's throat but Tamar
Saying, "You left the curtains open and the sun
Has nearly killed me," doubled it down again,
And David Cauldwell, trembling: "Will you attempt
Age and the very grave, uncovering your body
To move the old bones that seventy years have broken
And dance your bosoms at me through a mist of death?
Though I know that you and your brother have utterly despised
The bonds of blood, and daughter and father are no closer bound,
And though this house spits out all goodness, I am old, I am old, I am old,
What do you want of me?" He stood tottering and wept,
Covering his eyes and beard with shaken old hands,
And Tamar, having not moved, "Nothing," she said,
"Nothing, old man. I have swum too deep into the mud
For this to sicken me; and as you say, there are neither
Brother nor sister, daughter nor father, nor any love
This side the doorways of the damnable house.
But I have a wildbeast of a secret hidden
Under the uncovered breast will eat us all up
Before Lee goes." "It is a lie, it is a lie, it is all a lie.
Stella you must go out, go out of the room Stella,
Not to hear the sick and horrible imaginations
A sick girl makes for herself. Go Stella." "Indeed I won't,
David." "You — you — it is still my house." "To let you kill her with bad
    words
All out of the bible — indeed I won't." "Go, Stella," said Tamar,
"Let me talk to this old man, and see who has suffered
When you come back. I am out of pity, and you and Jinny

Will be less scorched on the other side of the door." After a third refusal
The old woman went, leading her charge, and Tamar: "You thought it was
    your house? It is me they obey.
It is mine, I shall destroy it. Poor old man I have earned authority." "You
    have gone mad," he answered.
And she: "I'll show you our trouble, you sinned, your old book calls it, and
    repented: that was foolish.
I was unluckier, I had no chance to repent, so I learned something, we must
    keep sin pure
Or it will poison us, the grain of goodness in a sin is poison. Old man, you
    have no conception
Of the freedom of purity. Lock the door, old man, I am telling you a
    secret." But he trembling,
"O God thou hast judged her guiltless, the Book of thy word spake it, thou
    hast the life of the young man
My son . . ." and Tamar said, "Tell God we have revoked relationship in
    the house, he is not
Your son nor you my father." "Dear God, blot out her words, she has gone
    mad. Tamar, I will lock it,
Lest anyone should come and hear you, and I will wrestle for you with
    God, I will not go out
Until you are His." He went and turned the key and Tamar said, "I told
    you I have authority.
You obey me like the others, we pure have power. Perhaps there are other
    ways, but I was plunged
In the dirt of the world to win it, and, O father, so I will call you this last
    time, dear father
You cannot think what freedom and what pleasure live in having abjured
    laws, in having
Annulled hope, I am now at peace." "There is no peace, there is none,
    there is none, there is no peace

But His," he stammered, "but God's." "Not in my arms, old man, on these
   two little pillows? Your son
Found it there, and another, and dead men have defiled me. You that are
   half dead and half living,
Look, poor old man. That Helen of yours, when you were young, where
   was her body more desirable,
Or was she lovinger than I? You know it is forty years ago that we revoked
Relationships in the house." "He never forgives, He never forgives, evil
   punishes evil
With the horrible mockery of an echo." "Is the echo louder than the voice,
   I have surpassed her,
Yours was the echo, time stands still old man, you'll learn when you have
   lived at the muddy root
Under the rock of things; all times are now, to-day plays on last year and
   the inch of our future
Made the first morning of the world. You named me for the monument in
   a desolate graveyard,
Fool, and I say you were deceived, it was out of me that fire lit you and
   your Helen, your body
Joined with your sister's
Only because I was to be named Tamar and to love my brother and my
   father.
I am the fountain." But he, shuddering, moaned, "You have gone mad, you
   have gone mad, Tamar,"
And twisted his old hands muttering, "I fear hell. O Tamar, the nights I
   have spent in agony,
Ages of pain, when the eastwind ran like glass under the peeping stars or
   the southwest wind
Plowed in the blackness of the trees. You — a little thing has driven you
   mad, a moment of suffering,
But I for more than forty years have lain under the mountains and looked
   down into hell."

"One word," she said, "that was not written in the book of my fears. I did indeed fear pain

Before peace found me, or death, never that dream. Old man, to be afraid is the only hell

And dead people are quit of it, I have talked with the dead." "Have you — with her?" "Your pitiful Helen?

She is always all about me; if you lay in my arms old man you would be with her. Look at me,

Have you forgotten — your Helen?" He in torture

Groaned like a beast, but when he approached the bed she laughed, "Not here, behind you." And he blindly

Clutching at her, she left the coverlet in his hands and slipping free at the other side

Saw in a mirror on the wall her own bright throat and shoulder and just beyond them the haggard

Open-mouthed mask, the irreverend beard and blind red eyes. She caught the mirror from its fastening

And held it to him, reverse. "Here is her picture, Helen's picture, look at her, why is she always

Crying and crying?" When he turned the frame and looked, then Tamar: "See that is her lover's.

The hairy and horrible lips to kiss her, the drizzling eyes to eat her beauty, happiest of women

If only he were faithful; he is too young and wild and lovely, and the lusts of his youth

Lead him to paw strange beds." The old man turned the glass and gazed at the blank side, and turned it

Again face towards him, he seemed drinking all the vision in it, and Tamar: "Helen, Helen,

I know you are here present; was I humbled in the night lately and you exulted?

See here your lover. I think my mother will not envy you now, your lover, Helen, your lover,

The mouth to kiss you, the hands to fondle secret places." Then the old
　　man sobbing, "It is not easy
To be old, mocked, and a fool." And Tamar, "What, not yet, you have not
　　gone mad yet? Look, old fellow.
These rags drop off, the bandages hid something but I'm done with them.
　　See . . . I am the fire
Burning the house." "What do you want, what do you want?" he said, and
　　stumbled toward her, weeping.
"Only to strangle a ghost and to destroy the house. Spit on the memory of
　　that Helen
You might have anything of me." And he groaning, "When I was young
I thought it was my fault, I am old and know it was hers, night after night,
　　night after night
I have lain in the dark, Tamar, and cursed her." "And now?" "I hate her,
　　Tamar." "O," said Tamar gently,
"It is enough, she has heard you. Now unlock the door, old father, and go,
　　and go." "Your promise,
Tamar, the promise, Tamar." "Why I might do it, I have no feeling of
　　revolt against it.
Though you have forgotten that fear of hell why should I let you
Be mocked by God?" And he, the stumpage of his teeth knocking together,
　　"You think, you think
I'll go to the stables and a rope from a rafter
Finish it for you?" "Dear, I am still sick," she answered, "you don't want to
　　kill me? A man
Can wait three days: men have lived years and years on the mere hope."

　　　　　　　　　　　　　　　　　　　　　　　　Meanwhile
　　the two old women
Sat in their room, old Stella sat at the window looking south into the
　　cypress boughs, and Jinny
On her bed's edge, rocking her little withered body backward and forward,
　　and said vacantly,

"Helen, what do you do the times you lock the door to be alone, and Lily
    and Stella
Wonder where David's ridden to?" After a while she said again, "Do tell
    me, sister Helen,
What you are doing the times you lock the door to be alone, and Lily and
    Stella wonder
Where David's ridden to?" And a third time she repeated, "Darling sister
    Helen, tell me
What you are doing the times you lock the door to be alone, and Lily and
    Stella wonder
Where David's riding?" Stella seemed to awake, catching at breath, and not
    in her own voice,
"What does she mean," she said, "my picture, picture? O! the mirror — I
    read in a book Jinny.
A story about lovers; I never had a lover, I read about them; — I won't look,
    though.
With all that blind abundance, so much of life and blood, that sweet and
    warming blaze of passion,
She has also a monkey in her mind." "Tell me the story about the picture."
    "Ugh, if she plans
To humble herself utterly . . . You may peek, Jinny,
Try if you can, shut both eyes, draw them back into your forehead, and
    look, look, look
Over the eyebrows, no, like this, higher up, up where the hair grows, now
    peek Jinny. Can't you
See through the walls? You can. Look, look, Jinny. As if they'd cut a
    window. I used to tell you
That God could see into caves: you are like God now: peek, Jinny." "I can
    see something.
It's in the stable, David's come from Monterey, he's hanging the saddle on a
    peg there . . ."
"Jinny, I shall be angry. That's not David,

It's Lee, don't look into the stable, look into the bedroom, you know, Jinny,
     the bedroom,
Where we left Tamar on the bed." "O that's too near, it hurts me, it hurts
     my head, don't scold me, Helen.
How can I see if I'm crying? I see now clearly."
"What do you see?" "I see through walls, O, I'm like God, Helen. I see the
     wood and plaster
And see right through them." "What? What are they doing?" "How can
     you be there and here, too, Helen?"
"It's Tamar, what is she doing?" "I know it's you Helen, because you have
     no hair
Under the arms, I see the blue veins under the arms." "Well, if it's me, what
     is she doing?
Is she on the bed? What is she saying?" "She is on fire Helen, she has white
     fire all around you
Instead of clothes, and that is why you are laughing with so pale a face."
     "Does she let him do
Whatever he wants to, Jinny?" "He says that he hates ... somebody ...
     and then you laughed for he had a rope
Around his throat a moment, the beard stuck out over it." "O Jinny it
     wasn't I that laughed,
It was that Tamar, Tamar, Tamar, she has bought him for nothing. She and
     her mother both to have him,
The old hollow fool." "What do they want him for, Helen?" "To plug a
     chink, to plug a chink, Jinny,
In the horrible vanity of women. Lee's come home, now I could punish her,
     she's past hurting,
Are they huddled together Jinny? What, not yet, not yet?" "You asked for
     the key but when he held it
You ran away from him." "What do I want, what do I want, it is frightful
     to be dead, what do I ...

Without power, and no body or face. To kill her, kill her?
There's no hell and curse God for it . . ."

                                    Lee Cauldwell childishly
Loved hearing the spurs jingle, and because he felt
"After to-morrow I shan't wear them again,
Nor straddle a pony for many a weary month and year,
Maybe forever," he left them at his heels
When he drew off the chaps and hung the saddle
On the oak peg in the stable-wall. He entered the house
Slowly, he had taken five drinks in Monterey
And saw his tragedy of love, sin, and war
At the disinterested romantic angle
Misted with not unpleasing melancholy,
Over with, new adventure ahead, a perilous cruise
On the other ocean, and great play of guns
On the other shore . . . at the turn of the stair he heard
Hands hammering a locked door, and a voice unknown to him
Crying, "Tamar, I loved you for your flame of passion
And hated you for its deeds, all that we dead
Can love or hate with: and now will you crust flame
With filth, submit? Submit? Tamar,
The defilement of the tideline dead was nothing
To this defilement." Then Lee jingling his spurs,
Jumped four steps to the landing, "Who is there? You,
Aunt Stella?" Old gray Aunt Jinny like a little child
Moaning drew back from him, and the mouth of Stella:
"A man that's ready to cross land and water
To set the world in order can't be expected
To leave his house in order." And Lee, "Listen, Aunt Stella,
Who are you playing, I mean what voice out of the world of the dead
Is speaking from you?" She answered, "Nothing. I was something

Forty years back but now I'm only the bloodhound
To bay at the smell of what they're doing in there."
"Who? Tamar? Blood?" "Too close in blood, I am the blood-stain
On the doorsill of a crime, she does her business
Under her own roof mostly." "Tamar, Tamar,"
Lee called, shaking the door. She from within
Answered "I am here, Lee. Have you said good-bye
To Nita and Conchita in Monterey
And your fat Fanny? But who is the woman at the door
Making the noise?" He said, "Open the door;
Open the door, Tamar." And she, "I opened it for you,
You are going to France to knock at other doors.
I opened it for you and others." "What others?" "Ask her,"
Said the young fierce voice from old Aunt Stella's lips,
"What other now?" "She is alone there," he answered,
"A devil is in you. Tamar," he said, "tell her
You are alone." "No, Lee, I am asking in earnest,
Who is the woman making the noise out there?
Someone you've brought from Monterey? Tell her to go:
Father is here." "Why have you locked it, why have you locked it?"
He felt the door-knob turning in his hand
And the key shook the lock; Tamar stood in the doorway
Wrapped in a loose blue robe that the auburn hair
Burned on, and beyond her the old man knelt by the bed,
His face in the lean twisted hands. "He was praying for me,"
Tamar said quietly. "You are leaving to-morrow,
He has only one child." Then the old man lifting a face
From which the flesh seemed to have fallen, and the eyes
Dropped and been lost: "What will you do to him, Tamar?
Tamar, have mercy.
He was my son, years back." She answered, "I am glad
That you know who has power in the house"; and he

Hid the disfigured face, between his wrists
The beard kept moving, they thought him praying to God.
And Tamar said, "It is coming to the end of the bad story,
That needn't have been bad only we fools
Botch everything, but a dead fool's the worst,
This old man's sister who rackets at the doors
And drove me mad, although she is nothing but a voice,
Dead, shelled, and the shell rotted, but she had to meddle
In the decencies of life here. Lee, if you truly
Lust for the taste of a French woman I'll let you go
For fear you die unsatisfied and plague
Somebody's children with a ghost's hungers
Forty years after death. Do I care, do I care?
You shan't go, Lee. I told the old man I have a secret
That will eat us all up . . . and then, dead woman,
What will you have to feed on? You spirits flicker out
Too speedily, forty years is a long life for a ghost
And you will only famish a little longer
To whom I'd wish eternity." "O Tamar, Tamar,"
It answered out of Stella's mouth, "has the uttermost
Not taught you anything yet, not even that extinction
Is the only terror?" "You lie too much," she answered,
"You'll enter it soon and not feel any stitch
Of fear afterwards. Listen, Lee, your arms
Were not the first man's to encircle me, and that spilled life
Losing which let me free to laugh at God,
I think you had no share in." He trembled, and said
"O Tamar have your sickness and my crime
Cut you so deep? A lunatic in a dream
Dreams nearer things than this." "I'd never have told you,"
She answered, "if his vicious anger — after I'd balanced
Between you a long time and then chose you —

Hadn't followed his love's old night-way to my window
And kindled fire in the room when I was gone,
The spite-fire that might easily have eaten up
And horribly, our helpless father, or this innocent
Jinny . . ." "He did it, he did it, forgive me, Tamar.
I thought that you gone mad . . . Tamar, I know
That you believe what you are saying but I
Do not believe you. There was no one." "The signal
Was a lamp in the window, perhaps some night
He'd come still if you'd set a lamp into my window.
And when he climbed out of the cypress tree
Then you would know him." "I would mark him to know.
But it's not true." "Since I don't sleep there now
You might try for the moth; if he doesn't come
I'll tell you his name to-morrow." Then the old man jerking
Like dry bones wired pulled himself half erect
With clutching at the bed-clothes: "Have mercy, Tamar.
Lee, there's a trick in it, she is a burning fire,
She is packed with death. I have learned her, I have learned her, I have
    learned her,
Too cruel to measure strychnine, too cunning-cruel
To snap a gun, aiming ourselves against us."
Lee answered, "There is almost nothing here to understand.
If we all did wrong why have we all gone mad
But me, I haven't a touch of it. Listen, dead woman,
Do you feel any light here?" "Fire — as much light
As a bird needs," the voice from the old woman
Answered, "I am the gull on the butt of the mast
Watching the ship founder, I'll fly away home
When you go down, or a swallow above a chimney
Watching the brick and mortar fly in the earthquake."
"I'll just go look at the young cypress bark

Under her window," he said, "it might have taken
The bite of a thief's hob-nails." When he was gone
And jingling down the stair, then Tamar: "Poor people,
Why do you cry out so? I have three witnesses,
The old man that died to-day, and a dead woman
Forty years dead, and an idiot, and only one of you
Decently quiet. There is the great and quiet water
Reaching to Asia, and in an hour or so
The still stars will show over it but I am quieter
Inside than even the ocean or the stars.
Though I have to kindle paper flares of passion
Sometimes, to fool you with. But I was thinking
Last night, that people all over the world
Are doing much worse and suffering much more than we
This wartime, and the stars don't wink, and the ocean
Storms perhaps less than usual." Then the dead woman,
"Wild life, she has touched the ice-core of things and learned
Something, that frost burns worse than fire." "O, it's not true,"
She answered, "frost is kind; why, almost nothing
You say is true. Helen, do you remember at all
The beauty and strangeness of this place? Old cypresses
The sailor wind works into deep-sea knots
A thousand years; age-reddened granite
That was the world's cradle and crumbles apieces
Now that we're all grown up, breaks out at the roots;
And underneath it the old gray-granite strength
Is neither glad nor sorry to take the seas
Of all the storms forever and stand as firmly
As when the red hawk wings of the first dawn
Streamed up the sky over it: there is one more beautiful thing,
Water that owns the north and west and south
And is all colors and never is all quiet,

And the fogs are its breath and float along the branches of the cypresses.
And I forgot the coals of ruby lichen
That glow in the fog on the old twigs. To live here
Seventy-five years or eighty, and have children,
And watch these things fill up their eyes, would not
Be a bad life . . . I'd rather be what I am,
Feeling this peace and joy, the fire's joy's burning,
And I have my peace." Then the old man in the dull
And heartless voice answered, "The strangest thing
Is that He never speaks: we know we are damned, why should He speak?
    The book
Is written already. Cauldwell, Cauldwell, Cauldwell, Cauldwell.
Eternal death, eternal wrath, eternal torture, eternity, eternity, eternity . . .
That's after the judgment." "You needn't have any fear, old father,
Of anything to happen after to-morrow," Tamar answered, "we have turned
    every page
But the last page, and now our paper's so worn out and tissuey I can read it
    already
Right through the leaf, print backwards."

                                    It was twilight in the room, the
    shiny side of the wheel
Dipping toward Asia; and the year dipping toward winter encrimsoned the
    grave spokes of sundown;
And jingling in the door Lee Cauldwell with the day's-death flush upon his
    face: "Father:
There are marks on the cypress: a hell of a way to send your soldier off: I
    want to talk to her
Alone. You and the women — " he flung his hand out, meaning "go." The
    old man without speaking
Moved to the door, propping his weakness on a chair and on the
    door-frame, and Lee entering

Passed him and the two women followed him — three, if Stella were one —
   but when they had passed the doorway
Old Cauldwell turned, and tottering in it: "Death is the horror," he said,
   "nothing else lasts, pain passes,
Death's the only trap. I am much too wise to swing myself in the stable on
   a rope from a rafter. Helen, Helen,
You know about death." "It is cold," she answered from the hallway;
   "unspeakably hopeless . . ." "You curse of talkers,
Go," he said, and he shut the door against them and said, "Slut, how many,
   how many?" She, laughing,
"I knew you would be sweet to me: I am still sick: did you find marks in
   the bark? I am still sick, Lee;
You don't intend killing me?" "Flogging, whipping, whipping, is there
   anything male about here
You haven't used yet? Agh you mouth, you open mouth. But I won't touch
   you." "Let me say something,"
She answered, standing dark against the west in the window, the death of
   the winter rose of evening
Behind her little high-poised head, and threading the brown twilight of the
   room with the silver
Exultance of her voice, "My brother can you feel how happy I am but how
   far off too?
If I have done wrong it has turned good to me, I could almost be sorry that
   I have to die now
Out of such freedom; if I were standing back of the evening crimson on a
   mountain in Asia
All the fool shames you can whip up into a filth of words would not be
   farther off me,
Nor any fear of anything, if I stood in the evening star and saw this dusty
   dime's worth
A dot of light, dropped up the star-gleam. Poor brother, poor brother, you
   played the fool too

But not enough, it is not enough to taste delight and passion and disgust
and loathing
And agony, you have to be wide alive, 'an open mouth' you said, all the
while, to reach this heaven
You'll never grow up to. Though it's possible if I'd let you go asoldiering,
there on the dunghills
Of death and fire . . . ah, you'd taste nothing even there but the officers'
orders, beef and brandy,
And the tired bodies of a few black-eyed French dance-girls: it is better for
you
To be lost here than there." "You are up in the evening star," he said, "you
can't feel this," flat-handed
Striking her cheek, "you are up on a mountain in Asia, who made you
believe that you could keep me
Or let me go? I am going to-morrow, to-night I set the house in order."
"There is nothing now
You can be sorry for," she answered, "not even this, it is out of the count,
the cup ran over
Yesterday." He turned and left the room, the foolish tune of the spurs
tinkled
Hallway and stair. Tamar, handling the fiery spot upon her cheek smiled in
the darkness,
Feeling so sure of the end. "Night after night he has ridden to the granite
at the rivermouth
And missed my light, to-night he will see it, the Lobos star he called it, and
look and look to be sure
It is not a ship's light nor a star's, there in the south, then he will come, and
my three lovers
Under one roof."

VII

Lee Cauldwell felt his way in the dark among the cypress trees, and turning
At the stable door saw the evening star, he felt for the lantern
Hung on the bent nail to the right of the door,
Lighted it, and in the sweet hay-dusty darkness
Found the black quirt that hung beside the saddle
And seemed a living snake in the hand, then he opened
A locker full of hunter's gear and tumbled
Leather and iron to the floor for an old sheath-knife
Under all the rest; he took the knife and whip
And Tamar in the dark of the westward bedroom heard him
Tinkle on the stair and jingle in the hall, slow steps
Moving to hers, the room that had been her room
Before this illness; she felt him as if she had been there
Lighting her lamp and setting it on the sill,
Then felt him look about the little room and feel it
Breathing and warm with her once habitancy
And the hours of hers and his there, and soften almost
To childish tears at trifles on the wall;
And then he would look at the bed and stiffen
In a brittle rage, feel with thrust under-lip
Virtuous, an outcrop of morality in him
To grow ridiculous and wish to be cruel,
And so return to her. Hastily, without light,
She redded up some of the room's untidiness,
Thrust into the stove the folds of bandage-cloth,
Straightened the bed a little, and laying aside
The loose blue robe lay down in the bed to await him,
Who, throwing open the door, "Tamar: I've got no right
To put my hands into your life, I see
That each of us lives only a little while

And must do what he can with it: so, I'm going
To-night; I'd nearly worked myself to the act
Of some new foolishness: are you there, Tamar?
The lamp?" He struck a match and saw her eyes
Shine on him from the pillow and when the lamp
Was lighted he began again: "It's all such foolishness.
Well, you and I are done. I set your lamp for a signal on the sill,
I'll take it away or help you to that room,
Whichever you like. That'll be my last hand in the game.
It won't take me ten minutes to pack and go, my plan's
Not to risk losing temper and have half decent
Thoughts of you while I'm gone, and you of me, Tamar."
She lay too quietly and the shining eyes
Seemed not to hide amusement, he waited for her
To acknowledge not in direct words perhaps
His generosity, but she silent, "Well, shall I leave the lamp?"
He said, not all so kindly, and Tamar, "I've no one else
If you are going. But if you'd stay I wouldn't
Touch you again, ever. Agh you can't wait
To get to France to crawl into strange beds,
But Monterey to-night. You — what a beast.
You like them dirty." He said, "You're a fool, Tamar.
Well, so I'll leave the lamp. Good-bye, Tamar."
"You said you'd help me down the hall." "Yes, even that.
What must I do, carry you?" "Is the bed together?
See whether there are sheets and covers on it."
He went, and returned icy-pale. "It hasn't been changed
Since I smelled fire and ran into the room
Six or eight days ago. The cupboard door-frame
Is all charcoal. By God, Tamar,
If I believed he'd done it — who is he, Andrews? —
You and your lies have made a horror in the house.

What, shall I go, shall I go?" "Me? who made *me*
Believe that I could keep you or let you go,
Didn't you say?" "You still believe it," he answered,
Doubling his fists to hold in anger, the passionate need
Of striking her like a torrent in his throat,
"Believe it, fool." "Poor brother. You will never see France,
Never wear uniform nor learn how to fasten
A bayonet to a gun-barrel." "Come. Stop talking.
Get up, come to your room." "Carry me," she answered.
"Though I am not really much too tired to walk.
You used to like me." "Well, to get done and be gone,"
He said, bending above her, she enlaced his neck
Softly and strongly and raised her knees to let
His arm slip under them, he like a man stung by a serpent
Felt weakness and then rage, panted to lift her
And staggered in the doorway and in the dark hallway
Grew dizzy, and difficultly went on and groaning
Dropped her on the bed in her own room, she did not move
To cover herself, then he drawing his palm
Across his forehead found it streaming wet
And said, "You whore, you whore, you whore. Well, you shall have it,
You've earned it," and he twisted himself to the little table
And took the whip, the oiled black supple quirt,
Loaded at the handle, that seemed a living snake in the hand,
And felt the exasperate force of his whole baffled
And blindfold life flow sideways into the shoulder
Swinging it, and half repenting while it dropped
Sickened to see the beautiful bare white
Blemishless body writhe under it before it fell,
The loins pressed into the bed, the breast and head
Twisting erect, and at the noise of the stroke
He made a hoarse cry in his throat but she

Took it silently, and lay still afterward,
Her head so stricken backward that the neck
Seemed strained to breaking, the coppery pad of her hair
Crushed on the shoulder-blades, while that red snake-trail
Swelled visibly from the waist and flank down the left thigh.
"O God, God, God," he groaned; and she, her whole body
Twitching on the white bed whispered between her teeth
"It was in the bargain," and from her bitten lip
A trickle of blood ran down to the pillow.

                                        That one light in the room,
The lamp on the sill, did not turn redder for blood nor with the
    whip-stripe
But shone serene and innocent up the northward night, writing a long
    pale-golden track
In the river's arm of sea, and beyond the river's mouth where the old lion's
    teeth of blunted granite
Crop out of the headland young Will Andrews kissed it with his eyes, rode
    south and crossed the river's
Late-summer sand-lock. Figures of fire moved in the hills on the left, the
    pasture-fires and brush-fires
Men kindle before rain, on a southerly wind the smell of the smoke
    reached him, the sea on his right
Breathed; when he skirted the darkness of the gum-tree grove at San Jose
    creek-mouth he remembered
Verdugo killed there; Sylvia Vierra and her man had lived in the little
    white-washed farm-hut
Under the surf-reverberant blue-gums; two years ago they had had much
    wine in the house, their friend
Verdugo came avisiting, he being drunk on the raw plenty of wine they
    thought abused

Nine-year-old Mary, Sylvia's daughter, they struck him from behind and
    when he was down unmanned him
With the kitchen knife, then plotted drunkenly — for he seemed to be
    dead — where to dispose the body.
That evening Tamar Cauldwell riding her white pony along the coast-road
    saw a great bonfire
Perilling the gum-tree grove, and riding under the smoke met evil odors,
    turning in there
Saw by the firelight a man's feet hang out of the fire; then Tamar never
    having suffered
Fear in her life, knocked at the hut's door and unanswered entered, and
    found the Vierras asleep
Steaming away their wine, but little Mary weeping. She had taken the child
    and ridden homeward.
Young Andrews thinking of that idyll of the country gulped at the smoke
    from the hills and tethered
His horse in the hiding of a clump of pines, and climbed the line-fence.

                                                        Turning
    a cypress thicket
He saw a figure sway in the starlight, and stood still, breathless. A woman:
    Tamar? Not Tamar:
No one he knew: it faced the east gables of the house and seemed twisting
    its hands and suddenly
Flung up both arms to its face and passed out of the patch of starlight. The
    boy, troubled and cautious,
Turned the other way and circling to the south face of the house peered
    from behind the buttressed
Base of a seventy-year-old trunk that yellow light on the other side clothed,
    and he saw
A lamp on the table and three people sitting by it; the old man,
    stiff-jointed as a corpse,

Grotesquely erect, and old Aunt Stella her lips continually in motion, and
old Jinny
Cross-legg'd having drawn up her ankles into her chair, nodding asleep. At
length Aunt Stella
Ceased talking, none of the three stirred. Young Andrews backed into the
wood and warily finishing
His circuit stood in the darkness under Tamar's window. The strong young
tree to help him to it
Still wore on its boughs her lamplight, then he climbed and set his hands
on the sill, his feet on the ledge
Under it, and Tamar came to the window and took up the lamp to let him
enter. Her face
White in the yellow lamp's glow, with sharp shadows under the eyes and a
high look of joy
He had never seen there frightened him, and she said, "I have been sick,
you know." "I heard," he answered,
"O Tamar, I have been lonely. We must let them know, we can't go on, my
place is with you
When you most need me." "We will tell them to-night," she said, and
kissed his mouth and called, "Lee, Lee,
Come. He has come." "What? Now?" he said. "I have told Lee. I was sick,
he was sorry for me, he is going
To camp to-morrow, he wants to see you and say good-bye." Lee entered
while she spoke and quietly
Held out his hand and Andrews took it. "Talk to each other," Tamar said,
"I am very tired
And must lie down." Lee muttered "She's been awfully sick, it scared us,
you were lucky, Bill Andrews,
Not to be here." "I didn't think so," he answered, "what was it, Lee?"
"Well, it's all over," Lee said
Shifting his feet, "I'm off to-morrow. I'm glad we're friends to say
good-bye. Be good to her, won't you."

And the other, "O God knows I will. All I can do. But of course . . . Lee
   . . . if they need me
She knows I won't beg off because I'm . . . married . . . maybe I'll see you
   over there." "O," said Tamar
Laughing, "you too?" and she sat up on the bed saying, "Lee: go and call
   father if he's able.
We ought to tell him, he ought to meet my — husband." "I'll see if he can,"
   Lee answered, "he was unwell
To-day, and if he's in bed . . ." He left the room, then Tamar: "Look.
   Bring the lamp. What Lee did to me."
She opened the blue robe and bared her flank and thigh showing the long
   whip-mark. "I have a story.
You must see this to believe it." He turned giddy, the sweet slenderness
Dazzling him, and the lamp shook in his hand, for the sharp spasm of
   physical pain one feels
At sight of a wound shot up his entrails. That long welt of red on the
   tender flesh, the blood-flecks
And tortured broken little channels of blood crossing it. "Tamar, Tamar!"
   "Put down the lamp,
And when they come I'll tell you the story." "What shall I do?" "Why,
   nothing, nothing. Poor boy," she said
Pityingly, "I think you are too glad of your life to have come
Into this house, you are not hard enough, you are like my mother, only
   stone or fire
Should marry into this house." Then he bewildered looking at the
   blackened door-frame, "Why yes,"
Laughed Tamar, "it is here, it has been here, the bridegroom's here already.
   O Will I have suffered . . .
Things I daren't tell." "What do you mean, Tamar?" "Nothing, I mustn't
   tell you, you are too high-tempered,
You would do something. Dear, there are things so wicked that nothing
   you can do can make them better,

So horrible now they are done that even to touch or try to mend or punish
　　them is only to widen
Horror: like poking at a corpse in a pool. And father's old and helpless."
　　"Your father, Tamar?"
"And not to blame. I think he hardly even knew what Lee —" "Lee?" "This
　　much I'll tell you,
You have to know it . . . our love, your love and mine, had . . . fruit,
　　would have been fruitful, we were going to have
A child, and I was happy and frightened, and it is dead. O God, O God, O
　　God, I wish
I too had been born too soon and died with the eyes unopened, not a cry,
　　darkness, darkness,
And to be hidden away. They did it to me; with other abuse, worse
　　violence." Meanwhile Lee Cauldwell
Finding his father with the two old women in the room down-stairs,
　　"Father," he said,
"Tamar was asking for you . . ." and Helen's voice through old Aunt Stella
　　answered, "She has enough,
Tell her she has enough." "Aunt Stella," he said, "how long will you keep it
　　up? Our trouble's clearing,
Let your ghosts be." "She has you and the other," she answered, "let me
　　have this one. Are we buzzards to quarrel
Over you dead, we ghosts?" Then Lee turning his shoulder at her, "You
　　must come up, father.
Do you remember the Andrews place that's up the valley? Young Andrews
　　is up-stairs with Tamar,
He wants to marry her. You know I have to go away to-morrow,
　　remember? and I'll go happier
To leave her . . . taken care of. So you'll see him, father?" "Who is it?"
　　asked the old man. "The bridegroom,"
Said Helen's voice, "a bridegroom for your Tamar, and the priest will be
　　fire and blood the witness,

Tamar (1917–23)　91

And they will live together in a house where the mice are moles." "Why do
     you plague me," he answered
Plaintively, and Lee: "Come, father," and he lifting his face, "I have prayed
     to the hills to come and cover me,
We are on the drop-off cliff of the world and dare not meet Him, I with
     two days to live, even I
Shall watch the ocean boiling and the sea curl up like paper in a fire and the
     dry bed
Crack to the bottom: I have good news for her, I will see her." "And I to
     tell her she may take
Two but not three," said Helen. "Stay here, stay here, be quiet," Lee
     answered angrily, "can I take up
The whole menagerie, raving?" He turned in the door and heard his father
     move behind him and said,
"If you come up be quiet," and at the door up-stairs, "Father is tired and
     sick, he'll only
Speak to you, Andrews, and must go to bed; he's worried about my going
     away to-morrow.
This is Bill Andrews, father." And Tamar coming to the door, "Let him
     come in, it's dark here,
No, bring him in. Father come in. What, shall the men that made your war
     suck up their millions,
Not I my three?" Then Andrews: "If Tamar is well enough to go to-night I
     will take her to-night.
You will be well when you are out of this house." "You hate it still," said
     Tamar. "He hates the house,"
She said to Lee, leading his eyes with the significance in hers to the
     blackened door-frame,
"Well, I will go with you to-morrow." And Lee, "Listen, Will Andrews, I
     heard from somebody
You know who set the fire here." "No, not that," he answered, "but I know
     other worse things

That have been done here." "Fire, fire," moaned the old man, "the fire of
  the Lord coming in judgment. Tamar,
It is well with us, be happy, He won't torture the wicked, He will rub them
  out and suddenly
With instant fire. We shall be nothing." "Come, Tamar," Andrews cried,
  "to-night. I daren't leave you."
"For fear I ask her," said Lee. "You did it, then. You set the fire." "No,
  that's too idiot
A lie to answer," he said, "what do I know about your fires? I know
  something
Worse than arson. And saw the horrible new scar of a whip
Not to be paid — this way!" He felt the jerk of his arm striking
And his fist hitting the sharp edge of the jawbone, but yet
When Lee staggered and closed in with a groan,
Clutching him, fumbling for his throat, Will thought "What a fool
To make a nasty show of us before Tamar
And the others, why does he want to fight?" and indignantly
Pushed him off and struck twice, both fists, Lee dropped
And scrabbled on hands and knees by the little table.
Then the old man cried, "We shall be nothing, nothing.
O but that's frightful."
And Will turning to Tamar saw such hatred
Wrinkle her face he felt a horrible surge
Of nausea in him, then with bare teeth she smiled at him
And he believed the hate was for her brother
And said, "Ah Tamar, come." Meanwhile the Helen
That spoke out of the lungs and ran in the nerves
Of old Aunt Stella caught the old man David Cauldwell
By the loose flapping sleeve and the lean arm,
Saying in a clotted amorous voice, "Come, David,
My brother, my lover, O honey come, she has no eyes for you,
She feasts on young men. But you to me, to me,

Are as beautiful as when we dared
Desperate pleasure, naked, ages ago,
In the room and by the sea." "Father," said Tamar,
"It is only an hour to the end, whom do you want
To-night? Stay here by me." "I was hunting for something," said Lee
    Cauldwell,
"Here it is, here it is," and had the sheath-knife bared
And struck up from the floor, rising, the blade
Ripped cloth and skin along his enemy's belly
And the leather belt catching it deflected the point
Into the bowels, Andrews coughed and fell backward
And Lee falling across him stabbed at his throat
But struck too high and opened the right cheek,
The knife scraping on bone and teeth, then Tamar
In a sea-gull voice, "I dreamed it in his face,
I dreamed a T cut in his face—" "You and your dreams
Have done for us," Lee groaned answer. "Akh, all blood, blood.
What did you say to make him hit me?"

                                        Though it is not thought
That the dead intervene between the minds
And deeds of the living, that they are witnesses,
If anything of their spirits with any memory
Survive and not in prison, would seem as likely
As that an exile should look longingly home:
And the mist-face of that mother at the window
Wavering was but a witness, could but watch,
Neither prevent nor cause: no doubt there are many
Such watchers in the world: the same whom Andrews,
Stepping like a thief among the cypress clumps an hour before
Saw twist her hands and suddenly fling up both vaporous arms and sway out
    of the starlight,

She now was watching at the down-stairs window
Old Jinny alone in the room, and saw, as the dead see, the thoughts
More clearly than the cloth and skin; the child mind
In that old flesh gathered home on itself
In coils, laboring to warm a memory,
And worked on by an effluence, petulantly pushing away
The easier memories of its open time
Forty years back, power flowing from someone in that house
Belting it in, pressing it to its labor,
Making it shape in itself the memory of to-day's
Vision, the watcher saw it, how could she know it
Or know from whence? a girl naked, no, wrapped in fire,
Filmed in white sheets of fire. "Why, I'm like God,"
Old Jinny had said, "I see through walls," a girl
Naked though clothed in fire, and under the arms
Naked, no hair, — "Ah to be like her, to be like her, probably
Cloth, hair, burned off": displaying herself before a wild old man
Who appeared part of the joy: "Ah to be like her,
Fire is so sweet, they never let me play with it,
No one loves Jinny, wouldn't fire be a father
And hold her in his arms? Fire is so sweet,"
She hovered the hot lamp, "sweet fire, sweet light,"
She held a rag of paper above it, "O dear, dear fire,
Come and kiss Jinny, no one's looking,
Jinny's alone. Dear star, dear light, O lovely fire
Won't you come out, why is it turning black,
Ah come, Ah come, hug Jinny." The hungry beautiful bird
Hopped from its bird-cage to her. "I've got my star,
Ah love, Ah love, and here's more paper
And a little of Jinny's dress, love, lovely light,
Jinny so loves you, Jinny's baby, Jinny's baby,
O," she screamed, "Oo, Oo, Oo," and ran to the window, folded

In a terrible wreath, and at her side the curtains
Danced into flame, and over her head; the gasp
That followed on a cry drew down a sword
Of flame to her lungs, pain ceased, and thinking "Father"
She dropped herself into the arms of the fire,
Huddling under the sill, and her spirit unprisoned
Filled all the room and felt a nuptial joy
In mixing with the bright and eager flame.
While from that blackened morsel on the floor
Fire spread to the wall and gnawed it through, and the window-glass
Crackling and tinkling a rush of south wind fed
The eagerness in the house. They heard up-stairs
That brutal arch of crying, the quick crescendo,
The long drop and the following moan, Will Andrews
Struggled to rise and like a gopher-snake that a child
Has mashed the head of with a stone, he waggled
The blood-clot of his head over the floor
Gulping "You devils, you devils." Lee would have run down
But Tamar clung to him, the old man on his knees
Muttered to God, and old Aunt Stella
In no voice but her own screamed, screamed. Then fire
Was heard roaring, the door leaked threads of smoke,
Lee caught up Tamar in his arms and turned
To the window, the cypress-ladder, but his first step,
Blind, with the burden in his arms, the smoke in his eyes,
Trampled his murdered man on the floor who turning
Caught the other ankle and Lee went down and Tamar
So lovingly wound him that he could not rise
Till the house was full of its bright death; then Tamar:
"I will not let you take me. Go if you want."
He answered, "You devil, shall I go?" "You wouldn't stay!

Think of your black-eyed French girls." "We are on the edge of it," he
    answered,
"Tamar, be decent for a minute." "I have my three lovers
Here in one room, none of them will go out,
How can I help being happy? This old man
Has prayed the end of the world onto us all,
And which of you leaves me?" Then the old man: "O what mountain,
What mountain, what mountain?" And Lee, "Father. The window.
We'll follow you." But he kneeling would not rise,
While the house moved and the floor sagged to the south
And old Aunt Stella through the opening door
Ran into the red and black, and did not scream
Any more; then Tamar, "Did you think you would go
Laughing through France?" And the old man, "Fierce, fierce light,
Have pity, Christ have pity, Christ have pity, Christ have pity,
Christ have pity,
Christ have pity . . ."
And Tamar with her back to the window embraced
Her brother, who struggled toward it, but the floor
Turned like a wheel.

                    Grass grows where the flame flowered;
A hollowed lawn strewn with a few black stones
And the brick of broken chimneys; all about there
The old trees, some of them scarred with fire, endure the sea-wind.

POINT JOE

Point Joe has teeth and has torn ships; it has fierce and solitary beauty;
Walk there all day you shall see nothing that will not make part of a poem.

I saw the spars and planks of shipwreck on the rocks, and beyond the
  desolate
Sea-meadows rose the warped wind-bitten van of the pines, a fog-bank
  vaulted

Forest and all, the flat sea-meadows at that time of year were plated
Golden with the low flower called footsteps of the spring, millions of
  flowerets,

Whose light suffused upward into the fog flooded its vault, we wandered
Through a weird country where the light beat up from earthward, and was
  golden.

One other moved there, an old Chinaman gathering seaweed from the
  sea-rocks,
He brought it in his basket and spread it flat to dry on the edge of the
  meadow.

Permanent things are what is needful in a poem, things temporally
Of great dimension, things continually renewed or always present.

Grass that is made each year equals the mountains in her past and future;
Fashionable and momentary things we need not see nor speak of.

Man gleaning food between the solemn presences of land and ocean,
On shores where better men have shipwrecked, under fog and among
  flowers,

Equals the mountains in his past and future; that glow from the earth was
   only
A trick of nature's, one must forgive nature a thousand graceful subtleties.

GALE IN APRIL

Intense and terrible beauty, how has our race with the frail naked nerves,
So little a craft swum down from its far launching?
Why now, only because the northwest blows and the headed grass billows,
Great seas jagging the west and on the granite
Blanching, the vessel is brimmed, this dancing play of the world is too
   much passion.
A gale in April so overfilling the spirit,
Though his ribs were thick as the earth's, arches of mountain, how shall one
   dare to live,
Though his blood were like the earth's rivers and his flesh iron,
How shall one dare to live? One is born strong, how do the weak endure it?
The strong lean upon death as on a rock,
After eighty years there is shelter and the naked nerves shall be covered
   with deep quietness,
O beauty of things go on, go on, O torture
Of intense joy I have lasted out my time, I have thanked God and finished,
Roots of millennial trees fold me in the darkness,
Northwest wind shake their tops, not to the root, not to the root, I have
   passed
From beauty to the other beauty, peace, the night splendor.

THE TREASURE

Mountains, a moment's earth-waves rising and hollowing; the earth too's
  an ephemerid; the stars —
Short-lived as grass the stars quicken in the nebula and dry in their
  summer, they spiral
Blind up space, scattered black seeds of a future; nothing lives long, the
  whole sky's
Recurrences tick the seconds of the hours of the ages of the gulf before
  birth, and the gulf
After death is like dated: to labor eighty years in a notch of eternity is
  nothing too tiresome,
Enormous repose after, enormous repose before, the flash of activity.
Surely you never have dreamed the incredible depths were prologue and
  epilogue merely
To the surface play in the sun, the instant of life, what is called life? I fancy
That silence is the thing, this noise a found word for it; interjection, a jump
  of the breath at that silence;
Stars burn, grass grows, men breathe: as a man finding treasure says "Ah!"
  but the treasure's the essence;
Before the man spoke it was there, and after he has spoken he gathers it,
  inexhaustible treasure.

Roan Stallion

1924-25

BIRDS

The fierce musical cries of a couple of sparrowhawks hunting on the headland,
Hovering and darting, their heads northwestward,
Prick like silver arrows shot through a curtain the noise of the ocean
Trampling its granite; their red backs gleam
Under my window around the stone corners; nothing gracefuller, nothing
Nimbler in the wind. Westward the wave-gleaners,
The old gray sea-going gulls are gathered together, the northwest wind wakening
Their wings to the wild spirals of the wind-dance.
Fresh as the air, salt as the foam, play birds in the bright wind, fly falcons
Forgetting the oak and the pinewood, come gulls
From the Carmel sands and the sands at the river-mouth, from Lobos and out of the limitless
Power of the mass of the sea, for a poem
Needs multitude, multitudes of thoughts, all fierce, all flesh-eaters, musically clamorous
Bright hawks that hover and dart headlong, and ungainly
Gray hungers fledged with desire of transgression, salt slimed beaks, from the sharp
Rock-shores of the world and the secret waters.

FOG

Invisible gulls with human voices cry in the sea-cloud
"There is room, wild minds,
Up high in the cloud; the web and the feather remember
Three elements, but here
Is but one, and the webs and the feathers
Subduing but the one
Are the greater, with strength and to spare." You dream, wild criers,
The peace that all life
Dreams gluttonously, the infinite self that has eaten
Environment, and lives
Alone, unencroached on, perfectly gorged, one God.
Caesar and Napoleon
Visibly acting their dream of that solitude, Christ and Gautama,
Being God, devouring
The world with atonement for God's sake . . . ah sacred hungers,
The conqueror's, the prophet's,
The lover's, the hunger of the sea-beaks, slaves of the last peace,
Worshippers of oneness.

BOATS IN A FOG

Sports and gallantries, the stage, the arts, the antics of dancers,
The exuberant voices of music,
Have charm for children but lack nobility; it is bitter earnestness
That makes beauty; the mind
Knows, grown adult.

           A sudden fog-drift muffled the ocean,
A throbbing of engines moved in it,
At length, a stone's throw out, between the rocks and the vapor,
One by one moved shadows
Out of the mystery, shadows, fishing-boats, trailing each other
Following the cliff for guidance,
Holding a difficult path between the peril of the sea-fog
And the foam on the shore granite.
One by one, trailing their leader, six crept by me,
Out of the vapor and into it,
The throb of their engines subdued by the fog, patient and cautious,
Coasting all round the peninsula
Back to the buoys in Monterey harbor. A flight of pelicans
Is nothing lovelier to look at;
The flight of the planets is nothing nobler; all the arts lose virtue
Against the essential reality
Of creatures going about their business among the equally
Earnest elements of nature.

PEOPLE AND A HERON

A desert of weed and water-darkened stone under my western windows
The ebb lasted all afternoon,
And many pieces of humanity, men, women, and children, gathering
  shellfish,
Swarmed with voices of gulls the sea-breach.
At twilight they went off together, the verge was left vacant, an evening
  heron
Bent broad wings over the black ebb,
And left me wondering why a lone bird was dearer to me than many
  people.
Well: rare is dear: but also I suppose
Well reconciled with the world but not with our own natures we grudge to
  see them
Reflected on the world for a mirror.

NIGHT

The ebb slips from the rock, the sunken
Tide-rocks lift streaming shoulders
Out of the slack, the slow west
Sombering its torch; a ship's light
Shows faintly, far out,
Over the weight of the prone ocean
On the low cloud.

Over the dark mountain, over the dark pinewood,
Down the long dark valley along the shrunken river,
Returns the splendor without rays, the shining of shadow,
Peace-bringer, the matrix of all shining and quieter of shining.
Where the shore widens on the bay she opens dark wings
And the ocean accepts her glory. O soul worshipful of her
You like the ocean have grave depths where she dwells always,
And the film of waves above that takes the sun takes also
Her, with more love. The sun-lovers have a blond favorite,
A father of lights and noises, wars, weeping and laughter,
Hot labor, lust and delight and the other blemishes. Quietness
Flows from her deeper fountain; and he will die; and she is immortal.

Far off from here the slender
Flocks of the mountain forest
Move among stems like towers
Of the old redwoods to the stream,
No twig crackling; dip shy
Wild muzzles into the mountain water
Among the dark ferns.

O passionately at peace you being secure will pardon
The blasphemies of glowworms, the lamp in my tower, the fretfulness
Of cities, the cressets of the planets, the pride of the stars.
This August night in a rift of cloud Antares reddens,
The great one, the ancient torch, a lord among lost children,
The earth's orbit doubled would not girdle his greatness, one fire
Globed, out of grasp of the mind enormous; but to you O Night
What? Not a spark? What flicker of a spark in the faint far glimmer
Of a lost fire dying in the desert, dim coals of a sand-pit the Bedouins
Wandered from at dawn . . . Ah singing prayer to what gulfs tempted
Suddenly are you more lost? To us the near-hand mountain
Be a measure of height, the tide-worn cliff at the sea-gate a measure of
    continuance.

The tide, moving the night's
Vastness with lonely voices,
Turns, the deep dark-shining
Pacific leans on the land,
Feeling his cold strength
To the outmost margins: you Night will resume
The stars in your time.

O passionately at peace when will that tide draw shoreward?
Truly the spouting fountains of light, Antares, Arcturus,
Tire of their flow, they sing one song but they think silence.
The striding winter giant Orion shines, and dreams darkness.
And life, the flicker of men and moths and the wolf on the hill,
Though furious for continuance, passionately feeding, passionately
Remaking itself upon its mates, remembers deep inward
The calm mother, the quietness of the womb and the egg,
The primal and the latter silences: dear Night it is memory
Prophesies, prophecy that remembers, the charm of the dark.

And I and my people, we are willing to love the four-score years
Heartily; but as a sailor loves the sea, when the helm is for harbor.

Have men's minds changed,
Or the rock hidden in the deep of the waters of the soul
Broken the surface? A few centuries
Gone by, was none dared not to people
The darkness beyond the stars with harps and habitations.
But now, dear is the truth. Life is grown sweeter and lonelier,
And death is no evil.

AUTUMN EVENING

Though the little clouds ran southward still, the quiet autumnal
Cool of the late September evening
Seemed promising rain, rain, the change of the year, the angel
Of the sad forest. A heron flew over
With that remote ridiculous cry, "Quawk," the cry
That seems to make silence more silent. A dozen
Flops of the wing, a drooping glide, at the end of the glide
The cry, and a dozen flops of the wing.
I watched him pass on the autumn-colored sky; beyond him
Jupiter shone for evening star.
The sea's voice worked into my mood, I thought "No matter
What happens to men . . . the world's well made though."

JOY

Though joy is better than sorrow joy is not great;
Peace is great, strength is great.
Not for joy the stars burn, not for joy the vulture
Spreads her gray sails on the air
Over the mountain; not for joy the worn mountain
Stands, while years like water
Trench his long sides. "I am neither mountain nor bird
Nor star; and I seek joy."
The weakness of your breed: yet at length quietness
Will cover those wistful eyes.

PHENOMENA

Great-enough both accepts and subdues; the great frame takes all creatures;
From the greatness of their element they all take beauty.
Gulls; and the dingy freightship lurching south in the eye of a rain-wind;
The air-plane dipping over the hill; hawks hovering
The white grass of the headland; cormorants roosting upon the guano-
Whitened skerries; pelicans awind; sea-slime
Shining at night in the wave-stir like drowned men's lanterns; smugglers signaling
A cargo to land; or the old Point Pinos lighthouse
Lawfully winking over dark water; the flight of the twilight herons,
Lonely wings and a cry; or with motor-vibrations
That hum in the rock like a new storm-tone of the ocean's to turn eyes westward
The navy's new-bought Zeppelin going by in the twilight,
Far out seaward; relative only to the evening star and the ocean
It slides into a cloud over Point Lobos.

from THE TOWER BEYOND TRAGEDY
[final scene]

ORESTES   I left the madness of the house,
    to-night in the dark, with you it walks yet.
    How shall I tell you what I have learned? Your mind is like a hawk's or like
        a lion's, this knowledge
    Is out of the order of your mind, a stranger language. To wild-beasts and
        the blood of kings
    A verse blind in the book.
ELECTRA   At least my eyes can see dawn graying: tell and
    not mock me, our moment
    Dies in a moment.
ORESTES   Here is the last labor
    To spend on humanity. I saw a vision of us move in the dark: all that we
        did or dreamed of
    Regarded each other, the man pursued the woman, the woman clung to the
        man, warriors and kings
    Strained at each other in the darkness, all loved or fought inward, each one
        of the lost people
    Sought the eyes of another that another should praise him; sought never his
        own but another's; the net of desire
    Had every nerve drawn to the centre, so that they writhed like a full
        draught of fishes, all matted
    In the one mesh; when they look backward they see only a man standing at
        the beginning,
    Or forward, a man at the end; or if upward, men in the shining bitter sky
        striding and feasting,
    Whom you call Gods . . .
    It is all turned inward, all your desires incestuous, the woman the serpent,
        the man the rose-red cavern,
    Both human, worship forever . . .

ELECTRA   You have dreamed wretchedly.

ORESTES   I have
    seen the dreams of the people and not dreamed them.

    As for me, I have slain my mother.

ELECTRA   No more?

ORESTES   And the gate's open, the
    gray boils over the mountain, I have greater

Kindred than dwell under a roof. Didn't I say this would be dark to you? I
    have cut the meshes

And fly like a freed falcon. To-night, lying on the hillside, sick with those
    visions, I remembered

The knife in the stalk of my humanity; I drew and it broke; I entered the
    life of the brown forest

And the great life of the ancient peaks, the patience of stone, I felt the
    changes in the veins

In the throat of the mountain, a grain in many centuries, we have our own
    time, not yours; and I was the stream

Draining the mountain wood; and I the stag drinking; and I was the stars

Boiling with light, wandering alone, each one the lord of his own summit;
    and I was the darkness

Outside the stars, I included them, they were a part of me. I was mankind
    also, a moving lichen

On the cheek of the round stone . . . they have not made words for it, to go
    behind things, beyond hours and ages,

And be all things in all time, in their returns and passages, in the
    motionless and timeless centre,

In the white of the fire . . . how can I express the excellence I have found,
    that has no color but clearness;

No honey but ecstasy; nothing wrought nor remembered; no undertone nor
    silver second murmur

That rings in love's voice, I and my loved are one; no desire but fulfilled; no
    passion but peace,

The pure flame and the white, fierier than any passion; no time but spheral
    eternity: Electra,
Was that your name before this life dawned —

ELECTRA   Here is mere death. Death
    like a triumph I'd have paid to keep you
A king in high Mycenae: but here is shameful death, to die because I have
    lost you. They'll say
Having done justice Agamemnon's son ran mad and was lost in the mountain; but
    Agamemnon's daughter
Hanged herself from a beam of the house: O bountiful hands of justice! This horror
    draws upon me
Like stone walking.

ORESTES   What fills men's mouths is nothing; and your threat
    is nothing; I have fallen in love outward.
If I believed you — it is I that am like stone walking.

ELECTRA   I can endure even to
    hate you,
But that's no matter. Strength's good. You are lost. I here remember the
    honor of the house, and Agamemnon's.

She turned and entered the ancient house. Orestes walked in the clear
    dawn; men say that a serpent
Killed him in high Arcadia. But young or old, few years or many, signified
    less than nothing
To him who had climbed the tower beyond time, consciously, and cast
    humanity, entered the earlier fountain.

ROAN STALLION

The dog barked; then the woman stood in the doorway, and hearing iron strike stone down the steep road
Covered her head with a black shawl and entered the light rain; she stood at the turn of the road.
A nobly formed woman; erect and strong as a new tower; the features stolid and dark
But sculptured into a strong grace; straight nose with a high bridge, firm and wide eyes, full chin,
Red lips; she was only a fourth part Indian; a Scottish sailor had planted her in young native earth,
Spanish and Indian, twenty-one years before. He had named her California when she was born;
That was her name; and had gone north.

She heard the hooves and wheels come nearer, up the steep road.
The buckskin mare, leaning against the breastpiece, plodded into sight round the wet bank.
The pale face of the driver followed; the burnt-out eyes; they had fortune in them. He sat twisted
On the seat of the old buggy, leading a second horse by a long halter, a roan, a big one,
That stepped daintily; by the swell of the neck, a stallion. "What have you got, Johnny?" "Maskerel's stallion.
Mine now. I won him last night, I had very good luck." He was quite drunk. "They bring their mares up here now.
I keep this fellow. I got money besides, but I'll not show you." "Did you buy something, Johnny,
For our Christine? Christmas comes in two days, Johnny." "By God, forgot," he answered laughing.

"Don't tell Christine it's Christmas; after while I get her something,
    maybe." But California:
"I shared your luck when you lost: you lost *me* once, Johnny, remember?
    Tom Dell had me two nights
Here in the house: other times we've gone hungry: now that you've won,
    Christine will have her Christmas.
We share your luck, Johnny. You give me money, I go down to Monterey
    to-morrow,
Buy presents for Christine, come back in the evening. Next day
    Christmas." "You have wet ride," he answered
Giggling. "Here money. Five dollar; ten; twelve dollar. You buy two bottles
    of rye whisky for Johnny."
"All right. I go to-morrow."

                        He was an outcast Hollander; not old, but
    shriveled with bad living.
The child Christine inherited from his race blue eyes, from his life a
    wizened forehead; she watched
From the house-door her father lurch out of the buggy and lead with due
    respect the stallion
To the new corral, the strong one; leaving the wearily breathing buckskin
    mare to his wife to unharness.

Storm in the night; the rain on the thin shakes of the roof like the ocean
    on rock streamed battering; once thunder
Walked down the narrow canyon into Carmel valley and wore away
    westward; Christine was wakeful
With fears and wonders; her father lay too deep for storm to touch him.

                                                            Dawn
    comes late in the year's dark,

Later into the crack of a canyon under redwoods; and California slipped from bed

An hour before it; the buckskin would be tired; there was a little barley, and why should Johnny

Feed all the barley to his stallion? That is what he would do. She tip-toed out of the room,

Leaving her clothes, he'd waken if she waited to put them on, and passed from the door of the house

Into the dark of the rain; the big black drops were cold through the thin shift, but the wet earth

Pleasant under her naked feet. There was a pleasant smell in the stable; and moving softly,

Touching things gently with the supple bend of the unclothed body, was pleasant. She found a box,

Filled it with sweet dry barley and took it down to the old corral. The little mare sighed deeply

At the rail in the wet darkness; and California returning between two redwoods up to the house

Heard the happy jaws grinding the grain. Johnny could mind the pigs and chickens. Christine called to her

When she entered the house, but slept again under her hand. She laid the wet night-dress on a chair-back

And stole into the bed-room to get her clothes. A plank creaked, and he wakened. She stood motionless

Hearing him stir in the bed. When he was quiet she stooped after her shoes, and he said softly,

"What are you doing? Come back to bed." "It's late, I'm going to Monterey, I must hitch up."

"You come to bed first. I been away three days. I give you money, I take back the money

And what you do in town then?" She sighed sharply and came to the bed.

                                                        He reaching his hands
    from it
Felt the cool curve and firmness of her flank, and half rising caught her by
    the long wet hair.
She endured, and to hasten the act she feigned desire; she had not for long,
    except in dream, felt it.
Yesterday's drunkenness made him sluggish and exacting; she saw, turning
    her head sadly,
The windows were bright gray with dawn; he embraced her still, stopping
    to talk about the stallion.
At length she was permitted to put on her clothes. Clear daylight over the
    steep hills;
Gray-shining cloud over the tops of the redwoods; the winter stream sang
    loud; the wheels of the buggy
Slipped in deep slime, ground on washed stones at the road-edge. Down
    the hill the wrinkled river smothered the ford.
You must keep to the bed of stones: she knew the way by willow and alder:
    the buckskin halted mid-stream,
Shuddering, the water her own color washing up to the traces; but
    California, drawing up
Her feet out of the whirl onto the seat of the buggy swung the whip over
    the yellow water
And drove to the road.

                        All morning the clouds were racing northward
    like a river. At noon they thickened.
When California faced the southwind home from Monterey it was heavy
    with level rain-fall.
She looked seaward from the foot of the valley; red rays cried sunset from a
    trumpet of streaming

Cloud over Lobos, the southwest occident of the solstice. Twilight came
    soon, but the tired mare
Feared the road more than the whip. Mile after mile of slow gray twilight.

                                                   Then,
    quite suddenly, darkness.
"Christine will be asleep. It is Christmas Eve. The ford. That hour of
    daylight wasted this morning!"
She could see nothing; she let the reins lie on the dashboard and knew at
    length by the cramp of the wheels
And the pitch down, they had reached it. Noise of wheels on stones,
    plashing of hooves in water; a world
Of sounds; no sight; the gentle thunder of water; the mare snorting,
    dipping her head, one knew,
To look for footing, in the blackness, under the stream. The hushing and
    creaking of the sea-wind
In the passion of invisible willows.

                              The mare stood still; the woman
    shouted to her; spared whip,
For a false leap would lose the track of the ford. She stood. "The baby's
    things," thought California,
"Under the seat: the water will come over the floor"; and rising in the
    midst of the water
She tilted the seat; fetched up the doll, the painted wooden chickens, the
    woolly bear, the book
Of many pictures, the box of sweets: she brought them all from under the
    seat and stored them, trembling,
Under her clothes, about the breasts, under the arms; the corners of the
    cardboard boxes
Cut into the soft flesh; but with a piece of rope for a girdle and wound
    about the shoulders

All was made fast. The mare stood still as if asleep in the midst of the
    water. Then California
Reached out a hand over the stream and fingered her rump; the solid wet
    convexity of it
Shook like the beat of a great heart. "What are you waiting for?" But the
    feel of the animal surface
Had wakened a dream, obscured real danger with a dream of danger.
    "What for? For the water-stallion
To break out of the stream, that is what the rump strains for, him to come
    up flinging foam sidewise,
Fore-hooves in air, crush me and the rig and curl over his woman." She
    flung out with the whip then;
The mare plunged forward. The buggy drifted sidelong: was she off
    ground? Swimming? No: by the splashes.
The driver, a mere prehensile instinct, clung to the side-irons of the seat
    and felt the force
But not the coldness of the water, curling over her knees, breaking up to
    the waist
Over her body. They'd turned. The mare had turned up stream and was
    wallowing back into shoal water.
Then California dropped her forehead to her knees, having seen nothing,
    feeling a danger,
And felt the brute weight of a branch of alder, the pendulous light leaves
    brush her bent neck
Like a child's fingers. The mare burst out of water and stopped on the slope
    to the ford. The woman climbed down
Between the wheels and went to her head. "Poor Dora," she called her by
    her name, "there, Dora. Quietly,"
And led her around, there was room to turn on the margin, the head to the
    gentle thunder of the water.
She crawled on hands and knees, felt for the ruts, and shifted the wheels
    into them. "You can see, Dora.

I can't. But this time you'll go through it." She climbed into the seat and
    shouted angrily. The mare

Stopped, her two forefeet in the water. She touched with the whip. The
    mare plodded ahead and halted.

Then California thought of prayer: "Dear little Jesus,

Dear baby Jesus born to-night, your head was shining

Like silver candles. I've got a baby too, only a girl. You had light wherever
    you walked.

Dear baby Jesus give me light." Light streamed: rose, gold, rich purple,
    hiding the ford like a curtain.

The gentle thunder of water was a noise of wing-feathers, the fans of
    paradise lifting softly.

The child afloat on radiance had a baby face, but the angels had birds'
    heads, hawks' heads,

Bending over the baby, weaving a web of wings about him. He held in the
    small fat hand

A little snake with golden eyes, and California could see clearly on the
    under radiance

The mare's pricked ears, a sharp black fork against the shining light-fall.
    But it dropped; the light of heaven

Frightened poor Dora. She backed; swung up the water,

And nearly oversetting the buggy turned and scrambled backward; the iron
    wheel-tires rang on bowlders.

Then California weeping climbed between the wheels. Her wet clothes and
    the toys packed under

Dragged her down with their weight; she stripped off cloak and dress and
    laid the baby's things in the buggy;

Brought Johnny's whisky out from under the seat; wrapped all in the dress,
    bottles and toys, and tied them

Into a bundle that would sling over her back. She unharnessed the mare,
    hurting her fingers

Against the swollen straps and the wet buckles. She tied the pack over her
shoulders, the cords

Crossing her breasts, and mounted. She drew up her shift about her waist
and knotted it, naked thighs

Clutching the sides of the mare, bare flesh to the wet withers, and caught
the mane with her right hand,

The looped-up bridle-reins in the other. "Dora, the baby gives you light."
The blinding radiance

Hovered the ford. "Sweet baby Jesus give us light." Cataracts of light and
Latin singing

Fell through the willows; the mare snorted and reared: the roar and thunder
of the invisible water;

The night shaking open like a flag, shot with the flashes; the baby face
hovering; the water

Beating over her shoes and stockings up to the bare thighs; and over them,
like a beast

Lapping her belly; the wriggle and pitch of the mare swimming; the drift,
the sucking water; the blinding

Light above and behind with not a gleam before, in the throat of darkness;
the shock of the fore-hooves

Striking bottom, the struggle and surging lift of the haunches. She felt the
water streaming off her

From the shoulders down; heard the great strain and sob of the mare's
breathing, heard the horse-shoes grind on gravel.

When California came home the dog at the door snuffed at her without
barking; Christine and Johnny

Both were asleep; she did not sleep for hours, but kindled fire and knelt
patiently over it,

Shaping and drying the dear-bought gifts for Christmas morning.

> She
hated (she thought) the proud-necked stallion.

He'd lean the big twin masses of his breast on the rail, his red-brown eyes
	flash the white crescents,
She admired him then, she hated him for his uselessness, serving nothing
But Johnny's vanity. Horses were too cheap to breed. She thought, if he
	could range in freedom,
Shaking the red-roan mane for a flag on the bare hills.

A man brought up

	a mare in April;
Then California, though she wanted to watch, stayed with Christine
	indoors. When the child fretted
The mother told her once more about the miracle of the ford; her prayer to
	the little Jesus
The Christmas Eve when she was bringing the gifts home; the appearance,
	the lights, the Latin singing,
The thunder of wing-feathers and water, the shining child, the cataracts of
	splendor down the darkness.
"A little baby," Christine asked, "the God is a baby?" "The child of God.
	That was his birthday.
His mother was named Mary: we pray to her too: God came to her. He
	was not the child of a man
Like you or me. God was his father: she was the stallion's wife — what did I
	say — God's wife,"
She said with a cry, lifting Christine aside, pacing the planks of the floor.
	"She is called more blessed
Than any woman. She was so good, she was more loved." "Did God live
	near her house?" "He lives
Up high, over the stars; he ranges on the bare blue hill of the sky." In her
	mind a picture
Flashed, of the red-roan mane shaken out for a flag on the bare hills, and
	she said quickly, "He's more

Like a great man holding the sun in his hand." Her mind giving her words
    the lie, "But no one

Knows, only the shining and the power. The power, the terror, the burning
    fire covered her over . . ."

"Was she burnt up, mother?" "She was so good and lovely, she was the
    mother of the little Jesus.

If you are good nothing will hurt you." "What did she think?" "She loved,
    she was not afraid of the hooves —

Hands that had made the hills and sun and moon, and the sea and the great
    redwoods, the terrible strength,

She gave herself without thinking." "You only saw the baby, mother?" "Yes,
    and the angels about him,

The great wild shining over the black river." Three times she had walked
    to the door, three times returned,

And now the hand that had thrice hung on the knob, full of prevented
    action, twisted the cloth

Of the child's dress that she had been mending. "Oh, Oh, I've torn it." She
    struck at the child and then embraced her

Fiercely, the small blond sickly body.

                                        Johnny came in, his face reddened
    as if he had stood

Near fire, his eyes triumphing. "Finished," he said, and looked with malice
    at Christine. "I go

Down valley with Jim Carrier; owes me five dollar, fifteen I charge him, he
    brought ten in his pocket.

Has grapes on the ranch, maybe I take a barrel red wine instead of money.
    Be back to-morrow.

To-morrow night I tell you — Eh, Jim," he laughed over his shoulder, "I say
    to-morrow evening

I show her how the red fellow act, the big fellow. When I come home." She
    answered nothing, but stood

In front of the door, holding the little hand of her daughter, in the path of
    sun between the redwoods,
While Johnny tied the buckskin mare behind Carrier's buggy, and bringing
    saddle and bridle tossed them
Under the seat. Jim Carrier's mare, the bay, stood with drooped head and
    started slowly, the men
Laughing and shouting at her; their voices could be heard down the steep
    road, after the noise
Of the iron-hooped wheels died from the stone. Then one might hear the
    hush of the wind in the tall redwoods,
The tinkle of the April brook, deep in its hollow.

                             Humanity is the start
   of the race; I say
Humanity is the mould to break away from, the crust to break through, the
    coal to break into fire,
The atom to be split.

                  Tragedy that breaks man's face and a white fire flies
   out of it; vision that fools him
Out of his limits, desire that fools him out of his limits, unnatural crime,
    inhuman science,
Slit eyes in the mask; wild loves that leap over the walls of nature, the wild
    fence-vaulter science,
Useless intelligence of far stars, dim knowledge of the spinning demons
    that make an atom,
These break, these pierce, these deify, praising their God shrilly with fierce
    voices: not in a man's shape
He approves the praise, he that walks lightning-naked on the Pacific, that
    laces the suns with planets,
The heart of the atom with electrons: what is humanity in this cosmos? For
    him, the last

Least taint of a trace in the dregs of the solution; for itself, the mould to break away from, the coal
To break into fire, the atom to be split.

                                     After the child slept, after the leopard-footed evening
Had glided oceanward, California turned the lamp to its least flame and glided from the house.
She moved sighing, like a loose fire, backward and forward on the smooth ground by the door.
She heard the night-wind that draws down the valley like the draught in a flue under clear weather
Whisper and toss in the tall redwoods; she heard the tinkle of the April brook deep in its hollow.
Cooled by the night the odors that the horses had left behind were in her nostrils; the night
Whitened up the bare hill; a drift of coyotes by the river cried bitterly against moonrise;
Then California ran to the old corral, the empty one where they kept the buckskin mare,
And leaned, and bruised her breasts on the rail, feeling the sky whiten. When the moon stood over the hill
She stole to the house. The child breathed quietly. Herself: to sleep? She had seen Christ in the night at Christmas.
The hills were shining open to the enormous night of the April moon: empty and empty,
The vast round backs of the bare hills? If one should ride up high might not the Father himself
Be seen brooding his night, cross-legged, chin in hand, squatting on the last dome? More likely
Leaping the hills, shaking the red-roan mane for a flag on the bare hills. She blew out the lamp.

Every fibre of flesh trembled with faintness when she came to the door;
 strength lacked, to wander
Afoot into the shining of the hill, high enough, high enough . . . the
 hateful face of a man had taken
The strength that might have served her, the corral was empty. The dog
 followed her, she caught him by the collar,
Dragged him in fierce silence back to the door of the house, latched him
 inside.

            It was like daylight
Out-doors and she hastened without faltering down the foot-path, through
 the dark fringe of twisted oak-brush,
To the open place in a bay of the hill. The dark strength of the stallion had
 heard her coming; she heard him
Blow the shining air out of his nostrils, she saw him in the white lake of
 moonlight
Move like a lion along the timbers of the fence, shaking the night-fall
Of the great mane; his fragrance came to her; she leaned on the fence;
He drew away from it, the hooves making soft thunder in the trodden soil.
Wild love had trodden it, his wrestling with the stranger, the shame of the
 day
Had stamped it into mire and powder when the heavy fetlocks
Strained the soft flanks. "Oh if I could bear you!
If I had the strength. O great God that came down to Mary, gently you
 came. But I will ride him
Up into the hill, if he throws me, if he tramples me, is it not my desire
To endure death?" She climbed the fence, pressing her body against the
 rail, shaking like fever,
And dropped inside to the soft ground. He neither threatened her with his
 teeth nor fled from her coming,
And lifting her hand gently to the upflung head she caught the strap of the
 headstall

That hung under the quivering chin. She unlooped the halter from the high
    strength of the neck
And the arch the storm-cloud mane hung with live darkness. He stood; she
    crushed her breasts
On the hard shoulder, an arm over the withers, the other under the mass of
    his throat, and murmuring
Like a mountain dove, "If I could bear you." No way, no help, a gulf in
    nature. She murmured, "Come,
We will run on the hill. O beautiful, O beautiful," and led him
To the gate and flung the bars on the ground. He threw his head downward
To snuff at the bars; and while he stood, she catching mane and withers
    with all sudden contracture
And strength of her lithe body, leaped, clung hard, and was mounted. He
    had been ridden before; he did not
Fight the weight but ran like a stone falling;
Broke down the slope into the moon-glass of the stream, and flattened to
    his neck
She felt the branches of a buck-eye tree fly over her, saw the wall of the
    oak-scrub
End her world: but he turned there, the matted branches
Scraped her right knee, the great slant shoulders
Laboring the hill-slope, up, up, the clear hill. Desire had died in her
At the first rush, the falling like death, but now it revived,
She feeling between her thighs the labor of the great engine, the running
    muscles, the hard swiftness,
She riding the savage and exultant strength of the world. Having topped
    the thicket he turned eastward
Running less wildly; and now at length he felt the halter when she drew on
    it; she guided him upward;
He stopped and grazed on the great arch and pride of the hill, the silent
    calvary. A dwarfish oakwood
Climbed the other slope out of the dark of the unknown canyon beyond;
    the last wind-beaten bush of it

Crawled up to the height, and California slipping from her mount tethered
    him to it. She stood then,
Shaking. Enormous films of moonlight
Trailed down from the height. Space, anxious whiteness, vastness. Distant
    beyond conception the shining ocean
Lay light like a haze along the ledge and doubtful world's end. Little vapors
    gleaming, and little
Darknesses on the far chart underfoot symbolized wood and valley; but the
    air was the element, the moon-
Saturate arcs and spires of the air.

                                Here is solitude, here on the calvary,
    nothing conscious
But the possible God and the cropped grass, no witness, no eye but that
    misformed one, the moon's past fullness.
Two figures on the shining hill, woman and stallion, she kneeling to him,
    brokenly adoring.
He cropping the grass, shifting his hooves, or lifting the long head to gaze
    over the world,
Tranquil and powerful. She prayed aloud "O God I am not good enough,
    O fear, O strength, I am draggled.
Johnny and other men have had me, and O clean power! Here am I," she
    said, falling before him,
And crawled to his hooves. She lay a long while, as if asleep, in reach of the
    fore-hooves, weeping. He avoided
Her head and the prone body. He backed at first; but later plucked the
    grass that grew by her shoulder.

The small dark head under his nostrils: a small round stone, that smelt
    human, black hair growing from it:
The skull shut the light in: it was not possible for any eyes
To know what throbbed and shone under the sutures of the skull, or a shell
    full of lightning

Had scared the roan strength, and he'd have broken tether, screaming, and
    run for the valley.

              The atom bounds-breaking,
Nucleus to sun, electrons to planets, with recognition
Not praying, self-equaling, the whole to the whole, the microcosm
Not entering nor accepting entrance, more equally, more utterly, more
    incredibly conjugate
With the other extreme and greatness; passionately perceptive of
    identity. . . .

            The fire threw up figures
And symbols meanwhile, racial myths formed and dissolved in it, the
    phantom rulers of humanity
That without being are yet more real than what they are born of, and
    without shape, shape that which makes them:
The nerves and the flesh go by shadowlike, the limbs and the lives
    shadowlike, these shadows remain, these shadows
To whom temples, to whom churches, to whom labors and wars, visions
    and dreams are dedicate:
Out of the fire in the small round stone that black moss covered, a crucified
    man writhed up in anguish;
A woman covered by a huge beast in whose mane the stars were netted, sun
    and moon were his eyeballs,
Smiled under the unendurable violation, her throat swollen with the storm
    and blood-flecks gleaming
On the stretched lips; a woman — no, a dark water, split by jets of lightning,
    and after a season
What floated up out of the furrowed water, a boat, a fish, a fire-globe?

                                            It had
    wings, the creature,

And flew against the fountain of lightning, fell burnt out of the cloud back
    to the bottomless water . . .
Figures and symbols, castlings of the fire, played in her brain; but the white
    fire was the essence,
The burning in the small round shell of bone that black hair covered, that
    lay by the hooves on the hill-top.

She rose at length, she unknotted the halter; she walked and led the stallion;
    two figures, woman and stallion,
Came down the silent emptiness of the dome of the hill, under the cataract
    of the moonlight.

The next night there was moon through cloud. Johnny had returned half
    drunk toward evening, and California
Who had known him for years with neither love nor loathing to-night
    hating him had let the child Christine
Play in the light of the lamp for hours after her bed-time; who fell asleep at
    length on the floor
Beside the dog; then Johnny: "Put her to bed." She gathered the child
    against her breasts, she laid her
In the next room, and covered her with a blanket. The window was white,
    the moon had risen. The mother
Lay down by the child, but after a moment Johnny stood in the doorway.
    "Come drink." He had brought home
Two jugs of wine slung from the saddle, part payment for the stallion's
    service; a pitcher of it
Was on the table, and California sadly came and emptied her glass. Whisky,
    she thought,
Would have erased him till to-morrow; the thin red wine. . . . "We have a
    good evening," he laughed, pouring it.
"One glass yet then I show you what the red fellow did." She moving
    toward the house-door his eyes

Followed her, the glass filled and the red juice ran over the table. When it struck the floor-planks

He heard and looked. "Who stuck the pig?" he muttered stupidly, "here's blood, here's blood," and trailed his fingers

In the red lake under the lamplight. While he was looking down the door creaked, she had slipped out-doors,

And he, his mouth curving like a faun's, imagined the chase under the solemn redwoods, the panting

And unresistant victim caught in a dark corner. He emptied the glass and went out-doors

Into the dappled lanes of moonlight. No sound but the April brook's. "Hey Bruno," he called, "find her.

Bruno, go find her." The dog after a little understood and quested, the man following.

When California crouching by an oak-bush above the house heard them come near she darted

To the open slope and ran down hill. The dog barked at her heels, pleased with the game, and Johnny

Followed in silence. She ran down to the new corral, she saw the stallion

Move like a lion along the timbers of the fence, the dark arched neck shaking the night-fall

Of the great mane; she threw herself prone and writhed under the bars, his hooves backing away from her

Made muffled thunder in the soft soil. She stood in the midst of the corral, panting, but Johnny

Paused at the fence. The dog ran under it, and seeing the stallion move, the woman standing quiet,

Danced after the beast, with white-tooth feints and dashes. When Johnny saw the formidable dark strength

Recoil from the dog, he climbed up over the fence.

The child Christine

waked when her mother left her

And lay half-dreaming, in the half-waking dream she saw the ocean come up out of the west

And cover the world, she looked up through clear water at the tops of the redwoods. She heard the door creak

And the house empty; her heart shook her body, sitting up on the bed, and she heard the dog

And crept toward light, where it gleamed under the crack of the door. She opened the door, the room was empty,

The table-top was a red lake under the lamplight. The color of it was terrible to her,

She had seen the red juice drip from a coyote's muzzle, her father had shot one day in the hills

And carried him home over the saddle: she looked at the rifle on the wall-rack: it was not moved:

She ran to the door, the dog was barking and the moon was shining: she knew wine by the odor

But the color frightened her, the empty house frightened her, she followed down hill in the white lane of moonlight

The friendly noise of the dog. She saw in the big horse's corral, on the level shoulder of the hill,

Black on white, the dark strength of the beast, the dancing fury of the dog, and the two others.

One fled, one followed; the big one charged, rearing; one fell under his fore-hooves. She heard her mother

Scream: without thought she ran to the house, she dragged a chair past the red pool and climbed to the rifle,

Got it down from the wall and lugged it somehow through the door and down the hill-side, under the hard weight

Sobbing. Her mother stood by the rails of the corral, she gave it to her. On the far side

The dog flashed at the plunging stallion; in the midst of the space the man,
  slow-moving, like a hurt worm
Crawling, dragged his body by inches toward the fence-line. Then
  California, resting the rifle
On the top rail, without doubting, without hesitance
Aimed for the leaping body of the dog, and when it stood, fired. It snapped,
  rolled over, lay quiet.
"O mother you've hit Bruno!" "I couldn't see the sights in the moonlight,"
  she answered quietly. She stood
And watched, resting the rifle-butt on the ground. The stallion wheeled,
  freed from his torment, the man
Lurched up to his knees, wailing a thin and bitter bird's cry, and the roan
  thunder
Struck; hooves left nothing alive but teeth tore up the remnant. "O
  mother, shoot, shoot!" Yet California
Stood carefully watching, till the beast having fed all his fury stretched neck
  to utmost, head high,
And wrinkled back the upper lip from the teeth, yawning obscene disgust
  over — not a man —
A smear on the moon-lake earth: then California moved by some obscure
  human fidelity
Lifted the rifle. Each separate nerve-cell of her brain flaming the stars fell
  from their places
Crying in her mind: she fired three times before the haunches crumpled
  sidewise, the forelegs stiffening,
And the beautiful strength settled to earth: she turned then on her little
  daughter the mask of a woman
Who has killed God. The night-wind veering, the smell of the spilt wine
  drifted down hill from the house.

The Women at Point Sur

1925-26

POST MORTEM

Happy people die whole, they are all dissolved in a moment, they have
 had what they wanted,
No hard gifts; the unhappy
Linger a space, but pain is a thing that is glad to be forgotten; but one who
 has given
His heart to a cause or a country,
His ghost may spaniel it a while, disconsolate to watch it. I was wondering
 how long the spirit
That sheds this verse will remain
When the nostrils are nipped, when the brain rots in its vault or bubbles in
 the violence of fire
To be ash in metal. I was thinking
Some stalks of the wood whose roots I married to the earth of this place
 will stand five centuries;
I held the roots in my hand,
The stems of the trees between two fingers: how many remote generations
 of women
Will drink joy from men's loins,
And dragged from between the thighs of what mothers will giggle at my
 ghost when it curses the axemen,
Gray impotent voice on the sea-wind,
When the last trunk falls? The women's abundance will have built roofs
 over all this foreland;
Will have buried the rock foundations

I laid here: the women's exuberance will canker and fail in its time and like
    clouds the houses
Unframe, the granite of the prime
Stand from the heaps: come storm and wash clean: the plaster is all run to
    the sea and the steel
All rusted; the foreland resumes
The form we loved when we saw it. Though one at the end of the age and
    far off from this place
Should meet my presence in a poem,
The ghost would not care but be here, long sunset shadow in the seams of
    the granite, and forgotten
The flesh, a spirit for the stone.

CLOUDS AT EVENING

Enormous cloud-mountains that form over Point Lobos and into the
  sunset,
Figures of fire on the walls of to-night's storm,
Foam of gold in gorges of fire, and the great file of warrior angels:
Dreams gathering in the curded brain of the earth,
The sky the brain-vault, on the threshold of sleep: poor earth, you like your
  children
By inordinate desires tortured make dreams?
Storms more enormous, wars nobler, more toppling mountains, more
  jewelled waters, more free
Fires on impossible headlands . . . as a poor girl
Wishing her lover taller and more desirous, and herself maned with gold,
Dreams the world right, in the cold bed, about dawn.
Dreams are beautiful; the slaves of form are beautiful also; I have grown to
  believe
A stone is a better pillow than many visions.

PELICANS

Four pelicans went over the house,
Sculled their worn oars over the courtyard: I saw that ungainliness
Magnifies the idea of strength.
A lifting gale of sea-gulls followed them; slim yachts of the element,
Natural growths of the sky, no wonder
Light wings to leave sea; but those grave weights toil, and are powerful,
And the wings torn with old storms remember
The cone that the oldest redwood dropped from, the tilting of continents,
The dinosaur's day, the lift of new sea-lines.
The omnisecular spirit keeps the old with the new also.
Nothing at all has suffered erasure.
There is life not of our time. He calls ungainly bodies
As beautiful as the grace of horses.
He is weary of nothing; he watches air-planes; he watches pelicans.

APOLOGY FOR BAD DREAMS

I

In the purple light, heavy with redwood, the slopes drop seaward,
Headlong convexities of forest, drawn in together to the steep ravine.
    Below, on the sea-cliff,
A lonely clearing; a little field of corn by the streamside; a roof under
    spared trees. Then the ocean
Like a great stone someone has cut to a sharp edge and polished to shining.
    Beyond it, the fountain
And furnace of incredible light flowing up from the sunk sun. In the little
    clearing a woman
Is punishing a horse; she had tied the halter to a sapling at the edge of the
    wood, but when the great whip
Clung to the flanks the creature kicked so hard she feared he would snap
    the halter; she called from the house
The young man her son; who fetched a chain tie-rope, they working
    together
Noosed the small rusty links round the horse's tongue
And tied him by the swollen tongue to the tree.
Seen from this height they are shrunk to insect size,
Out of all human relation. You cannot distinguish
The blood dripping from where the chain is fastened,
The beast shuddering; but the thrust neck and the legs
Far apart. You can see the whip fall on the flanks . . .
The gesture of the arm. You cannot see the face of the woman.
The enormous light beats up out of the west across the cloud-bars of the
    trade-wind. The ocean
Darkens, the high clouds brighten, the hills darken together. Unbridled and
    unbelievable beauty

Covers the evening world . . . not covers, grows apparent out of it, as Venus down there grows out

From the lit sky. What said the prophet? "I create good: and I create evil: I am the Lord."

II

This coast crying out for tragedy like all beautiful places,

(The quiet ones ask for quieter suffering: but here the granite cliff the gaunt cypresses crown

Demands what victim? The dykes of red lava and black what Titan? The hills like pointed flames

Beyond Soberanes, the terrible peaks of the bare hills under the sun, what immolation?)

This coast crying out for tragedy like all beautiful places: and like the passionate spirit of humanity

Pain for its bread: God's, many victims', the painful deaths, the horrible transfigurements: I said in my heart,

"Better invent than suffer: imagine victims

Lest your own flesh be chosen the agonist, or you

Martyr some creature to the beauty of the place." And I said,

"Burn sacrifices once a year to magic

Horror away from the house, this little house here

You have built over the ocean with your own hands

Beside the standing boulders: for what are we,

The beast that walks upright, with speaking lips

And little hair, to think we should always be fed,

Sheltered, intact, and self-controlled? We sooner more liable

Than the other animals. Pain and terror, the insanities of desire; not accidents but essential,

And crowd up from the core": I imagined victims for those wolves, I made them phantoms to follow,

They have hunted the phantoms and missed the house. It is not good to
　　forget over what gulfs the spirit
Of the beauty of humanity, the petal of a lost flower blown seaward by the
　　night-wind, floats to its quietness.

III

Boulders blunted like an old bear's teeth break up from the headland; below
　　them
All the soil is thick with shells, the tide-rock feasts of a dead people.
Here the granite flanks are scarred with ancient fire, the ghosts of the tribe
Crouch in the nights beside the ghost of a fire, they try to remember the
　　sunlight,
Light has died out of their skies. These have paid something for the future
Luck of the country, while we living keep old griefs in memory: though
　　God's
Envy is not a likely fountain of ruin, to forget evils calls down
Sudden reminders from the cloud: remembered deaths be our redeemers;
Imagined victims our salvation: white as the half moon at midnight
Someone flamelike passed me, saying, "I am Tamar Cauldwell, I have my
　　desire,"
Then the voice of the sea returned, when she had gone by, the stars to their
　　towers.
. . . Beautiful country burn again, Point Pinos down to the Sur Rivers
Burn as before with bitter wonders, land and ocean and the Carmel water.

IV

He brays humanity in a mortar to bring the savor
From the bruised root: a man having bad dreams, who invents victims, is
　　only the ape of that God.

He washes it out with tears and many waters, calcines it with fire in the red
   crucible,
Deforms it, makes it horrible to itself: the spirit flies out and stands naked,
   he sees the spirit,
He takes it in the naked ecstasy; it breaks in his hand, the atom is broken,
   the power that massed it
Cries to the power that moves the stars, "I have come home to myself,
   behold me.
I bruised myself in the flint mortar and burnt me
In the red shell, I tortured myself, I flew forth,
Stood naked of myself and broke me in fragments,
And here am I moving the stars that are me."
I have seen these ways of God: I know of no reason
For fire and change and torture and the old returnings.
He being sufficient might be still. I think they admit no reason; they are
   the ways of my love.
Unmeasured power, incredible passion, enormous craft: no thought
   apparent but burns darkly
Smothered with its own smoke in the human brain-vault: no thought
   outside: a certain measure in phenomena:
The fountains of the boiling stars, the flowers on the foreland, the
   ever-returning roses of dawn.

LOVE-CHILDREN

The trail's high up on the ridge, no one goes down
But the east wind and the falling water the concave slope without a name to
    the little bay
That has no name either. The fish-hawk plunges
Beyond the long rocks, rises with streaming silver; the eagle strikes down
    from the ridge and robs the fish-hawk;
The stunted redwoods neither grow nor grow old
Up the steep slope, remembering winter and the sea-wind; the ferns are
    maiden green by the falling water;
The seas whiten on the reefs; nothing has changed
For a thousand years, ten thousand. It is not a thousand, it is only seventy,
    since man and woman came down
The untrampled slope, forcing a trail through lupine
And mountain laurel; they built a hut against the streamside; the coast
    cannot remember their names.
They had light eyes and white skins, and nobody knew
What they fled, why they came. They had children in this place; loved
    while they clung to the breast but later
Naked, untaught, uncared for, as wild as foxes,
A boy and a girl; the coast remembers they would squat beside a squirrel's
    earth until the furred thing
Crept out, then what the small hands caught the teeth
Would tear living. What implacable flame of passion I wonder left its
    children forgotten
To eat vermin and the raw mussels of the rock?
Love at the height is a bad hearth-fire, a wolf in the house to keep the
    children. I imagine languors,
Sick loathing, miserable renewals, blind insolence
In the eye of the noon sun. They'd stripped to bathe, desire on the salted
    beach between the skerries

Came bronze-clawed like a hawk; the children to see

Was the deep pearl, the last abandonment. They lived twelve years in the
hut beside the stream, and the children

Died, and the hut is fallen and vanished, the paths

Filled with thicket and vanished utterly. Nothing remains. Certainly a flame
burned in this place;

Its lamps wandered away, no one knows whither.

The flaming oil-drops fell and burned out. No one imagines that ghosts
move here, at noon or at midnight.

I'm never sorry to think that here's a planet

Will go on like this glen, perfectly whole and content, after mankind is
scummed from the kettle.

No ghost will walk under the latter starlight.

The little phials of desire have all been emptied and broken. Here the
ocean echoes, the stream's like bird-song;

The stunted redwoods neither grow nor grow old

Up the steep slope, remembering winter and the sea-wind; the ferns are
maiden green by the falling water;

The seas whiten on the reefs; the fish-hawk plunges

Beyond the long rocks, rises with streaming silver; the eagle strikes down
from the ridge and robs the fish-hawk.

CREDO

My friend from Asia has powers and magic, he plucks a blue leaf from the young blue-gum

And gazing upon it, gathering and quieting

The God in his mind, creates an ocean more real than the ocean, the salt, the actual

Appalling presence, the power of the waters.

He believes that nothing is real except as we make it. I humbler have found in my blood

Bred west of Caucasus a harder mysticism.

Multitude stands in my mind but I think that the ocean in the bone vault is only

The bone vault's ocean: out there is the ocean's;

The water is the water, the cliff is the rock, come shocks and flashes of reality. The mind

Passes, the eye closes, the spirit is a passage;

The beauty of things was born before eyes and sufficient to itself; the heart-breaking beauty

Will remain when there is no heart to break for it.

PRELUDE

I drew solitude over me, on the lone shore,
By the hawk-perch stones; the hawks and the gulls are never breakers of
     solitude.
When the animals Christ is rumored to have died for drew in,
The land thickening, drew in about me, I planted trees eastward, and the
     ocean
Secured the west with the quietness of thunder. I was quiet.
Imagination, the traitor of the mind, has taken my solitude and slain it.
No peace but many companions; the hateful-eyed
And human-bodied are all about me: you that love multitude may have
     them.

But why should I make fables again? There are many
Tellers of tales to delight women and the people.
I have no vocation. The old rock under the house, the hills with their hard
     roots and the ocean hearted
With sacred quietness from here to Asia
Make me ashamed to speak of the active little bodies, the coupling bodies,
     the misty brainfuls
Of perplexed passion. Humanity is needless.
I said "Humanity is the start of the race, the gate to break away from, the
     coal to kindle,
The blind mask crying to be slit with eye-holes."
Well now it is done, the mask slit, the rag burnt, the starting-post left
     behind: but not in a fable.
Culture's outlived, art's root-cut, discovery's
The way to walk in. Only remains to invent the language to tell it.
     Match-ends of burnt experience
Human enough to be understood,

Scraps and metaphors will serve. The wine was a little too strong for the
   new wine-skins . . .

                        Come storm, kind storm.
Summer and the days of tired gold
And bitter blue are more ruinous.
The leprous grass, the sick forest,
The sea like a whore's eyes,
And the noise of the sun,
The yellow dog barking in the blue pasture,
Snapping sidewise.

                     When I remembered old rains,
Running clouds and the iron wind, then the trees trembled.
I was calling one of the great dancers
Who wander down from the Aleutian rocks and the open Pacific
Pivoting countersunwise, celebrating power with the whirl of a dance,
   sloping to the mainland.
I watched his feet waken the water
And the ocean break in foam beyond Lobos;
The iron wind struck from the hills.

                        You are tired and corrupt,
You kept the beast under till the fountain's poisoned,
He drips with mange and stinks through the oubliette window.
The promise-breaker war killed whom it freed
And none living's the cleaner. Yet storm comes, the lions hunt
In the nights striped with lightning. It will come: feed on peace
While the crust holds: to each of you at length a little
Desolation: a pinch of lust or a drop of terror:

Then the lions hunt in the brain of the dying: storm is good, storm is
    good, good creature,
Kind violence, throbbing throat aches with pity.

                              Onorio Vasquez,
Young seer of visions who lives with his six brothers
On the breast of Palo Corona mountain looking northward,
Watches his brother Vidal and Julio the youngest
Play with a hawk they shot from the mountain cloud,
The wing broken. They crucified the creature,
A nail in the broken wing on the barn wall
Between the pink splinters of bone and a nail in the other.
They prod his breast with a wand, no sponge of vinegar,
"Fly down, Jew-beak." The wind streams down the mountain,
The river of cloud streams over: Onorio Vasquez
Never sees anything to the point. What he sees:
The ocean like sleek gray stone perfectly jointed
To the heads and bays, a woman walking upon it,
The curling scud of the storm around her ankles,
Naked and strong, her thighs the height of the mountain, walking and
    weeping,
The shadow of hair under the belly, the jutting breasts like hills, the face in
    the hands and the hair
Streaming north. "Why are you sad, our lady?" "I had only one son.
The strange lover never breaks the window-latches again
When Joseph's at synagogue."

                         Orange eyes, tired and fierce,
They're casting knives at you now, but clumsily, the knives
Quiver in the wood, stern eyes the storm deepens.
Don't wince, topaz eyes.

The wind wearies toward evening,
Old Vasquez sends his boys to burn the high pastures
Against the rain: see the autumn fires on the mountain, creeping red lakes
    and crescents
Up the black slope in the slide of the year: that's Vasquez and his boys
    burning the mountain. The high wind
Holds, the low dies, the black curtain flies north.

Myrtle Cartwright
Locked the windows but forgot the door, it's a lonely canyon
When the waves flap in the creek-mouth. Andrew's driving
The calves to Monterey, he trusts her, he doesn't know
How all her flesh burned with lascivious desire
Last year, but she remembered her mother and prayed
And God quenched it. Prayer works all right: three times
Rod Stewart came down to see her, he might have been wood
For all she cared. She suffers with constipation,
Tired days and smothering dreams, she's young, life's cheerless,
God sent a little sickness to keep her decent
Since the great prayer. What's that in the west, thunder?
The sea rumbles like thunder but the wind's died down,
Soon it should rain.

Myrtle Cartwright
Could sleep if her heart would quit moving the bed-clothes;
The lighthouse-keeper's daughter little Faith Heriot
Says "Father the cow's got loose, I must go out
With the storm coming and bring her into the stable.
What would mother do without milk in the morning?"
(Clearly Point Pinos Light: stands back from the sea
Among the rolling dunes cupped with old pasture.

Nobody'd keep a cow on the rock at Point Sur.)
This girl never goes near the cowshed but wanders
Into the dunes, the long beam of the light
Swims over and over her head in the high darkness,
The spray of the storm strains through the beam but Faith
Crouches out of the wind in a hollow of the sand
And hears the sea, she rolls on her back in the clear sand
Shuddering, and feels the light lie thwart her hot body
And the sand trickle into the burning places.
Comes pale to the house: "Ah Bossy led me a chase,
Led me a chase." The lighthouse-keeper believes in hell,
His daughter's wild for a lover, his wife sickening toward cancer,
The long yellow beam wheels over the wild sea and the strain
Gathers in the air.

             O crucified
Wings, orange eyes, open?
Always the strain, the straining flesh, who feels what God feels
Knows the straining flesh, the aching desires,
The enormous water straining its bounds, the electric
Strain in the cloud, the strain of the oil in the oil-tanks
At Monterey aching to burn, the strain of the spinning
Demons that make an atom, straining to fly asunder,
Straining to rest at the center,
The strain in the skull, blind strains, force and counterforce,
Nothing prevails . . .

                 Oh in storm: storm's kind, kind violence,
When the swollen cloud ached — suddenly
Her charge and agony condensed, slip, the thick dark
Whelps lightning; the air breaks, the twin birth rain falls globed

From the released blackness high up in the air
Ringing like a bell for deliverance.

Many-folded hills
Mouth the black voice that follows the white eye
Opening, universal white eye widening and shut. Myrtle Cartwright's
One of those whom thunder shakes with terror: head covered
Against the flashes: "If it should find me and kill me
What's life been worth? Nothing, nothing, nothing, death's horrible,"
She hears it like a truck driven jolting through heaven
Rumble to the north. "And if I die old:
Nothing, nothing."

Vasquez' boys have gone home.

Deep after
    midnight the wind rises, turns iron again,
From east of south, it grinds the heads of the hills, the dunes move in the
    dark at Point Pinos, the sandstone
Lighthouse at Point Sur on the top of the rock is like an axhead held
    against a grindstone.
The high redwoods have quit roaring to scream. Oaks go down on the
    mountain. At Vasquez' place in the yellow
Pallor of dawn the roof of the barn's lifting, his sons cast ropes over the
    timbers. The crucified
Snaps his beak at them. He flies on two nails.
Great eyes, lived all night?
Onorio should have held the rope but it slid through his fingers. Onorio
    Vasquez
Never sees anything to the point. What he sees:
The planted eucalyptuses bent double

All in a row, praying north, "Why everything's praying
And running northward, old hawk anchored with nails
You see that everything goes north like a river.
On a cliff in the north
Stands the strange lover, shines and calls."

                                        In the morning
The inexhaustible clouds flying up from the south
Stream rain, the gullies of the hills grow alive, the creeks flood, the summer
    sand-bars
Burst from their mouths, from every sea-mouth wedges of yellow, yellow
    tongues. Myrtle Cartwright
Hears the steep cataracts slacken, and then thunder
Pushes the house-walls. "Hear me God, death's not dreadful.
You heard before when I prayed. Now," she whispers,
"I'll make the bargain," thunder leans on the house-walls, "life's no value
Like this, I'm going to Stewart's, I can't live empty.
Now Andrew can't come home for every canyon
Vomits its bridge, judgment is yours only,
Death's in your hands." She opens the door on the streaming
Canyon-side, the desperate wind: the dark wet oak-leaves
All in a moment each leaf a distinct fire
Reflect the sharp flash over them: Myrtle Cartwright
Feels the sword plunge: no touch: runs tottering up hill
Through the black voice.

                                Black pool of oil hidden in the oil-tank
In Monterey felt the sword plunge: touched: the wild heat
Went mad where a little air was, metal curled back,
Fire leaped at the outlet. "Immense ages
We lay under rock, our lust hoarded,

The ache of ignorant desire, the enormous pressure,
The enormous patience, the strain, strain, the strain
Lightened we lay in a steel shell . . . what God kept for us:
Roaring marriage."

                  Myrtle Cartwright wins up hill through the oak-scrub
And through the rain, the wind at the summit
Knocks her breasts and her mouth, she crouches in the mud,
Feels herself four-foot like a beast and the lightning
Will come from behind and cover her, the wolf of white fire,
Force the cold flesh, cling with his fore-paws. "Oh, death's
What I was after." She runs on the road northward, the wind behind her,
The lightnings like white doves hovering her head, harmless as pigeons,
    through great bars of black noise.
She lifts her wet arms. "Come doves."

                        The oil-tank boils with joy in the
    north, one among ten, one tank
Burns, the nine others wait, feel warmth, dim change of patience. This one
    roars with fulfilled desire,
The ring-bound molecules splitting, the atoms dancing apart, marrying the
    air.

    Myrtle Cartwright
Knocks on her door: "Oh, I've come. Here's what you wanted."

                              (In the
    yellow inland no rain but the same lightning,
And it lights a forest.) He leads her into the barn because there are people
    in the house.

In the north the oil-tanks
Catch from the first, the ring-bound molecules splitting, the atoms dancing
        apart, marrying the air.
The marriage-bound thighs opening, on the stiff white straw, the nerves of
        fire, the ganglia like stars.

Don't you see any vision Onorio Vasquez? "No, for the topazes
Have dulled out of his head, he soars on two nails,
Dead hawk over the coast. O little brother
Julio, if you could drive nails through my hands
I'd stand against the door: through the middle of the palms:
And take the hawk's place, you could throw knives at me.
I'd give you my saddle and the big bridle, Julio,
With the bit that rings and rings when the horse twirls it."
He smiles. "You'd see the lights flicker in my hair."
He smiles craftily. "You'd live long and be rich,
And nobody could beat you in running or riding."
He chatters his teeth. "It is necessary for someone to be fastened with nails.
And Jew-beak died in the night. Jew-beak is dead."

Cawdor

1926-28

BIRTH-DUES

Joy is a trick in the air; pleasure is merely contemptible, the dangled
Carrot the ass follows to market or precipice;
But limitary pain — the rock under the tower and the hewn coping
That takes thunder at the head of the turret —
Terrible and real. Therefore a mindless dervish carving himself
With knives will seem to have conquered the world.

The world's God is treacherous and full of unreason; a torturer, but also
The only foundation and the only fountain.
Who fights him eats his own flesh and perishes of hunger; who hides in the
    grave
To escape him is dead; who enters the Indian
Recession to escape him is dead; who falls in love with the God is washed
    clean
Of death desired and of death dreaded.

He has joy, but joy is a trick in the air; and pleasure, but pleasure is
    contemptible;
And peace; and is based on solider than pain.
He has broken boundaries a little and that will estrange him; he is
    monstrous, but not
To the measure of the God. . . . But I having told you —
However I suppose that few in the world have energy to hear effectively —
Have paid my birth-dues; am quits with the people.

THE BROKEN BALANCE

I. Reference to a Passage in Plutarch's
Life of Sulla

The people buying and selling, consuming pleasures, talking in the
    archways,
Were all suddenly struck quiet
And ran from under stone to look up at the sky: so shrill and mournful,
So fierce and final, a brazen
Pealing of trumpets high up in the air, in the summer blue over Tuscany.
They marvelled; the soothsayers answered:
"Although the Gods are little troubled toward men, at the end of each
    period
A sign is declared in heaven
Indicating new times, new customs, a changed people; the Romans
Rule, and Etruria is finished;
A wise mariner will trim the sails to the wind."

                              I heard yesterday
So shrill and mournful a trumpet-blast,
It was hard to be wise. . . . You must eat change and endure; not be much
    troubled
For the people; they will have their happiness.
When the republic grows too heavy to endure, then Caesar will carry it;
When life grows hateful, there's power . . .

II. To the Children

Power's good; life is not always good but power's good.
So you must think when abundance
Makes pawns of people and all the loaves are one dough.

The steep singleness of passion
Dies; they will say, "What was that?" but the power triumphs.
Loveliness will live under glass
And beauty will go savage in the secret mountains.
There is beauty in power also.
You children must widen your minds' eyes to take mountains
Instead of faces, and millions
Instead of persons; not to hate life; and massed power
After the lone hawk's dead.

III

That light blood-loving weasel, a tongue of yellow
Fire licking the sides of the gray stones,
Has a more passionate and more pure heart
In the snake-slender flanks than man can imagine;
But he is betrayed by his own courage,
The man who kills him is like a cloud hiding a star.

Then praise the jewel-eyed hawk and the tall blue heron;
The black cormorants that fatten their sea-rock
With shining slime; even that ruiner of anthills
The red-shafted woodpecker flying,
A white star between blood-color wing-clouds,
Across the glades of the wood and the green lakes of shade.

These live their felt natures; they know their norm
And live it to the brim; they understand life.
While men moulding themselves to the anthill have choked
Their natures until the souls die in them;
They have sold themselves for toys and protection:
No, but consider awhile: what else? Men sold for toys.

Uneasy and fractional people, having no center
But in the eyes and mouths that surround them,
Having no function but to serve and support
Civilization, the enemy of man,
No wonder they live insanely, and desire
With their tongues, progress; with their eyes, pleasure; with their hearts,
    death.

Their ancestors were good hunters, good herdsmen and swordsmen,
But now the world is turned upside down;
The good do evil, the hope's in criminals; in vice
That dissolves the cities and war to destroy them.
Through wars and corruptions the house will fall.
Mourn whom it falls on. Be glad: the house is mined, it will fall.

IV

Rain, hail and brutal sun, the plow in the roots,
The pitiless pruning-iron in the branches,
Strengthen the vines, they are all feeding friends
Or powerless foes until the grapes purple.
But when you have ripened your berries it is time to begin to perish.

The world sickens with change, rain becomes poison,
The earth is a pit, it is time to perish.
The vines are fey, the very kindness of nature
Corrupts what her cruelty before strengthened.
When you stand on the peak of time it is time to begin to perish.

Reach down the long morbid roots that forget the plow,
Discover the depths; let the long pale tendrils
Spend all to discover the sky, now nothing is good

But only the steel mirrors of discovery . . .
And the beautiful enormous dawns of time, after we perish.

V

Mourning the broken balance, the hopeless prostration of the earth
Under men's hands and their minds,
The beautiful places killed like rabbits to make a city,
The spreading fungus, the slime-threads
And spores; my own coast's obscene future: I remember the farther
Future, and the last man dying
Without succession under the confident eyes of the stars.
It was only a moment's accident,
The race that plagued us; the world resumes the old lonely immortal
Splendor; from here I can even
Perceive that that snuffed candle had something . . . a fantastic virtue,
A faint and unshapely pathos . . .
So death will flatter them at last: what, even the bald ape's by-shot
Was moderately admirable?

VI. Palinode

All summer neither rain nor wave washes the cormorants'
Perch, and their droppings have painted it shining white.
If the excrement of fish-eaters makes the brown rock a snow-mountain
At noon, a rose in the morning, a beacon at moonrise
On the black water: it is barely possible that even men's present
Lives are something; their arts and sciences (by moonlight)
Not wholly ridiculous, nor their cities merely an offense.

VII

Under my windows, between the road and the sea-cliff, bitter wild grass
Stands narrowed between the people and the storm.
The ocean winter after winter gnaws at its earth, the wheels and the feet
Summer after summer encroach and destroy.
Stubborn green life, for the cliff-eater I cannot comfort you, ignorant which color,
Gray-blue or pale-green, will please the late stars;
But laugh at the other, your seed shall enjoy wonderful vengeances and suck
The arteries and walk in triumph on the faces.

HURT HAWKS

I

The broken pillar of the wing jags from the clotted shoulder,
The wing trails like a banner in defeat,
No more to use the sky forever but live with famine
And pain a few days: cat nor coyote
Will shorten the week of waiting for death, there is game without talons.
He stands under the oak-bush and waits
The lame feet of salvation; at night he remembers freedom
And flies in a dream, the dawns ruin it.
He is strong and pain is worse to the strong, incapacity is worse.
The curs of the day come and torment him
At distance, no one but death the redeemer will humble that head,
The intrepid readiness, the terrible eyes.
The wild God of the world is sometimes merciful to those
That ask mercy, not often to the arrogant.
You do not know him, you communal people, or you have forgotten him;
Intemperate and savage, the hawk remembers him;
Beautiful and wild, the hawks, and men that are dying, remember him.

II

I'd sooner, except the penalties, kill a man than a hawk; but the great
    redtail
Had nothing left but unable misery
From the bones too shattered for mending, the wing that trailed under his
    talons when he moved.
We had fed him six weeks, I gave him freedom,
He wandered over the foreland hill and returned in the evening, asking for
    death,

Not like a beggar, still eyed with the old

Implacable arrogance. I gave him the lead gift in the twilight. What fell was
    relaxed,

Owl-downy, soft feminine feathers; but what

Soared: the fierce rush: the night-herons by the flooded river cried fear at
    its rising

Before it was quite unsheathed from reality.

BIXBY'S LANDING

They burned lime on the hill and dropped it down here in an iron car
On a long cable; here the ships warped in
And took their loads from the engine, the water is deep to the cliff. The car
Hangs half way over in the gape of the gorge,
Stationed like a north star above the peaks of the redwoods, iron perch
For the little red hawks when they cease from hovering
When they've struck prey; the spider's fling of a cable rust-glued to the
    pulleys.
The laborers are gone, but what a good multitude
Is here in return: the rich-lichened rock, the rose-tipped stone-crop, the
    constant
Ocean's voices, the cloud-lighted space.
The kilns are cold on the hill but here in the rust of the broken boiler
Quick lizards lighten, and a rattle-snake flows
Down the cracked masonry, over the crumbled fire-brick. In the rotting
    timbers
And roofless platforms all the free companies
Of windy grasses have root and make seed; wild buckwheat blooms in the
    fat
Weather-slacked lime from the bursted barrels.
Two duckhawks darting in the sky of their cliff-hung nest are the voice of
    the headland.
Wine-hearted solitude, our mother the wilderness,
Men's failures are often as beautiful as men's triumphs, but your returnings
Are even more precious than your first presence.

AN ARTIST

That sculptor we knew, the passionate-eyed son of a quarryman,

Who astonished Rome and Paris in his meteor youth and then was gone, at
his high tide of triumphs,

Without reason or good-bye: I have seen him again lately, after twenty
years, but not in Europe.

In desert hills I rode a horse slack-kneed with thirst. Down a steep slope a
dancing swarm

Of yellow butterflies over a shining rock made me hope water. We slid
down to the place,

The spring was bitter but the horse drank. I imagined wearings of an old
path from that wet rock

Ran down the canyon; I followed, soon they were lost, I came to a stone
valley in which it seemed

No man nor his mount had ever ventured, you wondered whether even a
vulture'd ever spread sail there.

There were stones of strange form under a cleft in the far hill; I tethered
the horse to a rock

And scrambled over. A heap like a stone torrent, a moraine,

But monstrously formed limbs of broken carving appeared in the rock-fall,
enormous breasts, defaced heads

Of giants, the eyes calm through the brute veils of fracture. It was natural
then to climb higher and go in

Up the cleft gate. The canyon was a sheer-walled crack winding at the
entrance, but around its bend

The walls grew dreadful with stone giants, presences growing out of the
rigid precipice, that strove

In dream between stone and life, intense to cast their chaos . . . or to enter
and return . . . stone-fleshed, nerve-stretched

Great bodies ever more beautiful and more heavy with pain, they seemed
     leading to some unbearable
Consummation of the ecstasy . . . but there, troll among Titans, the
     bearded master of the place accosted me
In a cold anger, a mallet in his hand, filthy and ragged. There was no
     kindness in that man's mind,
But after he had driven me down to the entrance he spoke a little.

                                                                  The
     merciless sun had found the slot now
To hide in, and lit for the wick of that stone lamp-bowl a sky almost, I
     thought, abominably beautiful;
While our lost artist we used to admire: for now I knew him: spoke of his
     passion.

          He said, "Marble?
White marble is fit to model a snow-mountain: let man be modest. Nor
     bronze: I am bound to have my tool
In my material, no irrelevances. I found this pit of dark-gray freestone,
     fine-grained, and tough enough
To make sketches that under any weathering will last my lifetime. . . .

The town is eight miles off, I can fetch food and no one follows me home.
     I have water and a cave
Here; and no possible lack of material. I need, therefore, nothing. As to
     companions, I make them.
And models? They are seldom wanted; I know a Basque shepherd I
     sometimes use; and a woman of the town.
What more? Sympathy? Praise? I have never desired them and also I have
     never deserved them. I will not show you
More than the spalls you saw by accident.

What I see is the enormous
beauty of things, but what I attempt
Is nothing to that. I am helpless toward that.
It is only to form in stone the mould of some ideal humanity that might be
worthy to *be*
Under that lightning. Animalcules that God (if he were given to laughter)
might omit to laugh at.

Those children of my hands are tortured because they feel," he said, "the
storm of the outer magnificence.
They are giants in agony. They have seen from my eyes
The man-destroying beauty of the dawns over their notch yonder, and all
the obliterating stars.
But in their eyes they have peace. I have lived a little and I think
Peace marrying pain alone can breed that excellence in the luckless race
might make it decent
To exist at all on the star-lit stone breast.

I hope," he said, "that when I
grow old and the chisel drops,
I may crawl out on a ledge of the rock and die like a wolf."

These
fragments are all I can remember,
These in the flare of the desert evening. Having been driven so brutally
forth I never returned;
Yet I respect him enough to keep his name and the place secret. I hope that
some other traveller
May stumble on that ravine of Titans after their maker has died. While he
lives, let him alone.

THE MACHINE

The little biplane that has the river-meadow for landing-field
And carries passengers brief rides,
Buzzed overhead on the tender blue above the orange of sundown.
Below it five troubled night-herons
Turned short over the shore from its course, four east, one northward.
    Beyond them
Swam the new moon in amber.
I don't know why, but lately the forms of things appear to me with time
One of their visible dimensions.
The thread brightness of the bent moon appeared enormous, unnumbered
Ages of years; the night-herons
Their natural size, they have croaked over the shore in the hush at sundown
Much longer than human language
Has fumbled with the air: but the plane having no past but a certain future,
Insect in size as in form,
Was also accepted, all these forms of power placed without preference
In the grave arrangement of the evening.

MEDITATION ON SAVIORS

I

When I considered it too closely, when I wore it like an element and
   smelt it like water,
Life is become less lovely, the net nearer than the skin, a little troublesome,
   a little terrible.

I pledged myself awhile ago not to seek refuge, neither in death nor in a
   walled garden,
In lies nor gated loyalties, nor in the gates of contempt, that easily lock the
   world out of doors.

Here on the rock it is great and beautiful, here on the foam-wet granite
   sea-fang it is easy to praise
Life and water and the shining stones: but whose cattle are the herds of the
   people that one should love them?

If they were yours, then you might take a cattle-breeder's delight in the
   herds of the future. Not yours.
Where the power ends let love, before it sours to jealousy. Leave the joys of
   government to Caesar.

Who is born when the world wanes, when the brave soul of the world falls
   on decay in the flesh increasing
Comes one with a great level mind, sufficient vision, sufficient blindness,
   and clemency for love.

This is the breath of rottenness I smelt; from the world waiting, stalled
   between storms, decaying a little,

Bitterly afraid to be hurt, but knowing it cannot draw the savior Caesar but
   out of the blood-bath.

The apes of Christ lift up their hands to praise love: but wisdom without
   love is the present savior,
Power without hatred, mind like a many-bladed machine subduing the
   world with deep indifference.

The apes of Christ itch for a sickness they have never known; words and the
   little envies will hardly
Measure against that blinding fire behind the tragic eyes they have never
   dared to confront.

II

Point Lobos lies over the hollowed water like a humped whale swimming
   to shoal; Point Lobos
Was wounded with that fire; the hills at Point Sur endured it; the palace at
   Thebes; the hill Calvary.

Out of incestuous love power and then ruin. A man forcing the
   imaginations of men,
Possessing with love and power the people: a man defiling his own
   household with impious desire.

King Oedipus reeling blinded from the palace doorway, red tears pouring
   from the torn pits
Under the forehead; and the young Jew writhing on the domed hill in the
   earthquake, against the eclipse

Frightfully uplifted for having turned inward to love the people: — that root
   was so sweet O dreadful agonist? —

I saw the same pierced feet, that walked in the same crime to its expiation;
    I heard the same cry.

A bad mountain to build your world on. Am I another keeper of the
    people, that on my own shore,
On the gray rock, by the grooved mass of the ocean, the sicknesses I left
    behind me concern me?

Here where the surf has come incredible ways out of the splendid west,
    over the deeps
Light nor life sounds forever; here where enormous sundowns flower and
    burn through color to quietness;

Then the ecstasy of the stars is present? As for the people, I have found my
    rock, let them find theirs.
Let them lie down at Caesar's feet and be saved; and he in his time reap
    their daggers of gratitude.

III

Yet I am the one made pledges against the refuge contempt, that easily
    locks the world out of doors.
This people as much as the sea-granite is part of the God from whom I
    desire not to be fugitive.

I see them: they are always crying. The shored Pacific makes perpetual
    music, and the stone mountains
Their music of silence, the stars blow long pipings of light: the people are
    always crying in their hearts.

One need not pity; certainly one must not love. But who has seen peace, if
    he should tell them where peace

Lives in the world ... they would be powerless to understand; and he is
    not willing to be reinvolved.

IV

How should one caught in the stone of his own person dare tell the people
    anything but relative to that?
But if a man could hold in his mind all the conditions at once, of man and
    woman, of civilized

And barbarous, of sick and well, of happy and under torture, of living and
    dead, of human and not
Human, and dimly all the human future: — what should persuade him to
    speak? And what could his words change?

The mountain ahead of the world is not forming but fixed. But the man's
    words would be fixed also,
Part of that mountain, under equal compulsion; under the same present
    compulsion in the iron consistency.

And nobody sees good or evil but out of a brain a hundred centuries
    quieted, some desert
Prophet's, a man humped like a camel, gone mad between the mud-walled
    village and the mountain sepulchres.

V

Broad wagons before sunrise bring food into the city from the open farms,
    and the people are fed.
They import and they consume reality. Before sunrise a hawk in the desert
    made them their thoughts.

VI

Here is an anxious people, rank with suppressed bloodthirstiness. Among
the mild and unwarlike
Gautama needed but live greatly and be heard, Confucius needed but live
greatly and be heard:

This people has not outgrown blood-sacrifice, one must writhe on the high
cross to catch at their memories;
The price is known. I have quieted love; for love of the people I would not
do it. For power I would do it.

— But that stands against reason: what is power to a dead man, dead under
torture? — What is power to a man
Living, after the flesh is content? Reason is never a root, neither of act nor
desire.

For power living I would never do it; they are not delightful to touch, one
wants to be separate. For power
After the nerves are put away underground, to lighten the abstract unborn
children toward peace . . .

A man might have paid anguish indeed. Except he had found the standing
sea-rock that even this last
Temptation breaks on; quieter than death but lovelier; peace that quiets the
desire even of praising it.

VII

Yet look: are they not pitiable? No: if they lived forever they would be
pitiable:

But a huge gift reserved quite overwhelms them at the end; they are able
   then to be still and not cry.

And having touched a little of the beauty and seen a little of the beauty of
   things, magically grow
Across the funeral fire or the hidden stench of burial themselves into the
   beauty they admired,

Themselves into the God, themselves into the sacred steep unconsciousness
   they used to mimic
Asleep between lamp's death and dawn, while the last drunkard stumbled
   homeward down the dark street.

They are not to be pitied but very fortunate; they need no savior, salvation
   comes and takes them by force,
It gathers them into the great kingdoms of dust and stone, the blown
   storms, the stream's-end ocean.

With this advantage over their granite grave-marks, of having realized the
   petulant human consciousness
Before, and then the greatness, the peace: drunk from both pitchers: these
   to be pitied? These not fortunate?

But while he lives let each man make his health in his mind, to love the
   coast opposite humanity
And so be freed of love, laying it like bread on the waters; it is worst turned
   inward, it is best shot farthest.

Love, the mad wine of good and evil, the saint's and murderer's, the mote in
   the eye that makes its object
Shine the sun black; the trap in which it is better to catch the inhuman
   God than the hunter's own image.

A REDEEMER

The road had steepened and the sun sharpened on the high ridges; the
stream probably was dry,
Certainly not to be come to down the pit of the canyon. We stopped for
water at the one farm
In all that mountain. The trough was cracked with drought, the moss on
the boards dead, but an old dog
Rose like a wooden toy at the house-door silently. I said "There will be
water somewhere about,"
And when I knocked a man showed us a spring of water. Though his hair
was nearly white I judged him
Forty years old at most. His eyes and voice were muted. It is likely he kept
his hands hidden,
I failed to see them until we had dipped the spring. He stood then on the
lip of the great slope
And looked westward over an incredible country to the far hills that
dammed the sea-fog: it billowed
Above them, cascaded over them, it never crossed them, gray standing
flood. He stood gazing, his hands
Were clasped behind him; I caught a glimpse of serous red under the
fingers, and looking sharply
When they drew apart saw that both hands were wounded. I said "Your
hands are hurt." He twitched them from sight,
But after a moment having earnestly eyed me displayed them. The wounds
were in the hearts of the palms,
Pierced to the backs like stigmata of crucifixion. The horrible raw flesh
protruded, glistening
And granular, not scabbed, nor a sign of infection. "These are old wounds."
He answered, "Yes. They don't heal." He stood
Moving his lips in silence, his back against that fabulous basin of
mountains, fold beyond fold,

Patches of forest and scarps of rock, high domes of dead gray pasture and
  gray beds of dry rivers,
Clear and particular in the burning air, too bright to appear real, to the last
  range
The fog from the ocean like a stretched compacted thunderstorm
  overhung; and he said gravely:
"I pick them open. I made them long ago with a clean steel. It is only a
  little to pay — "
He stretched and flexed the fingers, I saw his sunburnt lips whiten in a line,
  compressed together,
"If only it proves enough for a time — to save so many." I searched his face
  for madness but that
Is often invisible, a subtle spirit. "There never," he said, "was any people
  earned so much ruin.
I love them, I am trying to suffer for them. It would be bad if I should die, I
  am careful
Against excess." "You think of the wounds," I said, "of Jesus?" He laughed
  angrily and frowned, stroking
The fingers of one hand with the other. "Religion is the people's opium.
  Your little Jew-God?
My pain" he said with pride "is voluntary.
They have done what never was done before. Not as a people takes a land
  to love it and be fed,
A little, according to need and love, and again a little; sparing the country
  tribes, mixing
Their blood with theirs, their minds with all the rocks and rivers, their flesh
  with the soil: no, without hunger
Wasting the world and your own labor, without love possessing, not even
  your hands to the dirt but plows
Like blades of knives; heartless machines; houses of steel: using and
  despising the patient earth . . .

Oh as a rich man eats a forest for profit and a field for vanity, so you came west and raped
The continent and brushed its people to death. Without need, the weak skirmishing hunters, and without mercy.
Well, God's a scare-crow, no vengeance out of old rags. But there are acts breeding their own reversals
In their own bellies from the first day. I am here" he said — and broke off suddenly and said "They take horses
And give them sicknesses through hollow needles, their blood saves babies: I am here on the mountain making
Antitoxin for all the happy towns and farms, the lovely blameless children, the terrible
Arrogant cities. I used to think them terrible: their gray prosperity, their pride: from up here
Specks of mildew.

       But when I am dead and all you with whole hands think of nothing but happiness,
Will you go mad and kill each other? Or horror come over the ocean on wings and cover your sun?
I wish," he said trembling, "I had never been born."

His wife came from the door while he was talking. Mine asked her quietly, "Do you live all alone here,
Are you not afraid?" "Certainly not," she answered, "he is always gentle and loving. I have no complaint
Except his groans in the night keep me awake often. But when I think of other women's
Troubles: my own daughter's: I'm older than my husband, I have been married before: deep is my peace."

TOR HOUSE

If you should look for this place after a handful of lifetimes:
Perhaps of my planted forest a few
May stand yet, dark-leaved Australians or the coast cypress, haggard
With storm-drift; but fire and the axe are devils.
Look for foundations of sea-worn granite, my fingers had the art
To make stone love stone, you will find some remnant.
But if you should look in your idleness after ten thousand years:
It is the granite knoll on the granite
And lava tongue in the midst of the bay, by the mouth of the Carmel
River-valley, these four will remain
In the change of names. You will know it by the wild sea-fragrance of wind
Though the ocean may have climbed or retired a little;
You will know it by the valley inland that our sun and our moon were born
    from
Before the poles changed; and Orion in December
Evenings was strung in the throat of the valley like a lamp-lighted bridge.
Come in the morning you will see white gulls
Weaving a dance over blue water, the wane of the moon
Their dance-companion, a ghost walking
By daylight, but wider and whiter than any bird in the world.
My ghost you needn't look for; it is probably
Here, but a dark one, deep in the granite, not dancing on wind
With the mad wings and the day moon.

CAWDOR

I

In nineteen-nine a fire swept our coast hills,
But not the canyons oceanward; Cawdor's ranges
And farm were safe. He had posted sentinels,
His son George and his man Jesus Acanna,
On two hills and they watched the fire all night
Stream toward Cachagua; the big-coned inland pines
Made pillars of white flame.

                   Cawdor at dawn
Stood by his door and saw in the bronze light
That leaked through towers of smoke windowed with sanguine
Reflections of the burning, two does and a fawn
Spring down the creek-bed stones of his ravine
Fleeing from their terror, and then a tawny mountain-lion
With no eyes for the deer. Next walked a lame
Gray horse, a girl led it, a broken old man,
His face bound with a dirty cloth, clung weakly
To the limping withers. Cawdor recognized him
Though he was faceless, old Martial, who had got a place
In the hills two years before, a feeble old man
Marked for misfortune; his stock, the first year, sickened
With lump-jaw; when a cow died in the creek
Martial had let her lie there. Then Cawdor had ridden
And cursed him, and Cawdor with his man Acanna
Roped the horns to draw the carcass out of the stream,
But when they drew, it burst.
Now Martial came, he and his daughter Fera,

For refuge, having saved from the fire nothing
But their own lives and the lame horse.

                                    The old man
Reeled and was dumb with pain, but the girl asked
For Hood Cawdor, and Cawdor said "Not here.
He left last winter." Hood was his second son,
The hunter, with whom he had quarrelled. And Fera Martial:
"We've come," she pointed toward the smoke-towers, "from that.
You are Hood's father. You've the same drooping eyes, like a big animal's
That never needs look sideways. I'm sorry, you'll have to take us in. My
    father is burnt, he is blinded.
The fire was on us before we awoke. He tried to fetch a bridle out of the
    burning stable.
There was a drum of coal-oil against the wall exploded and blew fire over
    his face.
I dragged him out of the fire." He said "Bring him in." "It wasn't dark," she
    answered, "the oaks were like torches
And all the hill roared like a wave. He says we can go in, father, here is the
    door-step."
The old man groaned, lifting his hand to his face but not touching it, and
    hung back from the door.
"I wish to God you had left me at home." She said "Your home?" "To be a
    blackened log with the others
Lying quiet," he said, "in the burnt hollow under the hill, and not have any
    care and not come
Blind and crying to my enemy's place." He turned in her hands and said
    "Oh Fera, where is the sun?
Is it afternoon?" She stood and held him. "Dear, only dawn. I think it must
    have come up, it's hidden
In the hell of smoke." "Turn me that way before I go in,

To the good light that gave me so many days. I have failed, and failed, and
    failed. Now I'll go in
As men go into the grave, and not fail any more."

He was in fact passive from that time on,
Except the restlessness of pain in bed
While his face scarred and the eyes died in the dark.
After the pain was lulled he seemed content
With blindness, it made an end of labor.

                                        Cawdor meanwhile
Would somehow have sent him up coast to Monterey
To find other charity; but the girl Fera
Coming ragged and courageous out of the fire
With cool gray eyes, had troubled his tough heart.
He'd not seen her before that dawn; and the image
Of the young haggard girl streaked with the dirt of the fire
And her skirt torn to bandage her father's face
Lived like a plant in his blood. He was fifty years old,
And mocked at himself; she was nineteen, she said.
But being a beggar really, under the burden
Of that blind man to care for, discounted youth;
And Cawdor, whatever the next ten years might bring him,
Felt no weight in the fifty. He had been stronger
From his youth up than other men, and still
The strength seemed to increase, the only changes
Toward age were harder lines in the shaven face
And fewer ferocities; the black passions of anger
That used to blind him sometimes had almost ceased.
Perhaps for lack of cause, now the few people
He dealt with knew him too well to cross him. And he'd security
And rough abundance to offer.

When Martial was able
Fera led him out-doors about the house
To feel the sun. He said it had no solidness
So near the ocean. "At home in the dear cup of the hills it used to come
    down
Like golden hammers, yet I'm content. Now it's dulled. Is there a cloud?"
    She answered, "Cypresses planted
Around the house, but the wind has broken them so . . . Sit on this bench
    by the door, here it beats golden."
He sat, and soon handled a thing beside him on the warm plank. "What's
    this thing on the bench,
Like a saucer with little holes?" "An old sea-shell," she answered, "an
    abalone's. They grow on the ocean-reef;
All this black soil's full of their shells, the Indians brought up." He said:
    "Fera: while we stay here
Will you do something to lengthen the life you saved? When's the new
    moon? Go down when the tides drain out
In the dark of the moon and at full moon, gather me mussels and abalones,
    I'll drink the broth
And eat the meat, it is full of salts and nourishment. The ancestors of our
    life came from the sea
And our blood craves it, it will bring me years of health." She answered "He
    wants us to go to-morrow." "Go, where?"
"That I can't tell. Is the sun pleasant?" "Oh, we can't go," he said, "you
    needn't be troubled. The sun
Is faint but pleasant. Now is that Cawdor passing?" "No. Concha Rosas,"
    she answered. "She helps the cook.
She helped me when you were sick."

                              Fera with private thoughts
Watched the Indian-blooded woman about her work
Pass in the dooryard, and go after a moment,

Carrying a pan under her arm, to the halved cask
Against the lift of the hill, where water trickled
From a wood pipe; tall weeds and calla lilies
Grew in the mud by it; the dark fat woman
Sat on a stone among them, paring and washing
Whatever was in the pan; and Fera said carefully:
"She has a child with blue eyes and she is an Indian.
She and the boy had their rooms in the house
When we came here, but Mr. Cawdor has moved them
To the old adobe out-building where Acanna
Lives with his wife." Her father listened or not, and answered: "Fera,
Am I still in the sun?" "Oh? Yes." "It is faint," he said, "but pleasant. I
    suppose now you can see the ocean
With golden scales on the broad blue?" "No," she answered, "we face up
    the canyon, toward the dark redwoods."

Cawdor's daughter Michal came by,
A blue-eyed girl of fourteen, nearly as tall as Fera.
She had a trap in her hand, and a live ground-squirrel
Dangled from it by the crushed paws. Then Fera
Left her father a moment to go with Michal
To the eagle's cage, to watch the captive be fed.
Against a cypress, a wide wire-screened box; no perch in it
But a wood block, for the bird's wing was broken.
Hood Cawdor, Michal's brother, had shot it, the autumn
Before he went away, and Michal had kept it alive.

She laid the squirrel inside and opened the trap.
The girls, their arms lacing each other's shoulders,
Set their faces against the wire to watch
The great dark-feathered and square-shouldered prisoner
Move in his corner. One wide wing trailed through filth

Quickening a buzz of blow-flies; the fierce dark eyes
Had dropped their films, "He'll never be tame," Michal said sadly.
They watched the squirrel begin to drag its body
On the broken fore-paws. The indomitable eyes
Seemed never to have left the girls' faces but a grim hand
Came forward and gathered its prey under its talons.
They heard a whispering twitter continue
Below the hover of the dark plumes, until
The brown hackles of the neck bowed, the bleak head
Stooped over and stilled it.

     Fera turned at a shadow
And saw Cawdor behind her, who said "One thing it's good for,
It makes Michal catch squirrels. Well, Fera, you're ready to go to-morrow?"
  "Let me go back to my father,"
She said, "I've left him alone too long. No, we're not ready." He followed
  her; Michal remained.
She touched her father's hand and spoke of the sun.
Old Martial lifted his cloth face, that he wore
To hide the scars; his voice dulled through the cloth:
"It is faint but very pleasant. I've been asleep."
She said "Mr. Cawdor's here." And Cawdor: "How are you. Now that he's
  better, Fera, little Romano
(That's Concha Rosas' boy) could take him walking in the afternoons and
  let you have a free time
To ride with Michal. If you could stay here. It's pitiful to see youth chained
  to helpless old age.
However, I have to drive to Monterey in the morning. I've put it off as
  long as I could,
And now he's able." She looked at Cawdor's face and his hands, and said
  "He means, father, that we
Must go to-morrow. I told you." Who sighed and answered, "That would
  be a long journey for nothing at all.

Are people more kind there? Wherever an old pitiful blind man goes
Someone will have to lead him and feed him and find him a bed. The world is not so made, Fera,
That he could starve. There *is* a God, but in human kindness." Cawdor said gravely: "Now's the other fool's turn
To speak: it makes me mad to have to spread out my foolishness.
I never had time to play with colored ribbons, I was brought up hard. I did a man's work at twelve
And bossed a gang at eighteen. That gets you nowhere. I learned that ruling poor men's hands is nothing,
Ruling men's money's a wedge in the world. But after I'd split it open a crack I looked in and saw
The trick inside it, the filthy nothing, the fooled and rotten faces of rich and successful men.
And the sons they have. Then I came down from the city.
I saw this place and I got it. I was what you call honest but I was hard; the little Mexican
Cried when I got it. A canyon full of redwoods and hills guaranteed not to contain gold.
I'd what I wanted, and have lived unshaken. My wife died when Michal was born; and I was sorry,
She seemed frightened at the end; but life was not changed.
I am fifty years old, the boys have grown up; and now I'm caught with wanting something and my life is changed.
I haven't slept for some nights. You'd think I might have been safe at fifty. Oh, I'm still my own master
And will not beg anything of you. Old blind man your girl's beautiful, I saw her come down the canyon
Like a fawn out of the fire. If she is willing: if you are willing, Fera, this place is yours.
It's no palace and no kingdom: but you are a beggar. It might be better for you to live
In a lonely place than lead your old blind-man up the cold street

And catch dimes in his hat. If you're not willing:

I'll tell you something. You are not safe here, by God you're not. I've been
my own master;

But now I'm troubled with two wolves tearing each other: to kneel down
like a fool and worship you,

And the other thing." She whitened and smiled. "I'm not afraid: but I'm not
experienced. Marriage you mean?

There's no security in anything less. We are, as you say, beggars: we want
security." Old Martial

Groped and muttered against her. She laughed: "I'm driving a bargain: be
quiet father." Cawdor said sadly:

"I think that I am the one being made a fool of, old man, not you. Fera if
you were willing

We'd drive up and be married to-morrow. And then . . . there must be
something . . . clothes, clothes: you look ridiculous

Bursting through Michal's like the bud of a poppy." She stood quietly and
looked over the dooryard

At Concha Rosas peeling potatoes beside the fountain. "Who's that wide-
lapped dark o' the moon

Among the lilies?" He said, "Why: Concha. You know her." "Oh, Concha.
And now you've moved her out of the house."

"Yes," he said angrily. And Fera laughing: "There is nothing under the sun
worth loving but strength: and I

Had some but it's tired, and now I'm sick of it. I want you to be proud and
hard with me; I'm not tame

If you ever soften. Oh, yes, to your offer. I'd a friend once that had fine
dreams, she didn't look forward

Into her mist of moon on the roses — not Rosas — you remember Edith,

Father? — with half the heart that races me to meet to-morrow." Then
Cawdor shuddered with hope of love;

His face relaxing began to look like an old man's. He stooped toward Fera,
to fondle or kiss,

She drew herself back. "Not now. Oh, I'll be honest

And love you well." She took her father by the arm. "The sun's passed from
    the bench, father, come in.
I'll build a fire on the hearth if you want." And Cawdor: "That's it! You like
    horses, that's what I'll give you.
You liked mine but I'll buy you better; Morales has a pair of whites as
    beautiful as flowers.
We'll drive by there to-morrow. Like kittens they are." He followed her
    in-doors.

Blue kingfisher laughing laughing in the lit boughs
Over lonely water,
Is there no man not duped and therefore you are laughing?
No strength of a man
But falls on folly before it drops into dust?
Go wicked arrow down to the ocean
And learn of gulls: they laugh in the cloud, they lament also.
The man who'd not be seduced, not in hot youth,
By the angel of fools, million-worshipped success,
The self-included man, the self-armored,
And never beguiled as to a bull nor a horse,
Now in his cooled and craglike years
Has humbled himself to beg pleasure: even power was better.
Laugh kingfisher, laugh, that is their fashion.
Whoever has discerned the vanity of water will desire wind.

II

The night of Cawdor's marriage, his son
Hood Cawdor lay in the north on the open sand-beach
Of a long lake. He was alone; his friend in that country
Who hunted with him, had gone to the Indian camp.
Hood slept beside his fire and seemed to awake
And hear the faint ripple, and wind in far firs,

Then all at once a voice came from the south
As if it had flown mountains and wide valleys yet clearly heard
And like a dying man's, "Hood, Hood. My son." He saw
His father's face clearly a moment after
Distorted either with pain or approach of death.
But then the actual stars of the night came through it,
Like those of a winter evening, Orion rising,
Altair and Vega going west. When he remembered
It was early autumn, he knew it must be past midnight.
He laid a flare of twigs on the live coals
Before he lay down; eyes on the opposite shore
Would have seen the sharp stars in the black crystal
Of the lake cancelled by a red comet's tail.

That night and in the morning Hood had no doubt
His father had just died or approached death;
But dreams and visions are an obscure coinage
No sane person takes faithfully. He thought of writing
To his sister Michal; he had no habit of writing.
Months later, after the rains began and cramped
His migrant hunting, he thought not with much sorrow
Yet mournfully, of his father as dead; and thought
That he'd a share in the place unless he'd been,
As appeared likely, cut off by a written will.
No doubt it was too late to see the old man,
Yet he'd go south. He sold his horse and shot-gun, took his rifle and
    went south.

                He approached home
Over the hills, not by the coast-road from Monterey. Miles beyond miles a
    fire had devoured

Until he looked from the height into the redwood canyons pitching to the
    ocean, these were unhurt,
Dark green and strong. Then he believed his father could not have died.

                                                                The

    first canyon he entered
A mountain-lion stood stilted on a bare slope between alder and redwood
    watching him come down:
Like the owner of the place: he slid the rifle-stock to his cheek thinking
    "The hills have not been hunted
Since I've been gone"; he fired, and the lank August-pasture-colored body
    somersaulted
Over the ridge; he found it lying under a laurel-bush. The skinning was a
    long toil; Hood came
Burdened across the fall of twilight to the great dome of high-cliffed
    granite, they call it the Rock,
That stands out of the hill at the head of Cawdor's canyon.

                                                 Here, after

    the trivial violent quarrel
That sped him from home the year before, he had built a fire at dusk
    hoping Michal would see it
And come to bid him good-bye; she had seen and come. He stood now and
    saw, down the great darkening gorge,
The reddish-yellow windows glimmer in his father's house, the iron-dark
    ocean a bank beyond,
Pricked at the gray edge with one pin-point ship's light. Deep, vast, and
    quiet and sad. After a little
He gathered sticks under the oaks and made a fire on the Rock's head,
    wishing Michal might see it.

If not, he could go down in the morning, (he'd blanket and food) and see
   whether the place was changed.

Michal had gone in-doors but Acanna saw it,
A bright high blood-drop under the lump-shaped moon,
When he was stamping stable-yard muck from his boots
Before he went in to supper. He said to the new farmhand
Dante Vitello, the Swiss whom Cawdor had brought
From Monterey: "You seen strangers go through?
Some fellow's got a fire on the Rock." Then Michal
Hurried her meal and went out. The fire waned,
Rayless red star up the blue-shadow-brimming
Moon-silver-lipped gorge. Michal went doubtfully
Up the dim moon-path by the lone redwood that lately
Excited by her father's marriage
She'd made a secret marriage with, and a law
That she must always touch it in passing. She touched it
Without much ceremony, and climbed, and peered
Under the oaks at the man out on the Rock's head.
Oh, it was Hood, in the red ember-glow. They met gladly;
The edge of shadow and moongleam down the gulf of the canyon crept up
   out of sight
Under the Rock before she went home. Hood said "You'll ask the old man
   whether he'd like to see me.
But tell him that I'll not stay. No plowing, I'm not a farmer." "You're still
   only a hunter" she answered.

By the house under the broken cypresses;
The saffron dawn from which Hood had descended
Still hung in the V of the canyon; Cawdor with morning friendliness, "Stay
   for a week if you like. Don't fear,

I won't set you at plowing, we've done the plowing. My wife's father," he
    said, "has your old room,
But you can have the one on the north, used to be Concha's." Fera Martial
    came out; she had changed
Amazingly from the sallow girl that Hood
Had seen two years ago at the lean farm. The eyes had not changed. A wind
    blew from her eyes
Like sea-wind from the gray sea. "Here's Hood," said Cawdor. "He looks
    more like you," she said, "than either of the others."
"As long as you don't ask him to work. George works, but this
Is only a hunter. Let him have the little north room for a week." Hood
    unstrapped the raw stiffening
Puma-skin from his pack. "I owe you a wedding-present," he said to Fera,
    "if you'll take this
I'll get it tanned. I shot it yesterday." Fera took in both hands the eight-foot
    trophy, she made
To draw it over her shoulders, "Stop. It's not dry, you'll stain your dress."
    "Who am I," she said impatiently,
"Not to be stained?" She assumed it like a garment, the head with the slits
    for eyes hung on her breast,
The moonstone claws dangling, the glazed red fleshy under-side
Turned at the borders, her bare forearm crossing it. "Sticky," she said and
    took it in-doors. "Come in."
He carried his pack, she led him up-stairs to the north room. "This was
    not yours when you used to live here."
"No. Mine was where your father is now." "Then who had this one?"
He answered "I don't remember: nobody: I guess it was empty." "That
    Rosas woman," she answered, "had it.
But the bed's aired." She left him there and went down.

He went out-doors to find Michal again
And couldn't find her; he wandered about and played with the horses,

Then Michal was coming up from the field seaward.
She carried a trap in her hand, and a live ground-squirrel
Dangled from it by the crushed paws, the white-rimmed
Eyes dull with pain, it had lain caught all night.
"What's that, Michal, why don't you kill it?" "A treat for the eagle.
I've taught him to eat beef but he loves to kill.
Oh squirrels are scarce in winter." "What, you've still got the eagle?"
"Yes. Come and watch."

      Hood remembered great sails
Coasting the hill and the redwoods. He'd shot for the breast,
But the bird's fate having captivity in it
Took in the wing-bone, against the shoulder, the messenger
Of human love; the broad oar of the wing broke upward
And stood like a halved fern-leaf on the white of the sky,
Then all fell wrecked. He had flung his coat over its head,
Still the white talon-scars pitted his forearm.

The cage was not in the old place. "Fera," she said,
"She made me move it because it smells. I can't
Scrape the wood clean." Michal had had it moved
To the only other level on the pitch of the hill;
The earth-bench a hundred feet above the house-roof,
An old oak's roots partly upheld; a faint
Steep path trailed up there. One side of the low leaning
Bole of the tree was the eagle's cage, on the other
A lichened picket-fence guarded two graves,
Two wooden head-boards. Cawdor's dead wife was laid here
Beside a child that had died; an older sister
Of Hood's and Michal's.

                        They stood and watched
The dark square-shouldered prisoner, the great flight-feathers
Of the dragged wing were worn to quills and beetles
Crawled by the weaponed feet, yet the dark eyes
Remembered their pride. Hood said "You ought to kill him.
My God, nearly two years!" She answered nothing,
But when he looked at her face the long blue eyes
Winked and were brimmed. The grim hand took the squirrel,
It made a whispering twitter, the bleak head tore it,
And Michal said "George wanted to kill him too.
I can't let him be killed. And now, day after day
I have to be cruel to bring him a little happiness."
Hood laughed; they stood looking down on the house,
All roof and dormers from here, among the thirteen
Winter-battered cypresses planted about it.

III

The next day's noon Michal said, "Her old father
Believes that food from the sea keeps him alive.
The low tides at full moon we always go down."
When Fera came they took sacks for the catch
And brown iron blades to pry the shells from the rock.
They went to the waste of the ebb under the cliff,
Stone wilderness furred with dishevelled weed, but under each round
    black-shouldered stone universes
Of color and life, scarlet and green sea-lichens, violet and rose anemones,
    wave-purple urchins,
Red starfish, tentacle-rayed pomegranate-color sun-disks, shelled worms
    tuft-headed with astonishing
Flower-spray, pools of live crystal, quick eels plunged in the
    crevices . . . the three intrusive atoms of humanity

Went prying and thrusting; the sacks fattened with shell-vaulted meat.
   Then Fera said "Go out on the reef,
Michal, and when you've filled the sack with mussels call Hood to fetch it."
   "Why should I go? Let *him*."
"Go Michal, I need Hood to turn over the stones." When Michal was gone
And walked beyond hearing on the low reef, dim little remote figure
   between the blind flat ocean
And burning sky, Fera stood up and said suddenly: "Judge me, will you.
   Kindness is like . . .
The slime on my hands, I want judgment. We came out of the mountain
   fire beggared and blinded,
Nothing but a few singed rags and a lame horse
That has died since. Now you despise me because I gave myself to your
   father. Do then: I too
Hate myself now, we've learned he likes dark meat — that Rosas — a
   rose-wreath of black flesh for his bride
Was not in the bargain. It leaves a taste." Hood steadied himself against the
   wind of her eyes, and quietly:
"Be quiet, you are telling me things that don't concern me, true or not. I
   am not one of the people that live
In this canyon." "You can be cold, I knew that, that's Cawdor. The others
   have kindly mother in them.
Wax from the dead woman: but when I saw your face I knew it was the
   pure rock. I loved him for that.
For I did love him, he is cold and strong. So when you judge me, write in
   the book that she sold herself
For someone to take care of her blind father, but not without love. You
   had better go out on the reef
And help Michal."

            He went, and kneeling beside his sister to scrape the
stiff brown-bearded lives

From the sea face of the rock, over the swinging streaks of foam on the
    water, "Michal" he said
"I wish you could get free of this place. We must think what we can do.
    God knows I wouldn't want you
Like the girls in town, pecking against a shop-window." "What did she
    want to tell you?" "Nothing at all.
Only to say she loves the old man. Michal, keep your mind clean, be like a
    boy, don't love.
Women's minds are not clean, their mouths declare it, the shape of their
    mouths. They want to belong to someone.
But what do I know? They are all alike to me as mussels." The sack was
    filled; reluctance to return
Had kept him hewing at the thick bed of mussels, letting them slide on the
    rock and drop in the water,
When he looked up Fera had come. "Why do you waste them?" she said.
    "You're right, waste is the purpose
And value of . . . Look, I've something to waste." She extended her hand
    toward him, palm downward, he saw bright blood
Trickle from the tips of the brown fingers and spot the rock. "You're hurt?"
    "Oh, nothing. I turned a stone,
A barnacle cut me, you were so long coming I thought I could do without
    you. Well, have you judged me,
With Michal to help?" "Let me see the cut," he said angrily. She turned
    the gashed palm cup-shape upward
On purpose to let a small red pool gather. She heard his teeth grating, that
    pleased her. He said
"I can't see," then she flung it on the ocean. "But you're a hunter, you must
    have seen many a wild creature
Drain, and not paled a shade." He saw the white everted lips of the cut and
    suffered a pain
Like a stab, in a peculiar place. They walked

And were silent on the low reef; Hood carried the sea-lymph-streaming
    sack on his shoulder. Every third step
A cold and startling shadow was flung across them; the sun was on the
    horizon and the tide turning
The surf mounted, each wave at its height covered the sun. A river of gulls
    flowed away northward,
Long wings like scythes against the face of the wave, the heavy red light,
    the cold pulses of shadow,
The croaking voice of a heron fell from high rose and amber.

                               There were
    three sacks to bring up the cliff.
Hood sent his sister to fetch a horse to the cliffhead to carry them home,
    but Michal without an answer
Went home by herself, along the thread of gray fog
That ran up the great darkening gorge like the clue of a labyrinth. Hood,
    climbing, saw on the cliffhead, unreal
To eyes upward and sidelong, his head cramped by the load, like a lit pillar
    Fera alone
Waiting for him, flushed with the west in her face,
The purple hills at her knees and the full moon at her thigh, under her
    wounded hand new-risen.
He slid the sack on the grass and went down. His knees wavered under the
    second on the jags of rock,
Under the third he stumbled and fell on the cliffhead. They were not too
    heavy but he was tired. Then Fera
Lay down beside him, he laughed and stood up. "Where's Michal? I sent
    her to fetch a horse." And Fera shivering:
"I waited for you but Michal went on. My father says that life began in the
    ocean and crept
Like us, dripping sea-slime up the high cliff. He used to be a schoolmaster
    but mother left him,

She was much younger than he. Then he began to break himself on bad
    liquor. Our little farm
Was the last refuge. But he was no farmer. We had utterly failed
And fallen on hollow misery before the fire came. That sort of thing builds
    a wall against recklessness.
Nothing's worth risk; now I'll be mean and cautious all the rest of my life,
    grow mean and wrinkled
Sucking the greasy penny of security. For it's known beforehand, whatever I
    attempt bravely would fail.
That's in the blood. But see," she looked from the ocean sundown to the
    violet hills and the great moon,
"Because I choose to be safe all this grows hateful. What shall I do?" He
    said scornfully: "Like others,
Take what you dare and let the rest go." "That is no limit. I dare," she
    answered. He looked aside
At the dark presence of the ocean moving its foam secretly below the red
    west, and thought
"Well, what does she want?" "Nothing," she said as if she had heard him.
    "But I wish to God
I were the hunter." She went up to the house,
And there for days was silent as a sheathed knife,
Attending her sick father and ruling the housework
With bitter eyes. At night she endured Cawdor if he pleased
As this earth endures man.

                        A morning when no one
Was in the house except her father in his room,
She stole to Hood's room on the north to fall
On the open bed and nuzzle the dented pillow
With a fire face; but then sweating with shame
Rose and fetched water for some menial service

About her father's body; he had caught cold
And was helplessly bedfast again.

                              Meanwhile Hood Cawdor
With hunting deer at waterheads before dawn,
Evening rides with Michal, lucky shots at coyotes
And vain lying-wait and spying of creekside pad-prints
For the great mountain-lion that killed a calf,
Contentedly used six days of his quick seven
And would have gone the eighth morning. But the sixth night
The farm-dogs yelled furious news of disaster,
So that Hood snatched up half his clothes and ran out
Barefoot; George came behind him; they saw nothing.
The dogs were silent, two of them came at call
Under the late moonrise cancelled with cloud,
But would not quest nor lead. Then the young men
Returned to bed. In the white of dawn they found
The dog that had not come in the night, the square-jawed
Fighter and best of the dogs, against the door
So opened with one stroke of an armed paw
That the purple entrails had come out, and lay
On the stone step, speckled with redwood needles.

That postponed Hood's departure, he was a hunter
And took the challenge. He found the fighting-spot,
Scratched earth and the dog's blood, but never the slayer.

IV

                                        A sudden rainstorm
Beat in from the north ocean up a blue heaven and spoiled his hunting.
    The northwest wind veered east,

The rain came harder, in heavy falls and electric pauses. Hood had come
    home, he sat with Michal
Playing checkers; Fera was up-stairs with her father.
The blind man had grown feebler; he had been in fact dying since the fire;
    but now two days he had eaten
Nothing, and his lungs clogged. Most of the daytime
And half the night Fera'd spent by his bedside. He had lain deeply
    absorbed in his own misery,
His blindness concentrating his mood, until the electric streams and hushes
    of the rain vexed him,
Toward evening he fell into feverish talk of trivial
Remembered things, little dead pleasures. Fera gave patient answers until
    he slept. She then
Left him and slept heavily beside her husband.

                                    The rain had ceased,
    Hood saw a star from his window
And thought if the rain ceased he might give over his hunting and go
    to-morrow. But out of doors
Was little promise of the rain ceasing; the east wind had slipped south, the
    earth lay expectant. The house
Wore an iron stub for some forgotten purpose
Fixed upward from the peak of the roof; to one passing out-doors at
    midnight the invisible metal
Would have shown a sphered flame, before the thunder began.

                                            Fera
    before the first thunderclap
Dreaming imagined herself the mountain-lion that had killed the dog; she
    hid in leaves and the hunter
Aimed at her body through a gap in the green. She waited the fire, rigid,
    and through closed lids

Saw lightning flare in the window, she heard the crash of the rifle. The
    enthralling dream so well interpreted
The flash and the noise that she was not awakened but slept to the second
    thunder. She rose then, and went
To her father's room for he'd be awakened. He was not awakened.
He snored in a new manner, puffing his cheeks. Impossible to wake him.
    She called Cawdor. In the morning
They sent Acanna, for form's sake, not hope's, to fetch a doctor. Hood
    offered to ride, Acanna was sent.
The torrents of rain prevented his return, and the doctor's coming, to the
    third day. But northward
He rode lightly, the storm behind him.

                            The wind had shifted before
    dawn and grooved itself
A violent channel from east of south, the slant of the coast; the house-roof
    groaned, the planted cypresses
Flung broken boughs over the gables and all the lee slope of the gorge was
    carpeted green
With the new growth and little twigs of the redwoods. They bowed
    themselves at last, the redwoods, not shaken
By common storms, bowed themselves over; their voice and not the ocean's
    was the great throat of the gorge
That roared it full, taking all the storm's other
Noises like little fish in a net.

                    On the open pasture
The cattle began to drift, the wind broke fences.
But Cawdor, although unsure and thence in his times
Violent toward human nature, was never taken
Asleep by the acts of nature outside; he knew
His hills as if he had nerves under the grass,

What fence-lengths would blow down and toward what cover
The cattle would drift. He rode with George, and Hood
Rode after, thwart the current in the cracked oaks
To the open mercy of the hill. They felt the spray
And sharp wreckage of rain-clouds in the steel wind,
And saw the legs of the others' horses leaning
Like the legs of broken chairs on the domed rims
On the running sky.

                In the house Fera
Sat by her father's bed still as a stone
And heard him breathe, that was the master-noise of the house
That caught the storm's noises and cries in a net,
And captured her mind; the ruling tenth of her mind
Caught in the tidal rhythm lay inert and breathing
Like the old man's body, the deep layers left unruled
Dividing life in a dream. She heard not the roof
Crying in the wind, nor on the window
The endless rattle of earth and pebbles blasted
From the hill above. For hours; and a broken cypress bough
Rose and tapped the strained glass, at a touch the pane
Exploded inward, glass flew like sparks, the fury of the wind
Entered like a wild beast. Nothing in the room
Remained unmoved except the old man on the bed.

Michal Cawdor had crawled up the hill four-foot
To weight her eagle's cage with heavier stones
Against the storm, and creeping back to the house
Heard the glass crash and saw the gapped window. She got up-stairs
And saw in the eddying and half blinded glimmer
Fera's face like an axe and the window blocked

With a high wardrobe that had hidden the wall
Between the two windows, a weight for men
To strain at, but Fera whose nerves found action before
Her mind found thought had wrestled it into service
Instead of screaming, the instant the crash snapped her deep trance. When
    Michal came Fera was drawing
The table against the wardrobe to hold it firm, her back and shoulders
    flowing into lines like fire
Between the axe face and the stretched arms: "Ah shut the door," she said
    panting, "did Hood go with them?
He hasn't *gone?*" "Who? Hood?" "Coo if you like: has he gone?" "He went
    with father," she answered trembling,
"To herd the cows . . ." "Why are your eyes like eggs then, for he'll come
    back, Michal?" She went to the bedside
And murmured "He hasn't moved, it hasn't hurt him." But Michal: "Did
    you want Hood?" "Want him? I wanted
Someone to stop the window. Who could bear life
If it refused the one thing you want? I've made a shutter to hold although it
    sings at the edges.
Yet he felt nothing. Michal, it doesn't storm for a sparrow's death. You and
    I, Michal, won't have
A stir like this to speed us away in our times. He is dying." Michal
    answered "Dante Vitello's
Roping the hay-stacks, I'll fetch him Fera?" "What could he do while the
    wind continues, more than I've done?
We can stand draughts. Oh Michal, a man's life and his soul
Have nothing in common. You never knew my father, he had eagle
    imaginations. This poor scarred face
For whose sake neither nature nor man have ever stepped from the path
    while he was living: his death
Breaks trees, they send a roaring chariot of storm to home him.

Hood wouldn't leave without his rifle," she said,
"He didn't take the rifle when he went up?"
"Why no, not in this wind."

                              In the afternoon the wind
Fell, and the spray in the wind waxed into rain.
The men came home, they boarded the broken window.
The rain increased all night. At dawn a high sea-bird,
If any had risen so high, watching the hoary light
Creep down to sea, under the cloud-streams, down
The many canyons the great sea-wall of coast
Is notched with like a murderer's gun-stock, would have seen
Each canyon's creek-mouth smoke its mud-brown torrent
Into the shoring gray; and as the light gained
Have seen the whole wall gleam with a glaze of water.

V

There was a little acre in Cawdor's canyon
Against the creek, used for a garden, because they could water it
In summer through a wood flume; but now the scour
Devoured it; and after Cawdor had ditched the barns
Against the shoreless flood running from the hill,
In the afternoon he turned to save this acre.
He drove piling to stay the embankment; Hood pointed
The beams, and Cawdor drove them with the great sledge-hammer,
Standing to his knees in the stream.

                              Then Fera Cawdor
Came down the bank without a cloak, her hair
Streaming the rain, and stood among the brown leafless
And lavender shoots of willow. "Oh come to the house, Hood."

She struck her hands together. "My father is conscious,
He wants to speak to Hood, wants Hood." Who wondering
Gave the axe to his brother and went up.

They came to the room off the
short hallway; he heard
Through the shut door before they reached it the old man's breathing: like
nothing he'd ever heard in his life:
Slime in a pit bubbling: but the machine rhythm, intense and faultless. She
entered ahead
And drew a cloth over the wrinkled eye-pits; the bald scars in the beard and
the open mouth
Were not covered. "Ah shut the door," she said, "against the wind on the
stairway." He came reluctantly
Into the dreadful rhythm of the room, and said "When was he conscious?
He is not now." And Fera:
"He is in a dream: but *I* am in a dream, between blackness and fire, my
mind is never gathered,
And all the years of thoughtful wonder and little choices are gone. He is on
the shore of what
Nobody knows: but *I* am on that shore. It is lonely. I was the one that
needed you. Does he feel anything?"
He thought, this breathing-machine? "Why no, Fera."
"It is only because I am cold," she said wringing her hands, violently
trembling, "the cold rain-water
Rains down from my hair.
I hated my loose mother but this old man was always gentle and good even
in drunkenness.
Lately I had true delight in doing things for him, the feeding, cleaning, we'd
travelled so far together,
So many faces of pain. But now he has flown away, where is it?" She
mastered her shuddering and said

"All that I loved is here dying: and now if you should ask me to I would strike his face
While he lies dying." But he bewildered in the ice-colored wind of her eyes stood foolish without an answer,
And heard her: "Do you understand?" He felt the wind tempered, it fell in tears, he saw them running
By the racked mouth; she ceased then to be monstrous and became pitiful. Her power that had held him captive
Ceased also, and now he was meanly afraid of what she might do. He went through the house and found Michal,
And brought her up to the room. Then Fera lifted her face from the bed, and stood, and answered "Come Michal.
This is the place. Come and look down and despise us. Oh, we don't mind. You're kind: I am wicked perhaps
To think that he is repulsive as well as pitiful to you. You hunter with a rifle, one shot's
Mercy in the life: but the common hunter of the world uses too many; wounds and not kills, and drives you
Limping and bleeding, years after years,
Down to this pit. One hope after another cracked in his hands; the school he had; then the newspaper
He labored day and night to build up, over in the valley. His wife my shameful mother abandoned him.
He took whiskey for a friend, it turned a devil. He took the farm up here, hunted at last
To the mountain, and nothing grew, no rain fell, the cows died
Before the fire came. Then it took his eyes and now it is taking his life. Now it has taken
Me too, that had been faithful awhile. For I have to tell you, dear dear Michal, before he dies,
I love you — and Hood for your sake, Michal —
More than I do this poor old man. He lies abandoned." She stood above him, her thin wet clothing

In little folds glued to the flesh, like one of the girls in a Greek frieze, the
    air of their motion
Moulds lean in marble; Michal saw her through mist in the eyes and
    thought how lovely she was, and dimly
Heard her saying: "Do you not wish you were like this man, Hood? *I* wish
    I were like this man.
He has only one thing left to do. It is great and maybe dreadful to die, but
    nothing's easier.
He does it asleep. Perhaps we *are* like this man: we have only one thing left
    to do, Hood,
One burning thing under the sun. I love you so much, Michal, that you will
    surely forgive
Whatever it is. You'll know it is not done wickedly, but only from bitter
    need, from bitter need . . ."
She saw him frowning, and Michal's wonder, and cried quickly:
"You needn't pity him! For even in this deformity and shame of obscure
    death he is much more fortunate
Than any king of fat steers: under the bone, behind the burnt eyes
There have been lightnings you never dreamed of, despairs and exultations
    and hawk agonies of sight
That would have cindered your eyes before the fire came.
Now leave me with him. If I were able I would take him up, groaning to
    death, to the great Rock
Over your cramp cellar of a canyon, to flame his bitter soul away like a shot
    eagle
In the streaming sky. I talk foolishly. Michal you mustn't come back until
    he has died, death's dreadful.
You're still a child. Stay, Hood." But he would not.

                      He heard in the
  evening
The new farmhand talking with Concha Rosas,

His Alp-Italian accent against her Spanish-
Indian like pebbles into thick water. "This country
You cannot trust, it never need any people.
My old country at home she is not so kind
But always she need people, she never kill all.
She is our mother, can't live without us. This one not care.
It make you fat and soon it cutting your neck."
Concha answered inaudibly, and the other: "You Indian.
Not either you. I have read, you come from Ah-sia.
You come from Ah-sia, us from Europa, no one from here.
Beautiful *matrigna* country, she care for Indian
No more nor white nor black, how have she help you?"
Their talk knotted itself on miscomprehension
Until *matrigna* shaped into *madrastra*.
"Beautiful stepmother country."

                                      Hood ceased to hear them.
Why, so she was. He saw as if in a vision
The gray flame of her eyes like windows open
To a shining sky the north wind sweeps, and wind
And light strain from the windows. What wickedness in the fabric
Was driving her mad with binding her to old men?
He went to the door to look at the black sky.
He'd leave the house to-night but pity and the rain held him.
He heard the eaves gutter in their puddles and rush
Of rivulets washing the dark.

                                While he was there
She came from the stair and whispered: for they were alone
In the dark room, the others in the lamplit room
At the table: "If I were hurt in the hills,
Dying without help, you'd not sneak off and leave me.

Oh, nobody could do that. Pull the door to
On that black freedom. Perhaps my father will die
This drowning night, but can't you see that I am a prisoner
Until he does: the wrists tied, the ankles:
I can neither hold nor follow.
No, no, we have to let them take their time dying.
Why, even on Cawdor's, on your father's account
It would be wicked to call despair in here
Before it must come. I might do strangely
If I were driven. You'll promise. Put your hand here."
She caught it and held it under the small breast
Against the one dry thinness of cloth. She had changed then.
He felt it thudding. "I am being tortured you know."
He shook and said "Until he dies I'll not go.
Dear child, then you'll be quieter." "When you said *child*,
Your voice," she answered, "was as hard as your father's.
Hood, listen, all afternoon
I have been making a dream, you know my two white horses,
They are like twins, they mustn't be parted.
One for you, one for me, we rode together in the dream
Far off in the deep world, no one could find us.
We leaned and kissed . . ." He thrust her off, with violent fear,
And felt her throat sob in his hand, the hot slender
Reed of that voice of hers, the drumming arteries
Each side the reed flute. She went crouching and still
To the stair; he stood in the dark mourning his violence.

But she had gone up into the snoring rhythm
Neither day nor night changed. Cawdor had asked her
Whom she would have to watch with her all night,
"For you must sleep a little." She had chosen Concha
Rosas; and that was strange, he thought she had always

Hated Concha. He came at the end of evening
And brought the brown fat silent woman.

                              Then Fera
Looked up, not rising from the chair by the bed
And said with a difficult smile over the waves of noise:
"I was thinking of a thing that worried my father, in the old days. He made
    a bargain with a man
To pasture his horse, the horse died the first week. The man came asking
    pay for a year's pasture
For a dead horse. My father paid it at last, I wouldn't have paid it." "No,
    hardly," he answered. And Fera:
"The bargain ends when the man dies — when the horse dies." She looked
    at her dying father and said
Shuddering: "I'm sorry to keep you up all night, Concha; but you can sleep
    in your chair. He was always
A generous fool, he wasn't made for this world." Cawdor looked down at
    the bed through the dull noise
Like surf on a pebble shore, and said that he'd been out to look at the
    bridge; it was still standing.
The rain would break to-night, the doctor would come to-morrow. "That
    would be late, if there were hope,"
She answered, "no matter." "Dear child," he said hoarsely, "we all die."
    "Those that have blood in us. When you said *child*,
Your voice," she answered, "was as hard as a flint. We know that you and
    the Rock over the canyon
Will not die in our time. When they were little children
Were you ever kind?" "Am I not now?" "Oh, kind." She leaned sidewise
    and smoothed
The coverlet on the bed, but rather as a little hawk slips sidelong from its
    flapping vantage

In the eye of the wind to a new field. "But about blood in the stone veins,
  could Concha tell me?
Look, his face now Concha, pure rock: a flick and it shows. Oh," she said
  and stood up, "forgive me.
For I am half mad with watching him
Die like an old steer the butcher forgot. It makes me
Mad at your strength. He had none: but his mind had shining wings, they
  were soon broken."

When Cawdor went out
She said to Concha "It is growing cold. Wrap yourself in the blanket before
  you sleep in the chair."
When Concha nodded she went and shook her awake, by the fat shoulder.
  "Did Hood make love to anyone
In those old days? They're hot at sixteen." "He never. Oh no." "You didn't
  serve the father and the sons?
Whom did he love?" "Nobody. He love the deer.
He's only a boy and he go hunting." Fera whispered from the throat: "I
  wish to God, you brown slug,
That I had been you, to scrape the mud from his boots when he came in
  from hunting; or Ilaria Acanna
Cooking him little cakes in the oak-smoke, in the white dawns when the
  light shakes like water in a cup
And the hills are foam: for now who knows what will happen?
Oh sleep, cover your head with the blanket, nothing has changed."

She went about the room and rested in her chair.
The snoring rhythm took her mind captive again,
And in a snatch of sleep she dreamed that Michal
Had stolen her lion-skin, the one that Hood had given her,
And wore it in the hills and was shot for a lion.

Cawdor (1926–28)   213

Her dead body was found wrapped in the skin.
There was more, but this was remembered.

                        Perhaps the minds
That slept in the house were wrought to dreams of death
By knowledge of the old man's ebbing. Hood Cawdor
Dreamed also of a dead body; he seemed a child; at first
He dreamed it was his father lay dead in the house,
But afterwards his father held him by the hand
Without a break in the dream. They looked through a door
Into the room in which his mother lay dead.
There an old woman servant, who had now been gone
These many years, prepared his mother's body
For burial; she was washing the naked corpse.
Matrigna; madrastra. He awoke and lay in the dark
Gathering his adult mind, assuring himself
The dream grew from no memory; he remembered
His mother living, nothing of seeing her dead.
Yes, of the burial a little; the oak on the hill,
And the red earth. His thought of the grave calmed him
So that he was falling asleep.

                        But Fera remained awake
After her dream. How could one drive a wedge
Between the father and the son? There was not now
Any affection: but Hood was loyal: or afraid.
They had quarrelled the time before. The snatch of sleep
Had cleared her mind.

                      She heard the snoring rhythm
Surely a little slower and a little slower,
Then one of the old hands drew toward the breast.

The breathing failed; resumed, but waning to silence.
The throat clicked when a breath should have been drawn.
A maze of little wrinkles, that seemed to express
Surprised amusement, played from the hollow eye-pits
Into the beard.

VI

              The window was black still.
No cock had cried, nor shiver of dawn troubled the air.
The stale lamp shone and smelled. Ah, what a silence.
She crossed the room and shook Concha. "Get up, Concha.
He has died. I was alone and have closed his mouth.
Now I'll go out." She thought in the hallway,
"Besides, I am greedy to be caught in Hood's room.
We can but die, what's that. Where did this come from?"
She whispered, staring at the candle she held
Without a memory of having found nor lighted it.
She opened Hood's door and shut it behind her.

                            "He has died!"
No answer. Then Fera felt the tears in her eyes
Dried up with fear. "You haven't gone? Are you here Hood?"
She saw him lifting his face from the shadows like a sea-lion from the wave.
   "I dreaded
You'd slip away from here in my night. It is finished and I
Alone was by him, your father's flitch of dark meat snored in a corner. He
   has died. All the wild mind
And jagged attempts are sealed over." Her voice lifted and failed, he saw her
   sleep-walker face
Candle-lighted from below, the shadow of the chin covering the mouth and
   of the cheek-bones the eyes

To make it the mask of a strained ecstasy, strained fleshless almost. Herself
    was wondering what sacred fear
Restrained her, she'd meant to go touch, but here desire at the height
    burned crystal-separate. He said, staring:
"Have you called my father? I'll dress and come, what can I do?" "Do you
    think I will call," she said quietly,
"Cawdor?" She stopped and said: "Death is no terror, I have just left there.
    Is there anything possible to fear
And not take what we want, openly with both hands? I have been unhappy
    but that was foolish
For now I know that whatever bent this world around us, whether it was
    God or whether it was blind
Chance piled on chance as blind as my father,
Is perfectly good, we're given a dollar of life to gamble against a dollar's
    worth of desire
And if we win we have both but losers lose nothing,
Oh, nothing, how are they worse off than my father, or a stone in the field?
    Why, Hood, do you sleep naked?"
She asked him, seeing the candle's gleam on the arm and shoulder. "I
    brought no night-clothes with me," he sullenly
Answered, "I didn't expect people at night. What do you want?" "Nothing.
    Your breast's more smooth
Than rubbed marble, no hair like other men in the groove between the
    muscles, it is like a girl's
Except the hardness and the flat strength. No, why do you cover it, why
    may I not look down with my eyes?
I'd not hide mine. No doubt I'll soon die,
And happy if I could earn that marble to be my gravestone. You might cut
    letters in it. I know
It never would bleed, it would cut hard. *Fera Martial* you'd carve, the letters
    of a saved name,

Why should they fall like grains of sand and be lost forever
On the monstrous beach? But while I breathe I have to come back and beat
    against it, that stone, for nothing,
Wave after wave, a broken-winged bird
Wave after wave beats to death on the cliff. Her blood in the foam. If I
    were another man's wife
And not Cawdor's you'd pity me." "Being what you are," he answered: he
    rose in the bed angrily, her eyes
Took hold like hands upon the beautiful bent shoulders plated from the
    bone with visible power,
Long ridges lifting the smooth skin, the hunter slenderness and strength:
    "being what you are you will gather
The shame back on your mind and kill it. We've not been made to touch
    what we would loathe ourselves for
To the last drop." She said "What were you saying? Do you think I should
    be shameless as a man making
Love to reluctance, the man to you for a woman, if I had time, if you were
    not going to-morrow?
If I just had time, I'd use a woman's cunning manners, the cat patience and
    watchfulness: but shame
Dies on the precipice lip." "I hear them stirring in the house," he answered.
    "You lie, Hood. You hear nothing.
This little room on the north is separate and makes no sound, your father
    used to visit his thing here,
You children slept and heard nothing. You fear him of course. I can
    remember having feared something . . .
That's long ago. I forget what. Look at me once,
Stone eyes am I too horrible to look at? If I've no beauty at all, I have more
    than Concha had
When she was more fawn than sow, in her lean years, did your father avoid
    her? I must have done something

In ignorance, to make you hate me. If I could help it, would I come
Fresh from the death of the one life I have loved to make myself
Your fool and tell you I am shameless, if I could help it? Oh that's the
    misery: you look at me and see death,
I am dressed in death instead of a dress, I have drunk death for days, makes
    me repulsive enough,
No wonder, but you too Hood
Will drink it sometime for all your loathing, there are two of us here
Shall not escape.

                    Oh, but we shall though, if you are willing. There is
    one clean way. We'll not take anything
Of Cawdor's, I have two horses of my own. And you can feed us with the
    rifle. Only to ride beside you
Is all I want. But I would waken your soul and your eyes, I could teach you
    joy.

            I know that you love
Liberty, I'd never touch your liberty. Oh let me ride beside you a week,
    then you could leave me.
I'd be your . . . whatever you want, but you could have other women. That
    wouldn't kill me; but not to be with you
Is death in torture." Her hope died of his look. "I know we came from the
    fire only to fail,
Fail, fail, it's bred in the blood. But," she cried suddenly, "you lie when you
    look like that. The flesh of my body
Is nothing in my longing. What you think I want
Will be pure dust after hundreds of years and something from me be crying
    to something from you
High up in the air."

She heard the door open behind her, she turned on
the door. Cawdor had come.
She cried "Have you waked at last? You sleep like logs, you and your son.
He has died. I can wake nobody.
I banged your door, but this one was unlatched and when I knocked it flew
open. Yet I can't wake him.
Is it decent to leave me alone with the sow Concha in the pit of sorrow?"
His confused violent eyes
Moved and shunned hers and worked the room, with the ancient look of
men spying for their own dishonor
As if it were a lost jewel. "How long ago did you knock? I have been
awake." "What do I know
Of time? He has died." She watched him tremble, controlling with more
violence the violence in him; and he said:
"I know he has died. I came from that room." Then Fera, knowing
That Hood looked like a boy caught in a crime but herself like innocence:
"How did you dare to go in?
Oh yes, the dead never stand up. But how did you dare? You never once
hid your contempt
While he was living. You came and cursed him because our cow died in the
creek. Did he want it to die?
Then what have you done just now, spat in his face? I was not there, he lay
at your mercy." She felt
Her knees failing, and a sharp languor
Melt through her body; she saw the candle-flame (she had set the candle on
the little table) circling
In a short orbit, and Cawdor's face waver, strange heavy face with the
drooping brows and confused eyes,
Said something heavily, unheard, and Fera answered: "Certainly I could
have gone in and called you, but I
Was looking about the house for someone that loved him. You were one of
the hunters that hunted him down.

Cawdor (1926–28)   219

I thought that Hood ... but no, did he care? I couldn't awake him. This
     flesh will harden, I'll be stone too
And not again go hot and wanting pity in a desert of stones. But you ...
     you ... that old blind man
Whom you despised, he lived in the house among you a hawk in a
     mole-hill. And now he's flown up. Oh, death
Is over life like heaven over deep hell." She saw Michal in the door.
     "You're here too, Michal?
My father has died. *You* loved him."

                              She said in the hallway,
"Are you well, Michal? I'm not; but when I slept
A snatch of the early night I dreamed about you.
You wrapped yourself in the mountain-lion skin
That Hood gave me, and Jesus Acanna shot you for a lion."

VII

Cawdor remained behind in the room,
But Hood pretended to have been asleep and hardly
Awakened yet. Certainly he'd not betray
The flaming-minded girl his own simplicity
Imagined a little mad in her sorrow. He answered
Safe questions, but the more his intent was innocent
The more his looks tasted of guilt. And Cawdor:
"When are you going?" "To-day." "That's it? By God
You'll wait until the old blind man is buried.
What did she call you for,
Yesterday in the rain?" "She said her father
Was conscious, but when I came he was not conscious."
"Well, he's not now," he answered, his brows drooping
Between the dawn and the candle. Dawn had begun,

And Cawdor's face between the pale window
And the small flame was gray and yellow. "Get dressed," he said.
He turned to go, and turned back. "You were such friends
With that old man, you'll not go till he's buried."

He went and found Fera, in the room with the dead.
But seeing her bloodless face, and the great eyes
Vacant and gray, he grew somberly ashamed
Of having thought her passion was more than grief.
He had meant to charge Concha to watch her
While Hood remained in the house. He forgot that, he spoke
Tenderly, and persuaded Fera to leave
Concha to watch the dead, and herself rest
In her own room. Michal would sit beside her
All morning if she were lonely. "And Hood," he said,
Spying on her face even against his own will,
"Wanted to go to-day, I told him to wait.
Why did you call him, yesterday in the rain?"
"Yesterday?" "You came in the rain." "If that was yesterday:
Our nights have grown long. I think my father called him,
(My father was then alive) wishing to talk
Of the Klamath country. He too had travelled. He despised people
Who are toad-stools of one place." "Did they talk long?"
"I can't remember. You know: now he has died.
Now the long-laboring mind has come to a rest.
I am tired too. You don't think that the mind
Goes working on? That would be pitiful. He failed in everything.
After we fail our minds go working under the ground, digging, digging . . .
    we talk to someone,
The mind's not there but digging around its failure. That would be
    dreadful, if even while he lies dead

The painful mind's digging away ..." Cawdor for pity
Of the paper-white face shrunk small at dawn
Forbore then, he folded his doubts like a man folding
A live coal in his hand.

Fera returned
To her father's room; she said, "Concha, go down to breakfast. Michal,
Leave me alone for God's sake." Being left alone she knelt by the bed: "In
    that dim world, in that
Dim world, in that dim world, father? ... there's nothing. *I* am between
    the teeth still but you are not troubled.
If only you could *feel* the salvation."

She was mistaken. Sleep and delirium
    are full of dreams;
The locked-up coma had trailed its clue of dream across the crippled
    passages; now death continued
Unbroken the delusions of the shadow before. If these had been relative to
    any movement outside
They'd have grown slower as the life ebbed and stagnated as it ceased, but
    the only measure of the dream's
Time was the dreamer, who geared in the same change could feel none; in
    his private dream, out of the pulses
Of breath and blood, as every dreamer is out of the hour-notched arch of
    the sky. The brain growing cold
The dream hung in suspense and no one knew that it did. Gently with
    delicate mindless fingers
Decomposition began to pick and caress the unstable chemistry
Of the cells of the brain; Oh very gently, as the first weak breath of wind in
    a wood: the storm is still far,

The leaves are stirred faintly to a gentle whispering: the nerve-cells, by
    what would soon destroy them, were stirred
To a gentle whispering. Or one might say the brain began to glow, with its
    own light, in the starless
Darkness under the dead bone sky; like bits of rotting wood on the floor of
    the night forest
Warm rains have soaked, you see them beside the path shine like vague
    eyes. So gently the dead man's brain
Glowing by itself made and enjoyed its dream.

                         The nights of many years
    before this time
He had been dreaming the sweetness of death, as a starved man dreams
    bread, but now decomposition
Reversed the chemistry; who had adored in sleep under so many disguises
    the dark redeemer
In death across a thousand metaphors of form and action celebrated life.
    Whatever he had wanted
To do or become was now accomplished, each bud that had been nipped
    and fallen grew out to a branch,
Sparks of desire forty years quenched flamed up fulfilment.
Out of time, undistracted by the nudging pulse-beat, perfectly real to itself
    being insulated
From all touch of reality the dream triumphed, building from past
    experience present paradise
More intense as the decay quickened, but ever more primitive as it
    proceeded, until the ecstasy
Soared through a flighty carnival of wines and women to the simple delight
    of eating flesh, and tended
Even higher, to an unconditional delight. But then the interconnections
    between the groups of the brain

Failing, the dreamer and the dream split into multitude. Soon the altered
    cells became unfit to express
Any human or at all describable form of consciousness.

                                                    Pain and pleasure
        are not to be thought
Important enough to require balancing: these flashes of post-mortal felicity
    by mindless decay
Played on the breaking harp by no means countervalued the excess of
    previous pain. Such discords
In the passionate terms of human experience are not resolved, nor worth it.

                                                                    The
        ecstasy in its timelessness
Resembled the eternal heaven of the Christian myth, but actually the nerve-
    pulp as organ of pleasure
Was played to pieces in a few hours, before the day's end. Afterwards it
    entered importance again
Through worms and flesh-dissolving bacteria. The personal show was over,
    the mountain earnest continued
In the earth and air.

                        But Fera in her false earnestness
Of passionate life knelt by the bed weeping.
She ceased when Michal returned. Later in the morning
She sent Michal to look for Hood and ask him
Whether he would surely stay as Cawdor had said
Until they buried her father. "Tell him to come
Himself and tell me." Michal came back: "He said
That he was not able to come; but he would stay."
At noon she saw him. She dressed and went to the table,

Where Cawdor sat and watched them. Hood shunned her eyes;
She too was silent.

                             In the afternoon Cawdor came up
And said "The doctor has come." "Why Michal," she said, "but that's a pity.
Came all the sloppy way for nothing, the doctor." "No," Cawdor said. "I
    want you to see him, Fera.
You are not well." She went and saw him, in her father's room, where
    Concha with some childhood-surviving
Belief in magic had set two ritual candles burning by the bed of death. The
    doctor hastily
Covered the face, the candle-flames went over in the wind of the cloth. Fera
    stood quietly and said
She had no illness, and her father was dead. "I'm sorry you've come so far
    for nothing." "Oh, well," he answered,
"The coast's beautiful after the rain. I'll have the drive." "Like this old
    man," she said, "and the other
Millions that are born and die; come all the sloppy way for nothing and
    turn about and go back.
They have the drive." The young doctor stared; and Cawdor angrily
Wire-lipped like one who hides a living coal
In the clenched hand: "What more do you want?" "Oh," she answered,
"I'm not like that"; and went out.

                            After the doctor had gone
She vomited, and became so weak afterwards
That Michal must call Concha to help undress her.
After another spasm of sickness her dream
Was like a stone's; until Cawdor awakened her
In the night, coming to bed. She lay rigid
And saw the fiery cataracts of her mind
Pour all night long. Before the cock crew dawn
Sea-lions began barking and coughing far off

In the hollow ocean; but one screamed out like torture
And bubbled under the water. Then Fera rose
With thief motions. Cawdor awoke and feigned sleep.
She dressed in the dark and left the room, and Cawdor
Followed silently, the black blood in his throat
Stood like a knotted rope. She entered, however,
Her father's room.

     She was not surprised, no one was there
And Concha's candles had died. She fingered the dark
To find her father, the body like a board, the sheeted face,
And sat beside the bed waiting for dawn.
Cawdor, returned to his room, left the door open
To hear the hallway; he dressed, and waiting for dawn
Now the first time knew clearly for what reason
He had made Hood stay: that he might watch and know them,
What they had . . . whether they had . . . but that was insane:
One of the vile fancies men suffer
When they are too old for their wives. She in her grief?
He had not the faculty common to slighter minds
Of seeing his own baseness with a smile. When Hood had passed
The creaking hallway and gone down-stairs, and the other
Not moved an inch, watching her quiet dead,
Cawdor was cured of the indulgence jealousy,
He'd not be a spy again.

    But Fera had heard
Hood pass; she knew Cawdor was watching; she thought
That likely enough Hood had risen before dawn
To leave the canyon forever. She sat like a stone
Turning over the pages of death in her mind,
Deep water, sharp steel, poisons they keep in the stable
To wash the wounds of horses . . .

VIII

Hood coming in to breakfast from the fragrant light
Before sunrise, had set his rifle in the corner by the door.
George Cawdor left the table and going out-doors
Stopped at the door and took the rifle in his hands
Out of mere idleness. Hood sharply: "Mine. Put it down!"
He, nettled, carried it with him to the next room,
There opened the outer door and lined the sights
With a red lichen-fleck on a dead cypress-twig.
Hood came behind him and angrily touched his shoulder,
Reaching across his arm for the rifle; then George
Who had meant to tease him and give it back in a moment,
Remembered a grudge and fired. The sharp noise rang
Through the open house like a hammer-blow on a barrel.
Hood, in the shock of his anger, standing too near
To strike, struck with his elbow in the notch of the ribs,
His hands to the rifle. George groaned, yet half in sport still
Wrestled with him in the doorway.

      Hood, not his mind,
But his mind's eye, the moment of his elbow striking
The muscle over the heart, remembered his dream of the night.
A dream he had often before suffered. (This came to his mind later, not
  now; later, when he thought
There is something within us knows our fates from the first, our ends from
  the very fountain; and we in our nights
May overhear its knowledge by accident, all to no purpose, it never warns
  us enough, it never
Cares to be understood, it has no benevolence but only knowledge.) He
  struggled in his dream's twilight
High on the dreadful verge of a cliff with one who hated him

And was more powerful; the man had pale-flaming gray eyes, it was the
     wind blowing from the eyes,
As a wind blew from Fera's, that forced him to the fall
Screaming, for in a dream one has no courage nor self-command but only
     effeminate emotions,
He hung screaming by a brittle laurel-bush
That starved in a crack of the rock. From that he had waked in terror. He
     had lain and thought, if Fera should come
But yet once more pleading for love, he would yield, he would do what she
     wanted . . . but soon that sea-lion shrieking
From the hollow ocean thoroughly awaked him, his mind stepped over the
     weakness, even rubbed it from memory.
What came to him now was only the earlier dream
Mixed with its rage of fear, so that he used
No temperance in the strife with his brother but struck
The next blow with his fist shortened to the mouth,
Felt lips on teeth. They swayed in the gape of the door,
Hood the aggressor but George the heavier, entwined like serpents,
The gray steel rifle-barrel between their bodies
Appeared a lance on which both struggled impaled.
For still they held it heedfully the muzzle outward
Against the sky through the door.

                         Hood felt a hand
Close on his shoulder like the jaws of a horse
And force him apart from the other, he twisted himself
Without a mind and fought it without knowing whom
He fought with, then a power struck his loins and the hand
Snapped him over. He fell, yet with limbs gathered
Came up as he struck the floor, but even in the crouch
His mind returned. He saw his father, the old man
Still stronger than both his sons, darkening above him;

And George rigid against the wall, blue-faced
Beyond the light of the door; but in the light,
Behind Cawdor, Michal with pitiful eyes.
He said, "Give me the rifle." George, who still held it,
Sucked his cut lip and gave the rifle to Cawdor;
Then Hood rose and stood trembling.

                       But Fera on the stair behind
    them:
She had heard the shot and come down half way: "What have you killed,"
    she said, "the mountain-lion? You snapping foxes
What meat will you take and be quiet a little? Better than you
Lies quiet up here." But why did her voice ring rather with joy than anger?
    "You deafen the ears of the dead.
Not one of you there is worthy to wash the dead man's body." She
    approached the foot of the stair; her face
Was white with joy. "Poor Hood, has he hurt you? I saw him pluck you off
    with two fingers a beetle from a bread-crumb.
It's lucky for them they'd taken your gun away from you." Cawdor said
    somberly, "What do you want here? The boys
Have played the fool, but you can be quiet." "And George," she answered,
    "his mouth is bleeding. What dreams have stirred you
To make you fight like weasels before the sun has got up? I am a woman by
    death left lonely
In a cage of weasels: but I'll have my will: quarrel your hearts out."
Then Cawdor turned to Hood and gave him the rifle,
And said to George: "I'm going to the hill with Hood
And mark a place for the grave. Get down some redwood
From the shop loft, the twelve-inch planks, when I come down
I'll scribe them for you. And sticks of two-by-four
To nail to at the chest corners." Fera cried "What a burial.
A weasel coffin-maker and another weasel

To dig the grave, a man buried by weasels."
Cawdor said heavily, "Come Hood." And Fera, "The gun too?
Be careful after the grave's dug, I wouldn't trust him."
He turned in the door: "By God I am very patient with you
For your trouble's sake, but the rope frays."

They had gone and Fera said "What would he do,
Beat me perhaps? He meant to threaten me, Michal?
The man is a little crazy do you think, Michal?"
She walked in the room undoing the dark braids of her hair.
"Why should he blame me for what I say? Blame God,
If there were any.
Your father is old enough to know that nobody
Since the world's birth ever said or did anything
Except from bitter need, except from bitter need. How old are you
    Michal?"
"Fifteen," she said. "Dear, please ..." "Oh, you'll soon come to it.
I am better than you all, that is my sorrow.
What you think is not true." She returned up-stairs
To the still room where one window was blinded
But the other one ached with rose-white light from clouds,
And nothing breathed on the bed.

                            But Michal hasted
And went up the hill to look to her caged eagle.
Hood and her father, she feared, would have to move
The cage, to make room for the grave.

                            She returned and heard
A soft roaring in the kitchen of the house.
"Why have you got the stove roaring, Ilaria?"
"She want hot water," Ilaria Acanna answered,

"She put the boilers over and open the drafts,
I pile in wood." Fera came down. "Not boiling, not yet?
Put in more oak. Oh, are you there Michal?
Common water is fair enough to bathe in
At common times, but now. Let's look out-of-doors.
I want it hot, there are certain stains. Come on.
We'll be back when it's hot." In the wind out-doors
She trembled and said "The world changes so fast,
Where shall we go, to the shore?" Passing the work-shop
Beside the stable they heard a rhythmic noise
Of two harsh notes alternate on a stroke of silence.
Fera stopped dizzily still, and after a moment:
"Although it sounded like my father's breathing,
The days before he died, I'm not fooled Michal.
A weasel," she said, "gnawing wood. Don't be afraid."
She entered. George lifted his dark eyes
From the saw-cut in the wine-colored redwood planks,
And Fera: "Oh, have you planed them too? That's kind.
The shavings are very fragrant.
How long will these planks last in their dark place
Before they rot and the earth fills them, ten years?"
"These never will rot." "Oh, that's a story. Not redwood even.
There's nothing under the sun but crumbles at last,
That's known and proved. . . . Where's the other weasel?" He looked
Morosely into her face and saw that her eyes
Gazed past him toward the skin of the mountain-lion
That Hood had given her. It was nailed wide and flat
In the gable-end, to dry, the flesh side outward,
Smeared with alum and salt. "Your brother weasel,"
She said, "Hood, Hood. The one that nibbled your lip.
How it is swollen." Not George but Michal answered
That Hood was up on the hill; "they had to move

My eagle's cage." Fera looked up at the lion-skin:
"I'll take that, George, that's mine." "Hm, the raw skin?"
"No matter," she said, "get it down. It's for my father.
What else have we got to give him? I'll wrap him in it
To lie like a Roman among the pale people.
. . . On your fine planks!" "You're more of a child than Michal,"
He said compassionately. "When you said *child*,
Your face," she answered, "softened I thought.
It's not like Hood's." He climbed up by the work-bench and drew the tacks,
She stood under him to take the skin, Michal beside her. The scene in the
    dim workshop gable-end
Wakes a sunk chord in the mind . . . the scene is a descent from the cross.
    The man clambering and drawing
The tyrannous nails from the pierced paws; the sorrowful women standing
    below to receive the relic,
Heavy-hanging spoil of the lonely hunter whom hunters
Rejoice to kill: . . . that Image-maker, its drift of metaphors.
George freed the skin, Fera raised hands to take it.
Her small hard pale-brown hands astonished him, so pale and alive,
Folding the tawny rawhide into a bundle.
"Where's Cawdor," she said, "your father: on the hill with Hood?"
He had gone up to Box Canyon with Dante Vitello,
Michal answered. And Fera: "Oh, but how hard it is.
Perhaps it could be oiled? It is like a board.
I'll take it to him." But Michal remained with George,
Tired of her restlessness, and afraid of her eyes.

Fera went up carrying the skin in her arms
And took it into the house. Ilaria Acanna
Came out to meet her. "Your water's boiling." "Well, let it stand."
She laid, in the still room up-stairs, the hard gift
Over her father's body. "Oh, that looks horrible,"

She cried shuddering and twitched it off. To hide it from sight
She forced it into the wardrobe against the wall,
The one she had moved to block the broken window
In the wild time of storm. She stood and whispered to herself,
And eyed the bed; then she returned out-doors,
And up the hill to the grave, in the oak's earth-bench
Above the house. The pit was waist-deep already,
And Hood was in the pit lifting the pick-axe
Between the mounds of wet red earth and cut roots.
Acanna leaned on a shovel above the pit-mouth.
For lack of room they had dug west of the oak;
The two old graves lay east. The eagle's cage
Was moved a few feet farther west; Hood labored
Between the cage and the oak. Jesus Acanna
From under the low cloud of the oak-boughs, his opaque eyes
And Indian silence watched Fera come up the hill,
But the eagle from the cage watched Hood labor; the one
With dark indifference, the other
With dark distrust, it had watched all the grave-digging.

Fera stood among the cut roots and said,
Lifting her hand to her face: "I was worn out yesterday
With not sleeping; forgive me for foolish words.
I came up here to tell you: for I suppose
You'll go away to-night or to-morrow morning.
Well, I am taught.
I wish that when you go you'd take for a gift
One of my white ponies, they'll have to bear being parted.
Good-bye. Live freely but not recklessly. The unhappy old man
For whom you are digging the hole, lost by that.
He never could learn that we have to live like people in a web of knives, we
     mustn't reach out our hands

Or we get them gashed." Hood gazing up from the grave: "I'm sorry. Yes,
    early in the morning." He glanced at Acanna
And said, "One thing I know, I shan't find loveliness in another canyon, like
    yours and Michal's." She turned
Away, saying "That's no help," and seemed about to go down; but again
    turning: "I meant to gather
Some branches of mountain laurel. There are no flowers
This time of year. But I have no knife. It shouldn't be all like a dog's
    burial." "I'll cut some for you."
He climbed out of the grave and said to Acanna: "I'll soon be back. If you
    strike rock at this end,
Level off the floor." Fera pointed with her hand trembling: "The tree's in
    the gap behind the oak-trees.
It's farther but the leaves are much fresher. Indeed he deserves laurel, his
    mind had wings and magnificence
One dash of common cunning would have made famous. And died a cow's
    death. You and I, if we can bear
The knocks and abominations of fortune for fifty years yet, have as much to
    hope for. Don't come. I'm not
A cheerful companion. Lend me the knife."
He thought she had better not be trusted alone with it,
The mind she was in,
And went beside her, above the older graves,
He felt his knees trembling. Across the steep slope
To the far oaks. Dark aboriginal eyes,
The Indian's and the coast-range eagle's, like eyes
Of this dark earth watching our alien blood
Pass and perform its vanities, watched them to the far oaks.
But after the oaks had hidden them Acanna
Covetously examined the hunter's rifle
Left behind, leaning against the lichened fence

Of the older graves. It was very desirable. He sighed
And set it back in its place.

Fera in the lonely
Oak-shielded shadow under the polished laurel-leaves: "Before you came
I used to come here," she caught her quivering under lip with the teeth to
keep it quiet, "for solitude.
Here I was sure no one would come, not even the deer, not a bird; safer
than a locked room.
Those days I had no traitor in my own heart, and would gather my spirit
here
To endure old men.

That I have to die
Is nothing important: though it's been pitied sometimes when people are
young: but to die in hell. I've lived
Some days of it; it burns; how I'd have laughed
Last year to think of anyone taken captive by love. A girl imagines all sorts
of things
When she lives lonely but this was never ... Who knows what the dead
feel, and it is frightful to think
That after I have gone down and stilled myself in the hissing ocean: roll,
roll on the weed: this hunger
Might not be stilled, this fire nor this thirst ...
For how can anyone be sure that death is a sleep? I've never found the little
garden-flower temperance
In the forest of the acts of God ... Oh no, all's forever there, all wild and
monstrous
Outside the garden: long after the white body beats to bone on the
rock-teeth the unfed spirit
Will go screaming with pain along the flash of the foam, gnawing for its
famine a wrist of shadow,

Torture by the sea, screaming your name. I know these things. I am not one
   of the careful spirits
That trot a mile and then stand."

                              He had bared his knife-blade to cut the
   bough, enduring her voice, but Fera
Caught the raised wrist. "Let it be. We have no right. The trees are decent,
   but we! A redwood cut
To make the coffin, an oak's roots for the grave: some day the coast will
   lose patience and dip
And be clean. Ah. Is it men you love?
You are girl-hearted, that makes you ice to me? What do you love? What
   horror of emptiness
Is in you to make you love nothing? Or only the deer and the wild feet of
   the mountain and follow them
As men do women. Yet you could dip that little knife-blade in me for
   pleasure, I'd not cry out
More than a shot deer, but I will never leave you
Until you quiet me." She saw that his face was gray and strained as a spent
   runner's beaten at the goal.
"Will you kiss me, once, you are going away in a moment forever? What do
   you owe Cawdor, what price
Of kindness bought you? This morning it was: he struck you and flung you
   on the ground: you liked that?" He gathered his strength
And turned himself to be gone. She caught him and clung,
And fallen to her knees when he moved outward, "I swear by God," she
   said, "I will tell him that you have taken me
Against my will, if you go from here before I have spoken. You'll not be
   hurt, Hood, you'll be far off,
And what he can do to *me* is no matter." He said "You have gone mad.
   Stand up. I will listen." But she
Feeling at last for the first time some shadow of a power

To hold and move him would not speak nor stand up, but crouched at his
	feet to enjoy it. At length she lifted
Wide staring eyes and fever-stained face. "I am very happy. I don't know
	what has told me: some movement
Or quietness of yours." She embraced his thighs, kneeling before him, he
	felt her breasts against them, her head
Nuzzling his body, he felt with his hand the fire of her throat, "Nothing,"
	he said
"Is worse nor more vile than what we are doing." "What? With a little . . .
	sin if you call it . . . kill a great misery?
No one," she thought, "ever tastes triumph
Until the mouth is rinsed with despair." She sobbed "I have found you."
	But when he had dropped the knife at the tree's root
To free his hand, and lay by her side on the drifted fall of the crisp
	oak-leaves and curled brown laurel-leaves,
Then she who had wooed began to resist him, to lengthen pleasure. "I have
	lighted the fire, let me warm my hands at it
Before we are burned." The face of her exultation was hateful to him. He
	thought of the knife in the leaves
And caught it toward him and struck the point of the blade into the muscle
	of his thigh. He felt no pain
A moment, and then a lightning of pain, and in the lit clearance: "I am not
	your dog yet," he said easily,
"I am not your thing." He felt her body shudder and turn stone above him.
	"What have you done?" "A half inch
Into the blood," he answered, "I am better." He stood up. "You will be
	grateful
To-morrow, for now we can live and not be ashamed. What sort of life
	would have been left us?" "No life
Is left us," she said from a loose throat.
"This mountain is dry." She stood and whispered "I won't do anything
	mean or troublesome. I pitied my father's

Failures from the heart, but then quietness came." Her teeth chattered
    together, she said "I will now go down
If you will let me?" He followed, limping from the Attis-gesture,
Outside the oaks and watched her creep toward the house.
The blood gliding by his knee he rubbed a handful of earth
Against the stain in the cloth to embrown the color,
And went faintly to the work he had left.

IX

                          Michal
Came up after a time with meat for the eagle.
While she fed it they had sunk the grave though shallow
To the hard rock and ceased. "Have you seen Fera
Lately?" Hood asked, "she was here wanting some greens
Because there are no flowers, but seemed to be taken sick
With grief and went down." "No. I was into the house
But not up-stairs." "We'd better see how she is.
Bring down the axe and pick-axe," he said to Acanna,
"But leave the spades." He stepped short, to conceal
His lameness. Michal asked him "What's the long stain?"
"Sap from the oak-roots, they're full of water."

                          They looked for Fera
All over the house and found her lying on the floor
The far side of her father's bed. Hood watched in terror
While Michal touched; he thought she had killed herself.
He had held an obscure panic by force a prisoner
All day but now it was worse, it was a wish to be gone,
"There's nothing I wouldn't give to have gone yesterday.
Oh pitiful child." She moved; she was not self-slain. She rose
To Michal's tugging hands and was led to bed

In her own room, hanging back but in silence.
Toward evening she dressed herself with Concha helping
In the blue serge that was the darkest she had
And went with the others up the hill to the burial.

A man at each corner carried the oblong box,
Cawdor and his sons and Dante Vitello. But Hood was lame
And when his left foot slipped on a stone his right
Failed with the weight. The stiff unseasonable
Calla lilies that Michal had found by water
Fell down the tilted lid; she gathered them up,
And when the box was lowered into its place
Dropped them upon it. Jesus Acanna had brought
The cords to use for lowering. All was done awkwardly
By shame-faced people, and the eagle watched from the cage.
The coffin grounding like a shored boat, the daughter
Of the tired passenger sighed, she leaned in the blindness
Of sand-gray eyes behind Michal toward Hood.
Her hand touched his, he trembled and stepped aside
Beyond Concha Rosas. Then Fera pressed her knuckles to her mouth
And went down the hill; the others remained.

Because of the dug earth heaped at the oak's foot
They were all standing on the west side the grave
Or at either end, a curious group, Cawdor's gray head the tallest,
Nine, to count Concha's child,
Intent, ill at ease, like bewildered cattle nosing one fallen. Not one of them,
    now that Fera was gone,
Had any more than generic relation to the dead; they were merely man
    contemplating man's end,
Feeling some want of ceremony.

The sky had been overcast; between the
ocean and the cloud
Was an inch slit, through which the sun broke suddenly at setting, only a
fraction of his passing face,
But shone up the hill from the low sea's rim a reddening fire from a pit.
The shadows of the still people
Lay like a bundle of rods, over the shallow grave, up the red mound of
earth, and upward
The mass of the oak; beyond them another shadow,
Broad, startling and rectilinear, was laid from the eagle's cage; nine slender
human shadows and one
Of another nature.

Jesus Acanna
Saw something like a jewel gleam in the rays
On the heap of surface earth at his feet; he stooped
And picked it up; a knife-edged flake of wrought
Chalcedony, the smooth fracture was pleasant to feel.
He stood and fondled it with his fingers, not mindful
That his own people had chipped it out and used it
To scrape a hide in their dawn or meat from a shell.

Then Cawdor made a clearing noise in his throat
And said in heavy embarrassment: "We know nothing of God, but we in
our turn shall discover death.
It might be good to stand quietly a moment, before we fill in the dirt, and
so if anyone
Is used to praying" — he looked at Concha and Ilaria — "might say it in
their minds." They stood with their eyes lowered,
And Cawdor took up a shovel and said impatiently
"Let us fill in." The sun was gone under the wine-colored ocean, then the
deep west fountained

Unanticipated magnificences of soaring rose and heavy purple, atmospheres of flame-shot
Color played like a mountain surf, over the abrupt coast, up the austere hills,
On the women talking, on the men's bent forms filling the grave, on the oak, on the eagle's prison, one glory
Without significance pervaded the world.

                                    Fera had gone down
To the emptied room in the vacant house to do
What she had imagined in the afternoon. In the pain of her mind
Nothing appeared fantastic; she had thought of a way
To trick death from the hands that refused life.
From Hood's own hands. She'd not be forgotten. She drew
The mountain-lion skin from where it was crumpled away,
And clothed herself in it, the narrow shoulders
Over her shoulders, the head over her head.
She bound it with bits of string and smoothed the wrinkles.
It would fool a hunter in the twilight; only her face
Must be turned from him. She fled from the house and hid
In the oaks against the hill, not far from the door.
The rosy light had waned from the cloud, wilderness-hearted
Twilight was here, embrowning the leaves and earth.
Concha and Ilaria and Concha's child came talking
And entered the house; kitchen windows were lighted.
The others delayed. Blue smoke began to veil out
And be fragrant among the leaves. She crouched in the oak-bush,
As every evening the wild lives of the mountain
Come down and lie watching by lonely houses.

Hood, when they took the redwood box to the house,
Had left his rifle in the stable, he came with Michal,

Having fetched it. They walked mournfully together,
For this was their last evening, he'd leave at dawn
For the free north. But nothing remained to say;
And through their silence, drawing near the house-door, Michal
Heard the stiff oak-leaves move, she looked and perceived
A life among them, laying her hand on his arm
She pointed with the other hand. The head and slant shoulder
And half the side unsheathed themselves from the oak,
The hindquarters were hidden. The long beast lifted
On straightened forelegs and stood quartering away,
The head raised, turned up the canyon. Hood held his fire,
Astonished at it, wasn't it one of the dogs?
Both dogs were splatched with white, the brindle was dead,
No white on this, and light enough yet remained
To show the autumn color and the hair's texture;
Here were the paws that killed the brindle and the calf;
In vain hunted; chance-met.

                              But Fera supposed
His weapon was in his room in the house, he'd slip
Into the house to fetch it and she'd have fled
When he returned; hunting alone up the twilight hill
Might he not even now discover a woman
In the beast's hide, pity that woman? Already in her mind
She wavered away from the necessity of death;
If Michal had not been present she might have stood up
And shown ...
The stroke that ended her thought was aimed too low.
In the hunter's mind a more deep-chested victim
Stood in the dusk to be slain; what should have transpierced
The heart broke the left arm-bone against the shoulder
And spared the life.

He knew, as she fell. He seemed to himself
To have known even while he fired. That worm of terror
Strangled his mind so that he kept no memory
Of Cawdor and the others taking her into the house.
He was left in the dark with a bruised face, someone had struck him,
Oh very justly.

        He rose and stood reeling
Like a boy whom bad companions have filled with sweetened
Liquor, to make him their evening sport. The yellow
Windows of the house wavered, he fought the sickness
And went in-doors. Someone stared at him passing
Up-stairs; he heard from the door her moaning breath.
Cawdor examined the wound, George held the lamp
Over the naked arm and breast, Concha
Was dipping a sponge: it was the dark clot
Stringing from the red sponge that overcame him.
Cawdor's face, like a rock to break on, turned
To say hoarsely "You bastard get out of this place,"
And turned back to the wound; terrible face in the lamp-shadow
Black as the blood-clot.

        He stood outside the door
Half fainting against the wall. Wanted him to go?
Good God, did he want to stay? Michal came whispering:
"You can't do anything here; and I am afraid of father.
Please go. Please go. To-morrow I'll meet you somewhere.
Oh what can you do here?"

        While he limped on the stairway
Fera's moan sharpened and became a voice.
He found himself out of doors; the blanket-roll

He had rolled ready to start to-morrow at dawn
Was in his hand. He looked for his rifle
On the ground between the shot and the mark, and stumbled over it
After he had failed to find it.

                              The sky had cleared
With its local suddenness, full of nail-sharp stars
And a frosty dust of shining; he went up the dim star-path
By the lone redwood into wide night. His usurped mind
Unheeding itself ran in its track of habit,
So that he went from the oaks as before, upward
The gravelly slope of spoiled granite to the Rock.
He soon gathered dead twigs and kindled a fire
On the dome of the Rock, wishing Michal might see it
And bring him word in the morning. The night had turned
Frostily cold with its cleared sky.

X

                              Fera's moan became vocal, she flapped
    the hurt arm, the hand
Lying still and hooked, the marbled flesh working between the shoulder and
    the elbow. Michal remembered
Her eagle in the fresh of its wound waving the broken flag: another one of
    Hood's rifle-shots. Cawdor
Gripped the shoulder quiet with his hand, and clinked in the basin
From his right hand the small red splinter of bone he had fished from the
    wound. Fera's eye-lids, that hung
Half open on arcs of opaque white, widened suddenly, and fluttered shut,
    and stood wide open,
The liquid pools of night in the rayed gray rings dilating and contracting
    like little hearts,

Each sparked with a minute image of the lamp above them. She tongued
    her lips and the dry teeth
And moved her head. "This must be life, this hot pain.
Oh, the bad hunter! I fail in everything, like my father." Cawdor looked
    sideways to place in his mind
The strips of a torn sheet laid ready, and smooth straight sticks of
    pinewood kindling fetched from the kitchen;
He pressed a ragful of pungent liquid to the wound's mouths. Fera lay
    quiet, but Michal trembled
To see her lips retract from the teeth, and hear the teeth creaking together.
    Then Fera whispered:
"Horse-liniment. Of course you would. It burns." But Cawdor answered:
    "Hold the lamp, Michal. George, hold her quiet."
He gripped with his hands the shoulder and the upper arm. Then Fera:
    "Oh God! Oh no! No . . . no . . .
I'll tell you anything . . ." The ends of the fracture were heard touching;
    but she writhing her body whipped over
In George's and Concha's hands; Cawdor held without failure but her
    movement baffled him, the ends of bone
Were heard slipping. He shifted his grasp and said to the others
    "Loose-handed fools. Hold firm." But Fera
Straining her chalky and diminished face, the earth-stain still unwashed on
    her cheek, clear of the pillow:
"Oh please. Dearest! I'll not hide anything. I'm not to blame." His mind
    was fixed on his work, yet even
While his muscles were setting themselves again her words entered his
    understanding. His grip relaxed;
He looked at her face, the eyes stared bright terror but the mouth
Attempting a fawning smile: "I'll tell you everything, dearest, but don't
    torture me. I thought I had tasted
Torture before. How little I knew." Her teeth chattered together and she
    said "He forced me. Hood forced me.

He threw me down under the laurel tree

And stopped my mouth with his hand. So that I couldn't be your wife any
     more, darling. But I

Never loved him. I only tried to be killed. Oh, Oh, his face

Is like a nigger's. George save me! Michal!" He sighed, "You lie. Be quiet."
     "Darling," she pleaded, "I feel

Pain so much more than you understand. I can't *bear* pain? *Bear* pain? I am
     not made like the people

You're used to." He wavered his head as if a fringe hung over the eyes, and
     bent to the wound, but she:

"I only tried to be killed." He muttered, "I don't kill women." And Fera:
     "You'd be so kind. Oh

But the darkness was sweet." And feeling his hands, "Oh Concha," she cried,
     "I've told him everything and yet he'll hurt me.

Dear Concha pray to him for me, he used to love you. And I have never
     been mean to you because of that,

Concha." Then Cawdor suddenly turned to the Indian woman: "Is it true,
     what she says?" But Michal: "No, no,

Her mind," she stammered, "gone wrong. Ah you coward, Fera." "And
     what part," Cawdor said, "had *you* in the play?

By God, you all . . . When?" he said hoarsely to Fera. "Before he died,"
     she answered, her breath hissing

In little pulses. He gathered his strength and said, "Out, Michal." And
     when she had gone: "Was it in this room,

Or his?" She answered "Under the laurel tree

He threw me down: I was not to blame not to blame more

Than a murdered man is." George said, "She is lying. Her madness is fear
     of pain. She is sick." "Though I've been played

For the fool of the world I know more than that. They make lies for
     pleasure but not

Get killed for pleasure. You sick whore does it hurt? Here is a different bed
     from the brown leaves

And the panting dog." Her face looking no bigger than a broken doll's on
    the pillow answered: "I knew
You'd kill me, I didn't think torture, why must I suffer alone? If I am to
    blame a little is he
Not rich with blame? He has got away I suppose. I swear by God I never
    consented to him.
It was all violence, violence . . . Have pity: no pity? Sweetheart: I never
    called you before: Sweetheart,
Have mercy on me." He stood as if to go out of the room; he was heard
    breathing, and slowly his hands
Crept to his throat. He turned and came back and said: "It is not to punish
    you.
I must set the bone. You can't stay here and be kept, you'll need both arms
    to live with. I will use all
Gentleness: but you lie still, it will be done in a moment. I'll send for the
    doctor, but when he comes
It will be too swollen perhaps for mending. Indeed I have other business.
    People take pain like bread
When their life needs it. After it is set the ache
Will quiet, you'll sleep."

               Michal outside the door
Heard her screaming and went in; but then she had fainted
And Cawdor worked more easily. He bound the arm
And set the splints, and bound it again and passed
A leather belt about her body to fasten it
Against her side. He looked then at her face,
The dark lashes lying still, the parted white lips
Pencilled at the borders with fine blue lines,
Meek as a child's after the turn of fever
Folds its weakness in sleep. Concha prepared
To bathe the face but Cawdor: "Let her alone.

Let her have the poor mercy while it lasts.
Come George, I'll help you saddle. He'll come sooner
For you than another." He spoke quietly, but leaving
The room he walked against the wall by the door
And spread his hands both ways to feel the door-frame
Before he went out. He ran and found Hood's room
Empty, before he went with George to the stable.
"I think it has cleared," he said in the dark, "aren't the stars out?"
He saw the red star of Hood's fire on the Rock.
"Take your pick of the horses: I must go back
And warn the women: she will wake in delirium
And strain the bandages loose: I didn't speak of that,
That I remember? That I remember? Good-night,"
He said eagerly. He turned, then George went down
Alone, but Cawdor up the hill to the Rock
As one tortured with thirst toils up the sandhills
To the known rock spring. When he issued from the oaks
On the ridge of the steep neck of air-crumbled granite
The canyon redwoods were a stain of black shade
In the pit below, the gleam-powdered sky soared out of conception,
The starlight vastness and steepness were narrow to him
And no wind breathed. He was like one threading a tunnel
With anguished hunger of the air and light, all the arrows
Of desire strung to their heads on the pale spark
Of day at the end: so all the needs of his life
Hung on the speck of humanity by the red embers
On the rock dome. It heard him, and twitched and stood up.
He made in his mouth and waterless throat the words
"Come down," but no sound issued; he came nearer and said
"What did you steal? Come down." Hood screamed "Keep off,"
The same panic of brainless fear returning,
With a horror of his own cowardice, how could he bear

To run, but how could he bear to stand? He imagined
Fera had died. His very innocence of evil
Made the avenger unbearable, one of those hands
Could break his body, he snatched his rifle and stood
On the other side of the embers and sobbed "Stop there.
By God if you come nearer I'll fire. Keep off your hands.
I'm not hiding, I'll answer the law, not you.
I can't ... Keep off. Oh! Oh!" For Cawdor blindly
Came through the fire; Hood with the rifle at his waist
Unshouldered, flung up the muzzle and shot in the air
Over his father's head: at the flash Cawdor
Felt a bright fear, not of death but of dying mocked,
Overreached and outraged as a fool dies,
Explode on his mind like light breaking on blindness
So that the body leaped and struck while the mind
Astonished with hatred stood still. There had been no choice,
Nor from the first any form of intention.
He saw Hood's body roll away from the fire
Like a thing with no hands; he felt in the knuckles
Of both his hands that both had been bruised on bone,
He saw Hood's body twist on the fall of the dome
Over the precipice and hands like weak flames
Scratch at the starlight rock: then one sharp moment's
Knife-edge a shadow of choice appeared: for all
Passed in a moment: he might have dived prone
And clutched after the hands with his hands: more likely
Gone down the granite slide into the gulf
With the other: but the choice had no consciousness
And in a moment no choice. There was no cry.
The curving hands scrabbled on the round of the rock
And slipped silently down, into so dreadful a depth
That no sound of the fall: nothing returned:

Mere silence, mere vanishing. Cawdor could hear the water
Whispering below, and saw the redwood forest
A long irregular stain in the starlit gorge-bottom,
But over the round of the rock it was not possible
To see the foot of the Rock. A little steady breeze
Blew curving up over the granite verge
From the night's drift in the chasm.

                                  He turned and walked
Stealthily away, yet firmly, feeling no horror
But only a hollow unbearable sadness. But Hood had earned
The death he had got: not that he'd used violence
In adultery, that was incredible, the woman had lied:
But the crime however invited had no forgiveness,
Not even in death. Women are not responsible;
They are like children, little children grown lewd;
Men must acknowledge justice or their world falls
Piecemeal to dirty decay. Justice had been
Performed. He felt the sapping unbearable sadness
A little lightened, so muttered "Justice. Justice.
Justice": but the third time of saying it the word
Was pithed of meaning and became useless. He had come
Half way to the house and there remembered the things
Left on the Rock. He returned. Only his knowledge
Of what lay at the foot prevented him then
From casting himself down. Nor could he cast the rifle,
The silly rifle that Hood had loved,
For fear of its falling on the poor damned face.
He stood between the blanket-roll and the rifle
Beside a few burnt sticks and scattered red coals
On the bulge of the Rock. "Well, I have killed my son." Whether he
   continued living or quit living,

It would be a pity Michal should know. Quit, because it hurts? He thought
 he was not the make to do that.
His recent real temptation appeared a contemptible flourish of play-acting.
 "Well, I have killed my son.
He needed killing." The woman's story of the rape was now believed; it had
 become needful
To believe her story. "I will take these and bury them with him." When
 he'd again gone under the oaks
He heard one coming up the dark path. A moment of stupid horror he
 dreamed it was Hood coming
To claim the rifle. But Michal no doubt, Michal. He laid the things he
 carried into the darkness
Of the oaks by the path, and hardened his mind to meet Michal. Meet . . .
 whom? It brushed against the stiff leaves
Like something broken that crept and rested. With no terror but pity going
 down in the dark to meet it
He heard it snort and stamp hooves, a stray horse plunged from the path.
 "God damn you," he said and a voice answered
From down the path: "Hood, is that you?" She had been coming up to the
 Rock, and the strayed horse
Drifting ahead. She said "One of the horses: I guess it's gone. Oh Hood,
 Fera has said
Frightful . . . where are you?" She cried sharply "Who is that?" "The
 things were true," he answered, "all true." He heard her
Stop, and he seemed to feel her trembling. "Where's Hood," she said in a
 moment, trembling, "what have you done?"
"Nothing." He said in his heart "Well: I have killed him?" He possessed
 his voice in quietness and said, "I came
To ask him the truth, and he has confessed. It was all true." She sobbed and
 said "What have you done with him?"
"Nothing," he answered indifferently. "He ran when I came. A guilty
 conscience, Michal. He has done a thing

Never forgiven." He had reached her now; in the starless night of the oaks
    he saw the gleam of her face
Retreating, she moving slowly backward before him. He said "Like the scut
    of a deer." "What?" "When I came
He streaked up the hill into the starlight." "How did you make him
    confess?" "Oh Michal, a guilty conscience.
That does it. You know he wasn't a coward by nature, not a damned
    coward. I saw him run like a rabbit-scut
Between the hill and the stars. Come up to the Rock and call him." "I
    thought I heard a gun-shot," she faltered.
"I was in the house with ... Then I went out." "A gun-shot? No. Come
    up and call him; perhaps he'll come down.
I promise you not to touch him. Come up and call to him, Michal. If you
    call loudly." They climbed to the Rock.
She saw it was vacant, the ends of a few sticks glowed on the stone, pale in
    their ash-crusts. "Hood. Hood,"
She called, and he said "Call louder. He has gone far." She answered,
"No, I won't call. I wish never to see him."

Who lay under the sheer below them, his broken shoulders
Bulging his coat in lumps the starlight regarded.
The bone vessel where all the nerves had met
For counsel while they were living, and the acts and thoughts
Been formed, was burst open, its gray and white jellies
Flung on the stones like liquor from a broken flask,
Mixed with some streamers of blood.

                        The vivid consciousness
That waking or dreaming, its twenty years, infallibly
Felt itself unitary, was now divided:
Like the dispersion of a broken hive: the brain-cells
And rent fragments of cells finding

After their communal festival of life particular deaths.
In their deaths they dreamed a moment, the unspent chemistry
Of life resolving its powers; some in the cold star-gleam,
Some in the cooling darkness in the crushed skull.
But shine and shade were indifferent to them, their dreams
Determined by temperatures, access of air,
Wetness or drying, as the work of the autolytic
Enzymes of the last hunger hasted or failed.

Yet there appeared, whether by chance or whether
From causes in their common origin and recent union,
A rhythmic sympathy among the particular dreams.
A wave of many minute delicious enjoyments
Would travel across the spilth; then a sad fading
Would follow it, a wave of infinitesimal pains,
And a pause, and the pleasures again. These waves both lessened
In power and slowed in time; the fragments of consciousness
Beginning to lapse out of the frailties of life
And enter another condition. The strained peace
Of the rock has no repose, it is wild and shuddering, it travels
In the teeth of locked strains unimaginable paths;
It is full of desire; but the brittle iniquities of pleasure
And pain are not there. These fragments now approached
What they would enter in a moment, the peace of the earth.

XI

When Cawdor had left the house, Concha
At once busied herself to recall to life
The milk-faced bandaged one on the bed, then Michal
Had intervened: "He said to let her alone.

He said to let her have peace." But Concha: "She stay
Fainting too long, she stop breathing, she die."
"I think that would be better." But the Indian woman
Trembling went on, then Michal held up the basin
While the other bathed the pale face, gray jewels of water
Ran down in the hair. There was no response; then Michal
Herself began to be frightened. She knew that her father
Had kept a bottle of whiskey somewhere in the room;
She set the basin on the blue chair and went
Searching on shelves.

             Concha flung back the sheet
And blanket to bathe the breast. How the hard strap
That held the arm furrowed the flesh of the waist.
The fine-grained clear white skin was beautiful to her;
The coins of rose about the small nipples
Astonished her; hers were as black as the earth; she dipped her head
As if to a flower's fragrance and felt the quiet breasts
She had cooled with water move on her face: Fera
Moaned and then said faintly, "You are blind, father.
Both horses were white." She moved her head on her hair,
Her voice changed: "Do you love me Concha? You never were jealous,
I've wondered at you. Where's Cawdor?" Michal returned
And said sullenly: "I've found it, and there's no glass.
She'd better suck from the bottle." But Fera lay
Regardless of her, and dropping her right forearm
Across her breast explored the splints, and folds
On heavy folds of linen that shelled the shoulder
And the left arm; then with pain-dwindled lips,
"Well," she said, "give it to me. It's time for me now
To taste of my father's friend. Help me sit up, Concha."

She sipped and choked; it spilled on her chin, the burning fragrance
Filled all the room. Michal took back the bottle
And said, "Why did you lie? You lied. You lied.
Horrible things." Fera dull-eyed, with racked mouth,
The coughing had hurt her arm: "Not lies. Every word
Faithful as death. I lay between your father and your brother
Like a snake between the rock and the stone.
Give me the bottle, give it back to me Michal.
I have to hush this torment. Your father'll come back
And beat me with his fists like a wild beast,
He's like a beast in his rages." "Every word's lies.
But if it were true, why did you tell him?" "Because he tortured me."
Michal crossed the room to the corner and saw
In the east window high up in the dark pane
A little drop of red light. She pressed her face
Against the glass and cupped it with her two hands
To shut the lamplight away. Hood's waning fire,
Like a red star under the diamond stars.
"I'll go and ask him," she said turning. "He'll tell me
Every last word was a lie." "What did you see, Oh what did you see,
    Michal?"
Fera said shaking. "A fire on the Rock? It's only some vaquero from inland,
    Hood wouldn't build one,
Not to-night, not to-night." She answered "I saw nothing. I saw the sky
    and some stars. Concha,
Take care of her, will you. Get her to sleep." As Michal crossed to the door
    a dim noise like a gun-shot
Seemed to be heard, she said "Oh, what was that? Concha: you heard it?
    Listen." But Fera laughing
With an ashen face: "Lived here all her life long
And never has heard a wave slapping the sand at the creek-mouth."

When she'd
gone out, Fera said: "Concha,
My father's blindness was crystal to hers. How could she stay in the room
and let Cawdor go out
To find his prey in the night? Did she know *nothing*? Give me the bottle,
dear Concha. Dear Concha." She drank,
And said: "I'd no other way to keep him, he was going away. Poor hunter. I
set a beast on his track
That he's no match for. The gun's no good boy hunter, you might as well
toss acorns. Two bulls, Concha,
Fighting by starlight, the young one is gored. Ah: Concha:
One of my loves was locked in the hill by the oak, now the other's safe too.
Listen: my birthday's to-night.
Has to be kept," she stammered, "I've told no one but you. And here's my
father's friend to sit up with.
Go down and get two glasses, Concha, and a pitcher of water." She called
her back from the door. "Concha!
The water in the house is all stale.
Go out to the spring among the calla lilies
And fill the pitcher. Don't hurry, Concha, I'm resting now."

As Concha
went out Fera stealthily
Undid the belt that locked her arm to her side; when the Indian was gone
She passed one-handed the strap through the buckle, the tongue thrown
back
To let it slide free. She knotted the end of the strap
To the top of the carved bed-post, kneeling on the pillow,
Tightening the knot between her hand and her teeth.
She dropped the collar about her neck, and shuffled her knees
Until they slipped from the mattress. The right arm
Sustained the left one, to ease its pain in the fall.

She could have breathed by standing, but while her mind
Remained she would not, and then was unable.

                                        Concha, down-stairs,
Had much to tell Ilaria. Acanna was there too
In the kitchen, and Concha's boy Romano, and Dante
Vitello, the Swiss. All questioned her. She'd forgotten
The water and found the glasses, when little Romano
In his child voice: "Escucha: un raton. — Listen mother,
A mouse in the ceiling." But no one looked up nor down
Until he fetched the gray cat from under the stove
And wanted to take her up-stairs. Concha forbade him,
But listened, and heard the noise in the ceiling change
From a soft stroking to a dull shudder in the wood.
The shudder was Fera's agony; the backs of her feet
Stroking the floor; she hung as if kneeling. But Concha said:
"A trade-rat maybe: no mouse. But I must go up."
The noise had ceased.

                    She screamed in the hallway above
And flung the glasses on the floor. The people below
Stared at each other. Her cries were timed, rhythmic,
Mechanical, like a ground-squirrel's when he sits up
Beside his burrow and watches a dog hunting
On the other side of the fence. At length Acanna
Ran to the stair, the others followed, and little Romano
With gray puss in his arms. They looked past Concha
Who stood in the door not daring to enter.

                                        The girl
Appeared kneeling, only her knees were lifted
A little above the floor; her head devoutly
Drooped over. She was naked but the bandaged arm;

The coins about the small nipples were now
As black as Concha's; the lips dark, the fine skin
Mottled with lead-color. Ilaria pushed in and lifted
The body, Jesus Acanna then found his knife
And cut the strap. They stretched the slender body
On the bed and began to talk, but Dante Vitello
Remembered at length to pump the ribs with his hands.
They saw the lids of the eyes after a time
Flutter and close; the Swiss paused from his labor,
The breathing went on by itself.

                      Cawdor returned
From the Rock with Michal, but would not enter the house.
He seemed going toward the sea when she left him. He went
As far as the work-shop and fetched tools for digging,
A lantern, matches to light it. He chose the tools
With a clear mind; this work had to be done
Because of the coyotes. It proved more dreadful
Than he'd imagined; but when it was done the dreadfulness itself
Had purged his mind of emotion. He took no pains
To conceal the grave, for at this time discovery
Meant nothing to him, he desired nor feared nothing,
Not even to put back time and undo an act.
However, no person ever went up there.
He rolled stones on the grave against the coyotes,
And gathered the tools, but when he had carried them
Half way home, he threw them with the lantern too
Into the creek under the starless redwoods.
His mind ceased there, as if the tools had been strings
Between the world and his mind; these cut, it closed.

In the bright of dawn, before sunrise began,
The lank steers wheeled their line when he waved his arms.

He cursed them with obscene words . . . but why? . . . and there stood
Thirty in a row, all in a row like soldiers
Staring at him with strained-up heads. He was in the pasture
On the highest dome of the hill.
Wild fragrant wind blew from the burning east,
A handful of cloud high up in the air caught fire and vanished.
A point of more excessive light appeared
On the ridge by the lone oak and enlarged.
Without doubt, the sun. But if it were the horn of a flaming beast:
We'd have a horned beast to see by.
"What have I lost by doing through a blind accident
What I ought to have done in cold blood? Was Hood anything to me?
I have lost nothing." He'd have counted Fera
Lost, if he'd thought of Fera; she did not enter his mind.
"If I'd lost much: it's likely I'd not lie down
But gather again and go on." His flesh and bones were soaked
With aching weariness: but that was nothing either.
His eyes dazzled in the rivers of light
And the sea lay at his feet flat and lifeless
Far down but flecked with the steps of the wind. He went down to the
    house
And heard that Fera had hanged herself and been saved,
But that was nothing either. No, something. Where were you?
He said to Concha. "She send me down. She send me.
She send me down for water. When I come back: Oh!"
"I'll not see her this morning," he answered.
"Bring my clothes to the little room on the north
And change the bed there. Hood's gone for good." He had done justly,
And could sleep very well there.

                    Two days passed
Before he remembered the blanket-roll and the rifle

Dropped in the oaks when Michal came. He went and sought
But never found them. But that was nothing either.

XII

Her voice was still roughened with an off whisper
In the bruised throat, and the white of one of her eyes
Grained with a drop of red, a little blood-vessel
Had broken there when the strap drew. When she was alone
She lay pointed on the bed, stiffened to the attitude
Of formal death, feeling the ache in her arm
But hardly conscious of it, the hours and scenes
And the form as a whole of all her life incessantly
Moving behind the blank wide open eyes.
She lay and contemplated it with little emotion
And hardly a thought. She thought of herself as dead,
Although she knew perfectly that she was living,
And had said to Concha: "You needn't watch me, you and Ilaria.
I'll never try death again, now I understand
That to fail is the very soul of my soul.
Failure is not so sweet that one who feels it
Beforehand will go running to meet it again.
Though death is sweet. That will come in its time
When I'm as old as my father, I fear not sooner;
Never for the asking."

          She said to Concha another day:
"I wish you could get Michal to come and see me;
Or George even. Not one soul has come in,
Not since the doctor was here, and death is so lonesome.
I could get up, but when I begin to walk

Cawdor will send me away. You must never tell them
That I can get up." This was at noon; Concha
Painfully made a slow thought in her mind
All afternoon, and said to Cawdor in the evening,
Stammering, because her words were planned beforehand:
"She say that she is well enough to get up."
"Who says?" "Oh . . . she . . ." "You mean," he said frowning,
"My wife? Let her get up then." She turned sadly, and then said:
"When she get up you going to send her away?"
"What is that to you?" Then Concha recklessly: "You keep her
After she loving with Hood?" She curved her body
In fear of his hand; but he took hold of her wrist
And drove her up the stairway to Fera's room.

Who lay in the bed straightened to the shape of death
And looked at them with still eyes; the scarlet drop
In the white of the left one spoiled her eyes' peace. Cawdor
Put off the questions that had burned him to ask,
And stood still and then said: "You are well enough to get up,
Concha says, but you think I'd send you away."
She smiled at Concha. "I wondered whether you'd do it.
And then I thought you wouldn't, but it's no matter.
No: you won't send me," she said to Cawdor, "for I
Suffered my destruction in simple innocence.
Oh, certainly you'll not drink again from a mouthed cup,
But the cup's not blamed. You are much too just to punish the cup. There
  are more reasons." His face a moment
Was like her father's a scar; it formed itself to be dark metal again and he
  said: "No doubt
You were loving with him and so he went mad." She thought, and
  answered: "No. You did justice. I know what you did.
You'd better send out your brown tattle-tales

Before we say any more, she'd hear and go tell, wouldn't you Concha?
    Besides that her sour odor
Poisons the room. I've noticed lately, the living smell much worse than the
    dead. Oh never mourn them;
No one was ever sorry to have died." He shook his head, like the bull that
    has charged a man and found
Only the vacant flapping of a red blanket, and he said: "Be straight will you
    for once, I won't hurt you.
You hide in a smoke of words like lies. Perhaps" — his face hollowed with
    terror — "it was all a lie?
No, that can't be. You white poison you were in the boat with him and lied
To save your skin?" He turned on Concha: "Did you see her make love to
    him?" But the Indian woman feared to go on;
She shook her head, and looked aside at Fera, and shook her head. Cawdor
    made himself patient
And said, "Perhaps a kiss: or you saw her stroking his head: he had fine
    hair . . ." Fera lay faintly
Smiling and watched him; he looked, stooping his face to Concha's, like a
    tall old Jew bargaining, and said:
"Or you saw them . . . by God, you told me they kissed, you said that."
    She nodded her head, panting and shrinking backward,
Wiping her dark hands on her apron incessantly; and Fera: "She'll tell more
    lies if you make more faces,
And when that fails you could pinch her arm. How can you expect truth
    from such people, they're all afraid of you?"
He looked at Concha and said feebly: "If I could know.
I am stupid and things are hidden. What I have done. Was right, but the
    blood rushes me behind my eyes
And God sends chance. It all happened in the blindness of chance." Fera
    said quietly "Don't talk before her."
He looked at her eyes and said, "You have the secret, if I could trust you.
    That red drop comes from hanging

And will clear up. You seem quieter in mind

Than ever before. Do you know where I sleep now? Hood's room." "It was
    Concha's first." He groaned in his throat, feeling

That every thought in her mind was impure, how could he fish the truth
    from a dirty fountain? He said:

"And yet you'll tell me. It will make no difference to you but only to me. I
    will do nothing to punish you,

Whatever you say, nothing in your favor either." "I've told you already," she
    answered. "But whether you tempted him,

Invited him, you egged him on, you thought he was safe. A word: or only a
    damned smile: women

Can move hell with their eyes." She closed her eyes, and said keeping them
    closed: "What I said that night

Each word was true. You're right though, I've still a secret. Shoo tattle-tales
    out,

And then I'll tell you my secret." He said, "Concha: get out." She sighed
    and went out gladly, and Fera:

"Open the door; I won't have her at the door." However the hallway was
    empty, and Fera said:

"I was friendly with him, he was your son and Michal's brother. I never in
    act nor look nor thought

Stepped over that. Was he vicious when he was little? I never knew it. A
    beast lived in his blood,

But no one warned me and now he is gone." "That's the word: gone. You are
    safe to blacken him, he can't answer."

"If I should lie and whiten him," she said,

"And say he was innocent, some stitch of his nerves in him destroyed me
    but his heart was innocent: and you believed it:

How could you sleep? And after a night or two

That room you have taken might seem too little for you. You are very
    strong, you'd hold yourself quiet three nights,

Or four nights, and then wander on the hill scaring the cattle." He said
    gravely, " Does every one know?
Who told you this?" "No one," she answered. "And after a week of nights
    they'd find you with those big-boned
Fingers clenched in your throat quiet on the hill." "On the Rock," he said.
    "Oh, on the Rock. But since . . .
Or under the Rock. But since he was guilty you can sleep sound." The flesh
    of his face, that had sagged lately,
Was now become firm for danger, and he asked: "How do you know these
    things if no one watched me?" She answered
"I know you so well. I used to be near you, if you remember, before I was
    spoiled. And now, lying
Like this" — she lay pointed in the bed, her arms on her breast — "I mean
    alone and cut off from life,
I've had leisure and power to think of you plainly, so all your acts that night
    stand in my mind
Fixed and forever like pieces of stone. That's the way with us dead, we see
    things whole and never
Wonder at things." He said, "You lie here and dream and imagine. There's
    nothing in it." "So you won't send me,"
She answered, "to stay with strangers. I know too much and might tell:
    that's nothing to you: but as time darkens
You'll find me the only comforter you have. And I can teach you the way to
    blessedness: I've tasted life
And tasted death; the one's warm water, yellow with mud and wrigglers,
    sucked from a puddle in the road,
Or hot water that scalds you to screaming;
The other is bright and cool and quiet, drawn from the deep. You knocked
    the scummed cup from the boy's hand
And gave him the other: is that a thing to be sorry for? I know; I have both
    in my hands; life's on the broken

And splinted left so I never lift it. You did kindly, not terribly. If you were wise, you'd do
    As much for yourself. If you were loving you'd do
As much for me." He stood and listened, and said "Is that all?"
She nodded. "Then it's not much.
I see there are two of us here twisting in hell,
Smile as you like." "Why yes," she answered, "by the left arm.
That's true. But I taste both." He was leaving the room
And she cried after him: "Oh my dear, dear, be merciful.
Life is so tough to cut, I never would have dreamed.
I fail. But nothing stops *you*."

                    He went out-doors
And felt a seeming-irresistible desire
To go to the foot of the Rock and lie with those stones
On the soft earth, his mouth whispering against it.
But now, he must never give in to any desire;
Strain the iron forever. Never do anything strange:
For even now their eyes followed him strangely.
No matter; they'd keep in subjection; they might have watched it
And not dare speak: but a pity if little Michal . . .
The stars in the sparse boughs, the skies are never
Darkened any more, a naughty glitter.
How does one commonly spend a winter evening:
Not letting the stars glitter through the split boughs.
He entered the house and sat down. Strain the iron forever:
He had strength for that.

                    Fera had little strength,
And the long hollow night coming looked unendurable.
Her right arm was flung free of the cover and lay
Bent on her eyes; after a while her teeth

Found the wrist: ugh, what was this? She raised it and saw
The yellow and brown scabs of the laceration
Where she had gnawed it before.

                                    In the morning, when Concha
Came in to serve her, she said "Did you believe in heaven and hell
When you were little? (To-day I'll get up,
I've had enough of this bed, you'll help me dress.)
Because you know the dead rarely come back;
But I died and came back, and I can tell you
More than the priests know. Dying's not bad: Oh, bad enough,
But you can stand it, you have to. But afterwards . . . Ah, there's . . ."
She moaned, her tight small fist crept up to her cheek
And trembled there. She was playing a comedy, she played it so well
Her own flesh suffered and chilled. "Death is no sleep, Concha, death is
    eternal torment and terror
For all that die. Neither is there any heaven for anyone. I saw my father
    there crying blood
From the hollows of his blind eyes and tearing his beard with his hands. He
    said 'Oh my God have you come, Fera?
Who ever dreamed that death could be worse than life?' I said 'It is so,' and
    all the crowd of the dead
Began moaning 'It is so.' But then you managed to make me breathe with
    your hands and I could come back,
They said to me then, 'Never tell any living person what death is like, for if
    they imagined
What it's like, for they all must come, how could they live?
Who'd not go mad with fear to feel it approaching?'
Oh Concha, hug life with tooth and nail, for what
Comes after is the most horrible. And no end, no end.
(Come here and help me. We'll have to slit down the sleeve
And pin it over the shoulder.) I didn't tell you

To scare you, Concha. Don't think about it. Ah no,
Or we'd sit screaming.
I wasn't going to tell you but then I thought
That you can bear it as well as I can, after the trick
You played me last night, my rival!
Live. Live forever if you could. Oh it was frightful."

XIII

Though she was up, and began to live and go out,
She avoided Cawdor's presence, still fearing to be sent away
If seen too often. She kept her room at mealtimes,
And he was almost never about the house
The other hours of the day.

                      The first time she went out,
She only walked under the storm-broken cypresses
About the door and went in; but the next morning
She climbed the steep to the great oak by the graves.
Still weak and bloodless, dizzy with climbing, she lay
Face down on the dug earth, her mouth breathing against it
And whispering over her father's body below.
The grave retained its freshness, no rain had fallen
On the red earth. She heard after a time
A rustling and scraping noise and raised her head.
It was Michal's eagle hungrily astir in the cage;
She used to feed it about this time. Fera
Saw beak and eyes in the shadow, and the dark square
Of the box cage against the bright blue shining
Flat ocean and the arch of sky. She stood up, and walked
About the oak's bole; she seemed to be counting the graves,

But there were only three; the two ancient ones
Enclosed with pickets and the raw new one unfenced.

Michal came up with flesh and water for the eagle,
But Fera stood on the other side of the oak
Until she had come; then, coming forward from it:
"Why Michal, how strange to think that all these days,
No matter what's happened, you still go on steadily as sunrise.
My father dies of old age, I fish for death
And catch failure again, and Hood . . . but you and the sunrises
Go on as if our tears and our deaths were nothing.
He isn't glad to see you: I'd have been glad to see you
My lonely days in bed but you never came."
Michal had looked over her shoulder, her face
Growing white as it turned. She turned back to the cage.
"I didn't know you were here," she said, and poured out
The dirty water from the drinking-basin
Without turning again. "I see that you hate me,"
Fera said; "we'll not speak of that. I see that your father
Has thought *my* father's grave not worthy of a mark.
If the cold charity of the county had buried him
There'd be a stake with his name.
Yet he was here like a man among cattle,
The only mind in this ditch." Michal said nothing,
But rubbed the white slime from the basin and rinsed it,
And Fera said, "The oak's dying, they chopped its roots.
Or was it the storm that burned these baby leaves?
We ought to be friends, Michal." Michal set in
The filled basin and shut the door of the cage.
She opened her lips to speak, and then kept silence,
And Fera said "You'll listen, my dear, if you won't speak. Do you think I'll
    swallow

These white and hating looks as if they were earned? What have I done?
  Tried to die? Yes; I tried twice;
And that was stupid, but people are pitied for that, not hated. You were
  quite kind my days of sunshine,
And now you peck the feathers from the sick bird." Michal said trembling,
  "Oh, no. Not that I'm spiteful,
Only, I can't understand." "That's true," she answered, "how could you?
Your life has been sweet and full of ignorance. But I, when my father was
  drunk in town, would hear my mother
Take lovers in the house. *There* was somebody to hate. Yet they were white
  men;
They weren't the color of Concha . . . no more of that. The second time I
  died I almost made it, you know.
They pumped me alive with their hands and I was born again
From the dark air: since then I can understand much that was dark before.
  So you, Michal,
Will understand . . . many things that are dark . . . when some wild night
  kills childhood in you. That's coming:
But don't pray for it, my dear.
Oh Michal that's the reason I so much want you to listen to me. The
  inflamed and dark season
And bitterness will come, and then I dread your saying to yourself: 'Fera
  she hated life; Fera
Preferred death; Fera was wise.' I wasn't; at least you mustn't think so. I
  welched on my fate,
(And failed of course, failure's my root in nature) but I am ashamed. So
  you must listen to me, Michal,
My praise of life, by my dead father, by the dying oak. What I've lived has
  not been lucky you know,
If I can praise it, who'd not? But how good it is, Michal, to live! Good for
  what? Ah, there's the question.

For the pleasure of it? Hardly for that. Take your own life, mine's marked,
    mine's worse than usual. Your mother
Lies yonder; you never knew her, you missed the *pleasure* of knowing her.
    You missed the pains too; you might have hated her.
More likely you'd have loved her deeply; you'd have been sad then to see
    her wasting with age and pain,
Those years would come; and you'd have felt the salt fountains of loneliness
Drain from your eyes when the day came and she died. There's not a
    pleasure in the world not paid for, Michal,
In pain with a penny or two for interest. But youth, they say, is a shining
    time, and no doubt for you
The pleasures outsun the pains. Then the hair grays, and the teeth blacken
    or drop, and the sky blackens.
You've swollen ankles and shrunk thighs, and horrible hanging breasts that
    flap like a hound's ears,
Or death comes first ... Oh, but I'm wrong, it's life I was praising! And
    the pain to the pleasure is sun to candle.
Joy never kills, you know, the most violent joy
Never drove anyone mad. Pain kills, and pain drives mad; and extreme pain
    can feed for days
On the stretched flesh; the extremes of pleasure rot in two minutes.

                                                                    Oh yes,
        but, Michal,
Surely life's ... good? My father — his thoughts were deep,
Patient and wise — believed it was good because it was growing.
At first it was a morsel of slime on the sea,
It grew to be worms and fishes, lizards and snakes,
You see the progress, then things with hair and hot blood,
It was coming up from the ocean and climbing mountains,
Subduing the earth, moulding its bundle of nerves

Into the magnificent mind of man, and passing
Beyond man, to more wonders. That helped my father!
He loved that. You and me of course it can't help,
Because we know nothing goes on forever.
What good is better and better if best draws blank?
Here's the oak was growing upward a hundred years
And now it withers. Sometime the world
Will change, only a little too hot or too cold
Or too dry, and then life will go like the oak.
Then what will all my father's magnificent thoughts,
Michal, and all the dreams of your children be worth?
Well, we must praise life for some other reason.
For surely it's . . . good? We know it must be. Here every morning
You bring food to this bird to keep it alive:
Because you love it: in its filth, in misery, in prison. What's wretcheder than
     a caged eagle? Guess. I'll not tell.
And you'd be bitter cruel to keep it alive: sick-feathered, abject,
     broken-armed: only, you know
Life is so *good*. It's true the creature seems ungrateful: but I am not grateful
     either: to Dante
Vitello who pumped the breath into my body."
She stopped and looked at Michal's white face, and said
"You haven't heard from Hood yet? He went so suddenly,
He ought to write you." Michal said "No," and Fera:
"You know nothing about him?" She cried trembling:
"Why do you ask about Hood? Why do you ask about Hood?
Let me alone." "Ah," Fera said, "do you think
That something has happened to him?" "He'll never come back.
It was your fault." "I'm sure he'll never come back,"
She said with a still face. "Now let's go down.
But I can't joke about your eagle Michal.

The hopeless cage of pain is a lamp
Shining rays that go right through the flesh
And etch the secrets of bone. Mine aches. Oh no, Michal,
I couldn't do it: but George would kill him for you:
Or ask your father: that's better: those are the hands."

Another morning Fera went up
Secretly under the redwoods to the Rock's foot,
Where the great ribbed and battering granite face
Came down and found earth. In spring the cliff-swallows nest
A third of the way up, and a pair of duckhawks
Two thirds of the way. High in air the gray dome
Seemed swaying from the sweep of the small fibrous clouds.
Fera crept back and forth at the foot with pale
Spying eyes: but this loose earth was only a squirrel's mound,
And that was a gopher's digging: for hours: and she found
Stones had been rolled together, their brown earth-bellies
Turned up to the sky, and the gray lichenous backs
Downward, there was fresh earth below, with grass-blades
Half buried and ferns trampled. One rain had fallen.
She stood and gazed and said to him there: "Did I not say beforehand
That after we were dead I should have no rest after all but run moaning
On the gray shore, gnawing for my hunger a wrist of shadow?" She found a
    brown scurf on the slope rocks
Above, and thought, "This is the blood that burst from your mouth when
    you fell"; caressing with hers the doubtful
Crust, that was really a brown lichen. "Oh why would you not listen to me?
    You chose, to die
Rather than live. Ah, you'd learned wisdom somewhere, you were too
    young to be wise, when with one beautiful
Act of delight, lovely to the giver as the taker, you might have made

A star for yourself and for me salvation." She rose and said to the grave: "It
    was I that killed you. The old man
Who lives in hell for it was only my hands."

XIV

It was true; and it was Cawdor that paid the suffering.
The woman found ease in words and outcry; the man,
The more sensitive by sex and by his nature,
Had forbidden himself action because one act
Was grown his cancer; speech because speech betrays;
Even thought, in one regard, for if Hood's guilt
Were not monstrous the punishment became monstrous,
And if he had been solicited into adultery
His guilt was not monstrous but halved and natural;
There was evidence enough for that, and there
Thought was forbidden. Meanwhile his mind remained
Implacably clear for the rest, cloudless harsh light
On what he had done, memory not dimmed with time
But magnified and more real, not masked with any
Mysticism, that comes most often and stands
Between the criminal and his crime, a redeemer
Shifting the load onto fate; no failure toward unreason
Except the fantasy of his wife's innocence.

His loved canyon was grown hateful and terrible;
He longed to go away, go away, but that
Was cowardice, the set pride and code of his life
Prohibited that; he desired to kill himself,
But that was cowardice; to go and accuse himself,
But that was a kind of cowardice; all the outlets of action
Were locked and locked. But the most present desire,

And the most self-despised, was to ask advice
No matter of whom: of George, of Dante Vitello:
He yearned on them with his eyes: but that was cowardice
And ridiculous too. Day by day the tensions of his mind
Were screwed tighter in silence. He had some strength,
Though not the strength his vanity used to imagine,
And now in the deadlock of his powers endurance
Continued still. He felt the eyes of his house
That used to peer at him from behind now openly
Glitter before his face. He believed they all knew,
Save little Michal, and were kept quiet by fear,
They watched his face for weakness, as the blackbirds
In Carmel Valley watch the green fruit for softness.

After the flood in December the later rains
Fell scant, shrewd north wind heeling listless falls
Blew the hills dry; Cawdor discovered his mind
Building conjectural bridges between the drought
And the curse of his deed; he conquered the sick thought,
Another cowardice.

                    In March when the cows were calving
Came printed news of foot-and-mouth disease
Among the cattle in the north, it had come in
Through San Francisco from Asia. An infected herd
Had been destroyed. Cawdor read and feared nothing,
His herd in the isolation of the coast canyon
Would be the last. Yet he dreamed in the night
That he was slaughtering his herd. A bench was dug
To stand on, in the steep wall of a gully;
He stood there with the sledge-hammer and Jesus Acanna
All black on a black horse against the twilight

Drove in the cattle. One swing of the hammer for each
On the peak between the horns, but the white-faced heifer
Sidled her head and the blow crushed the horn.
Bawling and slopped with blood down the sleek shoulders,
Plunging among the carcasses ... The dream returned
Too many times; the plague increasing in the north
He warned his men to guard the pasture and watch
For strays; then the dream ceased; but the hurt heifer
Still troubled his dreams.

          His mind had relented toward Fera,
Innocent sufferer and as wretched as himself.
He saw now that both George and Michal hated her.
Her arm had knitted crooked, it pained always
In her pale eyes. He spoke to her kindly; she answered patiently.
He saw as in a vision that if he should choose
He might go back to his own room from Hood's
This very night, and all be as it was before.
To hell with the glittering eyes, they would keep quiet.
"No," he said and went out of the house. But she
Followed and overtook him under the cypresses
In the evening twilight.

         Michal and George were left
In the lamplight in the room, and Michal said
"I want you ..." she made more words but they were too mumbled
To understand; she stopped and drew breath and said
Astonishingly aloud, as if she were calling
Across a canyon: "I want you to kill my eagle.
I ought never to have kept it. Nothing but wretchedness.
George, will you kill it quickly and without pain
To-morrow morning?" He stared at her and said

"We've other troubles to think of." "Yes. If you won't
I'll do it myself." "I will. Don't cry, Michal."
She went up-stairs crying.

                                    In the twilight under the trees
Fera touched Cawdor's arm and said timidly: "The best
Would be not to've been born at all; but if we are bound to live why
   should we hate each other?"
He turned in surprise, he had forgotten her. "You are not bound." "By
   failures of nature. I am like a sick beast . . .
Like Michal's eagle . . . I can't do for myself. I've tried. Think of *me* a
   little. You did the other
No evil but eternal good. Forget him now, and if I can't end: failure's my
   peg that I hang on:
Mayn't we go back and live as we were before? You loved me once, when I
   was a child and you
Were a man." He stood silent thinking of another matter, suddenly he
   barked with laughter and said
"What am I now?" "A living God: you could answer prayer if you pleased."
   "Don't be troubled," he said,
"About God. You talk about God
The day before you go mad." "I can't do that either. Are you afraid to live,"
   she answered,
"Because they whisper? But they know nothing; they've not a thread of
   evidence. I've talked to them all, not one
But I, not one but I could betray you." She peered up at his face to see
   what it said in the twilight.
It said nothing; he was thinking of another matter, and walking the open
   way from the trees, slowly
Toward the sea's fading light. "Besides, they are all afraid of you. Oh
   listen!" she said. "We two alone

Have all the decision. Nobody but I can twitch the reins in your hands.
    Look at me." She caught his arm.
"Am I changed?" He looked, and suddenly laughed with pleasure. "Why
    ... like a blown-out candle. Perfectly changed.
The fragrance all gone, all the wind fallen." He failed to see the lightning
    pallor, he was so prisoned
In the surprise of his mind. "No more in my eyes than a dead stick. No
    more," he said in astonishment,
"Than Concha Rosas." He spoke with no intention of cruelty, his mind in
    the pain of its own bonds
Islanded alone, incapable of feeling another's. She clasped her throat with
    her hand and said shuddering:
"For this. No, not another time.
I went on my knees to Hood, I made myself a shameless beggar, I washed
    his feet with tears.
That's not done twice. To love me: and he would not.
Ah God how can I make you know it? I duped you too well. Ah dupe, Ah
    fool," she stammered, "Ah murderer.
Machine that one winds up and it goes and does it. I wound you, I was the
    one. Now the air's fire
To drink and the days and nights the teeth and throat of a dog: shall I hide
    your eyes with my hand always
From what you have done, to let you die in sweet ignorance?" He said "Go
    on. Strain it out, gasping, a heifer
With the first calf." "It's the only child I'll bear you. I hope you will like the
    child. You killed the other
Woman's but mine perhaps will spill *you*
From the same rock. For proofs: ask Michal, she heard me pray to him for
    love: ask Concha Rosas again,
The fat beast listened and saw, she heard me, she helped me fool you: ask
    Jesus Acanna,
Watched me lead Hood from my father's earth to the laurel to be my lover:
    I led him, *I* called him, *I* flung

Flowers and fire at his feet: he never at mine: and he refused me, he died
　　for that. Ask your eyes,
Heartless blue stones in their caves, wanted to be blind and they saw,
They saw me come down in the rain to call him, the rain steamed where it
　　struck, I was hot, I walked in a shameless
Burning heat; my father was dying but I ran down.
And again you saw me, Hood was naked in bed at dawn, you caught me in
　　his room. Had he received me
Gladly or kindly, had he raised his arms to receive me? I begged and he put
　　me by, I broke in to beg
And he was driving me out when you came. He remembered his father's
　　honor, he was a fool and faithful,
He's paid for it, he was faithful to you, you paid the wages. Ah, wait, I've
　　more.
It's precious to me to tell you these things, I've hardly desired honey-sweet
　　death a longer while."
"You lie too much," he answered, "I asked you before to tell me. Pour it
　　out."
He stood like a gray tree in the twilight, only a surface trembling, the axe
　　was blunted in the bark,
Fera thought; and she said: "I asked him to cut leaves from the laurel to lay
　　in my father's grave,
There are no flowers in this ditch,
And under the laurel I gave him my love. Are you glad that he had my love?
　　That saves you, that lets you live.
The old husband happy in his wife's pleasures.
Under the laurel it was, behind the concealing oaks, under the laurel it was.
　　Before,
I had only cried out and begged with tears, but there I gave him my body,
　　my arms about him, my breasts
Against him: be patient will you, this is not much, this is not the poison: I
　　gave him my flesh to eat,
As Michal takes up meat to the eagle, but he was wilder than the eagle.

He remembered his father's honor, he would not feed. My arms were his
    cage, I held the meat to his mouth,
He would not feed." Her face distorted itself and seemed to reflect flame,
    like the white smoke
Of a hidden fire of green wood shining at night, twisting as it rises. Gipsies
    crouch by the smoke's root
Watching strange flesh simmer in the pot between the forked sticks. When
    the wind varies their eyes prickle
And the shine of the smoke hides the gray stars. Her face writhed like the
    shining smoke and she cried and said:
"I wish the little rivers under the laughing kingfishers in every canyon were
    fire, and the ocean
Fire, and my heart not afraid to go down.
I broke my heart against his mouth like honeycomb, he would not take me,
    Oh the bitter honey, the black-blooded
Drops from the wax, no wonder he refused me. There was a lion-skin
I wore to my death, was it you stole it or Concha? He gave it to me, his
    one gift, but your house
Is a house of thieves. One boy was honest and so you killed him. The boy
    respected his father's possession.
He despised me, he spat me out. Then when I pressed him hard and set fire
    to his body: the heart and soul
I never could reach, they were both stones: he took his hunter's knife in his
    hand, he made the pain
Of the point in his flesh a servant against me. Into his thigh he drove it, he
    laughed and was lame, and triumphed,
And limped into the darkness of death."

                            She stood silent, and Cawdor
    remembered his son's lameness
Stumbling under the old man's coffin up the steep hill. He groaned aloud,
    then Fera's face

Gleaming spotted the darkness before his eyes. "I loved him," she said.
    "Love is a trap that takes
The trapper and his game in the same teeth. The first to die has the luck.
    They hang bleeding together.
But you were a mere dupe and a common murderer,
Not love but envy, dupe and fool, what will you do?"
He swayed against the dark hill, "You make the lies,"
He said hoarsely, "must I always believe them?
Time. Time. All my damnation draws
From having done in a haste. What do you want?"
"If I were you
And had your strength I'd kill the woman first,
Then cut out the eyes that couldn't tell my innocent
Boy's head from a calf's to butcher,
And smell my way to the Rock and take the jump."
"I asked you," he said, "because a known devil's
Word is a warning." She came and touched him. "The first's
Easiest," she said, "to kill the woman: the rest
Follows of its own accord." She stroked his face and said
"It is all easy." He took her throat in his hands,
She did not tremble nor flinch; he tightened his fingers
Slowly, as if he were dreaming the thing not doing it,
Then her mouth opened, but the ivory face
Kept its composure still; his fingers closed
A little harder and half checked the hot breath.
Suddenly she clawed at his hands with hers, she cried
"Have pity! I didn't mean it. Oh, Oh, I was lying.
Let me live!" He set her by and ran back to the house,
She heard him sob as he ran.

                  George was alone
In the lamplit room, Cawdor came in and said
"It's nothing," and went up-stairs, his eyes so sunken

That no gleam showed. He shut himself in the room
He used now, where Hood had slept before. George followed
Quietly and saw the crack under the door
Silent of light; he listened and heard no sound.
Then he returned down-stairs. Fera had come in;
She made a smile and passed him and went to her place.

XV

In the morning Cawdor failed to come down; Michal
At length knocked at his door. She listened, trembling,
And got no answer. She opened the door. He stood
Against the window and said "Is it you Michal?
I'm not well. Let me alone." She saw that the bed
Had not been slept in; she could not see his face
Against the shining light but his voice frightened her,
So gentle and forlorn. "Let me bring you some breakfast,
Father?" "No," he said, "no. But there's one thing
You could do for me." "What thing?" "To let me alone.
Nothing else. Nothing else." She saw that his face
Kept turning toward the bed, the eyes and features
Could hardly be seen against the morning light.
She thought he meant to lie down.

                       When Michal had gone
He locked the door, and leaning to the bed whispered:
"She didn't see you. How astonished she'd have been,
She thinks you're hunting in the north." He smiled fondly
And touched the pillow. "You always had fine hair
But now it has grown longer." A sad perplexity
Wrinkled his face; when he drew back his hand
His eyes were again serene. He went to the window

And stood with his back against the light. "From here
I see you the most clearly. Ah no, lie quiet.
You've had a fall," he said shaking, "don't speak.
This puts my eyes in heaven." He stood a long while
And his face darkened. "She keeps begging to die.
Plenty of others want that and make less noise.
It was only a sorrowful joke last night,
I'd not have done it. I made her beg off at least.
But when she squealed I hardly could let go,
My fingers cramped like the arms of breeding toads.
I've lived some months in pain."

                       He listened, and said:
"I know. Thank God. But if you had died, what then?
I had too much foolish pride to throw the game
Because it hurt." He paused and said "I thought
I needed punishment but death's no punishment.
I thought of telling the sheriff": he laughed. "I know him.
And a judge save me? I had to judge myself.
Run to a judge was only running away
From judgment: I thought I'd not do that; shame Michal
And do no good. Running away. I thought the same
Of killing myself. Oh, I've been thinking.
If I'd believed in hellfire I'd have done it
Most nights of the week." He listened, and shook his head.
"No value in needless pain? Oh yet if I lay
As damned with blood as I believed I was
I'd manage somehow. Tit for tat is good sense.
The debt was to myself as well as to you,
And mostly I've paid my debts. Well, I thank God.
This black's turned gray."

Michal had found her brother
Mending iron at the forge, the little shed
Behind the workshop; she'd heard the hammer and found him.
"Have you forgotten your promise?" "Why no," George answered,
"I'll do it for you. I thought you'd change your mind."
She was as pale as if a dear friend's death
Were being sealed in the plot. "Then do it quickly.
I think that father," she said, "is going to be sick.
Our lives perhaps will change, I'll not have time
For trapping squirrels to notch the dreary days
Of the cage with pitiful instants of pleasure." He frowned
And struck the iron, the red darkening, with scales
Of black, and white flecks.

While George went to the house
For his revolver, Michal climbed up the hill
Weeping; but when he came with death in his hand
She'd not go away, but watched. At the one shot
The great dark bird leaped at the roof of the cage
In silence and struck the wood; it fell, then suddenly
Looked small and soft, muffled in its folded wings.

The nerves of men after they die dream dimly
And dwindle into their peace; they are not very passionate,
And what they had was mostly spent while they lived.
They are sieves for leaking desire; they have many pleasures
And conversations; their dreams too are like that.
The unsocial birds are a greater race;
Cold-eyed, and their blood burns. What leaped up to death,
The extension of one storm-dark wing filling its world,
Was more than the soft garment that fell. Something had flown away. Oh
   cage-hoarded desire,

Like the blade of a breaking wave reaped by the wind, or flame rising from
    fire, or cloud-coiled lightning
Suddenly unfurled in the cave of heaven: I that am stationed, and cold at
    heart, incapable of burning,
My blood like standing sea-water lapped in a stone pool, my desire to the
    rock, how can I speak of you?
Mine will go down to the deep rock.

This rose,

Possessing the air over its emptied prison,
The eager powers at its shoulders waving shadowless
Unwound the ever widened spirals of flight
As a star light, it spins the night-stabbing threads
From its own strength and substance: so the aquiline desire
Burned itself into meteor freedom and spired
Higher still, and saw the mountain-dividing
Canyon of its captivity (that was to Cawdor
Almost his world) like an old crack in a wall,
Violet-shadowed and gold-lighted; the little stain
Spilt on the floor of the crack was the strong forest;
The grain of sand was the Rock. A speck, an atomic
Center of power clouded in its own smoke
Ran and cried in the crack; it was Cawdor; the other
Points of humanity had neither weight nor shining
To prick the eyes of even an eagle's passion.

This burned and soared. The shining ocean below lay on the shore
Like the great shield of the moon come down, rolling bright rim to rim
    with the earth. Against it the multiform
And many-canyoned coast-range hills were gathered into one carven
    mountain, one modulated

Eagle's cry made stone, stopping the strength of the sea. The beaked and
      winged effluence
Felt the air foam under its throat and saw
The mountain sun-cup Tassajara, where fawns
Dance in the steam of the hot fountains at dawn,
Smoothed out, and the high strained ridges beyond Cachagua,
Where the rivers are born and the last condor is dead,
Flatten, and a hundred miles toward morning the Sierras
Dawn with their peaks of snow, and dwindle and smooth down
On the globed earth.

It saw from the height and desert space of
      unbreathable air
Where meteors make green fire and die, the ocean dropping westward to
      the girdle of the pearls of dawn
And the hinder edge of the night sliding toward Asia; it saw far under
      eastward the April-delighted
Continent; and time relaxing about it now abstracted from being, it saw the
      eagles destroyed,
Mean generations of gulls and crows taking their world: turn for turn in
      the air, as on earth
The white faces drove out the brown. It saw the white decayed and the
      brown from Asia returning;
It saw men learn to outfly the hawk's brood and forget it again; it saw men
      cover the earth and again
Devour each other and hide in caverns, be scarce as wolves. It neither
      wondered nor cared, and it saw
Growth and decay alternate forever and the tides returning.

It saw, according to the sight of its kind, the archetype
Body of life a beaked carnivorous desire
Self-upheld on storm-broad wings: but the eyes

Were spouts of blood; the eyes were gashed out; dark blood
Ran from the ruinous eye-pits to the hook of the beak
And rained on the waste spaces of empty heaven.
Yet the great Life continued; yet the great Life
Was beautiful, and she drank her defeat, and devoured
Her famine for food.

                    There the eagle's phantom perceived
Its prison and its wound were not its peculiar wretchedness,
All that lives was maimed and bleeding, caged or in blindness,
Lopped at the ends with death and conception, and shrewd
Cautery of pain on the stumps to stifle the blood, but not
Refrains for all that; life was more than its functions
And accidents, more important than its pains and pleasures,
A torch to burn in with pride, a necessary
Ecstasy in the run of the cold substance,
And scape-goat of the greater world. (But as for me,
I have heard the summer dust crying to be born
As much as ever flesh cried to be quiet.)
Pouring itself on fulfilment the eagle's passion
Left life behind and flew at the sun its father.
The great unreal talons took peace for prey
Exultantly, their death beyond death; stooped upward, and struck
Peace like a white fawn in a dell of fire.

XVI

Cawdor in the room in the house, his eyes fixed
On the empty bed: "Age tells. I've known the time . . .
But now from having fasted a night of sleep
After some bad ones, my eyes have a dazzle in them
So that I sometimes lose your face, then instantly

The trouble returns. I was cut deep:
But never half my deserving." He heard a listener
Lean at the door and the latch move a little;
His face blanked and was still. After long silence
A gentle tapping, and spoken through the shut door:
"I think you are not well: let me in a moment.
Your voice has been going on and on like fever
And now why has it stopped?" Cawdor stood shaking
Like a gray horse tethered short to the fence,
Unable to rear or step back, a serpent rattling
Its passionate sistrum in the lupin by the hooves.
He extended hands toward the bed, his eyes widened
To hold their vision, but as he feared it vanished,
Then he was not able to restrain his hands
From feeling the length of the bed, patting and stroking
Where there was nothing but the smooth coverlet.
He stood and hardened himself, the knocking renewed.
"I have been deceived. It began in the dark,"
He whispered, "and I've dreamed on after dawn.
Men go crazy this way . . . not I. All's black again,
But the dream was sweet. Black, black, black. Ah,"
He said to the door, "keep still!"

                                    The knocking ceased
And steps retreated. Suddenly his black anguish
Compelled him to kneel by the bed. "What shall I do?
Kill that woman? I've promised not to kill
Fly nor stinking beetle. Nor myself: that
Would be a little too easy, I am a murderer
But not a coward yet. Nothing, is hardest to do.
Oh God show me a way. Nothing?" The prayer
And the attitude stiffened his nerves with self-contempt.

He ceased and stood up. "Nor this." Himself was responsible,
Himself must choose, himself must endure. He stood
And looked at the bed, remembering the sweet dream.

More steps came to the door and he drew it open
Before one knocked. Fera said "You are sick,
And I was afraid to come back alone. I brought
Concha Rosas." He looked from one to the other,
"Both my vomits," he said gently. "I'll never
Send you away. This is something." She whispered to him:
"You are in danger. Everyone here . . . knows.
Ask Concha. If you shut yourself up they'll tell; they've been asked;
Only the fear of your face stops them.
Jesus Acanna was asked in Monterey
When he drove in the steers." Cawdor said gently:
"Stay here. I'll keep you with me both days and nights
For a live spark between the eye-lid and the eye.
What ails you to bring good news?" "I knew he was going mad.
Good news? Why, they'll not hang you. I'll be your perfect
Witness to keep you alive. Buried alive
While all the strength you're proud of rots and drops off,
And all the stupid and deceived mind
Tears itself into red strips behind gray
Stones and black iron. Where is it, San Quentin? Oh, kill yourself Cawdor.
You have no better hope." "I am all you say,
Blind, blind, blind dupe," he answered, "but not a coward yet." " My God,
Watch the man cling, Concha. Who'd ever think
That *his* was sweet to live? But it's not love of life,
It's terror of death." He was not listening. He looked
With softened anxious eyes at the bed, his lips
Moved, though he did not speak. She, not in mockery:
"What do you see?" "A face that I know perfectly

Was crushed—what day of the month is it?—three months
And certain days ago, to a red lump
Of sudden destruction: but can you see?—he smiles at me.
I know there is nothing there." Fera laughed, "Concha
Has scuttled away. *I* see his angry eyes
And tumbled light brown hair and bare strong shoulders . . ."
"Yes: his hair." " . . . when I ran in here at dawn,
He lifted himself in the bed like a white sea-lion
Out of the running wave. His breast was bare.
And it was smooth, it was like smooth grooved stone.
You caught me here in the room." Cawdor looked down
And smiled and trembled. "Perhaps if I hadn't come.
Perhaps if I hadn't come." "You were pitiful enough,"
She said, "before. We'd both like to think that.
No, he was straight and true and faithful as light.
Hard as crystal, there was not a spot to hold by.
We two are damned." She watched him shaking
And thought that now he would make some end; but he
Looked downward sideways and said "It has faded now.
You needn't wait, I'll never again do anything
Until I have thought and thought. I'll find a way."
He said in the door, "I thought the woman was with you."
"Concha? She scuttled: I told you." "No, you said nothing."

She followed. When they were on the stair they heard
George's revolver-shot that killed the eagle,
And the quick echo. Cawdor stopped on the stair
And looked at Fera's face. "Why did you turn
So strangely," she said, "what do you see? I fear
You have waited too long already and now your mind
Is helpless among many voices and ghosts.

Kill yourself, Cawdor, and be safe from that,
For soon it will be too late." He said drearily,
"Since you fooled me my ears and eyes have the trick.
But," with a burrowing motion of the head forward,
"I'm not deceived. Not deceived. . . . Who has Hood's rifle?"
"Ah," she answered, "old fox, that hole won't hide you.
He fired because you were coming at him to kill him:
Your guilt's no less." "I lost it," he said, "in the night in the oaks.
I've often looked there, he loved it." They went out-doors
Under the twisted cypress trees and Cawdor said,
"What were you saying? He fired in the air, not at me.
If you were full of eyes you'd find no fault in him."
Fera laughed out, and pointing at the oak on the hill:
"Hurrah, she's done it. That was the shot. Oh, well done Michal.
See if I always fail. The bird shut in a box
Was eating bitter meat for years and now it is blessed. I've been begging
    her
To make it blessed. Its arm was like mine." "Killed it? I'm sorry," he said,
    "for Michal." Suddenly he ran
To the dim path and climbed. He shouted "George, George"; his heavy
    voice and the echo of his voice battered
Upward between the walls of the canyon.

                                        He came to the shelf of earth,
    and hoarse with breathlessness: "More killing?
You dog, have you got Hood's gun?" Michal looked at his face with startled
    wet eyes, George did not speak
But held out the revolver in the flat of his hand. "I forgot that," Cawdor
    said. "Oh Michal, you loved
This brave-eyed thing. You fed it for years." "It was unhappy, father." "By
    God, if you go killing

Unhappiness who'll be left in the houses? Forgive me," he said humbly, "I've
much to bear." She, trembling:
"Why . . ." she wetted her lips with her tongue . . . "why did you ask
about Hood's rifle, he wouldn't leave it?"
George, hastily: "His mind's on another matter. You told me to fix the
branding-iron shafts . . ." Fera had come
Behind Cawdor, and driving her face like an axe between them: "Let him
confess. He came to confess.
Listen to him for that will deliver his mind, thence he may win
Your eagle's quietness: we used to feel this cage like a black sun shining
darkness on the canyon.
Now you've put out the sun, you've cured the sky with a gun-shot, nothing
but a draggled feather-duster
Left in the cage. Let him confess." Cawdor said hoarsely: "I have learned
that Hood was innocent. This woman
So angered me that I threatened his life in the night. I am dull and easy to
lie to. Hood went away
Rather than quarrel with the fool his father; he left his rifle under my feet
by the fire; I lost it;
If I could find it I'd keep it for him." "Ai," Fera cried sharply, "this is no
good. Wait, that gray face
Will ripen by summer: you can't bear it forever. What did he use, his
revolver? Even so little
A creature as that is a key to peace." Cawdor said, "Let me see it again."
George clicked the cylinder
Out of the frame before he handed it to him. Cawdor took and returned it.
"If I were weak enough
I could find ways, though I am not wise." He saw a knife-edged flake of
chipped flint or chalcedony
On the earth at his feet; they stood by Fera's father's grave, and the spring
rains had failed and not grassed it.

Cawdor picked up the Indian-wrought stone. "There were people here
  before us," he said, "and others will come
After our time. These poor flints were their knives, wherever you dig you
  find them, and now I forget
What we came up for. Why do you fix your eyes on me?
For I can neither imagine what I must do
Nor what I should say. You are like shadows." George said "Father:
Send this woman away. This is the bitter fountain, this is your sickness."
  "For the rifle," she answered,
"Acanna has it. Send me away: do: I've a pretty story for strangers, I'll bring
  back eyes
And dig for the old dog's hoard of bones." She said to Cawdor: "Now
  you've grown gentle, you can't eat meat,
But the others know we'd venison Thursday, Jesus Acanna killed it. He says
  that he got his rifle
In Monterey, have you seen the rifle, Michal? You country people have
  quick minds." "Oh, this is nothing,"
Cawdor groaned, "What does Hood want with a gun? He hunts no more.
However . . . do you see the sun?" George took his arm: "Come, let's go
  down." "Now it's due south," he answered,
"And men come home from the starved fields for food.
We'll go and ask him." George made a sign to Michal
So that she stayed behind when the others went down.
And Cawdor, seeing it: "That was well done. I see you now.
A moment ago you were like shadows of moths
When lamplight falls on the earth outside the window.
If I could have caught you I couldn't have held you. Send away sweet Fera?
What should we do without her?" She said: "That flint
Came from an old man's grave you used to despise
For his great weakness; he was the only mind in this ditch;
But now you don't. What's it for, to nick an artery?"

"It is hard," he answered, "and pleasant in the hand.
Last night I threw my knife out of the window
For fear it might use itself of its own accord.
I'd a good dream."

                    He saw Acanna among the cypresses
And called him with the old strength of his voice. "I hear that you've got
     Hood's rifle, you found it in the little oaks
Near by the Rock. Oh keep it," he said, "keep it. That's nothing. Kill all
     the deer for Hood has quit hunting,
Buck, fawn and doe. They say they have foot-and-mouth disease
And carry it over the mountain. But if you see a white doe,
That's the worst kind. Cut out her tongue when she drops,
It's poison. . . . You know that I killed him.
You all know it. George knows it. You've been whispering for long,
Watching my face. You've been staunch and not told
For askings: but that was wrong, it makes you accessory.
Now you must ride and tell, don't stay for dinner.
Get meat in the house and eat on the road, for now
I've confessed: if you don't tell you'll be in the same
Sickness with Cawdor. Go. Go." He pushed by him,
And Acanna stood all twisted, as Cawdor's hands
Had left him, unable to move, looking for guidance. At length
George twitched his dead-white face and answered: "Go on.
Do what he says. He has chosen." While they stood, Cawdor
Faced the hill so that his back was toward them and drove
The point of the flint through fold and flesh of each eye
Drawing sidewise on the stroke, so that his sight
Was burst, and blood and water ran down to his feet.
He did not groan, but Fera saw the red stream
Fall by some yellow flowers. She cried "Have you done
Wisely at last? Not with that chip?" He groaned then

Cawdor (1926–28)   293

But answered nothing. Then George ran to him and saw
The bitter thing he had done, and moved with sudden
Ungovernable pity thrust the revolver
Into his hand. Cawdor said: "What's this? Oh,
This thing. Keep it for cage-birds.
We have other plans. The decent girl my pleasant companion
Has promised to lead me by the hand up to the Rock
And prove our wings." But Fera staggered and said,
Her arms hanging straight down, head drooped, and knees
Bent like weak age: "I am broken. It is finished."
She covered her eyes against him. "My courage is past.
I have always failed." He said, "I'd not have flown down.
I meant to sit up there and think my old thoughts
Until they come to-morrow and take me. It was mere indulgence.
These punishments are a pitiful self-indulgence.
I'd not the strength to do nothing.

                    Be kind to Michal:
But spring's weeping-time. Oh George it was her face
I fell into this darkness to hide myself from.
But when I am taken from the sight of my mountain
It is better to have no eyes. Has Acanna gone?
Your droughty hay-harvest will be a thin sight."
He extended his hands. "Lead me, whoever is here,
Into the house. My head is full of sharp lightnings
And the ground streams and falls under my feet."

Dear Judas

1928-29

HOODED NIGHT

At night, toward dawn, all the lights of the shore have died,
And a wind moves. Moves in the dark
The sleeping power of the ocean, no more beastlike than manlike,
Not to be compared; itself and itself.
Its breath blown shoreward huddles the world with a fog; no stars
Dance in heaven; no ship's light glances.
I see the heavy granite bodies of the rocks of the headland,
That were ancient here before Egypt had pyramids,
Bulk on the gray of the sky, and beyond them the jets of young trees
I planted the year of the Versailles peace.
But here is the final unridiculous peace. Before the first man
Here were the stones, the ocean, the cypresses,
And the pallid region in the stone-rough dome of fog where the moon
Falls on the west. Here is reality.
The other is a spectral episode; after the inquisitive animal's
Amusements are quiet: the dark glory.

EVENING EBB

The ocean has not been so quiet for a long while; five night-herons
Fly shorelong voiceless in the hush of the air
Over the calm of an ebb that almost mirrors their wings.
The sun has gone down, and the water has gone down
From the weed-clad rock, but the distant cloud-wall rises. The ebb
    whispers.
Great cloud-shadows float in the opal water.
Through rifts in the screen of the world pale gold gleams and the evening
Star suddenly glides like a flying torch.
As if we had not been meant to see her; rehearsing behind
The screen of the world for another audience.

HANDS

Inside a cave in a narrow canyon near Tassajara
The vault of rock is painted with hands,
A multitude of hands in the twilight, a cloud of men's palms, no more,
No other picture. There's no one to say
Whether the brown shy quiet people who are dead intended
Religion or magic, or made their tracings
In the idleness of art; but over the division of years these careful
Signs-manual are now like a sealed message
Saying: "Look: we also were human; we had hands, not paws. All hail
You people with the cleverer hands, our supplanters
In the beautiful country; enjoy her a season, her beauty, and come down
And be supplanted; for you also are human."

THE LOVING SHEPHERDESS

I

The little one-room schoolhouse among the redwoods
Opened its door, a dozen children ran out
And saw on the narrow road between the dense trees
A person — a girl by the long light-colored hair:
The torn brown cloak that she wore might be a man's
Or woman's either — walking hastily northward
Among a huddle of sheep. Her thin young face
Seemed joyful, and lighted from inside, and formed
Too finely to be so wind-burnt. As she went forward
One or another of the trotting sheep would turn
Its head to look at her face, and one would press
Its matted shoulder against her moving thigh.
The school-children stood laughing and shouting together.
"Who's that?" "Clare Walker," they said, "down from the hills.
She'd fifty sheep and now she's got eight, nine,
Ten: what have you done with all the others, Clare Walker?"
The joy that had lived in her face died, she yet
Went on as if she were deaf, with forward eyes
And lifted head, but the delicate lips moving.
The jeering children ran in behind her and the sheep
Drew nervously on before, except the old ram,
That close at her side dipped his coiled horns a little
But neither looked back nor edged forward. An urchin shouted
"You killed your daddy, why don't you kill your sheep?"
And a fat girl, "Oh where's your lover, Clare Walker?
He didn't want you after all."

                    The patriarch ram
That walked beside her wore a greasy brown bundle
Tied on his back with cords in the felt of wool,
And one of the little boys, running by, snatched at it
So that it fell. Clare bent to gather it fallen,
And tears dropped from her eyes. She offered no threat
With the bent staff of rosy-barked madrone-wood
That lay in her hand, but said "Oh please, Oh please,"
As meek as one of her ewes. An eight-year-old girl
Shrilled "Whistle for the dogs, make her run like a cat,
Call your dog, Charlie Geary!" But a brown-skinned
Spanish-Indian boy came forward and said
"You let her alone. They'll not hurt you, Clare Walker.
Don't cry, I'll walk beside you." She thanked him, still crying.
Four of the children, who lived southward, turned back;
The rest followed more quietly.

                    The black-haired boy
Said gently "Remember to keep in the road, Clare Walker.
There's enough grass. The ranchers will sick their dogs on you
If you go into the pastures, because their cows
Won't eat where the sheep have passed; but you can walk
Into the woods." She answered "You're kind, you're kind.
Oh yes, I always remember." The small road dipped
Under the river when they'd come down the hill,
A shallow mountain river that Clare skipped over
By stone after stone, the sheep wading beside her.
The friendly boy went south to the farm on the hill, "good-bye, good-bye,"
    and Clare with her little flock
Kept northward among great trees like towers in the river-valley. Her sheep
    sidled the path, sniffing

The bitter sorrel, lavender-flowering in shade, and the withered ferns.
    Toward evening they found a hollow
Of autumn grass.

II

                        Clare laughed and was glad, she undid the bundle from
    the ram's back
And found in the folds a battered metal cup and a broken loaf. She shared
    her bread with the sheep,
A morsel for each, and prettily laughing
Pushed down the reaching faces. "Piggies, eat grass. Leave me the crust,
    Tiny, I can't eat grass.
Nosie, keep off. Here Frannie, here Frannie." One of the ewes came close
    and stood to be milked, Clare stroked
The little udders and drank when the cup filled, and filled it again and
    drank, dividing her crust
With the milch ewe; the flock wandered the glade, nibbling white grass.
    There was only one lamb among them,
The others had died in the spring storm.

                                    The light in the glade suddenly
    increased and changed, the hill
High eastward began to shine and be rosy-colored, and bathed in so clear a
    light that up the bare hill
Each clump of yucca stood like a star, bristling sharp rays; while westward
    the spires of the giant wood
Were strangely tall and intensely dark on the layered colors of the winter
    sundown; their blunt points touched
The high tender blue, their heads were backed by the amber, the
    thick-branched columns
Crossed flaming rose. Then Clare with the flush

Of the solemn and glad sky on her face went lightly down to the river to
    wash her cup; and the flock
Fed on a moment before they looked up and missed her. The ewe called
    Frannie had gone with Clare and the others
Heard Frannie's hooves on the crisp oak-leaves at the edge of the glade.
    They followed, bleating, and found their mistress
On the brink of the stream, in the clear gloom of the wood, and nipped the
    cresses from the water. Thence all returning
Lay down together in the glade, but Clare among them
Sat combing her hair, with a gap-toothed comb brought from the bundle.
    The evening deepened, the thick blond strands
Hissed in the comb and glimmered in the brown twilight, Clare began
    weeping, full of sorrow for no reason
As she had been full of happiness before. She braided her hair and pillowed
    her head on the bundle; she heard
The sheep breathing about her and felt the warmth of their bodies, through
    the heavy fleeces.

                    In the night she moaned
And bolted upright. "Oh come, come,
Come Fern, come Frannie, Leader and Saul and Tiny,
We have to go on," she whispered, sobbing with fear, and stood
With a glimmer in her hair among the sheep rising. The halved moon had
    arisen clear of the hill,
And touched her hair, and the hollow, in the mist from the river, was a lake
    of whiteness. Clare stood wreathed with her flock
And stared at the dark towers of the wood, the dream faded away from her
    mind, she sighed and fondled
The frightened foreheads. "Lie down, lie down darlings, we can't escape it."
    But after that they were restless
And heard noises in the night till dawn.

                        They rose in the quivering
Pale clearness before daylight, Clare milked her ewe,
The others feeding drifted across the glade
Like little clouds at sunrise wandering apart;
She lifted up the madrone-wood staff and called them.
"Fay, Fern, Oh Frannie. Come Saul.
Leader and Tiny and Nosie, we have to go on."
They went to the stream and then returned to the road
And very slowly went north, nibbling the margin
Bushes and grass, tracking the tender dust
With numberless prints of oblique crossings and driftings.
They came to Fogler's place and two ruffian dogs
Flew over the fence: Clare screaming "Oh, Oh, Oh, Oh,"
An inarticulate wild-bird cry, brandishing
The staff but never striking, stood out against them,
That dashed by her, and the packed and trembling ball
Of fleeces rolling into the wood was broken.
The sheep might have been torn there, some ewe or the lamb
Against the great foundations of the trees, but Fogler
Ran shouting over the road after his dogs
And drove them home. Clare gathered her flock, the sobbing
Throats and the tired eyes, "Fay, Fern, Oh Frannie,
Come Leader, come little Hornie, come Saul"; and Fogler:
"You ought to get a good dog to help take care of them."
He eyed curiously her thin young face,
Pale parted lips cracked by the sun and wind,
And then the thin bare ankles and broken shoes.
"Are you Clare Walker? I heard that you'd gone away:
But you're Clare Walker, aren't you?" "We had a dog,"
She said, "a long time ago but he went away.
There, Nosie. Poor Frannie. There. These poor things
Can find their food, but what could I keep a dog with?

But that was some years ago." He said, "Are these all?
They're all gathered? I heard you'd thirty or forty."
Then hastily, for he saw the long hazel eyes
Filling with tears, "Where are you going, Clare Walker?
Because I think it will rain in a week or two,
You can't sleep out then." She answered with a little shudder,
"Wherever I go this winter will be all right.
I'm going somewhere next April." Fogler stood rubbing
His short black beard, then dropped his hand to scratch
The ram's forehead by the horns but Saul drew away.
And Fogler said: "You're too young and too pretty
To wander around the country like this.
I'd ask you to come here when it rains, but my wife . . .
And how could I keep the sheep here?" "Ah, no," she answered,
"I couldn't come back." "Well, wait," he said, "for a minute,
Until I go to the house. Will you wait, Clare?
I'll tie up the dogs. I've got some biscuit and things . . ."
He returned with a sack of food, and two old shoes
A little better than Clare's. She sat on a root;
He knelt before her, fumbling the knotted laces
Of those she had on, and she felt his hands tremble.
His wife's shoes were too short for the slender feet. When the others
Had been replaced, Fogler bent suddenly and kissed
Clare's knee, where the coat had slipped back. He looked at her face,
His own burning, but in hers nor fear nor laughter,
Nor desire nor aversion showed. He said "good-bye,"
And hurried away.

       Clare travelled northward, and sometimes
Half running, more often loitering, and the sheep fed.
In the afternoon she led them into the willows,
And choosing a green pool of the shallow stream

Bathed, while the sheep bleated to her from the shoals.

They made a pleasant picture, the girl and her friends, in the green shade

Shafted with golden light falling through the alder branches. Her body, the
    scare-crow garments laid by,

Though hermit-ribbed and with boyishly flattened flanks hardly a woman's,

Was smooth and flowing, glazed with bright water, the shoulders and
    breasts beautiful, and moved with a rapid confidence

That contradicted her mind's abstractions. She laughed aloud and jetted
    handfuls of shining water

At the sheep on the bank; the old ram stood blinking with pleasure, shaking
    his horns. But after a time Clare's mood

Was changed, as if she thought happiness must end.

She shivered and moved heavily out of the stream

And wept on the shore, her hands clasping her ankles,

Her face bowed on her knees, her knotted-up coils

Of citron-colored hair loosening. The ewe

That she called Nosie approached behind her and pressed

Her chin on the wet shoulder; Clare turned then, moaning,

And drew the bony head against the soft breasts.

"Oh what will you do," she whispered laughing and sobbing,

"When all this comes to an end?"

                              She stood and stroked off

The drops of water, and dressed hastily. They went

On farther; now there was no more forest by the road,

But open fields. The river bent suddenly westward

And made a pond that shone like a red coal

Against the shore of the ocean, under the sundown

Sky, with a skeleton of sand-bar

Between the pond and the sea.

                              When deepening twilight
Made all things gray and made trespass safe, Clare entered
The seaward fields with her flock. They had fed scantly
In the redwood forest, and here in the dead grass
The cattle had cropped all summer they could not sleep.
She led them hour after hour under the still stars.
Once they ran down to the glimmering beach to avoid
The herd and the range bull; they returned, and wandered
The low last bluff, where sparse grass labors to live in the wind-heaped
      sand. Silently they pastured northward,
Gray file of shadows, between the glimmer and hushing moan of the ocean
      and the dark silence of the hills.
The erect one wore a pallor of starlight woven in her hair. Before moonrise
      they huddled together
In a hollow cup of old dune that opened seaward, but sheltered them from
      the nightwind and from morning eyes.

III

The bleating of sheep answered the barking of sea-lions and Clare awoke
Dazzled in the broad dawn. The land-wind lifted the light-spun manes of
      the waves, a drift of sea-lions
Swung in the surf and looked at the shore, sleek heads uplifted and great
      brown eyes with a glaze of blind
Blue sea-light in them. "You lovely creatures," she whispered.
She went to the verge and felt the foam at her ankles. "You lovely creatures
      come closer." The sheep followed her
And stopped in the sand with lonesome cries. Clare stood and trembled at
      the simple morning of the world; there was nothing
But hills and sea, not a tree on the shore nor a ship on the sea; an edge of
      the hill kindled with gold,

And the sun rose. Then Clare took home her soul from the world and went
    on. When she was wandering the flats
Of open pasture between the Sur Hill sea-face and the great separate
    sea-dome rock at Point Sur,
Forgetting, as often before, that she and her flock were trespassers
In cattle country: she looked and a young cowboy rode down from the east.
    "You'll have to get off this range.
Get out of this field," he said, "your tallow-hoofed mutton." "Oh," she
    answered trembling, "I'm going. I got lost in the night.
Don't drive them." "A woman?" he said. He jerked the reins and sat
    staring. "Where did *you* drop from?" She answered faintly,
With a favor-making smile, "From the south." "Who's with you?"
    "Nobody."
"Keep going, and get behind the hill if you can
Before Nick Miles the foreman looks down this way."
She said to the ram, "Oh Saul, Oh hurry. Come Leader.
Tiny and Frannie and Nosie, we have to go on.
Oh hurry Fern." They huddled bleating about her,
And she in the midst made haste; they pressed against her
And moved in silence. The young cowboy rode on the east
As hoping to hide the flock from Nick Miles his foreman,
Sidelong in the saddle, and gazed at Clare, at the twisting
Ripple of pale bright hair from her brown skin
Behind the temples. She felt that his looks were friendly,
She turned and timidly smiled. Then she could see
That he was not a man but a boy, sixteen
Or seventeen; she felt more courage. "What would your foreman
Do if he saw us?" "He'd be rough. But," he said,
"You'll soon be behind the hill. Where are you going?"
She made no answer. "To Monterey?" "Oh . . . to nowhere!"
She shivered and sought his face with her eyes. "To nowhere, I mean."
"Well," he said sulkily, "where did you sleep last night?

Somewhere?" She said with eagerness, "Ah, two miles back,
On the edge of the sand; we weren't really in the field."
He stared. "You're a queer one. Is that old coat
All you've got on?" "No, no, there's a dress under it.
But scrubbed so often," she said, "with sand and water
Because I had no soap, it's nothing but rags."
"You needn't hurry, no one can see you now.
. . . My name's Will Brighton," he said. "Well, mine is Clare."
"Where do you live when you're at home, Clare?" "I haven't any."
They rounded the second spur of the hill. Gray lupine clothed the north
    flank, a herd of cattle stared down
From the pale slope of dead grass above the gray thicket. Rumps high, low
    quarters, they were part of the world's end sag,
The inverted arch from the Sur Hill height to the flat foreland and up the
    black lava rock of Point Sur;
In the open gap the mountain sea-wall of the world foam-footed went
    northward. Beyond the third spur Clare saw
A barn and a house up the wrinkled hill, oak-scrub and sycamores. The
    house built of squared logs, time-blackened,
Striped with white plaster between the black logs, a tall dead cube with a
    broken chimney, made her afraid;
Its indestructible crystalline shape. "Oh! There's a house.
They'll see us from there. I'll go back . . ." "Don't be afraid,"
He answered smiling, "that place has no eyes.
There you can turn your sheep in the old corral,
Or graze them under the buck-eyes until evening.
No one will come." She sighed, and then faintly:
"Nobody ever lives there, you're sure?" "Not for eight years.
You can go in," he said nervously; "maybe
You haven't been inside a house a good while?"
She looked up at his pleasant unformed young face,
It was blushing hot. "Oh, what's the matter with the house?"

"Nothing. Our owner bought the ranch, and the house
Stands empty, he didn't want it. They tell me an old man
Claiming to be God . . . a kind of a preacher boarded there,
And the family busted up." She said "I don't believe
Any such story." "Well, he was kind of a preacher.
They say his girl killed herself; he washed his hands
With fire and vanished." "Then she was crazy. What, spill
Her own one precious life," she said trembling,
"She'd nothing but that? Ah! no!
No matter how miserable, what goes in a moment,
You know . . . out . . ." Her head bowed, and her hand
Dug anxiously in the deep pads of wool
On the shoulder of the ram walking against her side;
When her face lifted again even the unwatchful boy
Took notice of tears.

              They approached the house; the fence in front was
   broken but the windows and doors were whole,
The rose that grew over the rotted porch steps was dead; yet the sleep of
   the house seemed incorruptible,
It made Clare and the boy talk low. He dropped out of the saddle and
   made the bridle hang down
To serve for tether. "Come round by the back," he whispered, "this door is
   locked." "What for?" "To go in," he whispered.
"Ah no, I have to stay with my sheep. Why in the world should I go in to
   your dirty old house?"
His face now he'd dismounted was level with hers; she saw the straw-
   colored hairs on his lip, and freckles,
For he'd grown pale. "Hell," he said, narrowing his eyes, hoping to be
   manly and bully her: but the heart failed him,
He said sadly, "I hoped you'd come in." She breathed "Oh," her mouth
   twitching,

But whether with fear or laughter no one could tell,
And said, "You've been kind. Does nobody ever come here?
Because I'd have to leave my poor friends out-doors,
Someone might come and hurt them." "The sheep? Oh, nobody.
No one can see them. Oh, Clare, come on. Look here,"
He ran and opened a gate, "the corral fence
Is good as new and the grass hasn't been touched."
The small flock entered gladly and found green weeds
In the matted gray. Clare slowly returned. The boy
Catching her by the hand to draw her toward the house,
She saw his young strained face, and wondered. "Have you ever
Been, with a woman?" "Ah," he said proudly, "yes."
But the honesty of her gaze dissolving his confidence
He looked at the ground and said mournfully, "She wasn't white.
And I think she was quite old . . ." Clare in her turn
Reddened. "If it would make you happy," she said.
"I want to leave glad memories. And you'll not be sorry
After I'm gone?"

        The sheep, missing their mistress,
Bleated and moved uneasily, forgetting to feed,
While Clare walked in the house. She said, "Oh, not yet.
Let's look at the house. What was the man's name
Whose daughter . . . he said he was God and suddenly vanished?"
"A man named Barclay," he said, "kind of a preacher."
They spoke in whispers, peering about. At length Clare sighed,
And stripped off the long brown coat.

                When they returned out-doors,
Blinking in the sun, the boy bent his flushed face
Toward Clare's pale one and said "Dear, you can stay here
As long as you want, but I must go back to work."

She heard the sheep bleating, and said "Good-bye.
Good luck, Will Brighton." She hurried to her flock, while he
Mounted, but when he had ridden three strides of a canter
Clare was crying "Oh help. Oh help. Oo! Oo!" He returned,
And found her in the near corner of the corral
On hands and knees, her flock huddling about her,
Peering down a pit in the earth. Oak-scrub and leafless
Buck-eyes made a dark screen toward the hill, and Clare
Stood up against it, her white face and light hair
Shining against it, and cried "Oh help me, they've fallen,
Two have fallen." The pit was an old well;
The hand-pump had fallen in, and the timbers
That closed the mouth had crumbled to yellow meal.
Clare lay and moaned on the brink among the dark nettles,
Will Brighton brought the braided line that hung at his saddle
And made it fast and went down.

                        The well-shaft was so filled up
With earth-fall and stones and rotting timbers, it was possible for the boy
    and girl to hoist up the fallen
Without other contrivance than the looped rope. The one came struggling
    and sobbing, Clare cried her name,
"Oh Fern, Fern, Fern." She stood and fell, and scrambled up to her feet,
    and plunged on three legs. The other
Came flaccid, it slipped in the rope and hung head downward, Clare made
    no cry. When it was laid by the well-brink
A slime of half-chewed leaves fell from its mouth. The boy climbed up.
    "While I was making your pleasure,"
Clare said, "this came. While I was lying there. What's punished is
    kindness." He touched the lifeless ewe with his foot,
Clare knelt against her and pushed him away. He said "It fell the first and
    its neck was broken." And Clare:

"This was the one that would nudge my hands
When I was quiet, she'd come behind me and touch me, I called her Nosie.
    One night we were all near frozen
And starved, I felt her friendly touches all night." She lifted the head. "Oh
    Nosie, I loved you best.
Fern's leg is broken. We'll all be like you in a little while." The boy ran and
    caught Fern, and said
"The bones are all right. A sprain I guess, a bad sprain. I'll come in the
    evening, Clare, if you're still here.
I'm sorry." She sat with the head on her lap, and he rode away. After a time
    she laid it on the earth.
She went and felt Fern's fore-leg and went slowly up the hill; her small flock
    followed.

IV

                Fern lagged and lagged,
Dibbling the dust with the mere points of the hoof
Of the hurt fore-leg, and rolling up to her shepherdess
The ache of reproachful eyes. "Oh Fern, Oh Fern,
What can I do? I'm not a man, to be able to carry you.
My father, he could have carried you." Tears from Clare's eyes
Fell in the roadway; she was always either joyful or weeping.
They climbed for half the day, only a steep mile
With many rests, and lay on the Sur Hill summit.
The sun and the ocean were far down below, like fire in a bowl;
The shadow of the hills lay slanting up a thin mist
Into the eastern sky, dark immense lines
Going out of the world.

                Clare slept wretchedly, for thirst
And anxious dreams and sorrow. She saw the lighthouse

Glow and flash all night under the hill;
The wind turned south, she smelled the river they had left,
Small flying clouds from the south crossed the weak stars.
In the morning Fern would not walk.

                                    Between noon and morning
A dark-skinned man on a tall hammer-headed
Flea-bitten gray horse rode north on the hill-crest.
Clare ran to meet him. "Please help me. One of my sheep
Has hurt her leg and can't walk. . . . Entiendes inglés?"
She faltered, seeing him Indian-Spanish, and the dark eyes
Gave no sign whether they understood, gazing through her with a blue light
    across them
Like the sea-lions' eyes. He answered easily in English, "What can I do?" in
    the gentle voice of his people;
And Clare: "I thought you might carry her down. We are very thirsty, the
    feed is all dry, here is no water,
And I've been gathering the withered grasses to feed her." He said, "We
    could tie her onto the horse." "Ah, no,
She'd be worse hurt. . . . She's light and little, she was born in the hills." The
    other sheep had followed their shepherdess
Into the road and sadly looked up, the man smiled and dismounted among
    them. "Where are you going?"
She answered "North. Oh come and see her. Unless you carry her
I don't know what we can do." "But it's two miles
Down to the river." The lame ewe, whether frightened
By the stranger and his horse, or rested at length,
Now rose and went quietly to Clare, the hurt fore-leg
Limping but serving. Clare laughed with pleasure. "Oh, now,
We can go down by ourselves. Come Fern, come Saul,
Fay, Frannie, Leader . . ." She was about to have called
The name of the one that died yesterday; her face

Changed and she walked in silence, Fern at her thigh.

The friendly stranger walked on the other side,

And his horse followed the sheep. He said: "I have seen

Many things, of this world and the others, but what are you?"

"My name's Clare Walker." "Well, I am Onorio Vasquez.

I meant, what are you doing? I think that I'd have seen you or heard of you

If you live near." "I'm doing? I'm taking care of my sheep." She looked at his face to be sure of kindness,

And said, "I'm doing like most other people; take care of those that need me and go on till I die.

But *I* know when it will be; that's the only. . . . I'm often afraid." Her look went westward to the day moon,

Faint white shot bird in her wane, the wings bent downward, falling in the clear over the ocean cloud-bank.

"Most people will see hundreds of moons: I shall see five.

When this one's finished." Vasquez looked intently at her thin young face, turned sideways from him, the parted

Sun-scarred lips, the high bridge of the nose, dark eyes and light hair; she was thin, but no sign of sickness; her eyes

Met his and he looked down and said nothing. When he looked down he remembered chiefly the smooth brown throat

And the little hollow over the notch of the breast-bone. He said at length, carefully, "You needn't be afraid.

I often," he murmured shyly, "have visions. I used to think they taught me something, but I was a fool.

If you saw a vision, or you heard a voice from heaven, it is nothing." She answered, "What I fear really's the pain.

The rest is only a kind of strangeness." Her eyes were full of tears and he said anxiously, "Oh, never

Let visions nor voices fool you.

They are wonderful but we see them by chance; I think they mean something in their own country but they mean

Nothing in this; they have nothing to do with our lives and deaths." She
    answered in so changed a voice that Vasquez
Stared; the tears were gone and her eyes were laughing. "Oh, no, it was
    nothing," she said, "in the way of that.
Visions? My trouble is a natural thing.
But tell me about those visions." He muttered to himself
With a shamed face and answered, "Not now." The south wind
That drove the dust of the little troop before them
Now increased and struck hard, where the road gained
A look-out point over the fork of the canyon
And the redwood forest below. The sheep were coughing
In the whirl of wind. At this point the lame ewe
Lay down and refused to rise, "Oh, now, now, now,"
Clare wrung her hands, "we're near the water too. We're all so thirsty.
Oh Fern!" Vasquez said sadly, "If she'd be quiet
Over my shoulders, but she won't." He heard a hoarse voice
Cry in the canyon, and Clare softly cried answer
And ran to the brink of the road. She stood there panting
Above the pitch and hollow of the gorge, her grotesque cloak
Blown up to her shoulders, flapping like wings
About the half nakedness of the slender body.
Vasquez looked down the way of her gaze, expecting
To see some tragical thing; he saw nothing but a wide heron
Laboring thwart wind from the shore over the heads of the redwoods. A
    heavy dark hawk balanced in the storm
And suddenly darted; the heron, the wings and long legs wavering in terror,
    fell, screaming, the long throat
Twisted under the body; Clare screamed in answer. The pirate death drove
    by and had missed, and circled
For a new strike, the poor frightened fisherman
Beat the air over the heads of the redwoods and labored upward. Again and
    again death struck, and the heron

Fell, with the same lost cry, and escaped; but the last fall
Was into the wood, the hawk followed, both passed from sight
Under the waving spires of the wood.

Clare Walker
Turned, striving with the gesture of a terrified child
To be quiet, her clenched fist pressed on her mouth,
Her teeth against the knuckles, and her blond hair
Wild on the wind. "Oh what can save him, can save him?
Oh how he cried at each fall!" She crouched in the wind
At the edge of the road, trembling; the ewe called Tiny
Crossed over and touched her, the others turned anxious looks
From sniffing the autumn-pinched leaves of the groundling blackberries.
When she was quieted Vasquez said, "You love
All creatures alike." She looked at his face inquiringly
With wide candid brown eyes, either not knowing
Or not thinking. He said, "It is now not far
Down to the running water; we'd better stretch her
Across the saddle" — he nodded toward the lame ewe —
"You hold her by the fore-legs and I by the hind ones,
She'll not be hurt." Clare's voice quieted the sheep
And Vasquez' the indignant horse. They came down at length
To dark water under gigantic trees.

V

She helped Fern drink before herself drooped eagerly
Her breast against the brown stones and kissed the cold stream.
She brought from the bundle what food remained, and shared it
With Vasquez and the munching sheep. There were three apples
From Fogler's trees, and a little jar of honey

And crumbled comb from his hives, and Clare drew a net
Of water-cress from the autumn-hushed water to freshen
The old bread and the broken biscuits. She was gay with delight
At having something to give. They sat on the bank, where century
After century of dropping redwood needles had made the earth, as if the
 dark trees were older
Than their own mother.

      Clare answered Vasquez' question and said she
 had come from the coast mountains in the south;
She'd left her home a long time ago; and Fogler, the farmer by the Big Sur,
 had given her this food
Because he was sorry his dogs had worried the sheep. But yesterday she was
 passing Point Sur, and Fern
Had fallen into a well by the house. She said nothing of the other ewe, that
 had died; and Vasquez
Seemed to clench himself tight: "What were you doing at Point Sur, it's
 not on the road?" "The sheep were hungry,
And I wandered off the road in the dark. It was wicked of me to walk in the
 pasture, but a young cowboy
Helped me on the right way. We looked into the house." He said, "Let no
 one go back there, let its mice have it.
God lived there once and tried to make peace with the people; no peace
 was made." She stared in silence, and Vasquez:
"After that time I bawled for death, like a calf for the cow. There were no
 visions. My brothers watched me,
And held me under the hammers of food and sleep."
He ceased; then Clare in a troubled silence
Thought he was lying, for she thought certainly that no one
Ever had desired death. But, for he looked unhappy
And said nothing, she said Will Brighton had told her

Something about a man who claimed to be God,
"Whose daughter," she said, "died." Vasquez stood up
And said trembling, "In the ruin of San Antonio church
I saw an owl as big as one of your sheep
Sleeping above the little gilt Virgin above the altar.
That was no vision. I want to hear nothing
Of what there was at Point Sur." He went to his horse
That stood drooping against the stream-bank, and rode
The steep soft slope between the broad butts of trees.
But, leaving the undisturbed air of the wood
For the rough wind of the roadway, he stopped and went back.
"It will rain," he said. "You ought to think of yourself.
The wind is digging water since we came down.
My father's place is too far. There's an old empty cabin
A short ways on." She had been crouching again
Over the stream to drink, and rose with wet lips
But answered nothing. Vasquez felt inwardly dizzy
For no reason he knew, as if a gray bird
Turned in his breast and flirted half open wings
Like a wild pigeon bathing. He said "You'll see it
Above the creek on the right hand of the road
Only a little way north." He turned and rode back,
Hearing her call "Good-bye," into the wind on the road.

This man was that Onorio Vasquez
Who used to live on Palo Corona mountain
With his father and his six brothers, but now they lived
Up Mill Creek Canyon beside the abandoned lime-kiln
On land that was not their own. For yearly on this coast
Taxes increase, land grows harder to hold,
Poor people must move their places. Onorio had wealth
Of visions, but those are not coinable. A power in his mind

Was more than equal to the life he was born to,
But fear, or narrowing fortune, had kept it shut
From a larger life; the power wasted itself
In making purposeless visions, himself perceived them
To have no meaning relative to any known thing: but always
They made him different from his brothers; they gave him
A kind of freedom; they were the jewels and value of his life.
So that when once, at a critical time, they failed
And were not seen for a year, he'd hungered to die.
That was nine years ago; his mind was now quieter,
But still it found all its value in visions.
Between them, he hired out his hands to the coast farms,
Or delved the garden at home.

Clare Walker, when he was gone, forgot him at once.
She drank a third draught, then she dropped off her shoes
And washed the dust from her feet. Poor Fern was now hobbling
Among the others, and they'd found vines to feed on
At the near edge of the wood, so that Clare felt
Her shepherdess mind at peace, to throw off
The coat and the rags and bathe in the slender stream,
Flattening herself to find the finger's depth water.
The water and the air were cold now, she rubbed her body
Hastily dry with the bleached rags of her dress
And huddled the cloak about her, but hung the other
Over a branch to dry. Sadly she studied
The broken shoes and found them useless at last,
And flung them into the bushes. An hour later
She resumed the dress, she called her flock to go on
Northward. "Come Fern, come Frannie. Oh Saul.
Leader and Hornie and Tiny, we have to go on."

VI

The sky had blackened and the wind raised a dust
When they came up to the road from the closed quiet of the wood,
The sun was behind the hill but not down yet. Clare passed the
    lichen-plated abandoned cabin that Vasquez
Had wished her to use, because there was not a blade of pasture about it,
    nothing but the shafted jealousy
And foodless possession of the great redwoods. She saw the gray bed of the
    Little Sur like a dry bone
Through its winter willows, and on the left in the sudden
Sea-opening V of the canyon the sun streaming through a cloud, the lank
    striped ocean, and an arched film
Of sand blown from a dune at the stream's foot. The road ahead went over
    a bridge and up the bare hill
In lightning zigzags; a small black bead came down the lightning, flashing at
    the turns in the strained light,
A motor-car driven fast, Clare urged her flock into the ditch by the road,
    but the car turned
This side the bridge and glided down a steep driveway.
When Clare came and looked down she saw the farmhouse
Beside the creek, and a hundred bee-hives and a leafless orchard,
Crossed by the wheeling swords of the sun.
A man with a gray mustache covering his mouth
Stood by the road, Clare felt him stare at the sheep
And stare at her bare feet, though his eyes were hidden
In the dark of his face in the shadow of the turbid light.
She smiled and murmured "Good evening." He giggled to himself
Like a half-witted person and stared at her feet.
She passed, in the swirls of light and dust, the old man
Followed and called "Hey: Missy: where will you sleep?"
"Why, somewhere up there," she answered. He giggled, "Eh, Eh!

If I were you. Ho," he said joyfully,
"If I were in your *shoes*, I'd look for a roof.
It's big and bare, Serra Hill. You from the south?"
"I've been in the rain before," she answered. She laid
Her hand on a matted fleece. "I've got to find them
Some feeding-place, they're hungry, they've been in the hungry
Redwoods." He stopped and peered and giggled: "One's lame.
But," he said chuckling, "you could go on all night
And never muddy your shoes. Ho, ho! Listen, Missy.
You ain't a Mexican, I guess you've had bad luck.
I'll fix you up in the hay-shed and you'll sleep dry,
These fellows can feed all night." "The owner," she said,
"Wouldn't let me. They'd spoil the hay." "The owner.
Bless you, the poor old man's too busy to notice.
Paying his debts. That was his sharp son
Drove in just now. They hated the old man
But now they come like turkey-buzzards to watch him die."
"Oh! Is he dying?" "Why, fairly comfortable.
As well as you can expect." "I think, we'll go on,"
She murmured faintly. "Just as you like, Missy.
But nobody cares whether you spoil the hay.
There's plenty more in the barn, and all the stock
'll soon be cleared out. I don't work for his boys.
Ho, it's begun already." Some drops were flying, and the sun
Drowned in a cloud, or had set, suddenly the light was twilight. The old
    man waved his hand in the wind
Over the hives and the orchard. "This place," he giggled, "meant the world
    to old Warfield: Hey, watch them sell.
It means a shiny new car to each of the boys." He shot up the collar of his
    coat, and the huddling sheep
Tucked in their rumps; the rain on a burst of wind, small drops but many.
    The sheep looked up at their mistress,

Who said, feeling the drift like needles on her cheek, and cold drops
Run down by her shoulder, "If nobody minds, you think, about our lying
    in the hay." "Hell no, come in.
Only you'll have to be out in the gray to-morrow, before the sharp sons get
    up." He led her about
By the bridge, through the gapped fence, not to be seen from the house.
The hay-shed was well roofed, and walled southward
Against the usual drive of the rain. Clare saw in the twilight
Wealth of fodder and litter, and was glad, and the sheep
Entered and fed.

               After an hour the old man
Returned, with a smell of fried grease in the gray darkness.
Clare rose to meet him, she thought he was bringing food,
But the odor was but a relic of his own supper.
"It's raining," he said; as if she could fail to hear
The hissing drift on the roof; "you'd be cosy now
On Serra Hill." He paused and seemed deeply thoughtful,
And said, "But still you could walk all night and never
Get your shoes wet. Ho, ho! You're a fine girl,
How do you come to be on the road? Eh? Trouble?"
"I'm going north. You're kind," she said, "people are kind."
"Why yes, I'm a kind man. Well, now, sleep cosy."
He reached into the dark and touched her, she stood
Quietly and felt his hand. A dog was heard barking
Through the hiss of rain. He said "There's that damn' dog.
I tied him up after I let you in,
Now he'll be yelling all night." The old man stumped off
Into the rain, then Clare went back to her sheep
And burrowed in the hay amongst them.

                              The old man returned
A second time; Clare was asleep and she felt
The sheep lifting their heads to stare at his lantern.
"Oh! What do you want?" "Company, company," he muttered.
"They've got an old hatchet-faced nurse in the house ...
But he's been dying for a month, he makes me nervous.
The boys don't mind, but *I'm* nervous." He kicked
One of the sheep to make it rise and make room,
Clare murmured sadly "Don't hurt them." He sat in the hay
In heavy silence, holding the lantern on knee
As if it were a fretful baby. The fulvous glimmer
Through one of his hands showed the flesh red, and seemed
To etch the bones in it, the gnarled shafts of the fingers
And scaly lumps in the skin. Clare heard the chained dog howling,
And the rain had ceased. She reached in pitying tenderness
And touched the old man's illuminated hand and said
"How hard you have worked." "Akh," he groaned, "so has he.
And gets ..." He moved his hand to let the warm light
Lie on her face, so that her face and his own were planets
To the lantern sun; hers smooth except the wind-blistered lips,
    pure-featured, pitying, with large dark eyes
The little sparkles of the reflected lantern had room to swim in; his bristly
    and wrinkled, and the eyes
Like sparks in a bush; the sheep uneasily below the faces moved formless,
    only Saul's watchful head
With the curled horns in the halo of light. The faint and farther rays of
    that sun touched falling spheres
Of water from the eaves at the open side of the shed, or lost themselves at
    the other in cobwebbed corners
And the dust of space. In the darkness beyond all stars the little river made
    a noise. The old man muttered,
"I heard him choking night before last and still he goes on.

It's a hell of a long ways to nothing....
You know the best thing to do? Tip this in the straw,"
He tilted the lantern a little, "end in a minute,
In a blaze and yell." She said "No! no!" and he felt
The hay trembling beside him. The unconscious motion of her fear
Was not inward but toward the sheep. He observed
Nothing of that, but giggled to himself to feel
The hay trembling beside him. He dipped his hand
And caught her bare foot; clutching it with his fingers
He scratched the sole with his thumb, but Clare sat quiet
In pale terror of tipping the lantern. The old man
Groaned and stood up. "You wouldn't sit like a stone
If I were twenty years younger. Oh, damn you," he said,
"You think we get old? I'm the same fresh flame of youth still,
Stuck in an old wrinkled filthy rawhide
That soon'll rot and lie choking." She stammered "Ah, no, no,
You oughtn't to think so. You're well and strong. Or maybe
At last it'll come suddenly or while you sleep,
Never a pain." He swung up the lantern
Before his hairy and age-deformed face. "Look at me. Pfah!
And still it's April inside." He turned to go out,
Clare whispered, "Oh! Wait." She stood wringing her hands,
Warm light and darkness in waves flushing and veiling
Her perplexed face, the lantern in the old man's fist
Swinging beyond his body. "Oh, how can I tell?"
She said trembling. "You see: I'll never come back:
If anything I could do would give you some pleasure;
And you wouldn't be sorry after I'm gone." He turned,
Stamping his feet. "Heh?" He held up the lantern
And stared at her face and giggled. She heard the sheep
Nestling behind her and saw the old man's mouth
Open to speak, a black hole under the grizzled thatch,

And close again on round silence. "I'd like to make you
Happier," she faltered. "Heh?" He seemed to be trembling
Even more than Clare had trembled; he said at length,
"Was you in earnest?" "I had a great trouble,
So that now nothing seems hard...
That a shell broke and truly I love all people.
I'll... it's a little thing... my time is short."
He stood giggling and fidgeting. "Heh, heh! You be good.
I've got to get my sleep. I was just making the rounds.
He makes me nervous, that old man. It's his stomach
Won't hold nothing. You wouldn't play tricks to-night
And the old man puking his last? Now, you lie down.
Sleep cosy," he said. The lantern went slowly winking away,
And she was left among the warm sheep, and thoughts
Of death, and to hear the stream; and again the wind
Raved in the dark.

        She dreamed that a two-legged whiff of flame
Rose up from the house gable-peak crying, "Oh! Oh!"
And doubled in the middle and fled away on the wind
Like music above the bee-hives.

        At dawn a fresh burst of rain
Delayed her, and two of the sheep were coughing. She thought that no
   unfriendly person would come in the rain,
And hoped the old man might think to bring her some food, she was very
   hungry. The house-dog that all night long
Had yapped his chain's length, suddenly ran into the shed, then Clare
   leaped up in fear for the sheep, but this
Was a friendly dog, loving to fondle and be fondled, he shook his sides like
   a mill-wheel and remained amongst them.
The rain paused and returned, the sheep fed so contentedly

Clare let them rest all morning in the happy shelter, she dulled her own
    hunger with sleep. About noon
She lifted her long staff from the hay and stood up. "Come Saul, come
    little Hornie,
Fay, Fern and Frannie and Leader, we have to go on.
Tiny, Tiny, get up. Butt and Ben, come on":
These were the two old wethers: and she bade the dog
"Good-bye, good-bye." He followed however; but at length
Turned back from the crooked road up the open hill
When cold rain fell. Clare was glad of that, yet she wished
She'd had something to give him.

VII

                    She gained the blasty hill-top,
The unhappy sheep huddling against her thighs,
And so went northward barefoot in the gray rain,
Abstractedly, like a sleepwalker on the ridge
Of his inner necessity, or like
Some random immortal wish of the solitary hills.
If you had seen her you'd have thought that she always
Walked north in the rain on the ridge with the sheep about her.
Yet sometimes in the need of a little pleasure
To star the gray, she'd stop in the road and kiss
One of the wet foreheads: but then run quickly
A few steps on, as if loitering were dangerous,
You'd have pitied her to see her.

                    Over Mescal Creek
High on the hill, a brook in a rocky gulch, with no canyon,
Light-headed hunger and cold and the loneliness unlocked

Her troubled mind, she talked and sang as she went. "I can't eat the cold
    cress, but if there were acorns,
Bitter acorns. Ai chinita que si,
Ai que tu dami tu amor. Why did you
Have to go dry at the pinch, Frannie? Poor thing, no matter. Que venga
    con migo chinita
A donde vivo yo.
I gave them all my bread the poor shipwrecked people and they wanted
    more." She trembled and said "They're cruel,
But they were hungry. They'll never catch us I think.
Oh hurry, hurry." With songs learned from the shepherd she came to the
    fall of the road into Mill Creek Canyon.
Two of the sheep were sick and coughing, and Clare looked down. Flying
    bodies of fog, an unending fleet
Of formless gray ships in a file fled down the great canyon
Tearing their keels over the redwoods; Clare watched them and sang, "Oh
    golondrina, Oh darting swallow,"
And heard the ocean like the blood in her ears. The west-covered sun
    stared a wan light up-canyon
Against the cataract of little clouds.

                        The two coughing sheep
Brought her to a stand; then she opened their mouths and found
Their throats full of barbed seeds from the bad hay
Greedily eaten; and the gums about their teeth
Were quilled with the wicked spikes; which drawn, thin blood
Dripped from the jaw. The folds of the throat her fingers
Could not reach nor relieve; thereafter, when they coughed,
Clare shook with pain. Her pity poisoned her strength.

                                        Unhappy
    shepherdess,

Numbed feet and hands and the face
Turbid with fever:
You love, and that is no unhappy fate,
Not one person but all, does it warm your winter?
Walking with numbed and cut feet
Along the last ridge of migration
On the last coast above the not-to-be-colonized
Ocean, across the streams of the people
Drawing a faint pilgrimage
As if you were drawing a line at the end of the world
Under the columns of ancestral figures:
So many generations in Asia,
So many in Europe, so many in America:
To sum the whole. Poor Clare Walker, she already
Imagines what sum she will cast in April.

                             She came by the farmhouse
At Mill Creek, then she wavered in the road and went to the door,
Leaving her sheep in the road; the day was draining
Toward twilight. Clare began to go around the house,
Then stopped and returned and knocked faintly at the door.
No answer; but when she was turning back to the road
The door was opened, by a pale slight young man
With no more chin than a bird, and Mongol-slanted
Eyes; he peered out, saying "What do you want?" Clare stood
Wringing the rain from her fingers. "Oh, Oh," she stammered,
"I don't know what. I have some sheep with me.
I don't know where we can stay." He stood in the door
And looked afraid. The sheep came stringing down
Through the gate Clare had left open. A gray-eyed man
With a white beard pushed by the boy and said
"What does she want? What, are you hungry? Take out your beasts,

We can't have sheep in the yard." Clare ran to the gate,
"Come Leader, come Saul." The old man returned in-doors
Saying, "Wait outside, I'll get you some bread." Clare waited
Leaning against the gate, it seemed a long while;
The old man came back with changed eyes and changed voice:
"We can't do anything for you. There isn't any bread.
Move on from here." She said through her chattering teeth,
"Come Saul, come Leader, come Frannie. We have to go on.
Poor Fern, come on." They drifted across the Mill Creek bridge
And up the road in the twilight. "The ground-squirrels," she said, "hide in
    their holes
All winter long, and the birds have perches but we have no place." They
    tried to huddle in the heart of a bush
Under a redwood, Clare crouched with the sheep about her, her thighs
    against her belly, her face on her knees,
Not sleeping, but in a twilight consciousness, while the night darkened.

                                                                    In
    an hour she thought she must move or die.
"Ah little Hornie," she said, feeling with shrivelled fingers the sprouts of the
    horns in the small arched forehead,
"Come Fern: are you there Leader? Come Saul, come Nosie . . . Ah no, I
    was dreaming. Oh dear," she whispered, "we're very
Miserable now." She crept out of the bush and the sheep followed; she
    couldn't count them, she heard them
Plunge in the bush and heard them coughing behind her. They came on
    the road
In the gray dark; there, though she'd meant to go north
She went back toward the farmhouse. Crossing the bridge
She smelled oak-smoke and thought of warmth. Grown reckless
Clare entered the farmhouse yard with her fleeced following,
But not daring enough to summon the door

Peered in a window. What she saw within
Mixed with her fever seemed fantastic and dreadful. It was nothing strange:
The weak-faced youth, the bearded old man, and two old women
Idle around a lamp on a table. They sat on their chairs in the warmth and
    streaming light and nothing
Moved their faces. But Clare felt dizzy at heart, she thought they were
    waiting for death: how could they sit
And not run and not cry? Perhaps they were dead already? Then, the old
    man's head
Turned, and the youth's fingers drummed on his chair. One of the blank
    old women was sewing and the other
Frowned and breathed. She lifted and spoke to white-beard, then the first
    old woman
Flashed eyes like rusty knives and sheathed them again
And sewed the cloth; they grew terribly quiet;
Only the white beard quivered. The young man stood up
And moved his mouth for a good while but no one
Of those in the room regarded him. He sighed and saw
Clare's face at the window. She leaped backward; the lamplight
Had fed her eyes with blindness toward the gray night,
She ran in a panic about the barren garden,
Unable to find the gate; the sheep catching her fear
Huddled and plunged, pricking the empty wet earth with numberless
    hoof-prints. But no one came out pursuing them,
The doors were not opened, the house was quiet. Clare found the gate
And stood by it, whispering "Dear Tiny. Ah, Fern, that's you. Come Saul,"
    she fumbled each head as it passed the gate-post,
To count the flock.

                    But all had not passed, a man on a horse
Came plodding the puddled road. Clare thought the world
Was all friendly except in that house, and she ran

To the road's crown. "Oh, Oh," she called; and Onorio
Vasquez answered, "I rode early in the morning
To find you and couldn't find you. I've been north and south.
I thought I could find the track of the sheep." She answered
Through chattering teeth, "I thought I could stand the rain.
I'm sick and the sheep are sick." He said gravely
"There's hardly a man on the coast wouldn't have helped you
Except in that house. There, I think they *need* help.
Well, come and we'll live the night." "How far?" she sighed
Faintly, and he said "Our place is away up-canyon,
You'll find it stiff travelling by day-light even.
To-night's a camp."

              He led her to the bridge, and there
Found dry sticks up the bank, leavings of an old flood, under the spring of
    the timbers,
And made a fire against the creekside under the road for a roof. He
    stripped her of the dripping cloak
And clothed her in his, the oil-skin had kept it dry, and spread her the
    blanket from under his saddle to lie on.
The bridge with the tarred road-bed on it was a roof
Over their heads; the sheep, when Clare commanded them, lay down like
    dogs by the fire. The horse was tethered
To a clump of willow in the night outside.

                    When her feet and her hands
    began to be warm he offered her food,
She ate three ravenous mouthfuls and ran from the fire and vomited. He
    heard her gasping in the night thicket
And a new rain. He went after while and dragged her
Back to the frugal fire and shelter of the bridge.

VIII

She lay and looked up at the great black timbers, the flapping fire-shadows,
And draggled cobwebs heavy with dirt and water;
While Vasquez watched the artery in the lit edge
Of her lean throat jiggle with its jet of blood
Like a slack harp-string plucked: a toneless trembling:
It made him grieve.

          After a time she exclaimed
"My sheep. My sheep. Count them." "What," he said, "they all
Are here beside you." "I never dreamed," she answered,
"That any were lost, Oh no! But my sight swam
When I looked at them in the bad light." He looked
And said "Are there not . . . ten?" "No, nine," she answered.
"Nosie has died. Count them and tell me the truth."
He stood, bowing down his head under the timbers,
And counted seven, then hastily the first two
A second time, and said "Nine." "I'm glad of that,"
She sighed, and was quiet, but her quill fingers working
The border of the saddle-blanket. He hoped she would soon
Sleep.

          The horse tethered outside the firelight
Snorted, and the sheep lifted their heads, a spot of white
Came down the dark slope. Vasquez laid his brown palm
Over Clare's wrists, "Lie still and rest. The old fellow from the house is
    coming.
Sleep if you can, I'll talk to him." "Is there a dog?" she whispered
    trembling. "No, no, the old man is alone."
Who peered under the heavy stringer of the bridge, his beard shone in the
    firelight. "Here," he shouted, "Hey!

Burn the road, would you? You want to make people stay home

And suck the sour bones in their own houses? Come out of that hole." But
　　Vasquez: "Now, easy, old neighbor. She wanted

Fire and a roof, she's found what you wouldn't give." "By God, and a man
　　to sleep with," he said, "that's lucky,

But the bridge, the bridge." "Don't trouble, I'm watching the fire. Fire's
　　tame, this weather." The old man stood twitching and peering,

And heard the sheep coughing in their cave

Under the road. He squinted toward Clare, and muttered at length meekly,
　　"Let me stay a few minutes.

To sit by the little road-fire of freedom. My wife and my sister have hated
　　each other for thirty years,

And I between them. It makes the air of the house. I sometimes think I can
　　see it boil up like smoke

When I look back at the house from the hill above." Vasquez said gravely

"I have often watched that." He answered "You haven't lived in it. They sit
　　in the house and feed on their own poison

And live forever. I am now too feeble with age to escape." Clare Walker
　　lifted her head, and faintly:

"Oh stay," she said, "I wish I could gather all that are unhappy

Before I die. But why do they hate each other?"

"Their nature," he answered, "old women." She sighed and lay down.

"I shan't grow old." "Young fellow," the old man said wearily

To Vasquez, "they all make that promise, they never keep it.

Life glides by and the bright loving creatures

Eat us in the evening. I'd have given this girl bread

And meat, but my hawks were watching me." He'd found a stone

On the edge of the creek, the other side of the fire, and squatted there, his
　　two fists

Closing his eyes, the beard shimmering between the bent wrists. His voice
　　being silent they heard the fire

Burst the tough bark of a wet branch; the wind turned north, then a gust of
  hail spattered in the willows
And checked at once, the air became suddenly cold. The old man lifted his
  face: "Ah can't you talk?
I thought you'd be gay or I'd not have stayed here, you too've grown old? I
  wish that a Power went through the world
And killed people at thirty when the ashes crust them. You, cowboy, die,
  your joints will begin to crackle,
You've had the best. Young bank-clerk you've had the best, grow fat and
  sorry and more dollars? Here, farmer, die,
You've spent the money: will bleed the mortgage
Fifty years more? You cunning pussy of the world, you've had the fun and
  the kissing, skip the diseases.
Oh you, you're an honest wife and you've made a baby: why should you
  watch him
Grow up and spoil, and dull like cut lead? I see, my dear, you'll never be
  filled till you grow poisonous
With eyes like rusty knives under the gray eye-brows. God bless you, die."
  He had risen from the stone, and trampled,
Each condemnation, some rosy coal fallen out at the fire's edge
Under his foot as if it had been a life. "Sharp at thirty," he said. Clare
  vaguely moaned
And turned her face to the outer darkness, then Vasquez
Misunderstanding her pain, thinking it stemmed
From the old man's folly: "Don't mind him, he's not in earnest.
These nothing-wishers of life are never in earnest;
Make mouths to scare you: if they meant it they'd do it
And not be alive to make mouths." She made no answer,
But lay and listened to her own rustling pulse-beat,
Her knees drawn up to her breast. White-beard knelt down and mended
  the fire,

And brushed his knees. "There's another law that I'd make: to burn the
    houses. Turn out the people on the roads,
And neither homes nor old women we'd be well off. All young, all gay, all
    moving, free larks and foolery
By gipsy fires." His voice fell sad: "It's bitter to be a reformer: with two
    commandments
I'd polish the world a-shining, make the sun ashamed."
Clare Walker stood up, then suddenly sought the dark night
To hide herself in the bushes; her bowels were loosened
With cold and fever. Vasquez half rose to follow her,
And he understood, and stayed by the fire. Then white-beard
Winking and nodding whispered: "Is she a good piece?
Hey, is she sick? I have to protect my son.
Where in hell did she get the sheep?" Vasquez said fiercely,
"You'd better get home, your wife'll be watching for you.
This girl is sick and half starved, I was unwilling
To let her die in the road." The old man stood up
As pricked with a pin at the thought of home. "What? We're free men,"
He said, lifting his feet in an anxious dance
About the low fire: "but it's devilish hard
To be the earthly jewel of two jealous women."
"Look," Vasquez said, "it seems to me that your house is afire.
I see rolls of tall smoke . . ." "By God," he answered,
"I wish it were," he trotted up to the road
While a new drift of hail hissed in the willows,
Softening to rain.

            When he was gone, Vasquez
Repaired the fire, and called "Clare! Come in to shelter.
Clare, come! The rain is dangerous for you. The old fool's gone home."
He stumbled in the dark along the strand of the creek
Calling "Clare, Clare!" then looking backward he saw

The huddle of firelit fleeces moving and rising,
And said "The sheep are scattering away to find you.
You ought to call them." She came then, and stood by the fire.
He heard the bleating cease, and looked back to see her
Quieting her friends, wringing the rain from her hair,
The fire had leaped up to a blaze. Vasquez returned
Under the bridge, then Clare with her lips flushed
And eyes brilliant with fever: "That poor old man, has he gone?
I'm sorry if he's gone.
My father was old, but after he'd plowed the hill-top I've seen him ride
The furrows at a dead run, sowing the grain with both hands, while he
    controlled the colt with his knees.
The time it fell at the furrow's end
In the fat clay, he was up first and laughing. He was kind and cruel." "Your
    father?" he said. She answered
"I can't remember my mother, she died to bear me, as I . . . We kept her
    picture, she looked like me,
And often my father said I was like her. — Oh what's become of the poor
    old man, has he gone home?
Here he was happy." "Yes, had to go home," he answered. "But you must
    sleep. I'll leave you alone if you like,
You promise to stay by the fire and sleep." "Oh I couldn't, truly. My mind's
    throwing all its wrecks on the shore
And I can't sleep. That was a shipwreck that drove us wandering. I
    remember all things. Your name's Onorio
Vasquez: I wish you had been my brother." He smiled and touched her
    cold hand. "For then," she said, "we could talk
Old troubles asleep: I haven't thought, thought,
For a long while, to-night I can't stop my thoughts. But we all must die?"
    "Spread out your hands to the fire,
Warm yourself, Clare." "No, no," she answered, her teeth chattering, "I'm
    hot.

My throat aches, yet you see I don't cough, it was Frannie coughing. — It
    was almost as if I killed my father,
To swear to the lies I told after he was killed, all to save Charlie. Do you
    think he'd care, after . . .
He was surely dead? You don't believe we have spirits? Nobody believes we
    have spirits." He began to answer,
And changed his words for caution. "Clare: all you are saying
Is hidden from me. It's like the visions I have,
That go from unknown to unknown." He said proudly,
"I've watched, the whole night of a full moon, an army of centaurs
Come out of the ocean, plunging on Sovranes reef
In wide splendors of silver water,
And swim with their broad hooves between the reef and the shore and go
    up
Over the mountain — I never knew why.
What you are saying is like that." "Oh, I'll tell you . . ." "To-morrow,"
He pleaded, remembering she'd eaten nothing and seeing
The pulse like a plucked harp-string jiggle in her throat;
He felt like a pain of his own the frail reserves of her body
Burn unreplenished. "Oh, but I'll tell you: so then
You'll know me, as if we'd been born in the same house,
You'll tell me not to be afraid: maybe I'll sleep
At the turn of night. Onorio — that's really your name?
How stately a name you have — lie down beside me.
I am now so changed: everyone's lovely in my eyes
Whether he's brown or white or that poor old man:
In those days nobody but Charlie Maurice
Seemed very dear, as if I'd been blind to all the others.
He lived on the next hill, two miles across a deep valley, and then it was
    five to the next neighbor
At Vicente Springs; people are so few there. We lived a long way south,
    where the hills fall straight to the sea,

And higher than these. He lived with his people. We used to meet near a
    madrone-tree, Charlie would kiss me
And put his hands on my breasts under my clothes. It was quite long before
    we learned the sweet way
That brings much joy to most living creatures, but brought us misery at
    last.

IX

        My father," she said,
"Had lived there for thirty years, but after he sold his cattle
And pastured sheep, to make more money, the neighbors
Were never our friends. Oh, they all feared my father;
Sometimes they threatened our shepherd, a Spanish man
Who looked like you, but was always laughing. He'd laugh
And say 'Guarda a Walker!' so then they'd leave him.
But we lived lonely.

                One morning of great white clouds gliding from
    the sea
When I was with Charlie in the hollow near the madrones, I felt a pleasure
    like a sweet fire: for all
My joy before had been in *his* pleasure: but this was my own, it frightened
    me." She stopped speaking, for Vasquez
Stood up and left her; he went and sat by the fire. Then Clare:
"Why do you leave me, Onorio? Are you angry now?"
"I am afraid," he answered, "of this love.
My visions are the life of my life: if I let the pitcher
Break on the rock and the sun kill the stars,
Life would be emptier than death." Her mind went its own way,
Not understanding so strange a fear: "The clouds were as bright as stars
    and I could feel them," she said,

"Through the shut lids of my eyes while the sweet fire
Poured through my body: I knew that some dreadful pain would pay for
    such joy. I never slept after that
But dreamed of a laughing child and wakened with running tears. After I
    had trembled for days and nights
I asked Tia Livia — that was our shepherd's cousin, she helped me keep
    house — what sign tells women
When they have conceived: she told me the moon then ceases
To rule our blood. I counted the days then,
Not dreaming that Tia Livia would spy and talk.
Was that not strange? I think that she told the shepherd too,
And the shepherd had warned my lover: for Charlie failed
Our meeting time, but my father was there with a gray face.
In silence, he didn't accuse me, we went home together.

I met my lover in another place. 'Oh Charlie,
Why do you wear a revolver?' He said the mountain
Was full of rattlers, 'We've killed twenty in a week.
There never have been so many, step carefully sweetheart.'
Sweetheart he called me: you're listening Onorio?
'Step carefully by the loose stones.' We were too frightened that day
To play together the lovely way we had learned.

The next time that I saw him, he and my father
Met on a bare hill-top against a gray cloud.
I saw him turn back, but then I saw that he was ashamed
To seem afraid of a man on the ridge of earth,
With the hills and the ocean under his feet: and my father called him. —
    What was that moan?" She stopped, and Vasquez
Heard it far off, and heard the sap of a stick whistle in the fire. "Nothing,"
    he said, "low thunder

Far out the ocean, or the surf in the creek-mouth." "—I was running up
    the steep slope to reach them, the breath in my heart
Like saw-grass cut me, I had no power to cry out, the stones and the
    broken stubble flaked under my feet
So that I seemed running in one place, unable to go up. It was not because
    he hated my father,
But he was so frightened. They stood as if they were talking, a noise of
    smoke
Blew from between them, my father turned then and walked
Slowly along the cloud and sat on the hill-top
As if he were tired.
I said after a time, without thinking,
'Go home, Charlie. I'll say that he killed himself.
And give me the revolver, I'll say it was his.'
So Charlie did.
But when the men came up from Salinas I told my lie
So badly that they believed I was the murderer.
I smelled the jail a long while. I saw the day moon
Down the long street the morning I was taken to court,
As weary-looking and stained as if it were something of mine.
I remembered then, that since I came there my blood
Had never been moved when the moon filled: what Livia'd told me.
So then I told them my father took his own life
Because the sheep had a sickness and I was pregnant.
The shepherd and Livia swore that they saw him do it.
I'd have been let home:
But the fever I'd caught gathered to a bursting pain,
I had to be carried from the courthouse to the hospital
And for a time knew nothing.
When I began to see with my eyes again
The doctor said: 'The influenza that takes
Many lives has saved yours, you'll not have a child.

Listen,' he said, 'my girl if you're wise.
Your miscarriage is your luck. Your pelvis — the bones down there
Are so deformed that it's not possible for you
To bear a living baby: no life can pass there:
And yours would be lost. You'd better remember,
And try not to be reckless.' I remember so well, Onorio.
I have good reason to remember. You never could guess
What a good reason.

My little king was dead
And I was too weak to care. I have a new king.

When I got home," she said patiently,
"Everybody believed that I was a murderer;
And Charlie was gone. They left me so much alone
That often I myself believed it. I'd lead the sheep to that hill,
There were fifty left out of three hundred,
And pray for pardon."

Sleep and her fever confused her brain,
One heard phrases in the running babble, across a new burst of hail.
    "Forgive me, father, for I didn't
Know what I was doing." And, "Why have you forsaken me, father?" Her
    mind was living again the bare south hill-top
And the bitter penitence among the sheep. "The two men that I loved and
    the baby that I never saw,
All taken away."

Then Vasquez was calling her name to break the black
    memories; she turned on her side, the flame-light
Leaped, and he saw her face puckering with puzzled wonder. "Not all
    alone? But how can that be?"

She sighed and said "Oh Leader, don't stray for awhile. Dear Saul: can you keep them here on the hill around me
Without my watching? No one else helps me. I'll lie down here on the little grass in the windy sun
And think whether I can live. I have *you*, dear stragglers. Thoughts come and go back as lightly as deer on the hill,
But as hard to catch. . . . Not *all* alone. Oh. Not alone at *all*.
Indeed it is even stranger than I thought."

                        She laughed and sat up. "Oh sweet warm sun. . . .
Are you there, Onorio? But where's the poor old man
Who seemed to be so unhappy? I wish he hadn't gone home,
For now I remember what I ought to tell him. I'm sadly changed
Since that trouble and sickness, and though I'm happy
I hardly ever remember in the nick o' time
What ought to be said. You must tell him
That all our pain comes from restraint of love."
The hail had suddenly hushed, and all her words
Were clear but hurried. "I learned it easily, Onorio,
And never have thought about it again till now. The only wonder's
Not to've known always. The beetle beside my hand in the grass and the little brown bird tilted on a stone,
The short sad grass, burnt on the gable of the world with near sun and all winds: there was nothing there that I didn't
Love with my heart, yes the hill though drunk with dear blood: I looked far over the valley at the patch of oaks
At the head of a field, where Charlie's people had lived (they had moved away) and loved them, although they'd been
Always unfriendly I never thought of it." Then Vasquez, for the first time forgetting the person a moment

To regard the idea: "You were cut off from the natural objects of love, you
     turned toward others." "Ah," she answered
Eagerly, "I'd always been turned to all others,
And tired my poor strength confining the joy to few. But now I'd no more
     reason to confine it, I'd nothing
Left to lose nor keep back.—Has the poor old man gone?
He seemed to be truly unhappy.
Wasn't he afraid we'd burn the bridge: we ought surely
To have drowned our fire. I was sick, or I'd have done … anything.
But old men are so strange, to want and not want,
And then be angry."

                    "He has gone," he answered.
"Now, Clare, if you could eat something, then sleep,
To fill the cup for to-morrow."
"I have to tell you the rest.—Why did he go?
Was he angry at me?—Oh, I feel better, Onorio,
But never more open-eyed.

                         There was one of those great owly hawks
That soar for hours, turning and turning below me along the bottom of the
     slope: I so loved it
I thought if it were hungry I'd give it my hand for meat.

                                        Then winter
came.
Then about Christmas time (because I'd counted the months and
     remembered Christmas) storm followed storm
Like frightened horses tethered to a tree, around and around. Three men
     came in the door without knocking,
Wherever they moved, water and black oil ran down. There'd been a
     shipwreck. I gave them the house, then one of them

Found the axe and began chopping firewood, another went back across wild
    rain to the fall of the hill
And shouted. He was so big, like a barrel walking, I ran in his shelter
And saw the great, black, masted thing almost on shore, lying on its side in
    the shadow of the hill,
And the flying steam of a fire they'd built on the beach. All that morning
    the people came up like ants,
Poor souls they were all so tired and cold, some hurt and some crying. I'd
    only," she said, "a few handfuls of flour
Left in the house." She trembled and lay down. "I can't remember any
    more."

            Vasquez made up the fire,
And went and drew up the blanket over Clare's shoulder.
He found her shuddering. "Now sleep. Now rest." She answered:
"They killed a sheep. They were hungry.
I'd grown to love so much the flock that was left.
Our shepherd, I think, had taken them away mostly
While I was kept in Salinas.
I heard her crying when they threw her down, she thought I could save her.
Her soft white throat.

That night I crept out in the thin rain at moonrise
And led them so far away, all that were left,
The house and the barn might hold a hundred hungry mouths
To hunt us all night and day and could never find us.
We hid in oak-woods. There was nothing to eat,
And never any dry place. We walked in the gray rain in the flowing gorges
    of canyons that no one
But the hawks have seen, and climbed wet stone and saw the storms racing
    below us, but still the thin rain

Sifted through the air as if it fell from the stars. I was then much stronger
Than ever since then.

A man caught me at last, when I was too weak to
run, and conquered my fear.
He was kind, he promised me not to hurt the poor flock,
But the half of them had been lost, I never could remember how. He lived
alone; I was sick in his cabin
For many days, dreaming that a monkey nursed me: he looked so funny,
he'd a frill of red hair
All around his face.

When I grew better, he wanted to do like Charlie. I
knew what the doctor had said,
But I was ashamed to speak of death: I was often ashamed in those days:
he'd been so kind. Yet terror
Would come and cover my head like a cold wave.
I watched the moon, but at the full moon my fear
Flowed quietly away in the night.

The spring and summer were full of pleasure and happiness.
I'd no more fear of my friend, but we met seldom. I went in freedom
From mountain to mountain, wherever good pasture grew,
Watching the creeks grow quiet and color themselves
With cool green moss, and the green hills turn white.
The people at the few farms all knew me, and now
Their minds changed; they were kind. All the deer knew me;
They'd walk in my flock.

In the midst of summer
When the moon filled, my blood failed to be moved,

The life that will make death began in my body.
I'd seen that moon when it was little as a chip
Over my left shoulder, from Palos ridge
By a purple cloud."

X

             "Oh, not till April," she said.
"All's quiet now, the bitterness is past, I have made peace
With death except in my dreams, those can't be ruled. But then, when I
    first
Began to believe and knew it had happened . . . I felt badly. I went back to
    my father's house,
Much was broken and chopped down, but I found
Little things that I'd loved when I was a child, hidden in corners. When I
    was drunk with crying
We hurried away. The lambs never seemed able to live, the mothers were
    glad to give me their milk,
We hid in the secret hills till it seemed desolate to die there. — Tell me,
    Onorio,
What month is this?"

             He answered, "Clare, Clare, fear nothing.
Death is as far away from you as from any one.
There was a girl (I've heard my brothers talking:
The road-overseer's daughter) was four or five months along
And went to a doctor: she had no trouble:
She's like a virgin again." Clare struck the earth with her hands
And raised her body, she stared through the red of the fire
With brilliant confused eyes. "Your face was like a devil's in the steamy
    glimmer:

But only because you don't understand. Why, Tia Livia herself ... you are
      too innocent, Onorio,
Has done so ... but women often have small round stones
Instead of hearts." "But," he answered, "if you're not able to bear it. Not
      even a priest would bid you die
For a child that couldn't be born alive. You've lived too much alone,
      bodiless fears have become
Giants in secret. I too am not able to think clearly to-night, in the stinging
      drift of the fire
And the strange place, to-morrow I'll tell you plainly. My mind is confused
As I have sometimes felt it before the clouds of the world
Were opened: but I know: for disease to refuse cure
Is self-murder, not virtue." She squatted upright
Wrapping the coat about her shoulders and knees,
And said, "Have you never seen in your visions
The golden country that our souls came from,
Before we looked at the moon and stars and knew
They are not perfect? We came from a purer peace
In a more perfect heaven; where there was nothing
But calm delight, no cold, no sickness, no sharp hail,
The haven of neither hunger nor sorrow,
But all-enfolding love and unchangeable joy
Near the heart of life." Vasquez turned from the fire
And stared at her lit face. "How did you learn
This wonder? It is true." "I remembered it,"
She answered, "when I was in trouble." "This is the bitter-sweet memory,"
He said, "that makes the breast of the earth bitter
After we are born and the dear sun ridiculous. We shall return there, we
      homesick."
"No," she answered. "The place was my mother's body before I was born.
      You may remember it a little but I've

Remembered plainly: and the wailing pain of entering this air. I've thought
   and thought and remembered. I found
A cave in a high cliff of white stone, when I was hiding from people: it was
   there I had the first memory.
There I'd have stayed in the safe darkness forever; the sheep were hungry
   and strayed out, so I couldn't stay.
I remembered again when I went home to our house and the door hung
   crazy
On a snapped hinge. You don't believe me, Onorio,
But after while you'll remember plainly, if some long trouble
Makes you want peace; or being handled has broken your shame. I have no
   shame now." He answered nothing
Because she seemed to speak from a frantic mind.
After a moment, "No matter," she said. "When I was in my worst trouble
I knew that the child was feeding on peace and happiness. I had happiness
   here in my body. It is not mine,
But I am its world and the sky around it, its loving God. It is having the
   prime and perfect of life,
The nine months that are better than the ninety years. I'd not steal one of
   its days to save my life.
I am like its God, how could I betray it? It has not moved yet
But feels its blessedness in its quietness; but soon I shall feel it move, Tia
   Livia said it will nestle
Down the warm nest and flutter like a winged creature. It shook her body,
   she said." But Vasquez, loathing
To hear these things, labored with the sick fire
In the steam of the wet wood, not listening, then Clare
Sighed and lay down. He heard her in a moment
Miserably sobbing, he went and touched her. "What is it?
Clare? Clare?" "Ai, when will morning come?
It is horrible to lie still," she said, "feeling

The black of April . . . it's nothing, it's nothing . . . like a cat
Tick tick on padded feet. Ah let me alone, will you?
Lying quiet does it: I'll have courage in my time."

A little later she asked for food, she ate,
And drank from the stream, and slept. She moved in her sleep
And tossed her arms, Vasquez would cover them again,
But the fever seemed quieted. He crossed the stream by the stones in the
      dull fire-glimmer
And fetched armfuls of flood-wood from under the opposite bridge-head.
      The fire revived; the earth turned past midnight;
Far eastward beyond the coasts of the continent morning troubled the
      Atlantic.

XI

                  Vasquez crouched by the fire
And felt one of those revelations that were in his own regard the jewels and
      value of his life
Approach and begin. First passed — as always
Since Barclay was gone, whom he had taken for incarnate God — ancestral
      forms against the white cloud,
The high dark heads of Indian migrations, going south along the coast,
      drawn down from the hungry straits and from Asia,
The heads like worn coins and the high shoulders,
The brown-lipped patient mouths below vulture beaks, and burnished fall
      of black hair over slant foreheads,
Going up to the Mayan and the Aztec mountains, and sowing the coast.
      They swept the way and the cloud cleared,
The vision would come: came instead a strong pause.

                                              A part of his mind
Wished to remember what the rest had forgotten,
And groping for it in the dark withstood the prepared
Pageant of dreams. He'd read in his curious boyhood
Of the child the mother is found incapable of bearing
Cut from the mother's belly. Both live; the wound
Heals: it was called the Caesarean section. But he, fearing
Whatever thought might threaten to infringe his careful
Chastity of mind, had quickly cancelled the memory;
That now sought a new birth; it might save Clare
If he could think of it.

                            That revived part
Made itself into the vision, all to no purpose,
His precious dreams were never to the point of life.
Only the imperial name, and the world's
Two-thousand-year and ten-thousand-miles-travelled
Caesarean memory appeared. He imagined at first that the voice
Cried "Ave Maria," but it cried "Ave Caesar."

                                        He saw the firelight-gilded
Timbers of the bridge above; and one of the ewes lifted her head in the
     light beside Clare sleeping;
The smoke gathered its cloud into a floating globe and these were
     forgotten. On the globe of the earth
The aquiline-headed Roman, who summed in his one person the powers
     and ordered science of humanity,
Stood and possessed his orb of empire and looked at the stars. Then the
     voice cried
"The pride of the earth."

But Vasquez laughed aloud, for the earth was a
grain of dust circling the fire,
And the fire itself but a spark, among innumerable sparks. The swarm of
the points of light drifting
No path down darkness merged its pin-prick eyelets into one misty
glimmer, a mill-stone in shape,
A coin in shape, a mere coin, a flipped luck-penny: but again Vasquez
Laughed out, for who was the spendthrift sowed them all over the sky,
indistinguishable innumerable
Fish-scales of light? They drew together as they drifted away no path down
the wild darkness; he saw
The webs of their rays made them one tissue, their rays that were their very
substance and power filled wholly
The space they were in, so that each one touched all, there was no division
between them, no emptiness, and each
Changed substance with all the others and became the others. It was
dreadful to see
No space between them, no cave of peace nor no night of quietness, no
blind spot nor no deaf heart, but the tides
Of power and substance flood every cranny; no annihilation, no escape but
change: it must endure itself
Forever. It has the strength to endure itself. We others, being faintly made
of the dust of a grain of dust
Have been permitted to fool our patience asleep by inventing death. A poor
comfort, he thought,
Yet better than none, the imaginary cavern, how we all come clamoring
To the gates of our great invention after few years.
Though a cheat, it works.

The speckled tissue of universes
Drew into one formed and rounded light, and Vasquez
Worshipped the one light. One eye . . . what, an eye?

A dark mountain with an eye in its cliff? A coal-black stallion
Eyed with one burning eye in the mid-brow?
Night has an eye. The poor little vision-seer
Groaned, that he never had wit to understand visions.
See all and know nothing. The eye that makes its own light
And sees nothing but itself. "I am seeing Barclay again,"
He marvelled, as who should say "I am seeing God:
But what is God?" He continued gazing,
And beads of sweat spilled from his forehead into the fire-edge
Ashes. He saw at last, neither the eyed mountain
Nor the stallion, nor Barclay, but his own eye
In the darkness of his own face.

                        The circuit was closed;
"I can endure all things," he thought, "forever. I am he
Whom I have sought.

                 And Clare loves all things
Because all things are herself. She has killed her father
And inherited. Her old enormous father
Who rode the furrows full tilt, sowing with both hands
The high field above the hills and the ocean. We kill steers for meat, and
    God
To be atoned with him. But I remain from myself divided, gazing beyond
    the flaming walls,
Not fortunate enough, and too faint-hearted."

                       He continued gazing
  across the wane of the fire at the dark
Vision of his own face turned sideways, the light of one eye. Clare turned
    in her place and awoke and said,
"How awfully little. Ooh, Ooh," in a dove's voice,

And then, "I forgot I wasn't alone, Onorio:
And here are the sheep. Have I slept a moment?
I did have a strange dream. I went out across the starlight
Knocking through flight after flight of the shiny balls
And got so far away that the sun and the great earth
And beautiful moon and all the stars were blended
Into one tiny light, Oh terribly little,
The flame of a pitiful little candle blown over
In the wind of darkness, in the fear of the night. It was so tiny
I wanted to be its comfort
And hold it and rock it on my breast. One wee flicker
In all the wild dark. What a dream." She turned anxiously
To touch the sheep, fondling their heads and naming them.
"Dear Fay, dear Fern. And here's Captain Saul. Ah bad little Hornie
Who taught you to be so bold?" Suddenly she cried
"Did Leader and Frannie go out — did two of the sheep
Go out lately?" But Vasquez, caught in his vision,
Answered "You also have broken
The fire-studded egg of heaven and we're together
In the world outside." "Ah Ah," she cried desolately,
"Did you lie when you counted them? When I was sick
And my eyes failed?" She ran into the darkness outside, calling their names;
The flock that remained stood up, in the edge of firelight, tremulously
    crying. Then Vasquez: "I hear a multitude
Of people crying, but why do you lament and cry? You particles of the eye
    of light, if some of you
Endure evil, the others endure good, the balance is perfect. The eye lives
    on mixed light and darkness,
Not either alone. And you are not many but one, the eye is not glad nor
    sorry, nor the dark face
Disquieted: be quiet, voices, and hear the real voice." Clare Walker came in
    from the dark with wide strained eyes,

In each iris the fire reflected made a red stain, and she cried:
"Onorio, for Christ's sake tell me, were they not with me?
Or have they slipped out?" He turned slowly an unanswering face
Of cool, dark and deaf stone, tempered to the mood
Of what he imagined . . . or perhaps perceived. And Clare:
"If I have slept and been dreaming while they're in danger
Or die in the dark: and they cried for me
In the dead night, while I slept and ate: I hope that all the miseries I ever
    feared for myself
Will come doubled, the rain on my hair be knives of ice, the sun whips of
    fire, the death I must die
Drawn out and dreadful like the dream of hell: Onorio, Oh come,
Help me to find them!" He rose, passively under command in the shrill of
    her voice, muttering: "I can't
Imagine what further's to find: yet I'll go along.
Is there another light or another darkness?"
"Oh," she answered, "it's black," and snatched the most eager brands
Out of the fire for a torch. He with deft fingers
Mimicking her act, but with a sleepwalker mindlessness,
Bound fire into a bundle of sallow twigs,
And calmly, twirling his torch to flame, followed
The red glow of her rod-ends. They ran on the bridge and wandered
Up the wet road, Clare calling her flock around her
And sobbing the names of the lost. The useless torches
Flared in the puddles and ruts of water, and ruddied
The plump backs of the sheep; so sanguine-outlined
The little ridiculous procession strayed up the road
In the lane of the trees, the great-trunked wood like storms
Of darkness on either hand. The torches died soon,
Then Clare stood still, desolately calling; weak dawn
Had washed all the world gray.

The heads of the little flock

Suddenly and all together were turned one way, then a limping ewe

Came out of the wood. Clare screamed with joy, and ran and dropped on
her knees to embrace the lean neck. "Oh Leader!

Leader! She's safe, Onorio. Oh Leader where's Frannie?" But then the
wound was discovered, the flap torn back

Red from the flank and hanging from the rump, and the blood-caked wool.
Clare moaned awhile with no words, and said,

"When I forgot you because I was sick, when I forgot to call you and count
you in the rain in the night:

I wish I had died. I have nothing but these

Onorio, to take care of, and lose and lose. She used to go first always, I
called her Leader:

And now she's hurt." Onorio heard Clare's teeth clacking together in the
thin cheeks, and her breath

Hissing between them, he answered calmly, still caught in his vision: "The
five claws of a lion. Look, Clare.

But don't grieve, the great river of the blood of life is always bursting its
banks, never runs dry,

Secret inexhaustible fountains feed it." She stared at his face and turned on
the forest her desert eyes

And wrung her hands. "Leader is hurt; and Frannie I think has died."

They
searched long; the fourth hour

Of daylight they found the half consumed body. The head was not
mangled, Clare fell beside it

On the wet earth and kissed the half open eyes,

Weeping and self-reproachful, but yet she lamented

Less violently than Vasquez had feared. At length

He said, "If you wish, Clare, I will fetch tools

And bury it here." She answered faintly, "No matter.

She feels nothing to-day, darkness nor light,

Teeth nor the grave. Oh, I loved her well: but now, see,

She's not living any more. Onorio . . . isn't that your name?

What a stately name! . . . this is the one that fed me with milk

Long after the others were dry, she was like a mother to me, when I might
  have starved.

She loved me, I know.

But even the udders are torn. Her name, Onorio, was Frannie."

She turned and said, "Poor Leader. Can you come now?

Come Fern, come Fay, come Tiny, we have to go on.

Come Saul."

                    Vasquez begged her to turn again

And stay at his father's place in the canyon

Until she was well. She had to go on, she answered.

And Vasquez: "My father is withered up with old age but he'd be kind; and
  my brothers

Would be your brothers. There's pasture for the sheep. We're only a sort of
  Indians but we can be kind. Come, Clare.

The place is pleasant and alone, up the deep canyon, beside the old quarry
  and the kilns where they burnt the lime.

A hundred laborers used to live there, but now the woods have grown back,
  the cabins are standing empty,

The roads are gone. I think the old masonry kilns are beautiful, standing
  like towers in the deep forest,

But cracked and leaning, and maidenhair fern grows from the cracks. The
  creek makes music below. Come, Clare.

It is deep with peace. When I have to go about and work on men's farms
  for wages I long for that place

Like someone thinking of water in deserts. Sometimes we hear the sea's
  thunder, far down the deep gorge.

The darkness under the trees in spring is starry with flowers, with redwood
    sorrel, colt's foot, wakerobin,
The slender-stemmed pale yellow violets,
And Solomon's-seal that makes intense islands of fragrance in April." "Oh,
    April," she said trembling,
"How exactly it follows. How could I rest? Ah, no,
Good-bye, good-bye, Onorio. Poor Leader, I am sure
We can go a little way before dark. Come, Saul, Saul."
She ran a few steps, panting hard.

                                    Vasquez perceived
No hope of staying her: "Then I'll go back to the bridge
And fetch my horse and my coat. I'll not leave you, Clare."
He went slowly, heavy and amazed. His horse
Had broken tether in the night, stung by the hail-stones.
Then Vasquez, still drunken with the dregs of his vision
To fatalist indifference, went hunting the horse
And found it late. He followed Clare the next morning,
But met another vision on the road, that waved
Impatient white hands against his passage, saying
"If I go up to Calvary ten million times: what is that to you?
Let me go up." Vasquez drew rein and sat staring.
He saw beyond the vision in the yellow mud
Prints of bare feet, dibbled about with many
Little crowding hoof-marks; he marvelled, feeling no sadness
But lonely thoughts.

XII

                        Clare Walker had crossed the ridge and gone down
To the mouth of Cawdor's Canyon. Japanese tenants
Now kept the house; short broad-faced men who planted

Lettuces in the garden against the creek-side
And beans on the hill. The barns were vacant, the cattle
Were vanished from the high pastures. The men were friendly,
Clare begged at their hands a little oil to soften
The bandage on Leader's wound; she'd torn her spent dress
In strips to bind it, and went now without clothing
But the long brown cloak.

                    She went northward, and on a foreland
Found vacant cabins around a ruined saw-mill;
And finding sacks of dry straw with a worn blanket
In one of the cabins, slept well and awoke refreshed
To travel on slowly northward in the glad sunlight
And sparkle of the sea. But the next day was dark,
And one of the wethers died, she never knew why,
She wept and went on.

                  Near Point Lobos, by a gate
Where Tamar Cauldwell used to lean from her white pony
To swing the bars, the lion-stricken ewe, Leader,
Groaned and lay down and died. Clare met much kindness there;
She was nursed in the house, helpless, for many days,
And the sheep were guarded and fed. The people clothed her
And calmed her wild mind; but she was not willing to tell them
Her griefs nor her cause of fear. They kept her by watchful force
Until she escaped, a great night of moonlight, and fled
With her small flock.

                Far up the Carmel Valley
The river became a brook, she watched a salmon
Row its worn body up-stream over the stones
And struck by a thwart current expose the bruised

White belly to the white of the sky, gashed with red wounds, but right
    itself
And wriggle up-stream, having that within it, spirit or desire,
Will spend all its dear flesh and all the power it has gathered, in the sweet
    salt pastures and fostering ocean,
To find the appointed high-place and perish. Clare Walker, in a bright
    moment's passage of anxious feeling,
Knowing nothing of its fate saw her own fate reflected. She drank, and the
    sheep drank; they went up the valley
And crossed, the next day, among the long-needled pines, the great thirsty
    sky-ridge.

        In the valley beyond
Clare journeyed northward again, anxiously avoiding
The travelled roads and hiding herself from people
In fear that someone's force or kindness might steal her
From the helpless flock; and later in habitual fear.

She was seen much later, heavily swollen
Toward child-birth, cowering from a thin April rain
By a little fire on the San Joaquin river-bank,
Sharing a camp of outcast men; no sheep
Remained with her, but when she moved in the morning
She called the names of many, Fern, Fay and Leader,
Nosie and Saul and little Hornie and the others,
"Dear Tiny, dear Frannie, come on, we have to go on."
The toothless tramp bandaging his foot by the fire
Looked up with a flicker of light in his slack face,
And the sickly sullen boy on the other side
Smiled without mockery. Clare had gone half a mile
And felt a grinding pang in her back, she clung to the fence
And saw the poplars planted along the road

Reach dreadfully away northward. When the pain ended
She went on northward; but after the second pain
She crept down to the river and hid her body
In a willow thicket. In the evening, between the rapid
Summits of agony before exhaustion, she called
The sheep about her and perceived that none came.

from DESCENT TO THE DEAD

Poems Written in Ireland and Great Britain

SHANE O'NEILL'S CAIRN

to U. J.

When you and I on the Palos Verdes cliff
Found life more desperate than dear,
And when we hawked at it on the lake by Seattle,
In the west of the world, where hardly
Anything has died yet: we'd not have been sorry, Una,
But surprised, to foresee this gray
Coast in our days, the gray waters of the Moyle
Below us, and under our feet
The heavy black stones of the cairn of the lord of Ulster.
A man of blood who died bloodily
Four centuries ago: but death's nothing, and life,
From a high death-mark on a headland
Of this dim island of burials, is nothing either.
How beautiful are both these nothings.

OSSIAN'S GRAVE

Prehistoric monument near Cushendall, in Antrim

Steep up in Lubitavish townland stands
A ring of great stones like fangs, the shafts of the stones
Grown up with thousands of years of gradual turf,
The fangs of the stones still biting skyward; and hard
Against the stone ring, the oblong enclosure
Of an old grave guarded with erect slabs; gray rocks
Backed by broken thorn-trees, over the gorge of Glenaan;
It is called Ossian's Grave. Ossian rests high then,
Haughtily alone.
If there were any fame or burial or monument
For me to envy,
Warrior and poet they should be yours and yours.

For this is the pure fame, not caged in a poem,
Fabulous, a glory untroubled with works, a name in the north
Like a mountain in the mist, like Aura
Heavy with heather and the dark gray rocks, or Trostan
Dark purple in the cloud: happier than what the wings
And imperfections of work hover like vultures
Above the carcass.

I also make a remembered name;
And I shall return home to the granite stones
On my cliff over the greatest ocean
To be blind ashes under the butts of the stones:
As you here under the fanged limestone columns
Are said to lie, over the narrow north straits
Toward Scotland, and the quick-tempered Moyle. But written reminders
Will blot for too long a year the bare sunlight

Above my rock-lair, heavy black birds
Over the field and the blood of the lost battle.

Oh but we lived splendidly
In the brief light of day
Who now twist in our graves.
You in the guard of the fanged
Erect stones; and the man-slayer
Shane O'Neill dreams yonder at Cushendun
Crushed under his cairn;
And Hugh McQuillan under his cairn
By his lost field in the bog on Aura;
And I a foreigner, one who has come to the country of the dead
Before I was called,
To eat the bitter dust of my ancestors;
And thousands on tens of thousands in the thronged earth
Under the rotting freestone tablets
At the bases of broken round-towers;
And the great Connaught queen on her mountain-summit
The high cloud hoods, it creeps through the eyes of the cairn.

We dead have our peculiar pleasures, of not
Doing, of not feeling, of not being.
Enough has been felt, enough done, Oh and surely
Enough of humanity has been. We lie under stones
Or drift through the endless northern twilights
And draw over our pale survivors the net of our dream.
All their lives are less
Substantial than one of our deaths, and they cut turf
Or stoop in the steep
Short furrows, or drive the red carts, like weeds waving
Under the glass of water in a locked bay,

Which neither the wind nor the wave nor their own will
Moves; when they seem to awake
It is only to madden in their dog-days for memories of dreams
That lost all meaning many centuries ago.

Oh but we lived splendidly
In the brief light of day,
You with hounds on the mountain
And princes in palaces,
I on the western cliff
In the rages of the sun:
Now you lie grandly under your stones
But I in a peasant's hut
Eat bread bitter with the dust of dead men;
The water I draw at the spring has been shed for tears
Ten thousand times,
Or wander through the endless northern twilights
From the rath to the cairn, through fields
Where every field-stone's been handled
Ten thousand times,
In a uterine country, soft
And wet and worn out, like an old womb
That I have returned to, being dead.

Oh but we lived splendidly
Who now twist in our graves.
The mountains are alive;
Tievebuilleagh lives, Trostan lives,
Lurigethan lives;
And Aura, the black-faced sheep in the belled heather;
And the swan-haunted loughs; but also a few of us dead
A life as inhuman and cold as those.

THE BROADSTONE
near Finvoy, County Antrim

We climbed by the old quarries to the wide highland of heath,
On the slope of a swale a giant dolmen,
Three heavy basalt pillars upholding the enormous slab,
Towers and abides as if time were nothing.
The hard stones are hardly dusted with lichen in nobody knows
What ages of autumns in this high solitude
Since a recordless tribe of an unknown race lifted them up
To be the availing hero's memorial,
And temple of his power. They gathered their slighter dead from the biting
Winds of time in his lee, the wide moor
About him is swollen with barrows and breaks upon many stones,
Lean gray guardians of old urned ashes,
In waves on waves of purple heather and blithe spray of its bells.
Here lies the hero, more than half God,
And nobody knows his name nor his race, in the bee-bright necropolis,
With the stone circle and his tribe around him.
Sometimes perhaps (but who'd confess it?) in soft adolescence
We used to wonder at the world, and have wished
To hear some final harmony resolve the discords of life?
— Here they are all perfectly resolved.

IN THE HILL AT NEWGRANGE

One of the three great prehistoric burial-mounds on the River Boyne

"Who is it beside me, who is here beside me, in the hollow hill?"
A foreigner I am. "You've dug for nothing. The Danes were here
A thousand years before you and robbed me of my golden bracelets,
Stinking red-haired men from the sea, with torches and swords."
Dead king, you keep a better treasure than bracelets,
The peace of the dead is dearer than gold, no one can rob you.

What do you watch, old king, from the cave? "In the north the muddy
    chippers of flint on the Antrim coast,
Their chests covered with hair and filth, shrewd eyes under bushes of brow,
    clicking the flints together.
How we used to hate those hunters. One squats in a cave-mouth and makes
    an axe, one in a dune shapes bolt-heads."
They have all (and we too, old king) been dead for thousands of years. I see
    in the north a red-haired woman
Meeting her lover by Shane O'Neill's cairn, her peasant husband is drunk
    at home, she drifts up the hill
In the sleeve of twilight. "Mary Byrnes is that you?" "Ye may kiss a hure
    but not name her. Ah, lad, come down.
When I was a wee maid I used to be loving Jesus,
All helpless and bleeding on the big cross. I'd never have married my
    drunkard only the cart ran over him.
He lay helpless and bleeding in the black lane. Och, laddie, not here now.
Carry me up to the cairn: a man lies bloodily under the sharp black stones,
    I love that man."
Mary Byrnes, when her lover has done and finished, before he stands up
To button his clothes together, runs a knife in his throat. "Oh Shane
    O'Neill it's you I was loving,
Never one else. You helpless and bleeding under the stones.

Do ye weary of stretching quiet the four long centuries? Take this lad's
    blood to hearten you, it drops through the stones.
Drips, drops in the stones.
Drink, Shane; drink, dear: who cares if a hure is hanged? We kill each
    other in Ireland to pleasure the dead."

Great upright stones higher than the height of a man are our walls,
Huge overlapping stones are the summer clouds in our sky.
The hill of boulders is heaped over all. Each hundred years
One of the enormous stones will move an inch in the dark.
Each double century one of the oaks on the crown of the mound
Above us breaks in a wind, an oak or an ash grows.

"I see in the south Cloyne round-tower burning: the Christians have built a
    spire, the thieves from the sea have burnt it,
The happy flame streams roaring up the stone tube and breaks from the
    four windows below the stone roof
Like four bright banners.
The holy men scream in their praying, the golden reliquaries are melted,
    the bell falls clanging."
They have all (and we too, old king) been dead for a thousand years. I see
    on the island mountain Achill,
In the west where wave after wave of the beaten tribes ran up and starved,
    an old woman, her head
Covered with a shawl, sits on Slieve Mor. Two thin sharp tears like knives
    in the yellow grooves of her face,
"My cow has died," she says, "and my son forgets me." She crouches and
    starves, in the quivering Atlantic wind,
Among the great skulls of quartz on the Achill mountain.

What do you watch, old king, from the cave? "A cause of mighty laughter
    in the mound on the hill at Dundalk.

They piled the earth on the blood of one of their spitfire princes, their
    bold watch-dog of the Ulster border.
After two handfuls of centuries
One Bruce, a younger drinker of battles, bloodily ceasing to be king of
    Ireland was buried above him.
Now a rich merchant has built his house on the mound's head, a living
    man. The old capon perches there trembling,
The young men of Ireland are passionate again, it is bad for a man of peace
    to have built on the hill of battles,
Oh his dear skin, Oh the papers of his wealth.
Cuchulain looks up at Bruce and Bruce at the sweating merchant. By God
    if we dead that watch the living
Could open our mouths the earth would be split with laughter."

I hear like a hum in the ground the Boyne running through the aging
Fields forever, and one of our great blue spiral-cut stones
Settle in the dark a hair's breadth under the burden of the hill.
"We hear from cairn to cromlech all over Ireland the dead
Whisper and conspire, and whinnies of laughter tinkle in the raths.
The living dream but the dead are awake."

High in Donegal, in the bitter waste north, where miles on miles of black
    heather dwindle to the Bloody Foreland,
Walks an old priest, near crazy with solitude and his peasants like cattle, he
    has wrestled with his mental Satan
Half his lifetime, and endured and triumphed. He feels the reward
    suddenly await him, the churchyard wall
Looks light and faint, the slabs and mounds by the entrance. In the midst
    of mass the crucified image trembles
Above the altar, and favorably smiles. Then Father O'Donnel
Gabbles the Latin faster to an end and turns himself once more and says to
    the people, "Go home now.

Missa est." In the empty church he screams and spits on the Christ,

He strikes it with his hand. Well done, old priest. "Is the man on the cross
his God, why does he strike his God?"

Because the tortured torturer is too long dying; because the strain in the
wounded minds of men

Leaves them no peace; but here where life is worn out men should have
peace. He desires nothing but unconsciousness,

To slip in the black bottomless lake and be still. Time for us also,

Old king, although no strain so many thousands of years has wounded our
minds, time to have done

With vision, as in the world's youth with desire and deed. To lie in the dark
in the hill until the stones crumble,

And the earth and the stars suck into nothing, the wheel slopes and returns,
the beautiful burden is renewed.

For probably all the same things will be born and be beautiful again, but
blessed is the night that has no glowworm.

GHOSTS IN ENGLAND

At East Lulworth the dead were friendly and pitiful, I saw them peek
  from their ancient earth-works on the coast hills
At the camps of the living men in the valley, the army-mechanics' barracks,
  the roads where they try the tanks
And the armored cars: "We also," they say, "trembled in our time. We felt
  the world change in the rain,
Our people like yours were falling under the wheel. Great past and
  declining present are a pitiful burden
For living men; but failure is not the worm that worries the dead, you will
  not weep when you come,"
Said the soft mournful shadows on the Dorset shore. And those on the
  Rollright ridge by the time-eaten stone-circle
Said nothing and had no wish in the world, having blessedly aged out of
  humanity, stared with great eyes
White as the hollowed limestone, not caring but seeing, inhuman as the
  wind.

       But the other ghosts were not good,
But like a moon of jackals around a sick stag.
At Zennor in the tumbled granite chaos, at Marazion and the angel's
  Mount, from the hoar tide-lines:
"Be patient, dead men, the tides of their day have turned," from the stone
  rings of the dead huts on Dartmoor,
The prison town like a stain of dirt on the distant hill: "We not the last,"
  they said, "shall be hopeless,
We not alone hunger in the rain." From Avebury in the high heart of
  England, in the ancient temple,
When all the cottages darkened themselves to sleep: "Send it along the
  ridge-ways and say it on the hilltops
That the bone is broken and the meat will fall."

There was also a ghost

of a king, his cheeks hollow as the brows

Of an old horse, was paddling his hands in the reeds of Dozmare Pool, in
the shallow, in the rainy twilight,

Feeling for the hilt of a ruinous and rusted sword. But they said "Be patient
a little, you king of shadows,

But only wait, they will waste like snow." Then Arthur left hunting for the
lost sword, he grinned and stood up

Gaunt as a wolf; but soon resumed the old labor, shaking the reeds with his
hands.

Northeastward to Wantage

On the chalk downs the Saxon Alfred

Witlessly walks with his hands lamenting. "Who are the people and who
are the enemy?" He says bewildered,

"Who are the living, who are the dead?" The more ancient dead

Watch him from the wide earth-works on White Horse Hill, peer from the
Ridge-way barrows, goggle from the broken

Mound and the scattered stones in the oval wood above Ashbury. They
whisper and exult.

In the north also

I saw them, from the Picts' houses in the black Caithness heather to the
bleak stones on Culloden Moor,

The rags of lost races and beaten clans, nudging each other, the blue lips
cracking with joy, the fleshless

Anticipatory fingers jabbing at the south. And on the Welsh borders

Were dead men skipping and fleering behind all the hedges. An island of
ghosts. They seemed merry, and to feel

No pity for the great pillar of empire settling to a fall, the pride and the
power slowly dissolving.

INSCRIPTION FOR A GRAVESTONE

I am not dead, I have only become inhuman:
That is to say,
Undressed myself of laughable prides and infirmities,
But not as a man
Undresses to creep into bed, but like an athlete
Stripping for the race.
The delicate ravel of nerves that made me a measurer
Of certain fictions
Called good and evil; that made me contract with pain
And expand with pleasure;
Fussily adjusted like a little electroscope:
That's gone, it is true;
(I never miss it; if the universe does,
How easily replaced!)
But all the rest is heightened, widened, set free.
I admired the beauty
While I was human, now I am part of the beauty.
I wander in the air,
Being mostly gas and water, and flow in the ocean;
Touch you and Asia
At the same moment; have a hand in the sunrises
And the glow of this grass.
I left the light precipitate of ashes to earth
For a love-token.

SUBJECTED EARTH

Walking in the flat Oxfordshire fields
Where the eye can find no rock to rest on but little flints
Speckle the soil, and the million-berried hedges
Tingle with birds at evening, I saw the somber
November day redden and go down; a flight of lapwings
Whirled in the hollow of the field, and half tame pheasants
Cried from the trees. I remembered impatiently
How the long bronze mountain of my own coast,
Where color is no account and pathos ridiculous, the sculpture is all,
Breaks the arrows of the setting sun
Over the enormous mounded eye-ball of ocean.

                                    The soft alien twilight
Worn and weak with too much humanity hooded my mind.
Poor flourishing earth, meek-smiling slave,
If sometime the swamps return and the heavy forest, black beech and
    oak-roots
Break up the paving of London streets;
And only, as long before, on the lifted ridge-ways
Few people shivering by little fires
Watch the night of the forest cover the land
And shiver to hear the wild dogs howling where the cities were,
Would you be glad to be free? I think you will never
Be glad again, so kneaded with human flesh, so humbled and changed.

Here all's down hill and passively goes to the grave,
Asks only a pinch of pleasure between the darknesses,
Contented to think that everything has been done

That's in the scope of the race: so should I also perhaps
Dream, under the empty angel of this twilight,
But the great memory of that unhumanized world,
With all its wave of good and evil to climb yet,
Its exorbitant power to match, its heartless passion to equal,
And all its music to make, beats on the grave-mound.

Notes to "Descent to the Dead"

It seems hardly necessary to stipulate that the elegiac tone of these verses reflects the writer's mood, and is not meant for economic or political opinion.

Shane O'Neill's cairn and the dateless monument called Ossian's Grave stand within a couple of miles of each other on the Antrim coast.

A dolmen is a prehistoric burial-house made of great stones set on end, roofed by a slab of stone. There are many still standing in Ireland and England.

Newgrange is one of three great artificial hills, on the Boyne west of Drogheda. Passages and cells were made of megalithic stonework, decorated with designs cut in the great stones, and the hills were heaped over them. No one assigns a reasonable date to these erections. Evidently they are burial mounds, like the pyramids.

The Irish round-towers are well known, of course, slender, tapering spires of stone and lime mortar, of mysterious origin, but probably belfries and towers of refuge, built between 600 and 1200 A.D. They are associated with the earliest Christian churches.

Antrim is the northeasternmost county of Ireland, only a few sea-miles from Scotland. Iona is the sacred island of the Hebrides.

Avebury is a little Wiltshire village inside a great prehistoric stone-circle and fosse. It was the religious and perhaps the political capital of southern England before Stonehenge was built, i.e. before 2000 B.C. probably. The circle and the remaining stones are greater than those at Stonehenge, but the stones were not hewn to shape. Most of them are gone now; broken up to build the village.

Dozmare Pool is in Cornwall, a little flat mere in a wide wilderness, said to be the water where the sword Excalibur was cast away when King Arthur died.

The ridge-ways are ancient grass-grown roads on the ridges of the hills, used by the pre-Celtic inhabitants of England, when the lowlands were impassable swamp and forest.

THE BED BY THE WINDOW

I chose the bed down-stairs by the sea-window for a good death-bed
When we built the house; it is ready waiting,
Unused unless by some guest in a twelvemonth, who hardly suspects
Its latter purpose. I often regard it,
With neither dislike nor desire: rather with both, so equalled
That they kill each other and a crystalline interest
Remains alone. We are safe to finish what we have to finish;
And then it will sound rather like music
When the patient daemon behind the screen of sea-rock and sky
Thumps with his staff, and calls thrice: "Come, Jeffers."

WINGED ROCK

The flesh of the house is heavy sea-orphaned stone, the imagination of
    the house
Is in those little clay kits of swallows
Hung in the eaves, bright wings flash and return, the heavy rock walls
    commercing
With harbors of the far hills and the high
Rills of water, the river-meadow and the sea-cloud. You have also, O sleepy
    stones,
The red, the white and the marbled pigeons
To beat the blue air over the pinewood and back again in a moment; and
    the bush-hidden
Killdeer-nest against the west wall-foot,
That is fed from many strange ebbs; besides the woodful of finches, the
    shoring gulls,
The sudden attentive passages of hawks.

Thurso's Landing

1930-31

THE PLACE FOR NO STORY

The coast hills at Sovranes Creek;
No trees, but dark scant pasture drawn thin
Over rock shaped like flame;
The old ocean at the land's foot, the vast
Gray extension beyond the long white violence;
A herd of cows and the bull
Far distant, hardly apparent up the dark slope;
And the gray air haunted with hawks:
This place is the noblest thing I have ever seen. No imaginable
Human presence here could do anything
But dilute the lonely self-watchful passion.

NEW MEXICAN MOUNTAIN

I watch the Indians dancing to help the young corn at Taos pueblo. The
old men squat in a ring
And make the song, the young women with fat bare arms, and a few
shame-faced young men, shuffle the dance.

The lean-muscled young men are naked to the narrow loins, their breasts
and backs daubed with white clay,
Two eagle-feathers plume the black heads. They dance with reluctance, they
are growing civilized; the old men persuade them.

Only the drum is confident, it thinks the world has not changed; the
beating heart, the simplest of rhythms,
It thinks the world has not changed at all; it is only a dreamer, a brainless
heart, the drum has no eyes.

These tourists have eyes, the hundred watching the dance, white Americans,
hungrily too, with reverence, not laughter;
Pilgrims from civilization, anxiously seeking beauty, religion, poetry;
pilgrims from the vacuum.

People from cities, anxious to be human again. Poor show how they suck
you empty! The Indians are emptied,
And certainly there was never religion enough, nor beauty nor poetry here
... to fill Americans.

Only the drum is confident, it thinks the world has not changed.
Apparently only myself and the strong
Tribal drum, and the rock-head of Taos mountain, remember that
civilization is a transient sickness.

NOVEMBER SURF

Some lucky day each November great waves awake and are drawn
Like smoking mountains bright from the west
And come and cover the cliff with white violent cleanness: then suddenly
The old granite forgets half a year's filth:
The orange-peel, egg-shells, papers, pieces of clothing, the clots
Of dung in corners of the rock, and used
Sheaths that make light love safe in the evenings: all the droppings of the
    summer
Idlers washed off in a winter ecstasy:
I think this cumbered continent envies its cliff then. . . . But all seasons
The earth, in her childlike prophetic sleep,
Keeps dreaming of the bath of a storm that prepares up the long coast
Of the future to scour more than her sea-lines:
The cities gone down, the people fewer and the hawks more numerous,
The rivers mouth to source pure; when the two-footed
Mammal, being someways one of the nobler animals, regains
The dignity of room, the value of rareness.

MARGRAVE

On the small marble-paved platform
On the turret on the head of the tower
Watching the night deepen.
I feel the rock-edge of the continent
Reel eastward with me below the broad stars,
I lean on the broad worn stones of the parapet-top
And the stones and my hands that touch them reel eastward.
The inland mountains go down and new lights
Glow over the sinking east rim of the earth.
The dark ocean comes up,
And reddens the western stars with its fog-breath
And hides them with its mounded darkness.

The earth was the world and man was its measure, but our minds have
    looked
Through the little mock-dome of heaven the telescope-slotted observatory
    eye-ball, there space and multitude came in
And the earth is a particle of dust by a sand-grain sun, lost in a nameless
    cove of the shores of a continent.
Galaxy on galaxy, innumerable swirls of innumerable stars, endured as it
    were forever and humanity
Came into being, its two or three million years are a moment, in a moment
    it will certainly cease out from being
And galaxy on galaxy endure after that as it were forever . . . But man is
    conscious,
He brings the world to focus in a feeling brain,
In a net of nerves catches the splendor of things,
Breaks the somnambulism of nature . . . His distinction perhaps,
Hardly his advantage. To slaver for contemptible pleasures
And scream with pain, are hardly an advantage.

Consciousness? The learned astronomer
Analyzing the light of most remote star-swirls
Has found them — or a trick of distance deludes his prism —
All at incredible speeds fleeing outward from ours.
I thought, no doubt they are fleeing the contagion
Of consciousness that infects this corner of space.

For often I have heard the hard rocks I handled
Groan, because lichen and time and water dissolve them,
And they have to travel down the strange falling scale
Of soil and plants and the flesh of beasts to become
The bodies of men; they murmur at their fate
In the hollows of windless nights, they'd rather be anything
Than human flesh played on by pain and joy,
They pray for annihilation sooner, but annihilation's
Not in the book yet.

              So, I thought, the rumor
Of human consciousness has gone abroad in the world,
The sane uninfected far-outer universes
Flee it in a panic of escape, as men flee the plague
Taking a city: for look at the fruits of consciousness:
As in young Walter Margrave when he'd been sentenced for murder: he was
    thinking when they brought him back
To the cell in jail, "I've only a moment to arrange my thoughts, I must
    think quickly, I must think clearly,
And settle the world in my mind before I kick off," but to feel the curious
    eyes of his fellow-prisoners
And the wry-mouthed guard's and so forth torment him through the steel
    bars put his mind in a stupor, he could only
Sit frowning, ostentatiously unafraid. "But I can control my mind, their
    eyes can't touch my will.

One against all. What use is will at this end of everything? A kind of
    nausea is the chief feeling . . .
In my stomach and throat . . . but in my head pride: I fought a good fight
    and they can't break me; alone, unbroken,
Against a hundred and twenty-three million people. They are going to kill
    the best brain perhaps in the world,
That might have made such discoveries in science
As would set the world centuries ahead, for I had the mind and the power.
    Boo, it's their loss. Blind fools,
Killing their best." When his mind forgot the eyes it made rapid capricious
    pictures instead of words,
But not of the medical school and the laboratories, its late intense interest;
    not at all of his crime; glimpses
Of the coast-range at home; the V of a westward canyon with the vibrating
Blue line of the ocean strung sharp across it; that domed hill up the valley,
    two cows like specks on the summit
And a beautiful-colored jungle of poison-oak at the foot; his sister half
    naked washing her hair,
"My dirty sister," whose example and her lovers had kept him chaste by
    revulsion; the reed-grown mouth of the river
And the sand-bar against the stinging splendor of the sea . . . and anguish
    behind all the pictures
(He began to consider his own mind again) "like a wall they hang on."
    Hang. The anguish came forward, an actual
Knife between two heart-beats, the organ stopped and then raced. He
    experimented awhile with his heart,
Making in his mind a picture of a man hanged, pretending to himself it was
    to happen next moment,
Trying to observe whether the beat suspended — "suspended," he
    thought — in systole or in diastole.
The effect soon failed; the anguish remained. "Ah my slack lawyer, damn
    him, let slip chance after chance.

Scared traitor." Then broken pictures of the scenes in court, the jury, the
   judge, the idlers, and not one face
But bleak with hatred. "But I met their eyes, one against all." Suddenly his
   mind became incapable
Of making pictures or words, but still wildly active, striking in all
   directions like a snake in a fire,
Finding nothing but the fiery element of its own anguish. He got up and
   felt the guard's eyes and sat down,
Turned side-face, resting his chin on his fist, frowning and trembling. He
   saw clearly in his mind the little
Adrenal glands perched on the red-brown kidneys, as if all his doomed
   tissues became transparent,
Pouring in these passions their violent secretion
Into his blood-stream, raising the tension unbearably. And the thyroids:
   tension, tension. A long course of that
Should work grave changes. "If they tortured a man like a laboratory dog
   for discovery: there'd be value gained: but by process
Of law for vengeance, because his glands and his brain have made him act
   in another than common manner:
You incredible breed of asses!" He smiled self-consciously in open scorn of
   the people, the guard at the door
To observe that smile — "my God, do I care about the turn-key's
   opinion?" — suddenly his mind again
Was lashing like a burnt snake. Then it was torpid for a while. This
   continued for months.

His father had come to visit him, he saw the ruinous white-haired head
Through two steel wickets under the bluish electric light that seemed to
   peel the skin from the face.
Walter said cheerfully too loudly, "Hullo. You look like a skull." The
   shaven sunk jaws in answer chewed

Inaudible words. Walter with an edge of pleasure thought "Once he was
    stronger than I! I used to admire
This poor old man's strength when I was a child," and said "Buck up, old
    fellow, it will soon be over. Here's nothing
To cry for. Do you think I'm afraid to die? It's good people that fear death,
    people with the soft streak
Of goodness in them fear death: but I, you know, am a monster, don't you
    read the papers? Caught at last:
I fought a hundred and twenty-three million people. How's Hazel? How's
    the farm? I could get out of this scrape
By playing dementia, but I refuse to, there's not an alienist living
Could catch me out. I'm the king of Spain dying for the world. I've been
    persecuted since I was born
By a secret sect, they stuck pins into me
And fed me regular doses of poison for a certain reason. Why do you
    pretend that you're my father?
God is. . . . Believe me, I could get by with it.
But I refuse."

        Old Margrave looked timidly at the two guards listening,
    and drew his brown tremulous hand
Across his eyes below the white hair. "I thought of going to try to see the
    governor, Walter."
"That's it!" "Don't hope for anything, Walter, they tell me that there's no
    hope. They say that I shan't even
Be allowed to see him." "By God," the young man said trembling, "you can
    if you want to. Never believe that lawyer.
If I'd had Dorking: but you couldn't afford him. Poor men have no right to
    breed sons. I'd not be here
If you'd had money to put me through college. Tell the governor
I know he won't pardon, but he can commute the sentence to life
    imprisonment. Then I can read and study,

I can help the penitentiary doctor, I can do something to help humanity.
   Tell him it's madness
To throw such a brain as mine into the garbage. Don't deny my guilt but
   tell him my reasons.
I kidnapped the little girl to get money to finish my medical education.
   What's one child's life
Against a career like mine that might have saved
Thousands of children? Say I'd isolated the organism of infantile paralysis:
   I'd have done more:
But that alone would save thousands of children. I was merciful; she died
   quietly; tell him that.
It was only pithing a little white frog.
Don't you think you can make him understand? I'm not a criminal: I judge
   differently from others. I wasn't
Afraid to think for myself. All I did
Was for money for my education, to help humanity. And tell him if I've
   done wrong — what's wrong? — I've paid for it
With frightful suffering: the more developed the brain the greater the
   agony. He won't admit that. Oh God,
These brains the size of a pea! To be juried
And strangled by a hundred and twenty-three million peas. Go down on
   your knees to him. You owe me that: you'd no right
To breed, you're poor.
But you itched for a woman, you had to fetch me out of the happy hill of
   not-being. Pfah, to hug a woman
And make this I. That's the evil in the world, that letter. I — I — Tell the
   governor
That I'm not afraid of dying, that I laugh at death. No, no, we'll laugh in
   private. Tell him I'm crazy.
I've come to that: after being the only sane mind among a hundred and
   twenty-three million peas.
Anything, anything . . ."

He had let his nerves go wild on purpose, to
    edge on the old man to action, now at last
Escaping utterly out of control they stumbled into a bog of thick sobs. The
    guards pulled him up
And walked him away as if he were half insensible. He was not insensible,
    but more acutely aware
Than ever in his life before of all that touched him, and of shame and
    anguish.

        You would be wise, you far stars,
To flee with the speed of light this infection.
For here the good sane invulnerable material
And nature of things more and more grows alive and cries.
The rock and water grow human, the bitter weed
Of consciousness catches the sun, it clings to the near stars,
Even the nearer portion of the universal God
Seems to become conscious, yearns and rejoices
And suffers: I believe this hurt will be healed
Some age of time after mankind has died,
Then the sun will say "What ailed me a moment?" and resume
The old soulless triumph, and the iron and stone earth
With confident inorganic glory obliterate
Her ruins and fossils, like that incredible unfading red rose
Of desert in Arizona glowing life to scorn,
And grind the chalky emptied seed-shells of consciousness
The bare skulls of the dead to powder; after some million
Courses around the sun her sadness may pass:
But why should you worlds of the virgin distance
Endure to survive what it were better to escape?

I also am not innocent
Of contagion, but have spread my spirit on the deep world.

I have gotten sons and sent the fire wider.
I have planted trees, they also feel while they live.
I have humanized the ancient sea-sculptured cliff
And the ocean's wreckage of rock
Into a house and a tower,
Hastening the sure decay of granite with my hammer,
Its hard dust will make soft flesh;
And have widened in my idleness
The disastrous personality of life with poems,
That are pleasant enough in the breeding but go bitterly at last
To envy oblivion and the early deaths of nobler
Verse, and much nobler flesh;
And I have projected my spirit
Behind the superb sufficient forehead of nature
To gift the inhuman God with this rankling consciousness.

But who is our judge? It is likely the enormous
Beauty of the world requires for completion our ghostly increment,
It has to dream, and dream badly, a moment of its night.

On the little stone-belted platform
On the turret on the head of the tower,
Between the stars and the earth
And the ocean and the continent.
One ship's light shines and eclipses
Very far out, behind the high waves on the hill of water.
In the east under the Hyades and rising Orion
Are many cities and multitudes of people,
But westward a long ways they are few enough.
It is fortunate to look westward as to look upward.
In the south the dark river-mouth pool mirrors a star

That stands over Margrave's farmhouse. The old man has lost it, he isn't
  there any more. He went down to the river-mouth
Last December, when recent rains had opened the stream and the salmon
  were running. Fishermen very solemnly
Stood all along the low sand like herons, and sea-lions off-shore in the
  rolling waves with deep wet voices
Coughed at each other; the sea-air is hoarse with their voices that time of
  year. Margrave had rambled since noon
Among the little folds of the seaward field that he had forgotten to plow
  and was trying to sell
Though he used to love it, but everything was lost now. He lay awhile on
  his face in the rotting stubble and random
Unsown green blades, then he got up and drifted over the ridge to the
  river-mouth sands, unaimed,
Pale and gap-eyed, as the day moon a clear morning, opposite the sun. He
  noticed with surprise the many
Fishermen like herons in the shallows and along the sands; and then that his
  girl Hazel was with him: who'd feared
What he might do to himself and had come to watch him when he lay face
  down in the field. "I know what they're doing,"
He said slyly, "Hazel, they're fishing! I guess they don't know,"
He whispered, "about our trouble. Oh no, don't tell them." She said,
  "Don't go down father, your face would tell them.
Sit here on the edge of grass, watch the brown river meet the blue sea. Do
  look: that boy's caught something.
How the line cuts the water and the small wheel sings." "If I'd been rich,"
Old Margrave answered, "they'd have fixed the hook for . . . Walter . . .
  with some other bait. It sticks in my mind that . . . Walter
Blames me too much." "Look," Hazel said, "he's landing it now. Oh, it's a
  big one." "I dreamed about fishing,
Some time ago," he answered, "but we were the fish. I saw the people all
  running reaching for prizes

That dangled on long lines from the sky. A lovely girl or a sack of money
    or a case of whiskey,
Or fake things like reputation, hackle-feathers and a hook. A man would
    reach up and grab and the line
Jerked, then you knew by his face that the hook was in him, wherever he
    went. Often they're played for half
A life-time before they're landed: others, like . . . my son . . . pulled up
    short. Oh, Oh,
It's not a dream." He said gently, "He wanted money for his education, but
    you poor girl
Wanted boy friends, now you've got a round belly. That's the hook. I
    wanted children and got
Walter and you. Hm? Hooked twice is too much. Let's walk." "Not that
    way: let's go up home, daddy.
It makes you unhappy to see them fishing." "No," he answered, "nothing
    can. I have it in my pocket." She walked behind him,
Hiding herself, ashamed of her visible pregnancy and her brother's fate; but
    when the old man stumbled
And wavered on the slope she went beside him to support him, her right
    hand under his elbow, and wreathed his body
With the other arm.

                    The clear brown river ran eagerly through the
    sand-hill, undercutting its banks,
That slid in masses; tall waves walked very slowly up-stream from the sea,
    and stood
Stationary in the throat of the channel before they dissolved. The rock the
    children call Red-cap stood
High and naked among the fishermen, the orange lichen on its head. At the
    sea-end of the sand
Two boys and a man had rifles instead of rods, they meant to punish the
    salmon-devouring sea-lions

Because the fish were fewer than last year; whenever a sleek brown head
    with the big questioning eyes
Broke sea they fired. Margrave had heard the shots but taken no notice, but
    when he walked by the stream
He saw a swimmer look up from the water and its round dark eye
Suddenly burst red blood before it went down. He cried out and twisted
    himself from Hazel's hand
And ran like a squirrel along the stream-bank. "I'll not allow it!" He
    snatched at a rifle. "Why should my lad
Be hanged for killing and all you others go free?" He wrestled feebly to
    gain the rifle, the sand-bank
Slid under his feet, he slipped and lay face down in the running stream and
    was hauled astrand. Then Hazel
Came running heavily, and when he was able to walk she led him away. The
    sea-beast, blinded but a painful
Vain gleam, starved long before it could die; old Margrave still lives.
    Death's like a little gay child that runs
The world around with the keys of salvation in his foolish fingers, lends
    them at random where they're not wanted,
But often withholds them where most required.

                           Margrave's son at this
    time
Had only four days to wait, but death now appeared so dreadful to him
    that to speak of his thoughts and the abject
Horror, would be to insult humanity more than it deserves. At last the
    jerked hemp snapped the neck sideways
And bruised the cable of nerves that threads the bone rings; the intolerably
    strained consciousness in a moment changed.
It was strangely cut in two parts at the noose, the head's
Consciousness from the body's; both were set free and flamed; the head's
    with flashing paradisal light

Like the wild birth of a star, but crying in bewilderment and suddenly
   extinguished; the body's with a sharp emotion
Of satisfied love, a wave of hard warmth and joy, that ebbed cold on
   darkness. After a time of darkness
The dreams that follow upon death came and subsided, like fibrillar
   twitchings
Of the nerves unorganizing themselves; and some of the small dreams were
   delightful and some slight miseries,
But nothing intense; then consciousness wandered home from the cell to
   the molecule, was utterly dissolved and changed;
Peace was the end of the play, so far as concerns humanity. Oh beautiful
   capricious little savior,
Death, the gay child with the gipsy eyes, to avoid you for a time I think is
   virtuous, to fear you is insane.

On the little stone-girdled platform
Over the earth and the ocean
I seem to have stood a long time and watched the stars pass.
They also shall perish I believe.
Here to-day, gone to-morrow, desperate wee galaxies
Scattering themselves and shining their substance away
Like a passionate thought. It is very well ordered.

FIRE ON THE HILLS

The deer were bounding like blown leaves
Under the smoke in front of the roaring wave of the brushfire;
I thought of the smaller lives that were caught.
Beauty is not always lovely; the fire was beautiful, the terror
Of the deer was beautiful; and when I returned
Down the black slopes after the fire had gone by, an eagle
Was perched on the jag of a burnt pine,
Insolent and gorged, cloaked in the folded storms of his shoulders.
He had come from far off for the good hunting
With fire for his beater to drive the game; the sky was merciless
Blue, and the hills merciless black,
The sombre-feathered great bird sleepily merciless between them.
I thought, painfully, but the whole mind,
The destruction that brings an eagle from heaven is better than mercy.

Give Your Heart to the Hawks

1931-33

A LITTLE SCRAPING

True, the time, to one who does not love farce,
And if misery must be prefers it nobler, shows apparent vices;
At least it provides the cure for ambition.
One does not crave power in anthills, nor praise in a paper forest;
One must not even indulge the severe
Romance of separateness, as of Milton grown blind and old
In his broken temple against the drunkards:
The ants are good creatures, there is nothing to be heroic about.
But the time is not a strong prison either.
A little scraping the walls of dishonest contractor's-concrete
Through a shower of chips and sand makes freedom.
Shake the dust from your hair. This mountain sea-coast is real,
For it reaches out far into past and future;
It is part of the great and timeless excellence of things. A few
Lean cows drift high up the bronze hill;
The heavy-necked plow-team furrows the foreland, gulls tread the furrow;
Time ebbs and flows but the rock remains.
Two riders of tired horses canter on the cloudy ridge;
Topaz-eyed hawks have the white air;
Or a woman with jade-pale eyes, hiding a knife in her hand,
Goes through cold rain over gray grass.
God is here, too, secretly smiling, the beautiful power
That piles up cities for the poem of their fall
And gathers multitude like game to be hunted when the season comes.

TRIAD

Science, that makes wheels turn, cities grow,
Moribund people live on, playthings increase,
But has fallen from hope to confusion at her own business
Of understanding the nature of things;—new Russia,
That stood a moment at dreadful cost half free,
Beholding the open, all the glades of the world
On both sides of the trap, and resolutely
Walked into the trap that has Europe and America;—
The poet, who wishes not to play games with words,
His affair being to awake dangerous images
And call the hawks;—they all feed the future, they serve God,
Who is very beautiful, but hardly a friend of humanity.

STILL THE MIND SMILES

Still the mind smiles at its own rebellions,
Knowing all the while that civilization and the other evils
That make humanity ridiculous, remain
Beautiful in the whole fabric, excesses that balance each other
Like the paired wings of a flying bird.
Misery and riches, civilization and squalid savagery,
Mass war and the odor of unmanly peace:
Tragic flourishes above and below the normal of life.
In order to value this fretful time
It is necessary to remember our norm, the unaltered passions,
The same-colored wings of imagination,
That the crowd clips, in lonely places new-grown; the unchanged
Lives of herdsmen and mountain farms,
Where men are few, and few tools, a few weapons, and their dawns are
    beautiful.
From here for normal one sees both ways,
And listens to the splendor of God, the exact poet, the sonorous
Antistrophe of desolation to the strophe multitude.

GIVE YOUR HEART TO THE HAWKS

I

The apples hung until a wind at the equinox,
That heaped the beach with black weed, filled the dry grass
Under the old trees with rosy fruit.
In the morning Fayne Fraser gathered the sound ones into a basket,
The bruised ones into a pan. One place they lay so thickly
She knelt to reach them.

                   Her husband's brother passing
Along the broken fence of the stubble-field,
His quick brown eyes took in one moving glance
A little gopher-snake at his feet flowing through the stubble
To gain the fence, and Fayne crouched after apples
With her mop of red hair like a glowing coal
Against the shadow in the garden. The small shapely reptile
Flowed into a thicket of dead thistle-stalks
Around a fence-post, but its tail was not hidden.
The young man drew it all out, and as the coil
Whipped over his wrist, smiled at it; he stepped carefully
Across the sag of the wire. When Fayne looked up
His hand was hidden; she looked over her shoulder
And twitched her sunburnt lips from small white teeth
To answer the spark of malice in his eyes, but turned
To the apples, intent again. Michael looked down
At her white neck, rarely touched by the sun,
But now the cinnabar-colored hair fell off from it;
And her shoulders in the light-blue shirt, and long legs like a boy's
Bare-ankled in blue-jean trousers, the country wear;
He stooped quietly and slipped the small cool snake

Up the blue-denim leg. Fayne screamed and writhed,
Clutching her thigh. "Michael, you beast." She stood up
And stroked her leg, with little sharp cries, the slender invader
Fell down her ankle.

              Fayne snatched for it and missed;
Michael stood by rejoicing, his rather small
Finely cut features in a dance of delight;
Fayne with one sweep flung at his face
All the bruised and half-spoiled apples in the pan,
A fragrant volley, and while he staggered under it,
The hat fallen from his head, she found one thoroughly
Soft-rotten, brown in the long white grass, and threw
For the crown of his dark head but perfectly missed,
Crying "Quits. We're even." They stood and warily smiled at each other
In the heavy-sweet apple air.

                  The garden was sunken lower than the little
    fields; it had many fragrances
And its own shadow, while the cows lay in the stream-bed, large sycamore
    leaves dropped on their flanks; the yellow
Heads of the hills quivered with sun and the straining sea-glare. Fayne said,
    "Where did it go, poor thing?"
Looking for the little serpent. Michael said gravely, "That's to remember
    me by. I wish I could do worse.
I'm going away." "What?" "From here again."
"Oh, no." "I am though." "No, Michael."
"Freckles," he answered, "didn't it ever occur to you
That it's fairly dull here? I'm going up to town again.
I've got to earn money and spend it and hear the motors."
She said dismally, "What about me? Who'll there be to talk to?"
"Lance of course." "I love him dearly: he's not fun exactly.

He wouldn't stick a rattlesnake up my leg."
"Gopher-snake," he shouted. They stood and laughed at each other,
And Michael: "I was over the ridge to Drunken Charlie's,
Fixing up a little party for Saturday.
There'll be a moon in the evening. I leave Monday."
Fayne said unhappily, "Help me pick up the apples
I poured on you."

II

        Michael was taking Mary Abbey;
The Dolmans came, and Will Howard with two girls,
And Leo Ramirez with his sister Nell, so that the youth
Of the coast was all there. They met at Fraser's
And crossed the ridge; and were picketing the horses
Where they could ride no farther, on the airy brink
Above the great slides of the thousand-foot cliff.
They were very gay, colorful mites on the edge of the world. The men
    divided the pack to carry;
Lance Fraser, being strongest, took most.

                        Far down below, the broad
    ocean burned like a vast cat's eye
Pupilled by the track of sun; but eastward, beyond the white-grassed hump
    of the ridge, the day moon stood bleak
And badly shaped, face of stained clay, above the limestone fang of one of
    the Ventana mountains
Just its own color. Lance, looking back, saw his wife talking to Michael, her
    cinnabar-colored hair
Like a flag of life against the pale east. That moment he saw the horses
    plunging against the sky

And heard a noise like a sharp head of water from a narrow pipe; a girl
    cried out,
Lance dropped his pack and returned. Will Howard was looking for stones
But found none, but Lance found a burnt fence-post, relic of an ancient
    fire. The snake lay with raised head,
The rattle of its tail making that noise of sharp water running; a big rattler,
    but very small
At bay in the circle of the laughing men. Lance struck for its head, but the
    snake that moment struck at the rope's end
That Michael was flicking at it, so that Lance's blow failed, the fence-post
    broke to bits in his hands,
The snake not harmed; then Michael laughing with pleasure whipped the
    creature to death with the doubled rope
And set his heel on the head; Lance damned all rotten wood, his blond face
    flushing
Dark through the sunburn. Michael cut off the victim's
Tail with the ten rattles to give to Mary;
The other young men quieted the horses, and caught
One that had dragged away the bush it was tied to.
Lance would not wait, he picked up his pack and went
Alone down the zigzag path; but after a moment
His temper cleared.

               Far down, short of the cat's eye ocean, they saw like a
    brown pebble
Drunken Charlie's hut in a gorge of the cliff, a feather of smoke, and his
    boat like a split berry
Of bladdery seaweed up the thin strand; and Lance stood waiting down the
    wild cliffside, his light brown hair
Golden with sun, his hat and the pack laid down. The warm wind up the
    mountain was wild with fragrance,
Chiefly the scent of the chiya bushes, that wear rosettes of seed

Strung on the stem. The girls squealed as they scrambled down, when the
    brittle traprock broke underfoot,
Small fragments ran over on the next below. When they came to the foot
    of the cliff Michael said, "Now," and offered
A bottle hot from his pocket. "It's time." Mary Abbey refused it but the
    others drank, from mouth to mouth,
Stinging fire from the slobbered bottle-neck.

                                        The sun was low
But had played all day on this southwestward
Cliff over the burning-glass water and the air
Still swirled with heat; the headland of Fraser's Point
Stopped off the trade-wind here. Fayne Fraser a little dizzily
Looked seaward, left of the blazing sun-track, and saw the track of the
    northwest gale and the running waves
Like an endless army of horse with banners going by off-shore; her eyes
    followed them, a ruled line southward
Of violent water, converging toward the bronze headland beyond headland
    of the mountain coast; and someone was saying,
"It's hot, we'll swim." "Before we eat," someone said.
The girls twittered together and clustered northward
To a little cove beyond a fair spit of rock;
The men remained on this side.

                                Fayne undressed beside Mary Abbey,
And was careful of words, because she'd sucked from the bottle more than
    she meant to, and had small experience of drinking.
She said carefully, "Where did those girls of Will Howard's come from?"
    "Nina told me," she answered: "waitresses
Down from the city on their vacation." "Honestly are they? I guessed it."
    "No," Mary said, "they're nice girls."

"That yellow-haired one, she's bad." "No," Mary said. Fayne said, "Did you
    see her face when she looked at Michael
Across that bottle?" "Oh, no," Mary answered. " . . . Well. Are you ready,
    Mary? Let's go."
They limped down to the waves, giggling and wincing.
Fayne had tied a broad handkerchief around her hair
To shed the spray; she swam out farther than others,
Mary remained along shore.

                    The other side of the rock-spit
The men had bathed, and had come up strand again
To dry by the driftwood fire; all except Michael,
Who loved to swim. Lance Fraser stood by the fire, his broad smooth chest,
    grooved between the square plates
Of heavy muscle, steamed and was ruddy in the glowing heat. He narrowed
    his eyes to look seaward
And saw Michael's left arm, over the speck of his head, lift, reach and dip,
Swimming side-stroke; two white arms flashing swanlike on either side of a
    handkerchief-hooded head
Emerged from the scales of light on the edge of the sun-dazzle. The
    swimmers approached each other,
And met this side the long brown stain of the breathing kelp-bed. Lance
    frowned,
But only thinking that they were too far out
And making a show of themselves.

                    On the pleasant water
Michael had called to Fayne, "I've something for you.
Come here a minute." She hardly dared, and thought
In the flashing joy of the sea, "Oh, the water covers us.
What have you got?" "Gin for girls.
We've got a fire on this side." They met laughing,

And reached the bottle from hand to hand and floated decorously
Separate again. Fayne looked toward shore, and saw the vast cliff in the flare
    of sundown soaring above
Like beaten gold, the imperfect moon-disk gold on its brow; the tiny
    distinct white shapes of men
Around their spot of fire in the flat blue sea-shadow. She breathed hard and
    said,
"My God how beautiful. Oh Michael, stay here at home."
He answered with a watery yell of pleasure, submerging his mouth
To roar as the sea-lions do.

                         Fayne trailed the bottle
And swam ashore. There was nothing to dry herself with;
The chill of the water had touched her blood, she sucked breath gustily
Through clicking teeth. She sipped from the salted bottle,
And dressed, but shivered still.

                             She sunned herself by the fire,
Watching with fascinated speculation of pain
The antennae of lobsters like spikes of jointed grass
Above the heating water in a five-gallon tin
Writhe at the sky, lives unable to scream.

III

Under the vast calm vaulting glory of the afterglow, low smoky rose and
    delicately
Stratified amber, soaring purple; then rose again, luminous and virginal
    floating the moon,
High up a scoured hollow of the cliff
Cormorants were settling to roost on the jags and ledges.
They writhed long negro snake-throats and shot

Sharp heads at each other, shaking out sooty wings
And angry complaining cries.

                        Below, on the thread of beach,
The lonely fisherman who was called Drunken Charlie,
Fire glowing on his drugged eyes, wide beard and lank hair,
Turned meat on the grid over the barbecue-pit
And talked to himself all the time. Michael Fraser knelt
By a turned chest that served for table and poured
From a jug into cups, fierce new distillate
From Charlie's cliff-hidden kettle.

                        Fayne Fraser shook half-dried hair,
The color of the coals at the heart of the fire
But darkening as light decreased, and went to Lance
Who stood alone at the waves' edge, turning his back on the world, and the
    wet sand
Raised by his weight on either side of his foot-soles ran water and glistened
    in the still light. Fayne said
"Are you cross, dear?" She pushed up his rolled sleeve and clasped her
    fingers on the broad trunk of his arm
Above the elbow, "Dear, are you sad?" "I? No," he said, "what about?"
    "You haven't spoken to anyone
Since we were swimming." "Why should I? You were out too far, though."
    "Oh, I can swim.
And Michael was there to help me if I'd got tired." "By God no," Lance
    said, with a sharp vision in his mind
Of her bright nakedness, the shining whiteness and the red hair. She
    understood and said softly, "Well,
I didn't need help. But he's our brother." "Certainly; I didn't mind him," he
    answered. "But I did hate

To think that rabble of girls could look at you; it isn't decent." She said,
   "They didn't seem interested.
Come, drink and eat. Those waitress-women are passing the paper plates."
   He saw that vision once more,
The form and whiteness, the little gay-colored flower of the pubic hair, and
   groaned, as a thick bull
Alone in the field groans to himself, not knowing why the hot brow and the
   hooves itch for destruction.
Fayne to cure his unhappiness hasted and returned
Fetching two cups of the fire Michael was pouring.

                                                After they had eaten,
   twilight and moonlight came;
The fire burned smaller and brighter; they were twelve around it; and
   drinks were poured. The bearded fisherman seemed
Stiffly asleep, with open eyes like a drowned man's
Glazed by the yellow firelight. Tom Dolman and Leo Ramirez
Roughed at each other, and Nina Dolman
Sitting between them cried out; then Michael said,
"Get up and wrestle." All but the fisherman turned
To watch them circle clumsily on the damp sand
And suddenly lock, into one quadruped body reeling
Against the dark band of ocean and the low sky.
Ramirez had the low hold but Dolman was the heavier man;
They tugged and sobbed; Ramirez was lifted high
And writhed on the other's shoulder by the evening star,
But the strained column staggered and crumbled, the Spaniard
Fell uppermost and was the first to rise up.
Michael asked very gravely, "Who was the winner?
The winner may challenge Lance." Ramirez gasping and laughing
Said, "Drunk: not to that extent." "Then gather firewood.
The fire's got low."

The yellow-haired one of the two girls Will Howard
    had brought
Sat in the sand beside Lance Fraser; she leaned on his shoulder and held a
    cup to his mouth and said
"Please drink it for me: things are beginning to go round in circles." He
    drank; then Fayne on his other side
Grew suddenly cool and quite clear; she leaned across him and said, "That
    hair in the cup! Well, you drank it.
Her bleaches have made it brittle so it keeps falling." "Oh," the other
    gasped, "that's not true." "It's pretty," Fayne said,
"Only the black half inch at the roots. Is your name Lois? What's your
    name?" "Lois." "Lean the other way,
Lois." Then Lance said angrily, "Be quiet will you," and got up
To fetch more firewood.

                A timber from one of the four ships
That have broken in half a century off Fraser's Point
Lay near and dry; Ramirez and Howard had brought it,
But the axe was lost in the sand. Lance up-ended it,
An ivory-white pillar under the moon,
Garnished with great iron bolts. He wedged his fingers
Into a crack and suddenly straining tore it in two;
The splitting made a great noise under the cliff,
The sea being quiet. Lance felt himself curiously
Numbed, as if the sharp effort had strained the whiskey
Out of his blood through the sheathes of his nerves;
His body obeyed as ever but felt a distance
Blocked off and alien. He took the halves of the timber
Under each arm and a bolt in his hand,
For two or three had fallen out of the wood,
This one straight, long and heavy. After he had laid
His logs on the fire he saw the fisherman's

Firelight-discolored eyes, and called "Hey! Charlie."
Still the man slept. Lance, wavering a little, reached
Over Will Howard's shoulder and took the cup from his hand,
Drank half, poured the other half on Charlie's long hair;
It dribbled into his beard; he coughed and awoke.
Lance said "D' you ever have rattlesnakes down here?
I snicked at one up the cliff with a rotten stick:
But this'd fix 'em." He gave him the iron bar;
Charlie posted it carefully up in the sand
Between his feet and answered, "Mm; but there's Injuns."
"What?" "All that was cleared out of the country.
Where did you think they got to? They ain't got ships.
Down here they are." The dark-haired girl that Will Howard had brought
Suddenly stood up from the fire, she went toward the sea and was heard
    vomiting. Charlie nodded and said,
"There's one o' them now. Most nights I see their fires away down the
    beach." Mary Abbey whispered to Michael,
"Don't take any more. Time to go home." "Ah no," he said, "dear, we just
    got here." Fayne came to Lance
And said, "Don't drink any more. Time to go home." He answered briskly,
    "Since when are you giving orders?"
"Since you're not fit to." She knew while the words made in her throat,
    "Now he'll be angry," a pale rush of anger
Ran to meet his; the memory of all his bad-tempered times, his heavy
    earnestness and lack of laughter,
Pierced like a mountain-peak the cloud in her mind, "Oh, I do hate you."
He stared, more astonished than angry, and saw her face
Lean, sharp, bled white, each freckle black as a mole
Against its moon-gleam pallor. "That's how you feel, ah?"
He turned his back. She thought, "He'll never forgive me:
Let him not," and saw the Dolmans, Nina and Tom,
Seeking the way up the cliff, Mary Abbey with them,

Fayne went and said, "Michael, I've lost my cup,
Aren't there any more cups?" "I'll hold the jug:
You hold your mouth." "Oo, I need water with it."
"No you don't." Half of the sip went strangling
Into her throat, half ran by her little chin
And trickled between her breasts. She looked at the fire,
Then at the moon, both blurred fantastically,
Red burrowed, white wavered high. Michael said, "My girl's gone."
Fayne said, "Oh, and yours?" He said "That's no sense. That's very."
She laughed and answered, "They don't."

                              The moon suspended in her
   great antelope-leap from the head of the cliff
Hung pouring whiteness along the narrow runway of sand and slide-rock
   under the continent's foot,
A watery glittering and secret place, walled from the world, closed by the
   cliff, ditched by the ocean.
Drunken Charlie dreamed by the dying fire;
Will Howard and Nell Ramirez were one slight point
Far down the white beach. Yellow-haired Lois
Spilled her drink and said, "Seeing is believing.
Come on, I'll show you." She smiled at Lance, "Come, dear.
Sadie's passed out; it's all right wi' Sadie,"
And to Leo Ramirez, "Come if you like, dark boy."
He swayed and stammered, "Responsible; sister Nell.
Keep an eye on young sister." "Ah, go and find her."
"Not till I see the picture on Sadie's stomach."
They wandered toward Drunken Charlie's little hollow skiff
And its black shadow, drawn up the moonlight sand.
Lance thought, "Here's a boat, let's break it," and thought with an ache of
   shame,

"I wouldn't think that, only being drunk." The center of his mind made
    savage war on rebellious out-liers
In breathless darkness behind the sweating forehead; while Leo Ramirez,
    seeing the bright fish-scales glued
With blood and slime to the boat-thwarts glitter like a night of stars, began
    to sing a stale song: "We'll always,
Be young and gay. We'll always, feel that way." Lois said "Shut up," and led
    them around the boat,
Her friend lay in the moonlight nestled against it. Lois knelt down and
    gently drew her by the shoulder;
She groaned in her sleep, resisting. Lois laughed, "The boys want to see it,
    Sadie," and tugged, and turned her
Onto her back, the stained pale face up to the moonlight; the teeth in the
    opened mouth glittered,
And sour breath crossed them, while Lois turned up the blouse, loosened
    the band and jerked up the linen shift
To show a three-masted sailing-ship tattooed with black and red inks on
    the soft white belly
Below the breasts. "My God," Ramirez said, "there it is."
Lois answered, "A fellow dared her," and looked for Lance,
Who trembled and said, "Cover her up, damn you."
Lois blinking drew down the blouse. Ramirez giggled,
"My God, a U.S. flag at the peak," and reached
Over Lois's shoulder to raise the cloth;
Lance struck and felled him, and stepping across him fallen
Leaned and strode toward the cliff and the red coals
That had been the fire.

                Drunken Charlie lay on the sand,
The iron bolt erect by his feet; Lance caught it up
And smashed the jug, and saw the remnant of whiskey
Glitter among the shards to sink into sand.

He ground his teeth; he saw in his mind in the stream of images
A second jug, and began to search for it.

                             The tide had fallen, the steep
    ribbon of beach was but little wider,
But the sea was become so flattened that no waves flashed. Enormous peace
    of the sea, white quiet of the cliff,
And at their angle and focus a few faint specks of humanity happy in liquor
    or released in sleep,
But Lance alone. Then noises like the cries of a woman screaming, bird
    after bird of sharp-colored sound
Flew on the face of the cliff, tattered wild wings against jagged rock. On
    the cliffhead the patient horses
Turned their ears, grooving small wrinkles about the roots of the cartilage,
    but did not lift up their heads;
And the sea was not moved, nor the moonlight quivered. Will Howard was
    lying beside Nell Ramirez; they'd fallen asleep
Before he had his desire; they sighed and stirred in the sand. He murmured
    "Oh, somebody's got hysterics,"
And wriggled his fingers, which had grown painfully numb between her
    plump knees. But Lois, Leo Ramirez
And Drunken Charlie heard the sounds nearer; they went in a wind of fear
    to find out their fountain,
And Sadie awoke in the sand and followed heavily,
Falling but once, catching her clothes that slipped,
Whining at the hollow pain in her skull.

                             Beyond a rock
Stood Lance, high white in the moonglaze, distorted, taller than human;
Lois said, "Dearie?" He babbled, "Oh Jesus Christ Oh Jesus Christ Oh Jesus
    Christ,"
Behind him in a great shadow of her hair darkened

By the rock-shadow Fayne turned her white wedge of face
With three holes in it. She was kneeling, bent S-shape,
And seemed to stare up from the very ground. She said "I think
It is finished. Water please. Water please.
He fell down from the cliff." Then Michael's feet were seen,
And thence the prone extended ridge of his body
Ending indefinitely under Fayne's face.
Lois cried, "He's hurt." But they dared not approach
For Lance standing between, high and twisted
Like a dead tree. Lance said "I . . ." Fayne cried,
"He fell down from the cliff." They all stood silent,
Lois's mouth opened and closed on silence
Three times, then asked, "Is he hurt?" Lance said, "Oh Christ.
I . . ." Fayne cried so that his words were hidden,
And stood up and said, "He has died. Michael.
He was climbing the cliff and fell, his foot caught in that bush;
He struck his head on that rock, on that edge of rock.
It is all — broken in. Oh, we loved him."
Ramirez said, "What for did he climb up there?"
"Have we drunk *water*?" Fayne said. But Lance began
To shake, like a tall dead mast of redwood that men are felling,
    It is half cut through, each dip of the axe the sonorous timber quivers from
    the root up to the cloud,
He said "I caught them . . ." "He caught him," Fayne cried, "when he fell
    but he could not save him." "I killed . . ." "You are wild with sorrow.
He fell head down — whether you'd tried to catch him or not. You are not
    to blame." He said, "It is horrible
To hear the lies from her mouth like bees from a hot hive: I am the one,"
    but Fayne running to him
Made an animal moan in her throat in time to hide what he said. She came
    to Lance, and her face
Like a held spear, and said, "Drunkard.

Too drunk to be understood. Keep still until you can talk and be
   understood." He drew backward from her,
Shuddering like a horse from a snake, but when his back was against the
   rock he stammered, "I
Will find my time." "Yes," she answered, "be quiet now. To-morrow when
   you are better they'll understand you."
"Is he dead?" "Keep still. Will you shame his end
With drunkard babbling? For he was the dearest," she said, "in the world to
   all of us. Lovelier than morning light
On the mountain before the morning. There is not one of us would not
   have died for him: *I* would, *I* would, *I* would,"
She cried writhing, "but not lose Lance too. How can I plan to save him,
   I've got what I can't bear?
You are all our friends."
She set her hands in the masses of red-dark hair, dark in the moonlight,
   and tearing it, with her white face
To the white moon: "*That* eye's blind. Like Juan Arriba's old mare he used
   to beat on the face,
Her eyes froze white like that. He was larking on the cliff and fell." She
   seemed to be treading a tragic dance,
She was scuffling sand to cover the bolt of shipwreck that lay in shadow of
   the rock; she wrung her hands
And knelt moaning by Michael's head; she rose with blood on her hand and
   fibers of hair, and ran
To the rock under the cliff. "This rock killed him. He fell on this edge,"
   she drew her hand on the edge
And the rock was stained. Then Sadie was heard gasping from her poor
   stained face. One or two looked at her. "O-uh,"
She whispered hoarsely, "we was having fun!"

                              Lance moved at length,
   like a dead man walking, toward his dead brother,

And stooped as one stoops to gather a sleeping child. Fayne ran and said,
     "No, the man. No, the man.
He has to come." Lance turned toward her his face like a paralyzed man's
Slack with peace, and said softly, "The man."
"He'd think wrong has been done. I can't think . . . coroner.
Don't take him up." "Home?" he said,
Seeming gently surprised; he gathered the body
Into his arms and walked along the foot of the cliff.
Fayne stayed behind a moment, the others following.
She cast quick looks over the rocks and sand;
One end of the rusty bolt was visible still;
She leaned toward it and fell on her face. She labored up
And went ten steps to the ebb and flung the iron
To the water edge.

                        Lance walked along the foot of the cliff.
He turned, not where the path went up, and walked
Into the face of the cliff, and stood there walking
Like an ox in a tread-mill, until Ramirez
Showed him the path. Fayne went up behind him.

                                            Half way up
He awoke a moment out of his automatism
To feel failure and pain, his breathing like knives, and the failure
Of his eyes; it was impossible to see the path;
He checked a step and fell forward.

                              Fayne came up to him
And stood; there was nothing that she could do. They lay
Very peacefully together, Lance's face
On his brother's breast. She looked across them;
Terribly far down the moonlight cliff crouched the dark sea.

Ramirez came up and stood. Fayne said they had not the strength to carry
     up either of the fallen, and so
They had to wait. They heard a faint breeze through the dry bushes; and
     the crying of sea-lions far down below,
Where eight or ten were lying in a circle by the softly heaving kelp-bed, as
     their custom is, and gazed
With great mild eyes at the sky and the night of water. Then they sing in
     their manner, lifting up sleek
Dark-shining muzzles to the white moon, making a watery noise of roaring
     and a lonely crying
For joy of life and the night.

                    At length Lance
Began to paw with his feet like a dreaming hound,
And some stones fell. He knelt and stood up
And took his burden and went up.

                         When they entered the sleeping
     farmstead,
Fayne led the horse; Lance held his brother and rode behind him.
It would be hard to tell which one was slain
If the moon shone on their faces. The horse stopped and sighed
By the garden-gate; Lance did not move to dismount,
But sat and held up his brother. Fayne came beside,
Reaching to help; Lance whispered "Ah, Ah, thank God."
"What?" "He may be saved, Fayne.
He is hot under the arms and I heard him breathe."
"You heard the horse breathe," she said. They lifted down
The unmanageable weight.

                    Oh ignorant penitents,
For surely the cause is too small for so much anguish.

To be drunk is a folly, to kill may call judgment down,
But these are not enormous evils,
And as for your brother, he has not been hurt.
For all the delights he has lost, pain has been saved him;
And the balance is strangely perfect,
And why are you pale with misery?
Because you have saved him from foolish labors and all the vain days?
From desires denied and desires staled with attaining,
And from fear of want, and from all diseases, and from fear of death?
Or because you have kept him from becoming old,
When the teeth drop and the eyes dim and the ears grow dull,
And the man is ashamed?
Surely it is nothing worse to be slain in the overflowing
Than to fall in the emptiness;
And though this moon blisters the night,
Darkness has not died, good darkness will come again;
Sometimes a fog will come in from sea,
Sometimes a cloud will crop all the stars.

IV

The moonlight from the west window was a square cloth
Laid on the floor, with one corner on the bed,
Lying over Michael's hand; they had taken him
To his own room. Fayne whispered: "Now we must tell them.
Your mother may die — her sick heart.
Don't let her die too bitterly. For this one night, dear,
Say nothing worse than 'Michael's gone.' Spare her something
Until she has cried. Four hours' mercy. By morning
That heart of hers will be seasoned." Fayne strained in the dark
To see his face. He answered in a short while,
"How many mornings I've come in here

And routed him out of bed. He always was a late sleeper.
Sound asleep mother." Fayne caught his arm. "Can't you hear me?"
"You," he said, "keep your hands off! ... Until morning
I'll say he fell."

 It was not morning, but the moon was down.
The old mother sat by the bed with her hand on Michael's, regularly her
 great fat-swollen body
Jerked with a sob, and tears were spurted from her closed eyes. Old Fraser
 sat with his fists evenly
Together on his knees, his bony face held erect, the brown eyes in their
 hollows red with lamplight.
Fayne heard the noise of a motor starting and left the room.

 He was
 backing out the big truck,
The shed was full of the headlight glare, the ruby taillight glowed by the
 axle. Before she could come
It had crept out; its light swung up the driveway by the stooping sycamore
And picked from darkness the heavy timbers of the high corrals and the
 white bee-hives remote on the hill;
Fayne ran down the river of light to the gate and closed it, and stood in the
 gate for fear he might smash through;
But Lance came wearily to open; stooping, tall,
Black on the light. She said, "Oh, where?" "You know.
Tell dad to come to Salinas and get the truck;
There wasn't enough gas in the little one."
She answered, "Can the sheriff make us happy again?
Or the judge make Michael alive again?" "Open the gate."
"Yes, dear. *Listen* to me. When Arriba and his boys
Stole cows of ours, did you run to the courthouse?
We take care of ourselves down here. What we have done

Has to be borne. It's in ourselves and there's no escaping,
The state of California can't help you bear it.
That's only a herd of people, the state.
Oh give your heart to the hawks for a snack o' meat
But not to men." When she touched him with her hands
Pleading, he sighed and said, "If I'd been nearer
My decent mind, it would have been you, not Michael.
Did y' love him? Or was it only because you're female
And were drunk, female and drunk?" "Oh. Hush. I was begging him
Not to leave us, as I'm begging you. He promised me, dear.
He said he'd not go away. I kissed him for that: he was our brother:
And you came behind." Lance's blackness of his leaning bulk
Vibrated in the light-beam. "It'd be a pity for me then.
I can't see clear, in the dirty streaming memories . . .
Don't be afraid: your part will be secret.
I'll say I killed him for nothing, a flea-bite quarrel,
Being beastly drunk." "He was killed," she answered, "for nothing."
"It's a great pity for me then.
Open the gate." She clung to the timber bolt
To hold it home in the slot, and felt his mind
Tearing itself. "Lance. Lance? Sweetheart:
Believe . . . whatever you need to save you.
I won't give you up. You can't remember what happened;
I tell you he fell from the cliff. But if your dreadful
Dream were true, I know you are strong enough
To give your heart to the hawks without a cry
And bear it in lonely silence to the end of life.
What else do you want? Ah. Confession's a coward
Running to officers, begging help. Not you."

                                            She heard
The scrape of slow boots on gravel outside the light-stream,

Across the pulses of the idling motor, and suddenly cried,
"He fell from the cliff." An old man said in the dark,
"They ain't got consideration. Where was you going
This time o' night, after what's happened? Your dad wants you.
Your ma's took bad." Lance moaned and stood still.
Fayne said, "He was going to Lobos to telephone
The doct . . . the coroner. Dearest, you ought to go in.
She suffered great pain before, she was near death.
Old Davie will drive up the coast for you
When daylight comes." "Oh," he said stilly, and turned
His face to the fountains of light; it gleamed without meaning
In the stream of radiance like a stake in a stream,
Except that from exhaustion the pupils of the eyes
Failed to contract, so that their secret interiors
Of their chambers returned the light all sanguine.
At length he kneaded them with his fists and said,
"I can't see well. You'll have to help me find the way in.
It's not a trick of yours, uh?"

V

His mother lay on the floor,
For Michael's body lay on the bed. The sun of pain at her heart had rays
    like skewers of anguish
Along the left arm and up by the jugular arteries. She dared not move; her
    face stood wet-white and still,
With live blue eyes; but the clay-pale lips opened and closed. Old Fraser
    had swathed her in hasty blankets.
Fayne entered; Lance behind her stood swaying and stooping in the door
    and saw his father
Crouched beside the great cocoon of the blankets; and Michael in the bed
    above, and trinkets of Michael's

That hung on the wall, gleam in the lamplight. The violence of pain was
    brief; she whispered "better," and breathed
With greedy shallow passion; her eyes found Lance.

                                  Daylight grayed
    slowly into the room;
The lamp ran dry unnoticed. Lance and his father
Labored and carried the heavy old woman to bed.
Fayne brought them food, but Lance refused it. In the afternoon
He walked out-doors for a time, but nothing farther
Than the cattle-pens. Fayne must have been watching for him,
Because she went and walked by his side, and said,
When they were turned from the house, "Mary Abbey was here.
It seems she expected to marry Michael, though he never told us.
She cried a lot." Lance made no sign of hearing her.
Fayne said, looking up sidelong at his cheek and jaw,
Where the flesh hung thin on the bone: "Her grief's not
Like ours, forever; but sharp at present. If she ever
Imagined that you . . . how could we bear her looks? You are too strong,
    dear,
To lay on weaker persons a burden
That you alone ought to bear." He strode faster
And stopped, muttering, "He lies up there, like that.
And my mother, like that: and I have done it;
And you talk about Mary Abbey." Fayne said, "I have no time
To choose names, for a man is coming to-day
To question us. He's sent for. I have to tell you that you must choose
    whether to relieve
Your own weakness . . . conscience I mean . . . by easy confession,
Or bear the whole weight unhelped. The first way's easy: you'll be
    acquitted: you'll be left humbled and soiled,

But free; for confession is not enough; and you were too lost to remember
     anything clearly; and I
Am the one witness. I saw him climb on the cliff and fall. So your
     conscience will be well comforted,
And fairly cheap. Only your mother perhaps will die of it; your father and I
     will swallow our portion;
And the crowd at Salinas
Will have had a good time watching your face in court. It would be harder,
     if you've a snake in your heart,
To keep it shut there."

                    He was silent, and drew sharp breath and said, "A
     red-haired one. Ah.
A white one with a red brush. Did you do it with him
Or not?" "Leave that," she said stilly; "this choice is *now*."
He groaned and answered, "My mind's not quick like yours.
. . . I'll not lie to them." "Let me show your mind to you:
Be patient a moment still: if I seem cruel,
That's to save, all that's left. Look at yourself:
A man who believes his own sweet brother's blood
Lies on his hands: yet
Too scrupulous to tell a lie, for his mother's life.
Our minds are wonderful." He meditated, and answered
Heavily, "The sunlight seems dull but red.
What makes it red?" "Your eyes are sick of not sleeping;
Or there's a forest-fire in the south." "Our minds? Little bottles
That hold all hell. I seem too tired to feel it, though.
I'll think, I'll think."
"You have no time for thinking. He will come probably
Within this hour." "Who? Let him come. I'll tell him
God made them male and female but men have made

So-and-so. . . . I fall asleep while I talk . . . whiskey eh?
Lighted the sticky fire. It's not possible
I'd ever done it except that I stumbled on you
In the heart of guilt. I know that." "Believe it then,"
She answered shrilly, and stood twitching her lips
In the white freckled face, in the reddish light of her hair,
"If that will help." "Oh," he said.
". . . I wish you had picked from another tree."
She answered: "You are to say that you found him dying.
You heard me cry, and he was down by the rock.
Isn't that the truth exactly, because you remember
No previous thing? You heard me cry out; you came;
Michael was dying or had died. That's all. You carried him home.
. . . I wish he'd come."

                    But the man did not come
Until afternoon the next day. Dark weather, for a stagnant ocean of clouds
        was hung on the sky,
And what light shone came colored like the taste of metal through smoke
        of burning forests far to the south
That veiled the coast, so that it seemed brown twilight
In the house, in Michael's room. A lamp was lighted,
The death-wound viewed. "*Who* saw him fall?" "I alone.
My husband and others came when I cried." "Where is your husband?"
"With his mother," she answered faintly. "She had an attack,
Her heart, angina, and has to lie still. Shall I
Call him, sir?" her voice hardening, her eyes
Growing hard and narrow. "Pretty soon. Was this young man
In trouble about anything?" "No." "A girl?" "He was engaged
To Miss Abbey." "They had a quarrel, ah?" "No."
"Did he seem cheerful?" "Very." "They always do.

Yesterday I had to drive by Elkhorn Slough
Because a very cheerful old man opened his throat
With his nephew's pen-knife. I was two hours
Finding that place; the farmers around there they couldn't tell you
Whether Jesus Christ died on the cross
Or at the battle of Bull Run."

                     Old Fraser had stood
Nerveless and dreaming over the livid face
Since they uncovered it; abruptly he turned his head
Above his bowed shoulder, saying "It's enough.
Dog, blaspheme not. Go to your own place.
My son found death in recklessness, I fear in folly;
Write that and leave us alone; go hence and leave us
To mourn and hope." "Well, Mr. Fraser. You understand . . ."
"I am very patient," the old man said, thrusting
His hollowed face toward the other, the closely set
Inflamed brown eyes pushing like the burnt end of a stick
That has been used to stir fire; the man stepped backward.
"Did he say patient! . . . Well, is your husband here?"
Fayne's mouth jerked and froze hard, her hands quieted.
"I will call him. Come to the room down-stairs."
She said at the foot of the stair, "This way, sir. It's dark.
Will you have to go . . . to see the cliff, to see
The cliff?" "Hm, what's that?" "Where he fell."
"Can we drive there?" "No, ride and walk." "Look here,"
He said, "I've come sixty-five miles already.
You're sure it was accidental?" "Yes." "Well.
I always try to save the family feelings
When the case is not clear." He tried his pen,
Shook it, and wrote. Fayne watched, quiet and cold, thinking that Lance

Would not have to be questioned; he was saved now;

And saw the man to his car. When he had gone

She thought that now she could laugh or cry if she wanted to,

Now Lance was saved, but her nerves and her mind stood quiet. She looked
    at the dusty gate and the dark house-gable

In the stagnant air against the black cloud, and perceived that all events are
    exact and were shaped beforehand,

And spaced in a steel frame; when they come up we know them; there is
    nothing for excitement.

                              She went in,

And found Lance in the dark at the head of the stair, bent forward like a
    great bird. "Has he gone, Fayne?"

"Did you *know* he was here?" "I will live on," he answered, "seems to be
    best. I loved him well; he died instantly,

No anger nor pain. Davis has dug a place by the children's graves."

                                                                On
    account of the dull weather

And closing twilight the group on the hill-top was hardly visible in their
    vast scene. It was quite evident

That not only Pico Blanco against the north, and the gray Ventanas, but
    even every dry fold

And gully of the humbler hills was almost by an infinite measure of more
    importance

Than the few faint figures on the bare height,

The truck, and three saddled horses,

And some persons.

The old man swayed and shook, standing praying

At the head of a dug slot

Beside the pile of pale earth.

The heavy great brown-furred sky that covered all things made a red point
    in the west, lost it and darkened,
And the Point Sur lighthouse made a thin stabbing from the northwest.

Swaying on his heels and toes the old man prayed:
"O Lord our God, when thy churches fell off from thee
To go a-whoring after organ-music,
Singing-women and lecturers, then my people
Came out from among them; and when thy last church,
Thy little band, thy chosen, was turned at length
To lust for wealth and amusement and worldly vanities,
I cried against them and I came forth from among them.
I promised thee in that day that I and my house
Would remain faithful, thou must never despair;
I said, though all men forget thee thou hast a fort
Here in these hills, one candle burning in the infidel world,
And my house is thy people.

                    My children died,
And I laid them in this place and begot more children
To be thy servants, and I taught them thy ways, but they fell away from
    thee.
They found their pleasure among the ungodly, and I believe
They made themselves drunk with wine, and my dear son is fallen.
He died on the shore. One half of the curse of Eli has fallen upon me."
He covered his face with his knotted hands and stood gasping,
And said, "I loved him. Here he is, Lord.
Surely thou hast forgiven his sins as I have forgiven them,
And wilt lift him to thy glory on the last day."
The old man stood silent, lifting his face, and fixed his deep close-set eyes,
    like the eyes of an old ape,

Small, dark and melancholy under the bar of the brow, between the wide
    cheek-bones, fixed them far off
Across the darkening ridges and ocean upon that single red spot that waned
    in the western sky,
And said "The world darkens and the end is coming.
I cannot beget more children; I am old and empty,
And my wife is old. All men have turned their faces away from thee;
I alone am thy church. Lord God, I beseech thee not to despair,
But remember thine ancient power, and smite the ungodly on their mouths
And the faithless churches with utter destruction. For Jesus' sake, amen."
    While he prayed, Fayne watched Lance
With pity and fear; and Mary Abbey, who was there with her father,
Kept stealing glances at Lance through her wet eye-lashes.
She whispered to Fayne: "Oh Lance looks dreadfully.
I never knew he loved him so dreadfully."
Fayne answered, "Yes, he did"; and looked up at Lance
With pity and fear. "He looks as if he'd fall sick,"
Mary said. Fayne answered, "No, he is strong.
He hasn't eaten since Michael died; maybe
He hasn't slept." Mary said, wiping her eyes,
"His face is so sad and fine, like carved marble.
They say he carried him all the way home, up that cliff."
The old man ended his prayer, the redwood box
Was lowered with ropes; Lance had the weight at one end,
Old Fraser and Davis at the other. The ropes cut grooves
In the earth edges. While they were shovelling earth,
Mary Abbey, with a sudden abandoned gesture
Of the hand that had the handkerchief in it, ran up to Lance
On the scraped ground. "*Don't* grieve so." She reached and touched
His hand on the spade-handle. "It makes me afraid for you.
We all loved him: life has to go on." He jerked his hand,
And looked down at her face with startled eyes

So pale gray-blue that all the light that remained in the world
Under the low black sky seemed to live in them,
Stammering, "No. *No.* He fell from the cliff." She said, "I know, Lance.
We have to bear it. I loved him too." He gathered his dreaming nerves
Into the bundle again and said, "Oh. All right. Please keep out of the way
    for the time.
We have this to do." "Good-bye," she answered patiently. "Father's calling
    me."

      The pit was filled full and mounded;
Fayne came and said, "What was she saying to you?" "Nothing. Who?"
    "Mary Abbey." "I didn't see her."
"What, Lance? She came and spoke to you." "I'd rather be there with
    Michael," he answered. "Dear, you must rouse yourself.
Life has to go on." "Somebody was saying so, I think.
There's not a hawk in the sky." She answered from a hoarse throat, "After
    dark? What are you dreaming?
See, Davie's turned on the headlights." "I hate them," he said, "killers, dirty
    chicken-thieves."

      The farm-truck headlights
Shone on the mounded earth, and cast its enormously lengthened shadow
    and the shadows of a few moving
Persons across the world, with the beam of light, over mound beyond
    mound of bare autumn hills, and black
Ocean under the black-roofed evening.

VI

      That night he returned again
To lie with Fayne in their bed, but like two strangers
Lying in one bed in a crowded inn, who avoid

Touching each other; but the fifth night
She laid her hand on the smooth strength of his breast,
He pretended to be asleep, she moved against him,
Plucking his throat with her lips. He answered, "After all?
You're right. If we're to live in this life
We'll keep its customs." He approached her confidently,
And had no power. The little irrational anger
At finding himself ridiculous brought to his mind
That worse rage, never before clearly remembered,
But now to the last moment; or imagined. He drew
His limbs from Fayne's without thinking of her, and lay still, with shut fists,
Sweating, staring up spirals of awful darkness, that spun away up and
    wound over his eyes
Around a hollow gray core with flecks in it. "I am damned unjustly. I did it
    in a moment."

                    But Fayne knew nothing
Of the shut agony beside her; only she was troubled at heart, and
    wondering
Whether he had ceased to love her said tenderly, "Sleep,
Darling. I didn't mean. I didn't want.
Only I love you." He felt her instinctive hand
Move downward fondling along the flat of his belly.
He set it aside and spoke, so low that her ears
Lost every word between the hair and the pillow.
"What, dearest?" "I know it," he said, "they're dogs: that was exactly
Fit to tell dogs. I can be damned
At home as well." "Hush, dear." "I don't make a good murderer,"
He said, "I sweat." She was silent and heard him breathing,
And mourned, "Oh cover your mind with quietness to-night.
In the morning you'll face it down again. This will get well with time.
It was really only a dreadful accident." "Very damnable," he said,

"Very true." Fayne said, "We'll live, sweetheart, to feel it
Only a dreadful accident, and the sad death
Of one we loved." "That's your smooth skin.
The fires fester on mine. Will you do something
For me?" "Dearest, with all my heart." "An easy kindness:
Shut up your mouth."

                    He got up after a time;
When he went out she followed, trembling. He turned on her
Outside the door. "I'm not going to Salinas,"
He whispered, "nor bump myself off either.
I'll not starve your hawks of their snatch o' meat.
Now let me alone for Christ's sake." She stood and saw him
Against the starlit window at the end steal down
The hallway, go past the stairhead, and enter the empty
Room of his brother. He slept there from that night on,
And seemed to regain calm strength.

VII

                              In the course of a month
Rain seemed at hand, the south wind whetting his knife on the long
     mountain and wild clouds flying;
Lance and his father set out to burn the hill to make pasture. They carried
     fire in forkfuls of straw
Along the base of the south wall of their valley; the horses they rode
     snorted against it, and smoke
Boiled, but the seaward end of the hill would only be burnt in patches.
     Inland, at the parched end,
A reach of high grass and sage might have led out the fire to the forest, and
     Lance rode up
To watch a flame down the wind to black out the danger.

He carried two barley-sacks and went to the Abbeys' trough
At the hill spring to dip them, to beat down the fire's
Creepings up wind. From that spur of the mountain
He saw the planted pine trees at Abbey's place,
And riding back with the dipped sacks, the vale
Of his own place, the smoke-mist, and Sycamore Creek
Wound like a long serpent down the small fields.
He set his fires and watched them rage with the wind,
Easily stifling their returns, riding herd
On the black line; then from the base of the hill
Red surf, and the dark spray rolled back by the wind,
Of the other fire came up roaring. The lines met
On the fall of the hill like waves at a river's mouth
That spout up and kill each other, and hang white spray
On cold clear wind.
A rabbit with blazing fur broke through the back-fire,
Bounding and falling, it passed by Lance and ran
Straight into the stem of a wild lilac bush,
He saw it was blind from the fire, and watching it struggle away
Up its dark pain, saw Mary Abbey coming down the black hill against the
    white sky,
Treading on embers. Lance turned and hardened in the saddle, and saw the
    vale below him a long trough of smoke
Spilled northward, then Mary came near and said, "I wanted to talk to you.
    I saw you ride by the water-trough."
He shuddered and said, "What? I'll watch the fire." "Fayne doesn't like me
    so well I think
Since Michael . . . . indeed I'm ashamed to be always around your house."
"I noticed you there," he said, carefully regarding
The dark braids of her hair, and the pale brown face
Seen from above. "I don't know," she said.
"My father says to go away for a time,

His sister lives on a place in Idaho.
But I wouldn't want to forget. But I told Fayne ...
So I don't know. We could see that you grieved for him
More deeply than anyone else, and all these great hills are empty."
He said, "Is that all?" "Ah ... ? Yes," she answered,
And turned away and looked back. Lance found that the bridle-leather
Had broken suddenly between his hands, and said "You won't get anything
    from Fayne; she's hard as iron.
Why do you follow us around? What do you think you'll find out?" She
    said, "Your grief is greater perhaps,
For you knew him longer. But you have Fayne and I have nobody: speak
    kindly to me. As I remember,
At first it came from seeing you and Fayne so happy in each other,
I wanted to be like that. I can't talk well, like Fayne,
But I read a great deal." He stared at her face and began to knot the bridle,
    his hands relaxing,
And said, "I must ride around by the oak-scrub and see that the fire has
    checked. I've got to be watchful always.
Will you stay here?" He went and returned and said, "Come down to our
    place whenever you are lonely, Mary.
My mother's quite well again. His death was ... do people talk much
    about it?" She looked in wonder at his face,
And he with numbed lips: "What lies do they ... can't you speak out?" "I
    never
Talked about it with anyone, since Nina Dolman
Told us that day. Truly there's nothing to be said by anyone
Except, he was bright with life and suddenly nothing, nothing, nothing,
    darkness."
Lance breathed and said sharply, "I wouldn't bet on it
If I were you. Mary, you are tender and merciful:
Don't come to the house; Fayne is like iron. You'd better
Run home and forget about us. Unless you should hear something

I ought to know." "What do you mean?" "Good-bye."
She saw his bridle-hand lift, she said "I've no pride,
I pray you not to leave me yet, Lance.
I loved him greatly, and now that bond hangs cut,
Bleeding on the empty world, it reaches after
You that were near him. Fayne and you. I was always
Without companions, and now I'd give anything
To be in your friendship a little." "Anything?" he said.
"You faithful women.
Fayne was five days. Mmhm, I have seen a vision.
My eyes are opened I believe."

                                He rode across the burnt hill,
Watching the wind swirl up the ashes and flatten
The spits of smoke. Past the singed oak-scrub he began to wonder,
If there was honey in the little tree, had . . . the dead
Tasted it before he died? "You'd better be off to Idaho.
. . . I shy from his name like a scared horse.
By God, I'd better get used to it; I've got to live with it."
He looked sharply all about the burnt solitude
To be sure of no hearers, and recited aloud:
"I killed Michael. My name is Lance Fraser.
I murdered my brother Michael. I was plastered,
But I caught 'em at it. I killed my brother Michael.
I'm not afraid to sleep in his room or even
Take over his girl if I choose. I am a dog,
But so are all."

                The tall man riding the little bay horse
Along the burnt ridge, talking loudly to nothing but the ash-drifting wind;
    a shadow passed his right shoulder;

He turned on it with slitted eyes, and saw through the strained lashes
    against the gray wind a ghastly old woman
Pursuing him, bent double with age and fury, her brown cloak wild on the
    wind, but when she turned up the wind
It was only a redtail hawk that hunted
On the burnt borders, making her profit in the trouble of field-mice. Lance
    groaned in his throat "Go up you devil.
Ask your high places whether they can save you next time."

VIII

Leo Ramirez rode down on business
About redwood for fence-posts; he asked in vain
For Lance, and had to deal with old Fraser. When he went out
He saw red hair around the corner of the house
And found Fayne in the garden, and asked for Lance.
"I couldn't tell you. I saw him ride to the south.
He'll be home soon for supper." Ramirez stood
In troubled silence, looking at the earth, and said
"I wonder ought I to tell him . . ." Fayne's body quivered
Ever so slightly, her face grew carefully blank.
"What, Leo?" "Will Howard, for instance. Mouths that can't
Shut up for the love of God." "He drives the coast stage,"
Fayne answered carefully. Ramirez looked over the creek
At the branded flanks of the south hill, and no rain had come
To streak them with gray relentings. "He didn't see it,"
He said; "and those two janes on vacation
Went back to town the next day." He giggled, remembering
The sailing-ship stippled on the white skin,
And fixed his mind smooth again. Fayne said, "How dares he
Lie about us?" Ramirez's brown soft eyes
Regarded her with mournful wonder and slid away.

He said, "You was very quick-thinking." "What?" she said, "you were
    there.
And when I cried to him to be careful you looked
And saw him larking on the rock, and you saw him fall,
You could see very plainly in the awful moonlight.
These are things, Leo, that you could swear to." He nodded,
And slid his red tongue along his dry lips and answered,
"Yes'm." "So Howard's a liar," she said. "But don't tell Lance;
He'd break him in two. We'll all do very well,
All wicked stories will die, long long before
Our ache of loss." "Yes'm." She walked beside him
To his tethered horse, and charmed him with an impulsive hand-clasp
After he was in the saddle.

                              She stood with her face high, the great sponge
    of red hair
Lying like a helmet-plume on her shoulders, and thought she was sure of
    conquering security but she was tired;
She was not afraid of the enemy world, but Michael would never be here
    laughing again. On the hill,
In the hill he lay; it was stranger than that, and sharper. And his killer
Ought to be hated a little in the much love. The smells on the wind were
    of ocean, the reedy creek-mouth,
Cows, and wood-smoke, and chile con carne on the kitchen stove; it was
    harder to analyze thoughts in the mind.
She looked at the dear house and its gables
Darkening so low against the hill and wide sky and the evening color
    commencing; it was Lance's nest
Where he was born, and his great white body grew high and beautiful. Old
    Davie shuffled up from the calf-pens
Into the house; then far and high, like a tiny horn on the hill against the
    green-saffron heaven

Lance grew into sight, the man and the horse and the evening peace. He
    was well again; he was sometimes cheerful
Since the early plowing; his muscles needed strong labor. He was like this
    mountain coast,
All beautiful, with chances of brutal violence; precipitous, dark-natured,
    beautiful; without humor, without ever
A glimmer of gayety; blind gray headland and arid mountain, and trailing
    from his shoulders the infinite ocean.
So love, that hunts always outside the human for his choice of metaphors,
Pictured her man on her mind. He dropped from sight
In the hill thickets. She thought, "That's the direction
From the Abbeys' or farther south. Mary Abbey's
Quit haunting our house." The sky grew ever more luminous pale,
The hills more solid purple. At the valley sea-mouth pale rose layered over
    amber, and over the rose
Pale violet, high over the lifted hawk-wings of divided hills, to one fine
    twist of flamingo-feather
Cloud flying in the wind and arch of the world.

                           A bat flitted up the still
    glimmer.
Fayne went up the drive and opened the gate
For Lance coming across the fields. He looked
As if he had fought, a victory; Fayne was silent;
He nodded, and said, "I've got it over with. You were right."
She saw a thin drift of blood on the bay's fore-leg;
A big brown bird hung from the saddle-thongs,
The half-spread sail of one wing clasped Lance's knee;
He had his rifle. "Another hawk, Lance?" "I've been there,"
He answered. "Oh, this? I pick 'em off when I see 'em.
I've been back to that place." "What place, dear?" "The . . .
Slaughter-house. Under the cliff. Ah: I looked around there.

And rubbed that . . . time into my eyes
Until it formed. Now I guess it won't mix
With every mouthful of air; I can call it to memory
Or shut it up." Fayne looked at his drawn face.
But she thought he seemed a degree restored
To natural goodness again, for he dismounted
And walked beside her. She smelled the prickly sweet fragrance
Of whiskey, and said: "That nasty old man was there.
Lance: you were careful with him?" "Care?" he said, "Hell.
We talked about fish. . . . I heard once about a fellow in jail
Kept banging his head on the wall until he died:
I'd liefer have done that than killed my brother.
I often . . . miss him." He stopped to tie up the hawk's feet
To the top wire of the fence; thence they went on
Without speaking.

                    At supper he said suddenly across the table, "Listen,
    dad.
Are not two sparrows sold for a farthing? When Mikey and I were little you
    used to have prayers in the evenings
And flogged us the times we snickered: why did you quit?" Old Fraser fixed
    his narrow-set apelike eyes
On Lance's face; they seemed to become one thrusting darkness, but he
    said nothing. After a time
Lance said, "But why did you quit?" "Because I grew old and powerless,"
    the old man answered. Lance: "What was that
You used to read about two sparrows for a farthing?" "The Book is there."
    He nodded toward the other room.
"Look it out for yourself." When they stood up from table Lance said, "I
    wish you would read it for us,
About the sparrows." "I will not," he said, "read for your mockery. I am
    utterly left alone on earth;

And God will not rise up in my time." But Lance: "Doesn't it say
No sparrow can fall down without God?" Fayne said, "Oh Lance: come
    on."
"No, no; I want him to read and pray.
What does that mean, fall to earth without God?
Does it mean that God fells it? Fayne and I
Know better than that: ah, Fayne? *We* know, ah?
But God connives.
Do read about the two sparrows." His roving glance
Came on his mother's blanched and full-moon face,
The pouched watery blue eyes, and the mouth always
Thirsting for breath. "No, no, I'll keep still, mother.
I didn't want to tease him, I was in earnest
To have prayers again."

                But he remained in the room
Until his mother had gone up to bed, then instantly
Said, "Listen, dad. Be a good sport.
Are not two sparrows sold for a farthing?" Fayne had watched him
Sitting stone-still, only twitching his hands,
His face hollow in the lamp-shadow: she went quickly
And touched his shoulder; she smoothed her hand on his throat,
Saying, "Please, Lance, no more of that. Why will you do it?"
"Sh," he said, "I have him by a raw spot: keep out.
He spooned the gospel down my throat when I was a cub:
Why's he so tight wi' that farthing? Once, dad, you whipped Mikey
For spelling the name of God backward
Until the red crucifixion ran down his legs.
Do you remember the brave little brown legs
All smeared and welted?" The old man eyed him and said,
"You lie. He had a thorn-scratch that opened." "Booh," Lance answered,
"I won't quarrel with you. I want the truth:

Are not two sparrows sold for a farthing?" Old Fraser
Groaned, and the straight edge of the lamp-shade shadow
That crossed his broad face obliquely over the burning
Blackness of the eyes, but left the stiff mouth and jaw
In the yellow light, shook with his passion. He said, "My Master also
Was mocked cruelly by those he loved, desiring to save them. You have a
    strong body, and if I struck you
You'd take me by the wrists like a little child. I am in my house and I have
    no one to help me.
I am old and worn out; my strength is gone and white hair has come, but
    honor has not come. I say that God
Is not mocked; but a feeble ailing old man, who loved his boys too
    indulgently and has seen the blithe hands
Reach out for damnation, and the happy feet . . . Oh . . .
Is rightly mocked. Oh Lance, over Michael's death." Lance, pale and
    mumbling: "We all have troubles, old man;
Yours have come late. Well. Are not two sparrows . . ." Fayne cried,
    "Lance, Lance, for pity
Hush, whatever he did to you when you were little.
He earns peace now." "Mm," he said, "where's that? I've
Been trying to get him to call me about those sparrows:
The old man won't play; we've an ace in the hole too.
Here it is for nothing, old man:
I rode by the Abbeys' line-fence along the steep
Over Wreck Beach, and there's a young deer, a spike-buck
Hanging dead on the wire, made a bad jump
From the low side. The barbs caught him by the loins,
Across the belly at the spring of the haunches, the top wire.
So there he hangs with his head down, the fore-hooves
Reaching the ground: they dug two trenches in it
Under his suspended nose. That's when he dragged at the barbs
Caught in his belly, his hind legs hacking the air.

No doubt he lived for a week: nothing has touched him: a young
    spike-buck:
A week of torture. What was that for, ah?
D' you think God couldn't see him? The place is very naked and open, and
    the sea glittering below;
He hangs like a sign on the earth's forehead, y' could see him from China.
    . . . But keep the wind side.
For a loving God, a stinking monument." "Bosh," the old man answered,
And stood up, and puckering a miminy mouth: "Your little buck!
There is not one soul in hell but would take his place on the wire
Shouting for joy . . . . and few men past fifty." Lance also,
Made surly by the slow death of whiskey in his blood,
Stood up: "Your merciful God, that made you whip little boys. We're dogs,
But done licking those feet." He bulked in the old man's way to the door,
    towering in the shadow, and forced him
Toward the near corner. Fayne ran between them. "Tell me the truth,"
    Lance said, "do you believe in your God?"
Old Fraser, who had stood glaring like a bayed cat, suddenly dwindled; and
    felt outside the walled cube
Of lamplight under gray stars no Scottish nor Palestinian uplands but the
    godless hills of America
Like vacant-eyed bison lying toward the sea, waiting for rain. He moved his
    lips without breath, he struck
His throat and said feebly: "I am choked and dried up with the running
    sands.
I have prayed a great deal in vain, and seen the whole earth
Shed faith like leaves;
And the faces of sin round as the sun and morality
Sneered to death. I cannot
Live unless I believe. . . . I cannot live";
And stood all shrunken. Lance, awed: "My God, who'd ever 'a' thought
He could be plagued into honesty?" The old man

Cried fiercely: "I believe. Ah: tell your people to be careful
Of the God they have backed into a snarling corner,
And laugh off like a dirty story." "That's it," Lance answered.
"Dogs. We all are." He stood backward, the old man
Passed slowly, staring, saying "Make yourself ready if you can.
For I see you are changed."

                              Fayne shuddered and said,
"What does he mean?" "He? Nothing. He means *two* sparrows
For a farthing." She said "Lance. . . . Lance?"
He moved to leave her; she breathed and said, "Can you hear?
We were doing, what you thought. It seemed . . . . usual
That night: both drunk: he was going away. . . . So what you did, Lance,
Was justice." "Agh," he said, "nudge me wi' that, still?
I know it perfectly. What does it matter, what farthing
Sold them?" Fayne, sobbing: "Oh, then, we did not. It is not true.
I lied." "It would not be possible to tell you," he said,
"How little I care." She, with both hands at her white throat, but lifting
    her face:
"Yes. I can bear that. We've sailed I think away past the narrows of
    common faithfulness. Then care for this:
To be able to live, in spite of pain and that horror and the dear blood on
    your hands, and your father's God,
To be able to go on in pure silence
In your own power, not panting for people's judgment, nor the pitiful
    consolation of punishing yourself
Because an old man filled you with dreams of sin
When you were little: you are not one of the sparrows, you are not a
    flock-bird: but alone in your nature,
Separate as a gray hawk." "The very thing I was thinking," he answered.
"If you'd take your red hair and spindly face

Out of my lamplight I'd be alone: it's like a burst blood-vessel
In the eye of thought."

IX

Old Mrs. Fraser
Caught cold and remained in bed, the bronchial pain
Frightened her heart with memories of worse anguish.
Fayne went back and forth from the stove to the bed
Heating flannels, to lay them on the white upland
Between the blond mountains of falling flesh
That had fed Lance. Going by the curtainless window
She looked whether she could see him, across the fields
Or up the burnt hill. Not Lance, but a smaller figure
Was coming down the black hill under white clouds:
Mary Abbey: her father had horses enough,
Was she walking down here?

Lance's mother
Wished for that wintergreen oil again; Fayne rubbed it
On the white plain and the roots of great soft udders.
She could feel in her finger-tips the suck and rattle
Of phlegm in the breathing-tubes, the old woman coughing
And saying "I see there was four sheets in the wash again
From you and Lance; well dearie, don't fret.
He's just his father all over, crazy as hawks.
They get to thinking Antichrist and the Jews and the wicked Pope in
    Rome
And scunner at every arrangement for human comfort.
Then they come home like hungry sailors from sea.
You're all worn out in the morning; my feet are cold."
She coughed and panted; Fayne rubbed the oil. The old woman said,

"My feet are cold." Fayne answered sadly "I'll rub them."
"No, if you'd get me an iron; a fine hot flat-iron
Done up in cloth is a great comfort in bed.
Right often it's been a husband to me when my old man
Was prophesying around and a fresh cow
Cried all the night."

                Fayne went down-stairs for the iron
And heard a wonderful sound behind the house; she heard Lance laughing.
She looked from the door and saw old Davie by the lime-washed
    hen-house, leaning both hands on a long shovel,
Gaze at the ground; Lance crouched near by, with blood on his hands and
    something between his knees, red feathers,
That fiery old half-bred game-cock, that sent the dogs
Yelping for mercy. A little Cooper's-hawk was tethered in front of Lance to
    a driven peg,
One wing bloodily trailing; Lance pushed the game-cock toward it and the
    hawk fell, tripped by its wing,
But crutched itself on the other and came up again,
Erect and watchful, holding the earth with its yellow feet.
Lance pushed and freed the game-cock, that eagerly
Staring-hackled in his battle-passion
Leaped up and struck down; the hawk tripped by its wing
Fell quivering under the spurs, but a long-fingered
Lean yellow hand reaching up out of ruin
Plucked at the red king's breast: who charged again: one hawk-wing
Waved, and the talons mysteriously accomplished
Many quick bitter acts, whence the red king
Reeled out of hope. He crouched beyond tether's reach,
Propping himself on both wings, but the sinking head
Still stretched for fight; then dull-eyed, at strength's end,
Went staggering to it again. The yellow hands

Easily made him what would never any more
Chirp over bright corn to the hens or subdue a rival.

Lance came, and the little hawk ran quickly and fell
Onto its broken shoulder at the tether's end. Lance picked up the dying
    game-cock;
Red grains of wheat from the torn crop fell down with the blood. Fayne
    watched from the open door; she saw him
Turn at the click of a gate, and Mary Abbey came up from the creek-bed
    path. At sight of Lance
She stopped; her hands went up to her throat. He, frowning: "What do you
    want ... Mary?" She lowered her hands
And stepping backward almost inaudibly said, "I ...
Came the back way. I ... came to see Fayne." She had hurried and was
    breathing hard. Lance stared at her,
And said "Go on in, confess your sins." He turned with his shoulder
    toward her; the bleeding bird in his hands
Stretched itself, thrusting back with the spurs as if it were killing its last
    rival, and suddenly died,
With a bright bubble of blood in the gaping beak. Old Davie laughed, but
    not Lance; the little hawk
Stood up and watched all with intent eyes. Mary stayed wringing her hands
    and Fayne came from the door,
Then Mary, half running toward her: "I hardly bear to see blood: let me go
    in." Fayne said to Lance:
"It won." "It will lose," he said in his throat, "when my heel is on it." She,
    gravely: "It fought well, Lance.
Have you hurt your hands?" "Ugh," he said, "nothing: the vermin." He
    moved toward the little captive, that looked up at him
With cold intentness; the blood had started again from its broken shoulder
    and striped the dead wing. Mary Abbey,

Shrilly, whipping the air with her hands: "Let me go!" Lance raised his
    foot to tread, but the victim's intent
Concentration of binocular eyes looked human; Mary cried shrilly: "They
    told me, my father said.....
And Nina told me ... Oh Fayne!" Lance, suddenly rigid: "What's that?"
    Fayne answered steadily and said, "Its life
Is little value to it with a broken wing. Come into the house." She
    answered "I am afraid."
But approached the door, whispering "What kind of a house, with blood
    sprinkled
Where you enter the door: what have you done?
His hands are red." Lance turned from the hawk and said with his teeth
    showing, "Tell your father
That I may soon be with this," he toed the dead cock, "our second-sighted
    old Scotchman has got a hunch.
But not with that, not caught alive." She fled from him
To the open door. Fayne, jerking her face but not
Her shoulders toward him said low: "You speak of things
Less real than nothing. It is not courage to make
Danger where there is none." She followed Mary Abbey
Into the door, saying: "Lance is not well. He loved his brother
Most deeply, and having heard of venomous talk
Makes the wound burn. Have you too been listening
To our enemies?" Mary, trembling in the house twilight:
"I know you couldn't speak calmly, if, if ... Oh Fayne.
But every person ... What have I done!" "Will you hush," Fayne said,
"Mrs. Gomez is probably not interested
In your girl dreams." Then Mary was silent, seeing
The dark ruler of the kitchen. Fayne took the iron,
And said on the stair, "I have to attend to Lance's mother:
You'd better stay with me. Then we'll walk." At the room door:
"Mary Abbey is here, mother."

                          Mary faltered
At the air of the room, the stove-heat and stale hangings in the air
Of wintergreen and eucalyptus. She stood close to the door,
And felt the weary mill turn in her mind,
Unable to think of any definite thing, painfully grinding, turning. Old Mrs.
     Fraser
Sniffed and said, "I can smell scorching cloth,
Did you try it with a wet finger? It ought to sizz
But if it whistles it will burn the sheets; Mary are you sick?
You look all blue by the mouth," she wagged her head in the pillow, "watch
     your heart." Fayne, kneeling
To slip the iron under the covers of the bed, tossed back her bright hair
     and said, "She's all right, mother.
Lance was having a kind of cock-fight in the back yard, that struck her pale:
     she's one of those delicate
Natures that die at seeing blood."

                          The weary mill of the mind struck a
     hard kernel and seemed to fall
Down hollow waters: Mary leaned on the door-frame, clenching her fists
     not to go down with it, biting
Her white lip, the circle of sight contracted until only the blood-splatch of
     Fayne's hair was visible
At the hub of the whirlpool. She slid with her back to the steep door-frame
     and did not fall; Fayne helped her
To escape the room, the old woman far off proclaiming "It is her heart."

                                                                Mary

     leaned on the newel
Of the stairhead to find her strength to go down, and said,
"I am so caught. And someone has daubed every
Beam of your house with it. All women have to bear blood

But mine has stopped. Please go first, Fayne,
For you don't hate me yet; now I can't bear
To meet . . . . anyone." Fayne slowly said, "It was Michael?"
"I am in terror," she answered, "of every living thing,
And him, and you." Fayne's triangular face,
The high cheek-bones and narrow jaw, thrust in the twilight
Opposite the other's white oval, as a small perching hawk
Thrusts with her head, forcing the shapes of things
To grow alive in the motion of the eyes
And yield up their hunted secrets: Fayne peered at her,
Trembling, and said, "Then follow."

                                        They went out the front way;
No one was seen; Fayne said: "It is horrible to be nearing New Year's
And still the dust and the sun, as if it could never rain. Would you like to
    be nurse to that old woman?
She's Lance's mother." Mary said faintly, stumbling on the plain path, "I
    have no mother: and the raging
Blue of your eyes hates me." "What you have heard," Fayne said, "is only
    the common lies of the shore.
It's natural for people to furnish a house with lies if it meets misfortune.
    When a man loses his property
He's called fool, or thief; when they see you crushed
By the sudden death of someone you love they begin to hint murder: it's
    human nature. If you're weak enough,
Believe them: it won't hurt us. But what are you here for?" She answered,
    leaning her hand on the post of the little gate
To steady her body: "I am not strong like you. I am in danger of killing
    myself, if . . .
Or if I believe them." "Better than you," Fayne said, "have died. Come on."
    A little way past the gate,

Mary said, "What is it? You too are trembling!" She answered, trembling,
  "Oh no: *my* life is easy. Dear,
We're friends, we mustn't make mysteries: tell me, won't you, what's all this
  web of trouble
You stare so white through? You can count on my loving friendship, and
  my
Forgiveness, if for any reason . . . My worst enemy
Will call me warm-hearted; and if I once had the name
Of being a jealous woman in my love for Lance:
Well," she said with a calm voice, her face twisting
Like a small white flame specked with flying ashes,
"That wears, it softens. And he . . . grows morose and strange,
Is not perfectly a splendor in my eyes any more.
I will confess that I cannot feel so warmly about him
As once I did. . . . Here above the bee-hives, Mary,
Nobody ever comes, and you could tell me
Everything safely; and if any advice of mine
Could help, though I am not wise."

                              They stood silently,
Turning their faces away from each other,
In a wind acrid with stale honey and the life of bees.
Mary Abbey shuddered and said, "I *came* here
To tell you. Oh, Oh. I used to seem to myself
Locked in, cold and unwishing; but . . . Michael's . . . love
Made April in me, and the sudden emptiness of death
Tore . . . I was much changed: you remember
How I clung to you in the desert of the days afterwards,
And tired you into dislike, until you turned
Hard eyes toward me. The first time I saw Lance alone
He was riding in fire and ashes; he was more unkind
Than you ever were." Fayne tasted

The crack in her bitten lip, and shut her eyes and said softly
"Go on, sweetheart"; but the dark-haired one
Only wept, and Fayne said "You've told me nothing,
Sweetheart." She answered "Are you still really my friend?
Don't look at me," and turned her face from Fayne,
Saying "I was so aching lonely. I only wanted
To be friends with someone: he really . . . he took me roughly
On the great lonely hill; it hurt, does it hurt at first
If you are loved?" Fayne had stopped trembling and stood
With bones and teeth showing through the skin of her face,
And trying to speak moaned slightly, and avoided
The little blind hand feeling for hers. "But still I
Strain and ache to be near him." Fayne took the hand,
And with her unfleshed mouth kissed Mary's hair,
And tried to speak, and with painful care: "Go . . . on . . .
Sweetheart?" "Then they told me that he killed Michael.
That was not true. Oh yes, I know, but I thought
If I loved where I ought to hate I would kill myself.
I have always been as regular as the new moon,
And this time, twelve days have passed. When I was troubling
About that, that was when they told me. I thought
About a coyote that was caught near our house
In two steel traps at once, so that it couldn't
Stand nor lie down." Fayne touched her teeth with her tongue
Until the stretched white lips came slowly to cover them,
And said, "Do you mean?" She answered, "I am so caught.
I know, I have a book about it. So I came here.
Your dooryard was full of blood." Fayne said, "Maybe you are.
He's travelled away past caring, and would let
Nature fly. I'd naturally. . . .
I have to control my starts, because Lance,
Who's worth ten thousand of *you*, hangs on the scale.

D' y' love him, *sweetheart?*" She turned her face toward her,

Saying, "Yes." Fayne mumbled and said, "I'd naturally . . .

It's babies like you . . . Listen to me.

I took Lance in my hand in that bad night

To fling at the world. We do not have to let the dogs judge for us. I told
   him that we are our own people

And can live by ourselves: if we could endure the pain of being lonely. Do
   you think *you* with Lance

Could strangle time? I am holding the made world by the throat

Until I can make it change, and open the knot that past time tied. To undo
   past time, and mend

The finished world: while you were busy teething your young virginity. I
   have to control myself.

Last year I'd 'a' let

Nature fly; changed your baby face wi' my hands,

Sweetheart: but I cannot risk: life has changed." "Oh Fayne! why did you
   say . . ." "I'm not a tame animal,"

She answered, "the wild ones are not promiscuous. What would you do,"
   her voice thinning to a wire, "if . . . Lance . . .

If it proved true, that you'd given your little dry heart and careful body

And anxious little savings of honor

For a prize to your lover's murderer: could you walk, eat, sleep,

While you knew that?" She said, "It is true then.

I had made up my mind: indeed I long for it.

Sleep: Oh, you'll see." Fayne drew in breath like one

Drinking in a desert passion, and said, "You've not

Enough courage." "Not for anything else," Mary answered;

"But that"; and began to go back down the dry hill.

Fayne followed, with eyes like the blue flame of sulphur

Under the fever of her hair, and lips reddening.

The moment of joy withered out of her face.

"I am fighting the whole people, do you think I'll risk:

For the pleasure of a small soft fool's removal,
Who'd weep it out to her father or leave a letter.... Oh, you: it's not
    true.
Lance is no murderer, you're innocent as far as that.
I saw with my eyes your unmourned lover
Clambering up the ledges in his happy drunkenness,
All alone, and the shale broke in his hands;
I saw him pitching down the white moonlight,
And heard the noise like a melon of his head on rock
In the clatter of the falling pebbles. Lance came up the sand
After I screamed." Mary Abbey stood swaying and said,
"If you knew my heart you'd pity me." Fayne, amazed: "Pity you
For having had Lance?" and said hoarsely, "When did you tell him
That you think you are pregnant?" "Oh, Oh," she stammered,
"Never. You hate me." "You're good at guessing," Fayne said.
"What do you want here, money to bribe a doctor?
We have no money here. Yet it seems I must help you,
Or worse will come. I know a woman in the city . . .
When you start east . . . But you must promise never to come back
Into the drawing net of our lives."

X

                             When Mary had gone,
Fayne went where Lance had been; but only the little hawk
Stood in the dust, hopeless and watchful, with its own misery
And a shadow of its own, between the privy and the hen-house and the
    back door. Fayne thought: would Lance
Be harmed if she should give it the gift? and fetched the axe from the
    wood-block, but forgot to be merciful
And went up-stairs. She washed herself, brushed her bright fleece, and came
    down.

She found Lance at the fence-corner
Where the north pasture comes down to drink. He had looped his belt
    around the neck of a yearling colt
That had a head like a barrel; the little body and long knotted legs of
    nature, but the head enormous,
Like a barrel-headed beast in a dream. "Oh Lance, what ails it?" He stared
    at her
And answered, faintly smiling, "I guess a little
Message from someone." "What?" she said. "Nothing. We don't have
    rattlers
In the middle of winter." "Is it a rattlesnake bite?"
"They sleep in the rocks and holes, twisted in bunches,
They won't strike if you dig them up: but here
On his lip are the pricks." He unhaltered
The shuddering colt. "Stumble away poor thing.
That was a mean trick, to sting the innocent."
Fayne said, "Was it a rattlesnake bite?" "Mm: but
What sent it up?" "This weather," she said, "the vicious sun."
"Fine hawk's-weather, ah? Did Mary what's-her-name
Tell you her young sins?" Fayne quivered, closing her eyes,
And answered at length, "She's sick." "So are we all."
"*I* am not. . . . Lance, you are generous: if you found a stranger
Starving, and gave her . . . *him* milk and bread, and came
Home and you found someone of yours starving;
Your father, whom you don't love, but you have to owe him
A kind of duty . . ." "Why didn't you say brother?"
She fixed her eyes on his face and sighed and said, "I am speaking
Of the living.
. . . And he begged you for the mouthed cup, and what was left
Of the broken loaf?" He made a sound of impatience
And turned, but Fayne took his hand, still marked by pressure
Of the strap that had held the struggling colt: "Would you let him starve?"

"No. What about it?" "That ... stranger ... you fed seems to be sorry
    about it. I suppose she was starving.
I have some angry rinsings of pride in me
Make begging bitter." "*That's* it," he said. "I could 'a' laughed at you
In the days before I was damned. I'm learning. The mares have their
    seasons but women always." "I will bear anything,"
She answered sighing, her narrow white face opaque with tolerance. "I was
    not always perfectly patient.
If you were safe I'd have twisted a knife in her fluty throat. My knife is
    patience." "I know the very
Place," he said. "Come on, I'll answer his note. The very place."

                                                                    They
    went up by the dry
Gully through the starved and naked pasture; the autumn hunger of horses
    and the patient hooves had left
Hardly roots of the grass, and the yellow dust was reddened with sundown.
    They saw lean horses drift off
Along the ridges on the darkening sky, and far on the last knoll
Three slabs of redwood standing like erect stones, quite black against the
    red streak and slate-color cloud,
Lonely and strange. Fayne, breathless with labor up the long slopes, cried
    hoarsely, "Where are you going? Oh Lance,
Not there?" "There," he said. "No. I won't. No.
What agony in you ... not here." "On his earth," he answered. "It would
    make us despise ourselves. Oh, do not hate him.
He did no wrong, he was happy and laughing-natured, and dear to us all."
    "Come on," he said, "or go home.
Choose." She went slowly away down the hill, and returned and said, "I
    love you and I want ... not what you think,
But near enough. And the dead know nothing." "I wouldn't bet on it," he
    said; "the drunk did." "You are wildly wrong,"

She answered, "Oh horribly," and embracing him strained up to his throat
Her whitened lips.

She felt the bare crumbled earth,
The dark home of the dead and serpents,
Under her back, and gave herself eagerly,
Desiring that gift that Mary meant to destroy,
And herself had never wanted before, but now
To accept what her rival dared not keep,
Take and be faithful where the other fled, had some bitter value;
And faith and the world were shaken; Lance might be lost,
The past might prove unconquerable: no, she could save him: but yet
She'd bind the future.

This time Lance did not fail.
She feared his caution and schemed against it, quite needlessly,
For he had wandered beyond prudent thoughts;
But when they were going away in the twilight, "Ah vile.
Vile," he said, "your hawks have worse poison in their hook beaks
Than any ground-nest of rattlers." She answered, "I am not to tell you
What my hope is." "On top of his bones, dogs in a boneyard."
She answered languidly and bitterly, "I ought to have let you
Go to Salinas. I did not know that your mind . . .
I would have waited for you all the long years.
I did not know that your mind needed men's judgment
And the helpless appraisals of the world to help you. You stood so strong,
Separate, clear, free in my eyes: and I did violence to you
When I kept you." She felt a trembling about him
And saw that he did not hear but was watching shadows
Fleet in the air: "Sea-gulls. They are gulls, Lance. Look how beautiful
The long sharp silent wings in the fading light
On the bare hill." "He took it very quietly," he answered;

"We are all dogs, every one." "Oh," she said, "the world's full
Of evil and foolishness but it is terribly beautiful.
If you could see that, Lance." "What? By God they won't, not alive.
But then comes hell." "I pray you, I pray you, dear,
Not to begin to think strangely: that's for your father, who often
Walks his road all staring between hedges
Of Christs and Satans: but you will rub your mind quiet
Like the face of a crystal; there is enough to see
In the dark lovely shoulders of hills, the cows and horses, the old gray rocks
    and the folk around us,
Without tapping strange dreams. . . . Oh, we'll live well."

XI

The rain held off; for two hundred and forty days there had been no rain
But one sun-drunken shower. The creek was dry rock and weary gray roots;
    the skin of the mountain crumbled
Under starved feet; the five carcasses of hawks that Lance had hung on the
    fence-wire dried without odor
In the north wind and rages of the sun.

                        Old Fraser walked under the
    moon along the farm-drive beside them,
Saying "Lord if thou art minded to burn the whole earth
And spat off the dust from thy hands, it is well done,
The glory and the vengeance: but if anywhere
Rain falls on hills, remember I beseech thee thy servant's place,
Or the beasts die in the field." While he was praying
The moon was dimmed; he felt a flutelike exultance
Flow up from the V of his ribs to his wrinkled throat:
He was not abandoned: and looked aloft and saw
A little many-colored man's-palm-size cloud

Coasting the moon from the southeast, the storm-side.

The old man exalted himself; he had power upon God; and anxiously
Repressing his joy for fear it waste the event
Beforehand, compelled his heart to remember bitterness,
His two sons lost, one dead, the other in rebellion,
And poverty and scorn and the starved cattle. "Oh Lord God,
As in old time thou didst choose one little people for thine out of all the
   earth,
So now thou hast chosen one man, one old man, foolish and poor: but if
   thy will was made up
To punish the earth, then heed not my voice but arise and punish. It is rank
   with defilement and infidelity
And the music of the evil churches." He saw a shining white form at the
   garden-gate, and for a high moment
Believed that some angel, as unto Abraham . . . It was Lance,
Perfectly naked, and Fayne his wife behind him
Walking in her white night-dress, who spoke pleadingly,
But Lance went on. He came with stiff hesitance,
And seemed not to look down at the latch but opened the gate.
The old man watched and waited in the tool-house shadow.
Lance passed the gate and stood in the open dust
Like a blind marble pillar-stone, the icy moonlight
Washing his body, pouring great shadows
Of the heavily moulded muscles on the hairless breast,
And the ripple of strength on the smooth belly; he stood
And babbled and called: "Mikey. Oh Mikey. Come home.
I'll be *it* to-morrow again. It's getting too dark to play,
Don't hide any more, buddy, for the owls are out.
If you'll come in I'll let you have my cornelian,
And the heron's eggs that I found." Fayne took his hand,
"Lance, Lance, wake up," and stroked the smooth power of his arm,
Her face caressing his shoulder. He said, "Hurry, they're blaming me.

They think you're lost." Fayne said, "I can't bear it, Lance.
Mikey's in the house. He's come in already." The old man
Came forward out of the shadow; Fayne heard and stared at him.
Lance said, "Damned liar. Ma's not . . . mare.
People ain't made like . . . dirty . . ." and babbled words
That could not be understood. Fayne said, "Sleep-walking.
Did he ever before . . . what can I do?" Lance moaned,
She reached her arm around him and stroked his face
With the other hand; the old man saw her hair
Against the wide white breast like a burst of blood
Deep in the moonlight, then Lance flung her aside
As white foam flies from the oar, saying still in the dream-drunken
Sing-song, "Oh no you don't: this is not dogs' meat.
Or you'll have to kill it before you paw it.
The angels wi' the hooky beaks. . . . What in hell," he said
Sharply, "who's there?" "I, Lance. Oh come to bed, dear.
You wandered out in your sleep." "No: that spying devil,"
He said, "hm?" "Your father, your father, Lance.
He was here when you came." "Oh. . . . Did I talk?"
"Hardly a word. Nothing, dear." "I sleep better
Alone," he said, "now."

                        The old man looked up at cloud-flecks
Like algae breeding on clear deep well-water around the moon,
And looked at Lance, and returned up the drive. Lance said, "Do you wear
    white? Hitch it up on your breast,
The teat is bare. Why did he turn away without speaking?" "He saw you'd
    wakened." "Black will look fine,"
He answered, "wi' the fiery hair. I want you to marry again, you'll have
    chances."

The sky in the morning
Was layered with cloud, and it drove from the southeast; the old man kept
  working his mouth in silent thanksgiving
For answered prayer; and the wind came down from heaven and smoked in
  the fields. The sky cleared for a time,
But that was natural; the wind increased. It ran quartering the little valley;
  ashes from the hill
And mountain dust entered all cracks of the house. It raged on the salt pool
  at the creek sea-mouth
By the caverned crag that storms have worn spongelike; it reaped the heads
  of the waves on the wide sea, and lay
Like a quivering steel blade on the necks of the herbless mountains.

                                                                        Far
  away northward in San Francisco
It blew the filth of the street into the faces
That walked there; one was Mary Abbey's little pale oval
Lost among thousands. She moved unevenly, fast and lagging,
And looked with terrified eyes at the gilt street-number
Scribed on a window; beyond a mean plush-curtained restaurant
The number stood over a door. She stood choking,
And read on a brass plate in the doorway: "Dr. Eisendraht,
Eye, ear, nose, throat"; a wind-scoop of sudden dust
Blurred the letters and filled her eyes. She went on
With faint small steps, and at the street-corner
Tried to stand still, and was jostled. Not wearing gloves
She spurred blood from the back of her left hand
With the nails of her right: the pain helped her go back
And enter the door and find the stairway. She had to sit long,
Waiting her turn; she was served impersonally

And dismissed, fainting or able, to the desert wind
And dust and multitude down the mean street.

                              At Sycamore Creek
Lance's mother was wiping the table oil-cloth
For the noon meal, the film of the wind's dust, and suddenly
Fell into a chair; Mrs. Gomez came in with knives and forks on the plates
    and found her, and Fayne
Came at the cry; they couldn't take her up-stairs until Lance came in. They
    helped her slip to the floor,
And brought a pillow, then Lance came in. Fayne said, "She is weak but
    better, the pain is passing." The old woman
Mountainous laid on the floor wished to lie still for a time. Lance knelt by
    her side. "All right, mother.
As long as you like. Fayne," he said gravely,
"Will you come to the door a minute?" Fayne went, and outside the door
    said, "What do you want, Lance? You scare her
Wi' that secret look." "I was not afraid to go in after him, I want you to see
    him. The question is
Whether my eyes have begun to sing lies to me.
He came from the orchard walk and went in the shed.
I know you have courage. A frightful branding. Oh," he sighed,
"That's the point." She looked at his face and followed him,
And reeled in the dry fierce wind in front of the house;
But he leaning his back on the stiff wind
So that his shirt moulded the groove between
The great bands of lean power from the shoulders: "Well. Do you see him?
In the shed door." "No." "It was closed, he opened it.
You can see that it's open? Now I'll catch him.
Come." He ran suddenly and leaped the garden-gate.
But Fayne must stop to unlatch it, and when she came
Lance had gone into the shed and around the motor-truck

That stood within. Fayne said, "Wind broke the peg
That held the clasp of the door: see, here's one piece.
That's why it's open." She heard the roof straining
Over the imprisoned storm. Lance said "Did he pass you?
Ah?" She answered, "We must go away from this place.
For you, it's haunted. Your mother, whom I think you love, is just now
Lying low between life and death, and you leave her
To chase the wind, and the foxes of your eyes. Do you love him so?
Or hate him?" He answered, "The fire's burnt through his cheek,
His back-teeth grinned at me through the horrible scar.
I'll be there soon." "What fire? . . . Are you dreaming punishment?
Oh, that's the vainest craziest falsehood of all.
Leave that to your poor old father." "We go down
Into blackness," he stiffly answered,
"And neither you nor I nor the old man
Knows what happens there. This was Michael: if I should dream him
I'd dream the skull knocked in, hm? What I saw's
The cheek burnt through." "I will not let go and lose you," she answered.
   "Probably," Lance said, "he'd have lied
If I could have caught him."

                    In the afternoon
Fayne saw from the window above the kitchen a small gray object
Making a singular dance in the flying dust.
The little hawk which Lance had shot but not killed
Was dying; they had dropped it a strip of beef that dried in the sun,
And given it a dish of water, and not again
Remembered it, though it stood up grimly and watched
Whoever passed to the privy. The water was blown
Out of the dish; no matter, it had never drunk.
Now it was flapping against the wind,
Fluttering the natural wing and trailing the broken one,

Grotesque in action as the blackcock at dawn
Making his dance of love; but this was of death.

In the night Fayne said: "That little hawk died. Oh be quiet now;
You've shot them out of the sky. . . . Dear, I am to blame
Like you, and yet I'd be as happy at heart
As a fed bird that glides through the high air
If you were not tearing yourself." He made no answer,
She heard the wind tear at the roof, and said,
"I love this place. But time has changed, let old Davie
And your dad farm it now, it is full of memories
And very fit for old men. You and I
Will take three horses for all our share of it,
And travel into the south by that deer-track
Where the planted foot is on the face of the mountain and the lifted foot
High over the gray face of the sea: four or five days
Only the eagles will see us, and the coasting ships
Our fires at evening, and so on southward. But when we get to Los Angeles,
    dear,
You'll put your great white shoulders to work
For passage-money, we'll sell the horses and ride
In a ship south, Mexico's not far enough,
The Andes are over the ocean like our hills here,
But high as heaven." "Fancy-work," he mumbled. "Ah. Low as hell."
Fayne said, "No. Listen: how the air rushes along the keel of the roof, and
    the timbers whining.
That's beautiful; and the hills around here in the cloud-race moon-glimmer,
    round rocks mossed in their cracks with trees:
Can't you see them? I can, as if I stood on them,
And all the coast mountain; and the water-face of the earth, from here to
    Australia, on which thousand-mile storms

Are only like skimming swallows; and the earth, the great meteor-ball of
    live stone, flying
Through storms of sunlight as if forever, and the sun that rushes away we
    don't know where, and all
The fire-maned stars like stallions in a black pasture, each one with his stud
    of plunging
Planets for mares that he sprays with power; and universe after universe
    beyond them, all shining, all alive:
Do you think all *that* needs us? Or any evil we have done
Makes any difference? We are a part of it,
And good is better than evil, but I say it like a prayer
That if you killed him, the world is all shining. It does not matter
If you killed him; the world's out of our power, the goodness and splendor
Are things we cannot pervert, although we are part of them,
And love them well." He heavily answered: "Have you finished?
Don't speak of . . . him . . . again." She began to answer,
Thought, and was silent.

XII

                      She fetched a pair of rawhide panniers
From the harness wall in the barn, remembering that Michael
Less than two years ago had whittled the frame, and Lance
Shaped the hairy leather and stitched it with sinew thongs.
That was the time they three in delight and love
Rode south by the sea-eagle trails to Point Vicente and Gamboa's
For seven days' hunting, when Fayne shivered with happiness,
Riding between the most beautiful and strongest man
For husband, and the gayest in the world for brother, on perfectly
Wild hills and by rushing streams.

She packed the panniers,
And balanced the weight, mixing her things with Lance's.
The wind had ceased and no rain had fallen, but the air grown colder
Whipped up her courage to believe Lance would go,
And find life, in new places. His mother was well again;
And on the farm all things had come to a pause; he was not needed.
The hay-loft was emptying fast: but Lance could not make it rain by
    staying!

           While she packed the panniers
A little agony was acting under the open window, between the parched lips
    of the creek.
One of those white-crowned sparrows that make sweet voices in the spring
    evenings in the orchard
Was caught by a shrike and enduring death, not the bright surgical mercy
    of hawks, but slow and strangling.
Its little screams quivered among the gray stones and flew in the window;
    Fayne sighed without noticing them,
And packed the panniers.

              When Lance came up at evening she showed
    him what she had done: "We'll go to-morrow."
He said he'd not leave the place in trouble, "Even dogs are faithful. After
    the first good rain I'll go."
The reasons she made only angered him.

             Late in January
Fell rain mingled with hail, and snow in the nights. Three or four calves
    died in a night, then Lance
Had occupation with what survived; and the north slopes of hills were
    sleeted with magic splendor
That did not melt.

Fayne was drying dishes while Mrs. Gomez washed
them; she dropped a cup
With the dazzle of the white hill in her eyes when the sun came out;
Then Lance's mother filled up the door and said,
"That Mary Abbey is here." Fayne answered clearly,
"I broke a cup. She is in Idaho I think."
The old woman: "She's thinner. Oh Fayne, there were only seven
Left of the dozen": she gasped, remembering Michael: six were enough.
"She's got something to tell you." Fayne said, "Being out of our net
Has she flown back? Where's Lance?" and passed the old woman
As one moves a door to pass through a doorway,
But found no one; neither in the front rooms
Nor on the garden path when she opened the house-door.
Then she returned to Lance's mother and asked,
"Where has she gone? Where was she?" but found no light in the answers,
Only that Mary looked waxy as a little candle,
Her heart must be terribly weak, she looked all blue by the mouth,
And must have come a wet way.

Fayne felt the jealous
Devil fingering her throat again, tightening her breath,
And hasted and found Lance; but he was alone;
In the lower creek-bed, lopping all the twigs from the willows, making a
    load, to be chopped fine
And mixed with little portions of hay. She saw him reaching up the dwarf
    stems, as tall as the trees,
The sky-cold knife, the purple twigs at his feet, and said, "Have you seen
    Mary Abbey?" "What?" "Mary Abbey."
"You said she'd gone." "Well, she did go: she was up at the house just
    now"; and knowing her own bitter absurdity
Fayne trembled, saying, "Was she here?" He looked into the hollow
    creek-bed behind him; what was Fayne seeing

To make her tremble? "No," he said. Fayne, trembling with anger: "I'll tell
    you what she went east for: she was pregnant.
She stopped in San Francisco to be fixed up." "That's bad," he said; "poor
    child";
He slashed the twigs. Fayne tortured her hands together until the pain in
    the knuckles made her able
To smell the wounds of the willows and say steadily, "What will you do
Now she's come back?" "Oh," he answered. She stood waiting; he slashed
    the twigs and dropped them, saying, "Let her stay there.
I've been thinking, Fayne. I've been able to think, now the heat's broken.
    We have no outlet for our bad feelings.
There was a war but I was too young: they used to have little wars all the
    time and that saved them,
In our time we have to keep it locked up inside and are full of spite: and
    misery: or blindly in a flash:
Oh," he said stilly; "rage
Like a beast and kill the one you love best. Because our blood grows fierce
    in the dark and there's no course for it.
I dream of killing all the mouths on the coast, I dream and dream." She
    said, "Will you go to-morrow?"
"No. When the grass grows up. I'm bound to save what I can for the old
    people, but knives and axes
Are a temptation. Two inches of grass." She stood gazing; he saw the blue
    of her defenceless eyes
Glance at his knife-hand. "Don't be a fool," he said, "I can be quiet forever.
    Have you seen the old man
When he looks at me? I think he knows." "That is impossible," Fayne
    answered. "Why?" "For his mind is like
A hanging rock; he'd go mad when you crossed his eyes. But if he learned it
    after you'd gone away
He could absorb it, like the other dreadful dreams that he eats." He
    answered, "Davis has known for weeks.

I can tell that." "We have friends," she said; "faithful ones." "Did you say
   that poor child
Was ... what did you say?" Fayne hardened and answered, "Your mother
   saw her."
"I mean ... no matter," he said.

                         In the night she lay
Unable to sleep; she heard the coyotes howl
And shriek on the white hill, and the dogs reply.
Omens and wraiths waked in her night-weakened nerves,
Reminders of the vague time when wolves were terrible
To one's ancestors; and through all the staring-gaps of the night
She kept thinking or dreaming of Mary Abbey,
Who had come to the house and then lacked courage to stay, and must no
   doubt
Be suffering something.
But Lance to-night slept quietly; he'd enjoyed the good fortune
Of useful and active labor out-doors, in the cold
Beautiful weather. He was so concentrated
On the one spot of anguish
That nothing else in the world was real to him. The Abbey girl
Was never real to him; not even while ... Fayne heard her own teeth
Chipping each other in the angry darkness ...
Nor whether she'd been in trouble.

                         The little wolves on the hill
Lifted their tumult into a tower of wailing; Fayne saw clearly in her mind
   the little muzzles
Lifted straight up, against the star-lit gray shoal of snow, and the
   yellow-gray clamor shot up the night
Like a church-spire; it faded and floated away, the crackling stars remained.
   "They smell," Fayne thought,

"The dead calves, and no doubt have found them. They've feasted,
And now they sing. . . . Nothing is real to Lance but his wound;
But when we get away from this luckless place,
Which yet I love,
Then gradually the glory of the outer world
Will become real; when he begins to perceive the rushing and shining
    storm and fragrance of things,
Then he'll be well."

                A drift of thin rain fell in the morning;
The white vanished from the hill. The third day,
Fayne, going to spy for fear Mary might come
Where Lance was working, found old Davis in the driveway
Talking to a tall thin man on a red horse;
A Spanish man whom Fayne had not seen before,
But felt that she'd seen the horse. She eyed them and said,
"What does he want?" Davis, turning his back on the stranger,
Covertly touched his forehead and drooped an eye-lid.
"He works at Abbey's. This is the famous Onorio Vasquez,
The cowboy that sees the visions. He wants to tell you: you can send him
    off if you want to. Have you heard
About Abbey's girl?" "What?" Fayne asked, her eyes narrowed, lips thinned.
    "He says she put herself out.
The young they ain't got consideration for nobody." "What do you mean?"
    "Jumped off a pier I believe.
A telegram came in their mail yesterday. Her dad's gone up to San
    Francisco to view the body.
— So his hired man can roam." Fayne's mouth jerked, her eyes widened. "I
    cannot understand what you mean,
Davie," she said; but gazed at the Spanish-Indian, the hollow brown eyes
With a bluish glaze across them, in the shadow of his hat, in his bony face.
    "Jumped off a pier,"

Davis answered with patient enjoyment; "it seems she kept her address in
    her hand-bag on account of traveling,
So they telegraphed." "Did you say that she died!" He nodded, "Mmhm:
    wa'n't made for a fish, didn't have gills.
The young ain't got consideration for things like that." "Mary!" Fayne said,
    her hand at her throat.
She drew deep breath, and sharply lifting her face toward the silent
    horseman: "What are you waiting for,
Your news is told?" He, in better English than one expected,
In the soft voice of his race: "You are very sorry:
Excuse me please. I only saw her a little and she went away
After I came to work: she was beautiful with patient eyes but I think it is
    often good to die young.
I often wish." "She came to this house," Fayne said, "two days ago: how
    could she . . . in the city? She was here
The day before yesterday." "No, that was the day," he answered, "she died."
    Fayne stared at him
Without speaking; he was half dazzled by the wide blue of her eyes below
    the fire-cloud of hair,
He looked at the brown earth. "What time did she . . .
What time?" Fayne asked. "Don't know." She said slowly,
"I think it is . . . strange." She hardened. "Nothing. Have you come
To tell us any other thing?" "Yes," he said proudly,
"I ride on the hill and see a vision over this house. You have heard of
    Onorio
Vasquez? That is my name." Old Davis made a derisive noise in his throat;
    Fayne, thinking "Visions?
Apparently we too . . ." said quietly, "I never heard of you." He, saddened:
    "It does not matter." But Davis, the grizzled
Thatch of his lip moving to make a smile:
"Now that's too bad: for the man's famous. He's got six brothers
And every one of them knows him, every Vasquez on the coast.

If they can't steal meat nor borrow a string of peppers they listen to brother
    Onorio
Telling his dreams all through a winter night;
They don't need nothing." She answered, "If you have nothing to do here,
Go and help Lance." And to Vasquez: "Tell me what it is
You have to say." "You know a place in the south call' Laurel Spring? No?"
    he said. "Near Point Vicente.
I never been: my brother Vidal has been. He told me a rock and an old
    laurel tree
Is cut by the wind into the shape of the rock, and the spring runs down.
    He made a beautiful place
The way he told; we are much Indian, we love such places."
Fayne answered, "I am busy just now." He: "Excuse me please.
I ride on the hill and every day
Watch the old war in the sky over this house;
I hurt my heart with my eyes. Sometimes a naked man
Fighting an eagle, but a rattlesnake bitten him;
Sometimes a lion fighting a tide of dogs;
But sometimes terrible armies out of the east and west, and the hacking
    swords." Fayne gazed at him
And said, "Is that all?
I have just heard that my best friend has died:
I cannot think of these things." He said "The two armies
Destroyed each other, except one man alone
Walking among the bodies of horses and men
That blocked the sky; then I heard someone say,
'Let him lie down with the others.' Someone say, 'No.
At Laurel Spring he will wash off the blood,
And be cured of his wound.' I cannot live
Until I tell you." "Is it on the way
Into the south?" Fayne said. "Yes: on the trail.
My brother Vidal . . ." "I believe many lies

Are told about us," she said. "Have you heard talk
About this house?" He picked at the hair rope of the halter
On the horn of the saddle. She said, "I can guess
What you have heard. . . . May I call you Onorio?
Because it was kind of you to come down: and thank you
For telling me about your vision." She went nearer to him,
To reach his eyes under the eaves of his hat.
"Do you know Leo Ramirez?" "Him? Yes." "Have you talked to him?
He could tell you about it. He and I alone
Saw my husband's brother climb on the cliff and fall.
Ask him and he will tell you the truth. The others lie:
To amuse idleness I guess. If they had your great power
And saw the spirits of the air, they'd never do so.
But would you think the spirits of the dead?" Her face
Flashed at him, soft and hard at once, like a wet stone.
"Nothing," she said. "This present world is enough
For all our little strength. Good-bye Onorio. If you hear anything
Come down and tell me . . . at Abbey's or anywhere . . .
For nobody comes down to see us any more,
On account of those wicked . . . lies . . ." While she spoke
A sob broke through and she hid her face. He from above
Looked down at her bent head and the wild color
And foam of her hair; he reached and touched her hair
As if it were a holy thing. Fayne, in a moment
Quelling her tears: "I'll remember
About the way south, that fountain. I am very unhappy
For my lost friend." She turned hastily away
And left him, and found Lance.

                               She sobbed, "Mary Abbey
Will never come back. I . . . I liked her well enough

If she had not . . . Oh Lance." He was flaying the leather from a white and
    red calf, kneeling to work.
He rested his red-stained hands on the carcass and looked up with vague
    eyes. Fayne remembered, "At Laurel Spring
He'll wash the blood . . ." "Hm?" he said, "what?" "Mary . . . What am I
    doing," Fayne thought, "I oughtn't to tell him
While his mind is like this"; and clearing her face if she could, making a
    smile, said carefully, "What
Do you want the skin for?" "I've nothing to do," he said, "for the time.
    Rawhide has uses. I ground my knife
After all the willows were cut. Occupation." "A sort of bloody one," Fayne
    said carefully. "Well," he said,
And tugged at the skin with his left hand, making small cuts with the knife
    against the cling of the flesh.
She stood and watched, and furtively wiped her eyes. He looked up again:
    "No fat to scrape off." He dipped
The knife in the shrunken flesh between ribs. "Amazing," he said, "how the
    beasts resemble us, bone for bone,
And guts and heart. What did you say about Mary Abbey?" "No," she
    answered, "nothing. I was too unkind.
I think how lonely she was." "Oh. You mean Mary Abbey. I wish to
    God . . ."
He stopped speaking and tugged the skin, making small cuts
At the tearing-place. Fayne said, "Did you ever hear
Of Laurel Spring, down the coast?" She saw his wide shoulders
Suddenly stiffen, a shadow shot over in the air
And Lance's white-blue eyes rolled after the bird,
A big black one, with bent-up wing-tips, a flesh-color head
That hung and peered. He sighed and pulled at the skin, slicing the fiber.
Fayne said, "A vulture. They're living high now." "Mm," he said, "*they
    know*: they're always stooping over my head.

I thought it was something else." "You've shot them out of the sky," she
    answered, "there are no hawks." "Aren't there!"
He said, and hushed.

                        After a time Fayne left him, and looked back
When she came to the ridge of the hill. She saw the brown breast of earth
    without any grass, and the lean brown buck-eye
Thicket that had no leaves but an agony of stems, and Lance
Furiously stabbing the flayed death with his knife, again and again, and
    heard his fist hammer
On the basket-work of the ribs in the plunges of the hiltless blade. She
    returned; when he saw her he was suddenly still.
She said, "Whom were you thinking of?" He gazed in silence as if he
    thought that he ought to remember her
But could not. "Who was being stabbed . . . in your mind, Lance?"
    "Nobody. We are all dogs. Let me amuse myself."
"Me?" she said steadily. "No." She sighed and said, "I was going to tell you
    . . . I will. Mary Abbey's dead."
She watched his blood-flecked face and his eyes, but they stood still. "Oh,"
    he said coldly. "What did she die of?"
"Unhappiness. She drowned herself." "Too bad." He said no more, and
    Fayne stared and said: "When your mother saw her
That day, she was not real but a pleading spirit; she was dying in the north.
    We never pitied her."
"Is she frightened?" he said. "Who? Your mother? I have not told her."
    "Don't then."

XIII

                He stood up slowly,
And wiped the knife on the hair side of the skin;
He looked up the darkening wind and said, "It is going to rain."

Fayne said, "Then will you go?" seeing his fixed face
Against the lit cloud, so that the sanguine flecks
And smear under the cheek-bone were not apparent,
Only the ridge of the face, the unrounded chin
Higher than her eyes. He turned in silence and passed
Heavily over the grassless earth, but soon
Fayne had to run to keep up. Near the house
They came to Davis pouring water into the hand-pump
Of the old well to prime it; who said, "The water's
Quit in the pipes; the crick's not dry up yonder,
I guess a rat in the intake . . ." Lance answered hoarsely,
"Fish it out then. Where's the old man?" Fayne said
"What do you want, Lance?" "The old man." Old Davis gaped
At his changed face; Fayne saw the water clamber
Up the sides of the can in the shaking hand
In little tongues that broke and ran over, "Hey, hey,"
Davie stammered, "y' got to consider," but Lance touched him
With only the finger-tips, then the man raised
One arm and pointed northwestward, slant up the hill.
Lance turned and ran; Fayne followed him, but could not now
Keep up, old Davis hobbled panting behind them;
At lengthening intervals the little ridiculous chase
Crossed over the creek-bed under sycamore trees,
Past buck-eye clumps, and slant up the bare hill
Below the broad moving sky.

       Tall spikes of a tough weed
With leather leaves grew at a place on the hill;
A few staring-flanked cows tongued the gray leaves
But would not crop them, and broke the stalks. Old Fraser stood
Against a fence-post and watched; he saw the herd

A red and white stippling far down the slope, and the serpent-winding
    creek-bed, the salt pool of its end
Behind the sand-bar, and the sandstone fang in the mouth of the valley,
    from which the shore hills over sky and water
Went up each way like the wings of a sombre archangel. Lance came from
    behind
And said, "I have run my course. I cannot go on forever." The old man,
    broken out of his revery,
Looked blindly at the wide chest, red hands and stained face, as if a pillar
    of mist had come up and stood
Threatening above him. "You," he said harshly, "what do you want?"
    "Judgment. I cannot go on alone,"
And in a boy's voice, "Oh judgment. I have done . . .
I need, I need." The old man's brown apelike eyes got him clear at length,
    and became after their manner
A force of thrusting, like a scorched bar of fire-hardened wood. "Go
    home," he said, "drunkard.
If there is no work in the field for your . . . hands . . . what blood is that?"
    "My brother's," Lance said. Fayne came too late,
And sobbed for breath, in her throat a whining, and said, "He was skinning
    a calf down there, he was . . ." Lance passed
Between them and leaned on the fence-wire with his hands together and
    dragged the palms of his hands to the right and left
So that the barbs of the wire clicked on the bones of his hands through the
    torn flesh. "And mine," he said.
Fayne heard the tough noise of tearing, and felt in her own entrails through
    the groin upward an answering anguish.
Lance turned, hissing with pain, and babbled: "For no reason on earth.
I was angry without a cause and struck him with iron and killed him. The
    beast in me
That wants destruction. I mean Michael you know, Michael I mean." Old
    Fraser staggered, saying quietly,

"Has he had drink?" Fayne said "He..." she looked up at Lance's
    beautiful head and stained gray face,
But the lower zone of her vision could not avoid his hands, and thick blood
    falling from the shut knuckles:
Where was that readiness of mind, her thoughts were wailing away on the
    wind like killdeer, which flitter singly
Crying all through the white lofts of the moonlight sky, and you never see
    them. "Am I going to tip over
For blood, like Mary?" She stammered: "He...
Ah God. I'll tell you...." Lance said, "This is mine. I have come. Keep
    that woman away from me until I speak.
She fooled me into concealment, time and again, Oh cunningly. I have
    fallen through flight after flight of evil
And harmed many." Fayne gathered her mind and said, "This is it. This is
    the thing. He made love
With a girl and she has just died: now he hates me and he hopes
To take all the sins of the world onto his shoulders, to punish himself. It is
    all like a mad saint.
You trained him to it. But I saw Michael..." Lance said, "I remember an
    iron bolt for my shipwreck
Stood in my hand": he opened the ripped palm and the red streamed: "I
    struck." "Climb," Fayne said,
"Up the awful white moon on the cliff and fall, I saw him. It is Mary
    Abbey
Has killed herself." Lance said, "How your power's faded. You'll never
Fool me or the world again. I would not die
Until I had told."

            Davis came up, and saw
Lance head and shoulders against the sky like a dead tree
On which no bird will nest; the others at his base

On the brown hill, Fayne saying "Oh weak as water,
How will this help you bear it?" Davis, choked
With haste on the hill: "Ah. Ah. What's he been doing?" Lance held
His two hands toward his father, suppliant, but clenched
To save the blood. "What shall I do?" The old man
Stepped backward without an answer. Fayne said, "Because
The Abbey girl drowned herself, Lance thinks his finger
Helped push her down: but she was sick in her dreams
And might 'a' done it for anyone: the rest's invention
To punish himself. I am the one to hate him
Meddling with that sick child, but I love him
And will not lose." Davis, eyeing certain flakes
And scraps on the red thorns of the wire, sighed "Ah
That was a ghastly thing," and stood swaying,
Yellow and withered. Old Fraser's burnt wandering eyes
Fixed on him, the old man said: "Which is the liar?
Did Lance do it?" Lance opened his palms toward him
As if they would take and hold, saying "Tell the truth.
I will not bear to live in the dark any more."
Davis groaned "Ay. It's true I guess." Fayne: "Ah Ah coward.
Because he held his hands at you." She said to old Fraser:
"People hate you and your enemies made this story
Because you still had a son after Michael died.
This is what they have whispered so long, and Lance has heard it
And uses it to stab himself." Lance said, "It is horrible
To hear the lies from her mouth like bees from a hive
Hot in the sun. I was Michael's death;
And I cannot bear it in silence. Only I pray you all to keep it
Hidden from my mother: you can do that
With a little care, with a little care, she cannot live long.
Make a story to save her." Old Fraser, suddenly

Covering his face: "*Me* ... has anyone cared a little to save
Lest I live to the bitterness?" He passed among them
With tottering steps, tasting the way with his hands,
And down the hill toward home. Lance stood and muttered,
"What did he say, did he answer me?
He's honest, I bank on that."

                    A short way down
The old man stumbled and nearly falling stood still a moment;
Then turned his course up the hill and seemed to make haste
With short weak steps. Lance watched him and followed soon,
But turned fiercely on old Davie: "Back to work. Off.
That rat in the intake." And to Fayne: "How death
Makes even a rat powerful, they swell like clouds.
Leave me, will you." She answered, "I will never leave you.
But you, Davie, go home." "Hm?" Lance said, "never? You take your time.
Tie up my hands then; I think the seepage dulls me
More than the hurt helps. Here's a handkerchief:
Your dress is old." She tore it, and while she bandaged him
They stood, the old man trotted on. Lance dully wondered:
"Why did I come to him; because he believes in God?
What the hell good is that? Hm? Oh, to put it
Out of its misery." "I know you have been in torture," Fayne said.
"And now you have done unwisely but yet we'll live: not here, but certainly,
    fully
And freely again. You might have spared that old man.
Our joined lives are not weak enough to have gone down
In one bad night. ... Oh Lance," she prayed suddenly, "have mercy on
    me. While you tear and destroy yourself
It is me that you tear."

    He went on, she followed. On the high knoll
ahead
Stood the bleak name-posts of those three burials, one new and two old,
  erect against the sinking gray sky,
And seemed to rise higher as the clouds behind went down. The old man
  was struggling across a gully this side.
Fayne breathlessly said, "Lance, Lance, can you hear me? He is going up to
  Michael's grave, where his wild mind, that you've
Not spared, is to find some kind of fall, some kind of decision. Do you
  remember, dear, that you took me
To Michael's grave a while back? You were so angry.
But that was the break of our bitter frost.
And maybe there, or maybe afterwards at home in bed: sometime you put
  new life in my body.
Do you remember that I begged you for it? I could not bear
That that sick child and not I . . .
Through *me* you go on, the other threw you away. Remember, whatever
  destroying answer
Is to gore us now,
A spark of your life is safe and warm in my body and will find the future.
  There is some duty in the parcel
With being a father; I think some joys too. But not to destroy yourself,
Not now I think." "Sing to yourself," Lance answered.
"I am sorry if she died sadly, I've worse to think of."

Fayne saw old Fraser, crooked and black against the light cloud,
Totter up the hill-top and drop himself down
By the new name-post, but he stood up again
Before Lance and Fayne came. He screamed, "Keep off,"
And picked up clods of the herbless earth and threw them,
But Lance went up without noticing. "What must I do?"
He prayed, "I cannot live as I am." Old Fraser

Suddenly kneeling covered his face and wept,
And said "What has God done? I had two sons and loved them too much,
And He is jealous. Oh Lance, was there no silence in the streaming world
To cover your mouth with, forever against me?
I am not. Not hangman. Tell your story
Where it belongs. Give yourself up.
Must I take you?" "That's what I thought of at the very first,
But have been deluded awhile," Lance answered quietly,
And turned to go down. Fayne cried, "What good is this? Oh but how
    often,
Father, you have spoken of the godless world: is that what Lance is to go to
    for help and punishment?
When they came to put a serum into your cows, what did you say? You
    would not trust an old cow to them,
Will you trust Lance? If he were as red as Cain . . . when hunters come
    and break down your fences here
Do we run to the law? Must we run to it
For a dearer cause? What justice or what help or what understanding? I told
    him to give his heart
To the wild hawks to eat rather than to men." Lance gripped her elbow
    with the tips of his fingers,
And pointing at the empty air past the old man: "See, he looks pleased wi'
    me,
And happy again." She looked first at Lance, then at the vacant air. "How
    could he help but forgive you,"
She answered, "he knows it was not hatred but madness.
Why must you punish yourself, you loved each other": and to the old man:
    "Is God's hand lamed? Tell Lance
To lean on your God; what can man do for him? I cannot remember," she
    said trembling, "how Cain ended.
There were no prisons I am sure?" Lance said, "He looks well.
No scar at all and his eyes laughing. Ah, Ah, look!

He waved his hand at his grave and laughed. I'll tell you, though,
He's not real. Don't mistake him. It makes me glad,
But it's bright nothing. Now it's gone: see?" The old man, suddenly
Erect and shaking against the gray cloud: "I will have no part in this
    matter.
It is written that sevenfold vengeance on the slayer of Cain. Go. Go. To be
    a fugitive and be a vagabond,
And tramp the earth hard that has opened her mouth for thy brother's
    blood. No wonder the sweet rain could not fall.
I say flee quickly, before the dogs . . . . should I give
My son to be judged by dogs?" Fayne said, "Do you hear him, Lance, he
    has answered you. We must go away south,
As I've been praying." Lance said, "It has all been useless and blind. I am
    back in hell." He sighed and went down
The way Fayne led, old Fraser behind them crying:
"If you had listened in the days before: now it is night,
And who shall hear? but the sharp feet of pursuers: yet look how Christ's
    blood
Flows like a fiery comet through heaven and would rain sweetness
The fields refuse."

            Fayne said, "I am going to tell your mother
That you've got work as foreman on a farm in the south,
A dairy I'll say, near Paso Robles. You've got to go and earn wages
Because we're to have a baby. But next summer
She'll see us again: we'll come visiting: do you understand?
You must not let her think that you're going for good;
She couldn't bear that perhaps; but cheerfully say good-bye,
You'll save the sorrow, that's your wish, perhaps even
The ticking of her tired heart. Can you do it, Lance?
No," she said sadly when she looked at his face.
"I'll say that you've gone ahead. You had to go suddenly

To get the job." "By God," he said, "I can do my own lying,
And smooth a face of my own, come on and watch me.
It is *my* mother." "Your hands, Lance." He moaned impatiently.
"How will you say they were hurt?" He moaned, "Hobbled, hobbled.
Never an inch. That's the first rule in hell,
Never to step one inch until it is planned.
. . . In the feed-cutter." Fayne said "I daren't. Yes, at the end.
I'll find clean cloth to bandage them. You must wash.
Get Davie to help you ready the horses.
The pack is ready, only we must put food in it."
He answered, "I am sick of life. I have beaten at the last door
And found a fool."

XIV

Beyond Abbey's place
The trail began to wind up to the streaming cloud.
Fayne looked back: Abbey's was hidden, the awful-memoried cliff
Crouched indistinguishable. Lance said fiercely,
"What do you see?" "Nothing." Fayne led the packhorse
To save torture of his hands; Lance rode behind.
He stopped on the rounding of a high fold of the hillside
And turned himself in the saddle, with his finger-tips
On the withers and on the croup. Fayne stopped. "Did you see," Lance
    said,
"The look of the man that watched us by Abbey's fence?"
"What, Lance? I am quite sure you are wrong: there has been no one
Since we left home." "Then I was mistaken.
. . . I see nobody following. If they come after me
I'll kill them; I am not going to be interfered with now.
My trouble's my own affair. I'd cut my heart out

To make him live: that's out of the question. I have beaten like a blind bird
　　at every window of the world.
No rational exit. No cure. Nothing. Go on. No," he said, "wait.
You know it's our last chance to see home. There are our hills but the
　　valley's hidden. There's Fraser's Point,
Do you see? The small jag: like a beak, ah? And," he said slowly, "the curve
On this side, glimmering along . . . that cliff you know.
Looks like flat shore." "Dear," she said faintly, "it would be better not to
　　look back. We're going far. Come."
"Worn flat I suppose by my thoughts, walking around, up and down,
　　walking around. Don't talk about it.
I can even pick out the hill where we stood this morning, that posted hill.
　　I'm a little run down in health,
Perhaps these haggles in my hands will poison. Go on: I've seen enough."
Around the corner of the hill, where wet earth hushed
The stony hooves, "Did you tell me," Lance said,
"That my mother saw Mary . . . what did you tell me?
When she died?" Fayne felt a tired hope of joy:
He was thinking of someone else than Michael at least.
"Your mother saw her the day she died; probably the hour
And very moment. She thought that she asked for me,
But when I came, the presence had disappeared."
"What about it?" he said, "there's no sense in it." "No.
That's the manner of . . . spirits. She had a clear sweet nature,
Candid and loving." Lance answered, "I am much troubled
About leaving my mother. The skin looked bluish again
Around her nostrils: we ought not to have left her." Fayne heard
An angry repeated crying high up in the air;
She was careful not to look up, but stealthily
Looked back at Lance; and said, "She was happy, dear,
When I told her about the baby; she was full of plans.
And we'll write often." He was glaring up at the sky,

His face menacing and pale. Fayne said, "Lance?"
And when he did not answer, herself looked up and watched a great soaring
    bird,
White-tailed, white-headed, a bald eagle, wide over the mountain and shore
    scribing his arc of flight,
Tormented by a red-tail hawk that sailed above. The hawk dived,
    screaming, and seemed to strike,
The eagle dipped a wing with reluctant dignity
And sailed his course. "Oh, you can't kill them all,"
Fayne said, "from here to Mexico." "I don't want to.
They win, damn them."

                              They climbed at length to the cloudy ridges
Where the high trail went south; they rode through the clouds and in
    windy clearings
Would see enormous declivities tilting from the hooves of the horses down
    wells of vapor to the sudden shore's
Thin white surf on a rock like a grain of sand. Two or three times
Fayne heard Lance stop; she sat in the cloud and waited until he came.
    When the ridge and the trail widened
They rode abreast; then she saw that he'd stripped
The bandage from his right hand, but one thin layer
The wound gaped through. "Oh Lance, it is all exposed: was it too tight?"
    "Too stiff." "I must fix it.
Have you thrown the linen away?" He said with a shamed face, "Let's be
    friends, Fayne. I feel somebody
Behind us; and I can tell you I won't be caught. I have my gun: I can't
    manage the trigger
Wi' that muff on my hand." "You are right," she answered with a flash of
    joyful fear; "but it is certain
That no one's following. Your wrist looks swollen." "No," he said; "but it is
    strange and pleasant to have left the place

Along with you. Your hair is like a fire in the cloud." She answered, "We
   have changed worlds." "Wait for me,"
He said, and turned and went back. Hearing him speak, but not able to see
   him through the blind vapor,
She struggled in a kind of nightmare to turn the packhorse
To go back to him; she dropped the hair rope and struck
Her mount with fists and heels. As it leaped, Lance
Grew out of the fog, towering on his little horse.
"What was it? What did you see?" "Ah, nobody.
I could 'a' sworn."

                         He was always listening as they went on,
And looking back, if the steam of the world cleared
Over the draft from a gorge. Fayne suddenly stopped
In the blind coil and drizzle of the cloud. "Are you there, Lance?
Are you all right?" "Hm? Yes," he answered, "I know it.
But I never can see him." Fayne said quietly, "Perhaps he is.
As when your mother saw Mary Abbey. But they're not real,
As you and I are, and the hard mountains and the horses and the wet cloud.
   He is not an enemy: we never
A moment hated him, but always loved and were sorry. But he is only an
   echo of our own troubled
And loving thoughts." Lance laughed like the sudden bark of a dog:
   "Eavesdroppers
Have got to take what they get. But *what's* real, ah? How do you know?" "I
   never thought of it," she answered,
"But I can tell you. What eyes, ears, fingers, can feel; and come again the
   next day
And feel again: that's real. You may see visions but you cannot touch them;
   but if you could touch them too,
Yet they don't last. . . . Did you ever hear of a place called Laurel Spring?"
   "No. Any water would do.

It's growing toward night." "I was thinking about a man named Vasquez," she answered,
"That sees visions."

The trail had come lower,
They rode in dropping skeins of the cloud, a slight cattle-track
On a steeple-roof slope so sheer and high
That every stone the hooves kicked out rolled down
Into deep water; but had dwindled from sight down the pitch of distance
The first quarter of its fall. The sea-west heaven
Opened an eye, whence the last of the sun
Flamed, like a fire fallen into a well
Flashing before it is drowned, that makes the black disk of water
As bright as blood; and the wild angry light streams from the bottom up the stained wall
And washes with color every cold stone: so from the floor of the world a fountain and flood of roses
Flew up to the height, those two riders might have seen
Their own blue shadows on the red cloud above them;
Then the eye of the west closed. Color was there
But no radiance, here the gray evening gathered.
Lance's mount suddenly stumbled; Fayne cried out;
And they rode on. Lance said, "Now he's ahead of us;
The horse shied when he passed; I couldn't see him.
It's trembling still." Fayne said, "No wonder. If it had fallen
It would roll from here to the sea; Oh keep your feet
Light in the stirrups. Your bay's getting too old, Lance.
To-morrow it must take the pack; you'll ride the pinto."
"*To-morrow!*" he said. Fayne turned and looked and said nothing, feeling intolerable sadness
Grow over her mind like the gray darkness covering the world; for a moment it seemed they were not escaping

But only dragging the trap; and the twilight darkened. There was no
    stopping here;
They rode like flies upon the face of a wall;
The tired horses must stick if they could, and go in darkness
Until some flat place found. Fayne was tired too,
And shook in the cold. "Lance, Lance, ride carefully.
If you should fall I'll follow. I will not live
Without you." He laughed "Ha!" like the bark of a dog.
"No danger here, we are going in the perfect owl's eye.
Michael has gone ahead to make ready for us.
You know: a camp." "What?" she said. "*You* know: a camp.
We'll come to it." "Oh Lance, ride carefully." A kind of shoulder on the
    wall
Showed in the dark, and a little noise
That Fayne thought was the sea. Lance called behind her,
"Hello. Are you there?" She said, "Here, Lance." "Uhk-hm.
The other fellow; not you." She thought "I can't bear it,"
And said quietly, "It's water my horse has found.
It must be a little creek; I can hear it falling."
They stopped and drank under the whispering bushes,
And found no place to lie down. There were no stars,
But three ship's lights crept on the cavernous depth
And made a constellation in the under-world;
Lance said "Damn you, go on." Fayne understood
By the useless curse how his mind stared. The horses
Paced on with heads down, and around the fold of the hill
Stopped of themselves. Here in a shallow gully
There seemed to be room to camp, between the sharp slope
And a comb of bushes.

                    Fayne saw a glimmer move in the dark
And sobbed to restrain a cry; it was Lance's hand

From which he had slipped the bandage; the wound and its wet exudate

Shone phosphorescent: the right hand: the hand that had done it. Or can
   pain shine? In a moment Fayne thought more quietly:

"Is it infected, could infection shine in the dark like decaying wood?" He
   was feeling the earth for sticks

To start a fire; she dipped in the pannier and found the matches. In the red
   firelight she examined his hand:

Feverish, a little; but less than his lips and eyes: Oh when would the strain
   end? "Let's make a big fire,

This our first night of freedom, and keep ghosts away." She took the
   short-handled axe from the pannier side

And broke dead wood with it. "We'll make a bright eye up here for the
   night, in the high blackness, for the hollow night,

For the ships to wonder what star. . . . I'll tell you what star,

You streaming ships: the camp-fire of Lance and Fayne is the star; we are
   not beaten, we are going to live.

We have come out of the world and are free, more hawk than human, we've
   given our hearts to the hawks to keep

In the high air." Lance laughed "Ha! Owls you mean. Welcome." He kept
   his hands

From the fire-heat, and would take no food.

XV

                                        The famished horses
Moved in the dark; Lance ground his teeth in sick sleep;
Wind whispered; the ocean moaned; that tinkling water
Fell down the rock. Fayne lay and was cold; she wondered
Whether it was Laurel Spring perhaps; then perfectly knowing
That all the leaves were oak, she was compelled
To creep away in the darkness and crush leaves
To smell their nature. "I was not like this

A year ago," she thought wistfully, "to lie wakeful
And stare at the words of a fool; in the high sweetness
Of mountain night." Her solitary mind
Made itself a strange thought: that Lance would be saved and well,
But she herself would die at the baby's birth,
After some happy months: it seemed to lead hope
Into the line of nature again; for nobody ever
Comes off scot free.

                She slept a little; Lance woke
And felt his hands aching, and thought, "It cannot be true
That I killed. Oh yes, it is. At every waking.
And there is no way to change it." Night was grown pale
In the way to dawn, and many dark cold forms
Of bush and rock stood quietly. But moving creatures
Troubled the stillness, Lance heard the steps of pursuit
Along the trail from the north, more than one rider;
Then his long-frustrate and troublesome life
Flaming like joy for the meeting, shook its bewildered elements
To one sharp edge. He was up, and moved quietly,
Willing to let Fayne sleep, in the sunset cloud
And pillow of her hair. His puffed hot fingers buckled
In a moment without fumbling the holstered belt
That had the gun; he caught the short-handled axe
That magnetlike drew his hand; and the world was suddenly
Most cool and spacious.

              Four lean steers
Led by a barren cow were along the path.
They had come to drink in the dawn twilight, and now
Remembered a grass-plot southward. Where Lance met them
The trail was but a hair of passage stepped in the face

Of a leaning clay cliff; the leader stopped,
Was pushed from behind, and trying in her fear to turn,
Splayed with both fore-feet over the slippery edge,
Felt the axe bite her neck; so leaping out blindly
Slid down the pit. They were horsemen to Lance, his enemies,
Albeit a part of his mind was awake and faintly
Knew what they were; the master part willed them to be
Men pursuing a murderer; they were both cattle and men
At the one moment. For being men, hated; for being cattle,
The hand was more free to strike, the fiery delight
More pure of guilt. The steer came on, not angrily,
Dull and unable to turn, dipping his new-moon horns,
Lance whining with joy and reckless of his own body
With both hands on the axe-helve drove the sharp steel
Into the shoulder; it broke right through the shoulder-blade
And nicked the broad ribs below. At the same moment
The curve and base of a horn found Lance's thigh
And pushed; but he with his weight flung forward
In the fury of the axe-blow went over the head
Onto the shoulder, and a moment clung there, as when an old
    mountain-lion
Has hunted under the spite of fortune for many days, until his bright hide
    is ruffled, and the ribs
Lift up the hair; he comes by a secret way and crouches in the alder-leaves
    an hour before dawn
Over a pool where the deer drink; but not a deer but a cow-elk comes to
    the pool,
And stands in the glimmer and the trembling twilight, and stoops her head:
    the puma watches, his lustful mind
Can even taste the hot flesh through the rough hide, and smell the soft
    heavy fountain of blood; he springs,

And sticks on the shoulder, blunting his teeth against the great bones of the
    neck; but the elk does not fall,
But runs, and beats her death against the low branches, and scrapes him off:
So Lance fell off from the steer's shoulder, and was ground
Between the flank and the cliff, as the numbed fore-leg
Failed and recovered. The weight lifting, he stood
With his back to the steep wall and violently
Pushed the great hairy quarters with all his power
Of both his arms; the hind hooves fell over the edge,
And the fore-legs, one crippled, scraped the stiff clay
In vain for foot-hold, the great hurt bulk went down
Standing, but fell in a moment and slid in the chasm.
The others had turned and fled.

                      Fayne saw her lover
Come swaying and shining against the gray sky
Over the abyss of darkness, and she had seen the steer fall.
Lance held the axe. "Ah, Ah," Fayne cried, "strike then. Strike. Finish it.
    We have not lived pleasantly,
And I have failed." He threatened her, laughing with pleasure. "I have not
    had such pleasure in the days of my life.
Did the dogs think they were hunting rabbit? Surprised them, ah, ah?" She
    said, "Your hands have opened again
And dripping fast." "More?" he said, hearing the horses that stamped and
    snorted beyond. "Oh, good. If they get me,
Remember it's a grand end." He ran and struck
The nearest; it was holding its head ready for the axe, backing and straining
On the taut halter, and went down on its knees; the second stroke
Chopped horribly along the neck, the third ended the pain. Lance crouched
    and looked at the head, and wearily

Rose, and said slackly, "There was no way out, here, either. My own horse
   you see.
I must 'a' been . . . I have been troubled.
Beating my face on every glass gap and porthole . . .
And get a beaten face.
Were those more horses?" Fayne had stood rigid; she said,
"Steers." "Why didn't they shoot? . . . Oh . . . Steers. *That's* it.
Yet I hate blood.
See how it springs from the ground: struck oil at last, ah?
I felt like this, that time. So we've tried a long time
And never found
My exit: I think there's none: the world's closed.
A brave fellow, a tethered horse.
A natural butcher."

            One of the fallen fore-legs
Paddled its hoof on the earth and Lance said faintly, "I've come to the
   point
I cannot even put him out of his pain."
He dropped the red axe; Fayne saw his own blood spring from his palm
When he let go. "I think," he said, "have I got the gun on me?
Will *you* finish him off?" "He is dead," she answered.
"Listen, Lance." Her throat was twisting and beating upward with hot
   nausea; she swallowed and said,
"Dearest. This is only a stumble on the way. We are going on. You will be
   well after this.
You are dreadful with blood but you are too beautiful
And strong to fail. Look, dear,
How the clear quivering waters and white of dawn fill the whole world; they
   seem to wash the whole mountain

All gently and white, and over the sea, purifying everything. If I were less
    tired
I could be full of joy." She pressed her hands to her throat and swallowed
    and said, "Where you and I
Have come to, is a dizzy and lonely place on a height: we have to peel off
Some humanness here or it will be hard to live. If you could think that all
    human feelings, repentance
And blood-thirst too, are not very important in so vast a world; nor
    anyone's life;
Nor love either, the unlucky angel
That has led me so far: we'll go on, we'll not fail. All over the mountain
The eagles and little falcons and all the bright cold hawks — you've made
    friends with them now — are widening
Their wings to wash them in the cool clearness, and over the precipices
    launching their bodies like ships
On the high waves of dawn. For us too
Dawn brings us wandering; and any ghost or memory that wants to follow
    us will be sore in the feet
Before the day's end. We're going until the world changes, you and I like
    the young hawks
Going hunting; we'll take the world by the throat and make him give us
What we desire."

                He stood bent over, smiling sidewise, watching the drip
    from his hands, and said,
"You do it quite bravely. No doubt you are right, and I must take your
    guidance without a word
From this time on. What next? I'll go wash. Faugh.
What a hell of red to be stuck in; you're out o' luck,
Loving a butcher." She answered with her hands at her mouth, struggling
    against her sickness, "I'll come in a moment

And help you to clean your hands and bandage them again." He went back
    by the trail, but she
Vomited with grievous labor a little water and followed him.

                                          Now all the
    world was quite clear
And full of dawn, so that Fayne saw from the trail
The jutting shoulder of the hill, guessed at in darkness,
Was a great rock, lengthened by thick hard foliage
Of mountain laurel, which grew above it, and the wind had carved
Into the very nature and form of the rock
That gave it shelter, but green for gray. She remembered
With a wild lift of the heart, "He'd wash the blood
In Laurel Spring, and be healed of his wounds,"
But Lance had not gone to the stony basin, but stood
Out on the ledge of the rock, and was looking down
The straight vast depth, toward the beauty of the ocean
Like a gray dove's breast under the dawn-light. She could not call to him
Before he leaped and went down. He was falling erect
With his feet under him for a long time,
But toward the bottom he began turning in the air.
One of the roots of the mountain concealed his end
On the shore rocks. Fayne lay down in the trail
And thought that when she was able she would go down to him,
One way or another. " . . . That would be happiest.
But then he'd be extinguished forever, his last young spark
That lies warm in my body, bought too dear
For gulls to eat . . . . and I never could help you at all,
And now has come the wild end.
I could not keep you, but your child in my body
Will change the world."

She climbed slowly down,
Rock to rock, bush to bush. At length she could see him
Lying softly, and there was somebody bending above him,
Who was gone in a moment. It was not so dreadful
As she had feared; she kissed the stained mouth,
And brought smooth stones from the shore until she had covered
Her love against the vultures and salty gulls;
Then climbed up, rock to rock, bush to bush.

Solstice

1933-35

RETURN

A little too abstract, a little too wise,
It is time for us to kiss the earth again,
It is time to let the leaves rain from the skies,
Let the rich life run to the roots again.
I will go down to the lovely Sur Rivers
And dip my arms in them up to the shoulders.
I will find my accounting where the alder leaf quivers
In the ocean wind over the river boulders.
I will touch things and things and no more thoughts,
That breed like mouthless May-flies darkening the sky,
The insect clouds that blind our passionate hawks
So that they cannot strike, hardly can fly.
Things are the hawk's food and noble is the mountain, Oh noble
Pico Blanco, steep sea-wave of marble.

LOVE THE WILD SWAN

"I hate my verses, every line, every word.
Oh pale and brittle pencils ever to try
One grass-blade's curve, or the throat of one bird
That clings to twig, ruffled against white sky.
Oh cracked and twilight mirrors ever to catch
One color, one glinting flash, of the splendor of things.
Unlucky hunter, Oh bullets of wax,
The lion beauty, the wild-swan wings, the storm of the wings."
— This wild swan of a world is no hunter's game.
Better bullets than yours would miss the white breast,
Better mirrors than yours would crack in the flame.
Does it matter whether you hate your . . . self? At least
Love your eyes that can see, your mind that can
Hear the music, the thunder of the wings. Love the wild swan.

THE CRUEL FALCON

Contemplation would make a good life, keep it strict, only
The eyes of a desert skull drinking the sun,
Too intense for flesh, lonely
Exultations of white bone;
Pure action would make a good life, let it be sharp-
Set between the throat and the knife.
A man who knows death by heart
Is the man for that life.
In pleasant peace and security
How suddenly the soul in a man begins to die.
He shall look up above the stalled oxen
Envying the cruel falcon,
And dig under the straw for a stone
To bruise himself on.

DISTANT RAINFALL

Like mourning women veiled to the feet
Tall slender rainstorms walk slowly against gray cloud along the far verge.
The ocean is green where the river empties,
Dull gray between the points of the headlands, purple where the women
    walk.
What do they want? Whom are they mourning?
What hero's dust in the urn between the two hands hidden in the veil?
Titaness after Titaness proudly
Bearing her tender magnificent sorrow at her heart, the lost battle's beauty.

ROCK AND HAWK

Here is a symbol in which
Many high tragic thoughts
Watch their own eyes.

This gray rock, standing tall
On the headland, where the sea-wind
Lets no tree grow,

Earthquake-proved, and signatured
By ages of storms: on its peak
A falcon has perched.

I think, here is your emblem
To hang in the future sky;
Not the cross, not the hive,

But this; bright power, dark peace;
Fierce consciousness joined with final
Disinterestedness;

Life with calm death; the falcon's
Realist eyes and act
Married to the massive

Mysticism of stone,
Which failure cannot cast down
Nor success make proud.

SHINE, REPUBLIC

The quality of these trees, green height; of the sky, shining; of water, a
  clear flow; of the rock, hardness
And reticence: each is noble in its quality. The love of freedom has been
  the quality of western man.

There is a stubborn torch that flames from Marathon to Concord, its
  dangerous beauty binding three ages
Into one time; the waves of barbarism and civilization have eclipsed but
  have never quenched it.

For the Greeks the love of beauty, for Rome of ruling; for the present age
  the passionate love of discovery;
But in one noble passion we are one; and Washington, Luther, Tacitus,
  Eschylus, one kind of man.

And you, America, that passion made you. You were not born to
  prosperity, you were born to love freedom.
You did not say "en masse," you said "independence." But we cannot have
  all the luxuries and freedom also.

Freedom is poor and laborious; that torch is not safe but hungry, and often
  requires blood for its fuel.
You will tame it against it burn too clearly, you will hood it like a kept
  hawk, you will perch it on the wrist of Caesar.

But keep the tradition, conserve the forms, the observances, keep the spot
  sore. Be great, carve deep your heel-marks.
The states of the next age will no doubt remember you, and edge their love
  of freedom with contempt of luxury.

SIGN-POST

Civilized, crying how to be human again: this will tell you how.
Turn outward, love things, not men, turn right away from humanity,
Let that doll lie. Consider if you like how the lilies grow,
Lean on the silent rock until you feel its divinity
Make your veins cold, look at the silent stars, let your eyes
Climb the great ladder out of the pit of yourself and man.
Things are so beautiful, your love will follow your eyes;
Things are the God, you will love God, and not in vain,
For what we love, we grow to it, we share its nature. At length
You will look back along the stars' rays and see that even
The poor doll humanity has a place under heaven.
Its qualities repair their mosaic around you, the chips of strength
And sickness; but now you are free, even to become human,
But born of the rock and the air, not of a woman.

FLIGHT OF SWANS

One who sees giant Orion, the torches of winter midnight,
Enormously walking above the ocean in the west of heaven;
And watches the track of this age of time at its peak of flight
Waver like a spent rocket, wavering toward new discoveries,
Mortal examinations of darkness, soundings of depth;
And watches the long coast mountain vibrate from bronze to green,
Bronze to green, year after year, and all the streams
Dry and flooded, dry and flooded, in the racing seasons;
And knows that exactly this and not another is the world,
The ideal is phantoms for bait, the spirit is a flicker on a grave; —
May serve, with a certain detachment, the fugitive human race,
Or his own people, or his own household; but hardly himself;
And will not wind himself into hopes nor sicken with despairs.
He has found the peace and adored the God; he handles in autumn
The germs of far-future spring.

                              Sad sons of the stormy fall,
No escape, you have to inflict and endure: surely it is time for you
To learn to touch the diamond within to the diamond outside,
Thinning your humanity a little between the invulnerable diamonds,
Knowing that your angry choices and hopes and terrors are in vain,
But life and death not in vain; and the world is like a flight of swans.

from AT THE BIRTH OF AN AGE
[vision of the self-hanged God]

Pain and their endless cries. How they cry to me: but they are I: let them
   ask themselves.
I am they, and there is nothing beside. I am alone and time passes, time
   also is in me, the long
Beat of this unquiet heart, the quick drip of this blood, the whirl and
   returning waves of these stars,
The course of this thought.
My particles have companions and happy fulfilments, each star has stars to
   answer him and hungry night
To take his shining, and turn it again and make it a star; each beast has
   food to find and his mating,
And the hostile and helpful world; each atom has related atoms, and
   hungry emptiness around him to take
His little shining cry and cry it back; but I am all, the emptiness and all,
   the shining and the night.
All alone, I alone.

            If I were quiet and emptied myself of pain, breaking
   these bonds,
Healing these wounds: without strain there is nothing. Without pressure,
   without conditions, without pain,
Is peace; that's nothing, not-being; the pure night, the perfect freedom, the
   black crystal. I have chosen
Being; therefore wounds, bonds, limits and pain; the crowded mind and the
   anguished nerves, experience and ecstasy.

Whatever electron or atom or flesh or star or universe cries to me,
Or endures in shut silence: it is my cry, my silence; I am the nerve, I am
   the agony,

I am the endurance. I torture myself
To discover myself; trying with a little or extreme experiment each nerve
    and fibril, all forms
Of being, of life, of cold substance; all motions and netted complications of
    event,
All poisons of desire, love, hatred, joy, partial peace, partial vision.
    Discovery is deep and endless,
Each moment of being is new: therefore I still refrain my burning thirst
    from the crystal-black
Water of an end.

GRAY WEATHER

It is true that, older than man and ages to outlast him, the Pacific surf
Still cheerfully pounds the worn granite drum;
But there's no storm; and the birds are still, no song; no kind of excess;
Nothing that shines, nothing is dark;
There is neither joy nor grief nor a person, the sun's tooth sheathed in
    cloud,
And life has no more desires than a stone.
The stormy conditions of time and change are all abrogated, the essential
Violences of survival, pleasure,
Love, wrath and pain, and the curious desire of knowing, all perfectly
    suspended.
In the cloudy light, in the timeless quietness,
One explores deeper than the nerves or heart of nature, the womb or soul,
To the bone, the careless white bone, the excellence.

RED MOUNTAIN

Beyond the Sierras, and sage-brush Nevada ranges, and vast
Vulture-utopias of Utah desert,
That mountain we admired last year on our summer journey, the same
Rose-red pyramid glows over Silverton.
Whoever takes the rock pass from Ouray sees foaming waterfalls
And trees like green flames, like the rocks flaming
Green; and above, up the wild gorge, up the wild sky,
Incredibly blood-color around the snow-spot
The violent peak. We thought it was too theatrical to last;
But if we ship to Cape Horn, or were buying
Camels in Urga, Red Mountain would not turn pale for our absence.
We like dark skies and lead-color heights,
But the excellence of things is really unscrupulous, it will dare anything.

Such Counsels You Gave to Me

1935-38

REARMAMENT

These grand and fatal movements toward death: the grandeur of the mass
Makes pity a fool, the tearing pity
For the atoms of the mass, the persons, the victims, makes it seem
   monstrous
To admire the tragic beauty they build.
It is beautiful as a river flowing or a slowly gathering
Glacier on a high mountain rock-face,
Bound to plow down a forest, or as frost in November,
The gold and flaming death-dance for leaves,
Or a girl in the night of her spent maidenhood, bleeding and kissing.
I would burn my right hand in a slow fire
To change the future ... I should do foolishly. The beauty of modern
Man is not in the persons but in the
Disastrous rhythm, the heavy and mobile masses, the dance of the
Dream-led masses down the dark mountain.

THE PURSE-SEINE

Our sardine fishermen work at night in the dark of the moon; daylight
   or moonlight
They could not tell where to spread the net, unable to see the
   phosphorescence of the shoals of fish.
They work northward from Monterey, coasting Santa Cruz; off New Year's
   Point or off Pigeon Point
The look-out man will see some lakes of milk-color light on the sea's
   night-purple; he points, and the helmsman
Turns the dark prow, the motor-boat circles the gleaming shoal and drifts
   out her seine-net. They close the circle
And purse the bottom of the net, then with great labor haul it in.

                                                        I cannot
   tell you
How beautiful the scene is, and a little terrible, then, when the crowded
   fish
Know they are caught, and wildly beat from one wall to the other of their
   closing destiny the phosphorescent
Water to a pool of flame, each beautiful slender body sheeted with flame,
   like a live rocket
A comet's tail wake of clear yellow flame; while outside the narrowing
Floats and cordage of the net great sea-lions come up to watch, sighing in
   the dark; the vast walls of night
Stand erect to the stars.

                              Lately I was looking from a night mountain-top
On a wide city, the colored splendor, galaxies of light: how could I help
   but recall the seine-net
Gathering the luminous fish? I cannot tell you how beautiful the city
   appeared, and a little terrible.

I thought, We have geared the machines and locked all together into
    interdependence; we have built the great cities; now
There is no escape. We have gathered vast populations incapable of free
    survival, insulated
From the strong earth, each person in himself helpless, on all dependent.
    The circle is closed, and the net
Is being hauled in. They hardly feel the cords drawing, yet they shine
    already. The inevitable mass-disasters
Will not come in our time nor in our children's, but we and our children
Must watch the net draw narrower, government take all powers, — or
    revolution, and the new government
Take more than all, add to kept bodies kept souls, — or anarchy, the
    mass-disasters.

                    These things are Progress;
Do you marvel our verse is troubled or frowning, while it keeps its reason?
    Or it lets go, lets the mood flow
In the manner of the recent young men into mere hysteria, splintered
    gleams, crackled laughter. But they are quite wrong.
There is no reason for amazement: surely one always knew that cultures
    decay, and life's end is death.

THE WIND-STRUCK MUSIC

Ed Stiles and old Tom Birnam went up to their cattle on the bare hills

Above Mal Paso; they'd ridden under the stars' white death, when they
     reached the ridge the huge tiger-lily

Of a certain cloud-lapped astonishing autumn sunrise opened all its petals.
     Ed Stiles pulled in his horse,

That flashy palamino he rode — cream-color, heavy white mane, white tail,
     his pride — and said

"Look, Tom. My God. Ain't that a beautiful sunrise?" Birnam drew down
     his mouth, set the hard old chin,

And whined: "Now, Ed: listen here: I haven't an ounce of poetry in all my
     body. It's cows we're after."

Ed laughed and followed; they began to sort the heifers out of the herd.
     One red little deer-legged creature

Rolled her wild eyes and ran away down the hill, the old man hard after
     her. She ran through a deep-cut gully,

And Birnam's piebald would have made a clean jump but the clay lip

Crumbled under his take-off, he slipped and

Spilled in the pit, flailed with four hooves and came out scrambling. Stiles
     saw them vanish,

Then the pawing horse and the flapping stirrups. He rode and looked down
     and saw the old man in the gully-bottom

Flat on his back, most grimly gazing up at the sky. He saw the earth banks,
     the sparse white grass,

The strong dark sea a thousand feet down below, red with reflections of
     clouds. He said "My God

Tom are you hurt?" Who answered slowly, "No, Ed.

I'm only lying here thinking o' my four sons" — biting the words

Carefully between his lips — "big handsome men, at present lolling in bed
     in their ... silk ... pyjamas ...

And why the devil I keep on working?" He stood up slowly and wiped the
    dirt from his cheek, groaned, spat,
And climbed up the clay bank. Stiles laughed: "Tom, I can't tell you: I
    guess you like to. By God I guess
You like the sunrises." The old man growled in his throat and said
"Catch me my horse."

                    This old man died last winter, having lived
    eighty-one years under open sky,
Concerned with cattle, horses and hunting, no thought nor emotion that all
    his ancestors since the ice-age
Could not have comprehended. I call that a good life; narrow, but vastly
    better than most
Men's lives, and beyond comparison more beautiful; the wind-struck music
    man's bones were moulded to be the harp for.

MEMOIR

I saw the laboratory animals: throat-bandaged dogs cowering in cages, still obsessed with the pitiful
Love that dogs feel, longing to lick the hand of their devil; and the sick monkeys, dying rats, all sacrificed
To human inquisitiveness, pedantry and vanity, or at best the hope
Of helping hopeless invalids live long and hopelessly.

                    I left that great light room where pain was the air
And found my friends dehorning cattle in the field above Rio Piedras Canyon. (The buyers require it now,
So many horned beasts have injured each other in the gorged trucks
And crowded cattle-cars up to Calvary.) I watched the two Vasquez boys, great riders, drive the scared steers
Into the frame that clamps them and holds them helpless. Bill Flodden with a long-handled tool like pruning-shears
Crushed off the horns and the blood spouted; Ed Stiles, our knower of bawdy stories, the good-natured man,
Stands by to cake the blood-fountains with burning alum. These fellows are fit for life, sane men, well-buttoned
In their own skins; rarely feel pain outside their own skins: whilst I like a dowser go here and there
With skinless pity for the dipping hazel-fork.

                    Blank rises the limestone
Mountain Pico Blanco, blue runs the sea. No life here but some gray bushes, lupine and sage,
No creditor of pity, sage and satisfied plants, for it rained this morning. Here in the sanctuary
I need not think beyond the west water, that a million persons

Are presently dying of hunger in the provinces of China. I need not think
    of the Russian labor-camps, the German
Prison-camps, nor any of those other centers
That make the earth shine like a star with cruelty for light. I need not think
    of the tyrannies, that make the tyrants
Ignoble and their victims contemptible. I need not think of the probable
    wars, tyranny and pain
Made world-wide; I need not . . . know that this is our world, where only
    fool or drunkard makes happy songs.

NOVA

That Nova was a moderate star like our good sun; it stored no doubt a little more than it spent
Of heat and energy until the increasing tension came to the trigger-point
Of a new chemistry; then what was already flaming found a new manner of flaming ten-thousandfold
More brightly for a brief time; what was a pin-point fleck on a sensitive plate at the great telescope's
Eye-piece now shouts down the steep night to the naked eye, a nine-day super-star.

It is likely our moderate
Father the sun will sometime put off his nature for a similar glory. The earth would share it; these tall
Green trees would become a moment's torches and vanish, the oceans would explode into invisible steam,
The ships and the great whales fall through them like flaming meteors into the emptied abysm, the six-mile
Hollows of the Pacific sea-bed might smoke for a moment. Then the earth would be like the pale proud moon,
Nothing but vitrified sand and rock would be left on earth. This is a probable death-passion
For the sun's planets; we have no knowledge to assure us it may not happen at any moment of time.

Meanwhile the sun shines wisely and warm, trees flutter green in the wind, girls take their clothes off
To bathe in the cold ocean or to hunt love; they stand laughing in the white foam, they have beautiful
Shoulders and thighs, they are beautiful animals, all life is beautiful. We cannot be sure of life for one moment;

We can, by force and self-discipline, by many refusals and a few assertions,
  in the teeth of fortune assure ourselves
Freedom and integrity in life or integrity in death. And we know that the
  enormous invulnerable beauty of things
Is the face of God, to live gladly in its presence, and die without grief or
  fear knowing it survives us.

THE ANSWER

Then what is the answer? — Not to be deluded by dreams.
To know that great civilizations have broken down into violence, and their
    tyrants come, many times before.
When open violence appears, to avoid it with honor or choose the least
    ugly faction; these evils are essential.
To keep one's own integrity, be merciful and uncorrupted and not wish for
    evil; and not be duped
By dreams of universal justice or happiness. These dreams will not be
    fulfilled.
To know this, and know that however ugly the parts appear the whole
    remains beautiful. A severed hand
Is an ugly thing, and man dissevered from the earth and stars and his
    history . . . for contemplation or in fact . . .
Often appears atrociously ugly. Integrity is wholeness, the greatest beauty is
Organic wholeness, the wholeness of life and things, the divine beauty of
    the universe. Love that, not man
Apart from that, or else you will share man's pitiful confusions, or drown in
    despair when his days darken.

THE BEAKS OF EAGLES

An eagle's nest on the head of an old redwood on one of the
precipice-footed ridges
Above Ventana Creek, that jagged country which nothing but a falling
meteor will ever plow; no horseman
Will ever ride there, no hunter cross this ridge but the winged ones, no one
will steal the eggs from this fortress.
The she-eagle is old, her mate was shot long ago, she is now mated with a
son of hers.
When lightning blasted her nest she built it again on the same tree, in the
splinters of the thunderbolt.
The she-eagle is older than I; she was here when the fires of 'eighty-five
raged on these ridges,
She was lately fledged and dared not hunt ahead of them but ate scorched
meat. The world has changed in her time;
Humanity has multiplied, but not here; men's hopes and thoughts and
customs have changed, their powers are enlarged,
Their powers and their follies have become fantastic,
The unstable animal never has been changed so rapidly. The motor and the
plane and the great war have gone over him,
And Lenin has lived and Jehovah died: while the mother-eagle
Hunts her same hills, crying the same beautiful and lonely cry and is never
tired; dreams the same dreams,
And hears at night the rock-slides rattle and thunder in the throats of these
living mountains.

It is good for man
To try all changes, progress and corruption, powers, peace and anguish, not
to go down the dinosaur's way
Until all his capacities have been explored: and it is good for him
To know that his needs and nature are no more changed in fact in ten
thousand years than the beaks of eagles.

ALL THE LITTLE HOOF-PRINTS

Farther up the gorge the sea's voice fainted and ceased.
We heard a new noise far away ahead of us, vague and metallic, it might
have been some unpleasant bird's voice
Bedded in a matrix of long silences. At length we came to a little cabin lost
in the redwoods,
An old man sat on a bench before the doorway filing a cross-cut saw;
sometimes he slept,
Sometimes he filed. Two or three horses in the corral by the streamside
lifted their heads
To watch us pass, but the old man did not.

                                    In the afternoon we returned
the same way,
And had the picture in our minds of magnificent regions of space and
mountain not seen before. (This was
The first time that we visited Pigeon Gap, whence you look down behind
the great shouldering pyramid-
Edges of Pico Blanco through eagle-gulfs of air to a forest basin
Where two-hundred-foot redwoods look like the pile on a Turkish carpet.)
With such extensions of the idol-
Worshipping mind we came down the streamside. The old man was still at
his post by the cabin doorway, but now
Stood up and stared, said angrily "Where are you camping?" I said "We're
not camping, we're going home." He said
From his flushed heavy face, "That's the way fires get started. Did you
come at night?" "We passed you this morning.
You were half asleep, filing a saw." "I'll kill anybody that starts a fire
here . . ." his voice quavered
Into bewilderment . . . "I didn't see you. Kind of feeble I guess.

My temperature's a hundred and two every afternoon." "Why, what's the
    matter?" He removed his hat
And rather proudly showed us a deep healed trench in the bald skull. "My
    horse fell at the ford,
I must 'a' cracked my head on a rock. Well sir I can't remember anything
    till next morning.
I woke in bed the pillow was soaked with blood, the horse was in the corral
    and had had his hay," —
Singing the words as if he had told the story a hundred times. To whom?
    To himself, probably, —
"The saddle was on the rack and the bridle on the right nail. What do you
    think of *that* now?" He passed
His hand on his bewildered forehead and said, "Unless an angel or
    something came down and did it.
A basin of blood and water by the crick, I must 'a' washed myself." My wife
    said sharply, "Have you been to a doctor?"
"Oh yes," he said, "my boy happened down." She said "You oughtn't to be
    alone here: are you all alone here?"
"No," he answered, "horses. I've been all over the world: right here is the
    most beautiful place in the world.
I played the piccolo in ships' orchestras." We looked at the immense
    redwoods and dark
Fern-taken slip of land by the creek, where the horses were, and the yuccaed
    hillsides high in the sun
Flaring like torches; I said "Darkness comes early here." He answered with
    pride and joy, "Two hundred and eighty-
Five days in the year the sun never gets in here.
Like living under the sea, green all summer, beautiful." My wife said,
    "How do you know your temperature's
A hundred and two?" "Eh? The doctor. He said the bone
Presses my brain, he's got to cut out a piece. I said All right you've got to
    wait till it rains,

I've got to guard my place through the fire-season. By God," he said
   joyously,
"The quail on my roof wake me up every morning, then I look out the
   window and a dozen deer
Drift up the canyon with the mist on their shoulders. Look in the dust at
   your feet, all the little hoof-prints."

CONTEMPLATION OF THE SWORD

(April, 1938)

Reason will not decide at last; the sword will decide.

The sword: an obsolete instrument of bronze or steel, formerly used to kill men, but here

In the sense of a symbol. The sword: that is: the storms and counter-storms of general destruction; killing of men,

Destruction of all goods and materials; massacre, more or less intentional, of children and women;

Destruction poured down from wings, the air made accomplice, the innocent air

Perverted into assassin and poisoner.

The sword: that is: treachery and cowardice, incredible baseness, incredible courage, loyalties, insanities.

The sword: weeping and despair, mass-enslavement, mass-torture, frustration of all the hopes

That starred man's forehead. Tyranny for freedom, horror for happiness, famine for bread, carrion for children.

Reason will not decide at last, the sword will decide.

Dear God, who are the whole splendor of things and the sacred stars, but also the cruelty and greed, the treacheries

And vileness, insanities and filth and anguish: now that this thing comes near us again I am finding it hard

To praise you with a whole heart.

                              I know what pain is, but pain can shine. I know what death is, I have sometimes

Longed for it. But cruelty and slavery and degradation, pestilence, filth, the
    pitifulness
Of men like little hurt birds and animals ... if you were only
Waves beating rock, the wind and the iron-cored earth, the flaming insolent
    wildness of sun and stars,
With what a heart I could praise your beauty.

                                    You will not repent, nor
    cancel life, nor free man from anguish
For many ages to come. You are the one that tortures himself to discover
    himself: I am
One that watches you and discovers you, and praises you in little parables,
    idyl or tragedy, beautiful
Intolerable God.

                    The sword: that is:
I have two sons whom I love. They are twins, they were born in nineteen
    sixteen, which seemed to us a dark year
Of a great war, and they are now of the age
That war prefers. The first-born is like his mother, he is so beautiful
That persons I hardly know have stopped me on the street to speak of the
    grave beauty of the boy's face.
The second-born has strength for his beauty; when he strips for swimming
    the hero shoulders and wrestler loins
Make him seem clothed. The sword: that is: loathsome disfigurements,
    blindness, mutilation, locked lips of boys
Too proud to scream.

                    Reason will not decide at last: the sword will decide.

OH LOVELY ROCK

We stayed the night in the pathless gorge of Ventana Creek, up the east
fork.
The rock walls and the mountain ridges hung forest on forest above our
heads, maple and redwood,
Laurel, oak, madrone, up to the high and slender Santa Lucian firs that
stare up the cataracts
Of slide-rock to the star-color precipices.

                        We lay on gravel and kept a
little camp-fire for warmth.
Past midnight only two or three coals glowed red in the cooling darkness; I
laid a clutch of dead bay-leaves
On the ember ends and felted dry sticks across them and lay down again.
The revived flame
Lighted my sleeping son's face and his companion's, and the vertical face of
the great gorge-wall
Across the stream. Light leaves overhead danced in the fire's breath,
tree-trunks were seen: it was the rock wall
That fascinated my eyes and mind. Nothing strange: light-gray diorite with
two or three slanting seams in it,
Smooth-polished by the endless attrition of slides and floods; no fern nor
lichen, pure naked rock . . . as if I were
Seeing rock for the first time. As if I were seeing through the flame-lit
surface into the real and bodily
And living rock. Nothing strange . . . I cannot
Tell you how strange: the silent passion, the deep nobility and childlike
loveliness: this fate going on
Outside our fates. It is here in the mountain like a grave smiling child. I
shall die, and my boys

Will live and die, our world will go on through its rapid agonies of change and discovery; this age will die,

And wolves have howled in the snow around a new Bethlehem: this rock will be here, grave, earnest, not passive: the energies

That are its atoms will still be bearing the whole mountain above: and I, many packed centuries ago,

Felt its intense reality with love and wonder, this lonely rock.

OCTOBER WEEK-END

It is autumn still, but at three in the morning
All the magnificent wonders of midwinter midnight, blue dog-star,
Orion, red Aldebaran, the ermine-fur Pleiades,
Parading above the gable of the house. Their music is their shining,
And the house beats like a heart with dance-music
Because our boys have grown to the age when girls are their music.
There is wind in the trees, and the gray ocean's
Music on the rock. I am warming my blood with starlight, not with girls'
    eyes,
But really the night is quite mad with music.

STEELHEAD, WILD PIG, THE FUNGUS

I

The sky was cold December blue with great tumbling clouds, and the
　　little river
Ran full but clear. A bare-legged girl in a red jersey was wading in it,
　　holding a five-tined
Hay-fork at her head's height; suddenly she dartled it down like a heron's
　　beak and panting hard
Leaned on the shaft, looking down passionately, her gipsy-lean face, then
　　stooped and dipping
One arm to the little breast she drew up her catch, great hammered-silver
　　steelhead with the tines through it
And the fingers of her left hand hooked in its gills, her slender body
Rocked with its writhing. She took it to the near bank
And was dropping it behind a log when someone said
Quietly "I guess I've got you, Vina." Who gasped and looked up
At a young horseman half hidden in the willow bushes,
She'd been too intent to notice him, and said "My God
I thought it was the game-warden." "Worse," he said smiling. "This river's
　　ours.
You can't get near it without crossing our fences.
Besides that you mustn't spear 'em, and . . . three, four, you little bitch
That's the fifth fish." She answered with her gipsy face, "Take half o' them,
　　honey. I loved the fun."
He looked up and down her taper legs, red with cold, and said fiercely,
　　"Your fun.
To kill them and leave them rotting." "Honey, let me have one o' them,"
　　she answered,
"You take the rest." He shook his blond head. "You'll have to pay a terrible
　　fine." She answered laughing,

"Don't worry: you wouldn't tell on me." He dismounted and tied the
   bridle to a bough, saying "Nobody would.
I know a lovely place deep in the willows, full of warm grass, safe as a
   house,
Where you can pay it." Her body seemed to grow narrower suddenly, both
   hands at her throat, and the cold thighs
Pressed close together while she stared at his face, it was beautiful, long
   heavy-lidded eyes like a girl's,
"I can't do that, honey . . . I," she said shivering, "your wife would kill
   me." He hardened his eyes and said
"Let that alone." "Oh," she answered; the little red hands came down from
   her breast and faintly
Reached toward him, her head lifting, he saw the artery on the lit side of
   her throat flutter like a bird
And said "You'll be sick with cold, Vina," flung off his coat
And folded her in it with his warmth in it and carried her
To that island in the willows.

                              He warmed her bruised feet in his hands;
She paid her fine for spearing fish, and another
For taking more than the legal limit, and would willingly
Have paid a third for trespassing; he sighed and said
"You'll owe me that. I'm afraid somebody might come looking for me,
Or my colt break his bridle." She moaned like a dove, "Oh Oh Oh Oh,
You are beautiful, Hugh." They returned to the stream-bank. There,
While Vina put on her shoes — they were like a small boy's, all stubbed and
   shapeless — young Flodden strung the five fish
On a willow rod through the red gills and slung them
To his saddle-horn. He led the horse and walked with Vina, going part way
   home with her.

Toward the canyon sea-mouth
The water spread wide and shoal, fingering through many channels down a
    broad flood-bed, and a mob of sea-gulls
Screamed at each other. Vina said, "That's a horrible thing." "What?"
    "What the birds do. They're worse than I am."
When Flodden returned alone he rode down and watched them. He saw
    that one of the thousand steelhead
Which irresistible nature herded up-stream to the spawning-gravel in the
    mountain, the river headwaters,
Had wandered into a shallow finger of the current, and was forced over on
    his flank, sculling uneasily
In three inches of water: instantly a gaunt herring-gull hovered and
    dropped, to gouge the exposed
Eye with her beak; the great fish writhing, flopping over in his anguish,
    another gull's beak
Took the other eye. Their prey was then at their mercy, writhing blind,
    soon stranded, and the screaming mob
Covered him.

            Young Flodden rode into them and drove them up; he
    found the torn steelhead
Still slowly and ceremoniously striking the sand with his tail and a bloody
    eye-socket, under the
Pavilion of wings. They cast a cold shadow on the air, a fleeting sense of
    fortune's iniquities: why should
Hugh Flodden be young and happy, mounted on a good horse,
And have had another girl besides his dear wife, while others have to
    endure blindness and death,
Pain and disease, misery, old age, God knows what worse?

II

Perhaps their wildness will never die from these mountains.
The eagle still dawns over the ridges like a dark sun, the deer breed, the
    puma hunts them, the rattler
Has his fangs, fleet hawks have the air. The timber-wolves were all killed,
    some rancher's German shepherd-dogs
Ran with coyotes and bred a new kind of wolves, strong and more cunning,
    fierce killers. And the grizzlies
Extinct, a wealthy amateur up the Carmel Valley brought in wild pigs
From the Urals to stock his hunting-park: they overswarmed it and broke
    his borders and roam the coast-range, beautiful
Monsters, full of fecundity, bristled like a hedge at midnight; and the boars
    with long naked
Knives in their jaws. They lair all day in impenetrable manzanita-thickets
    of the farther mountain
And whet their knives at night on the farmer's apple-trees.

                                                A gang of
    them returning toward the gray of dawn
Through Flodden's plowland, old Bill Flodden and his boy Harry ran out
When the dogs yelled, but Hugh stayed warm in bed beside his young wife;
    only when he heard rifle-shots
Yawned, stretched himself and went out. It was raining softly, things were
    dim gray and black and the trembling sky,
The dogs making a noise far away, the old man calling them. They had
    bayed something
In the steep chaparral at the base of the mountain. Hugh went up and said
    "Pig?" The old man said "I
Pinked him in the butt, he's too mad to run." The dogs raved in the thicket
    and as light increased, oozing
Down the black mountain-sides like water from a sponge

To spread on the gray floor of the valley, you saw the chaparral surface
    waving in ship's keel wakes
Where the boar charged the dogs, little quick rushes, one of them jagged
    up into a piercing death-scream,
A dog was caught, but nothing to be seen except the greasewood-
Tops waving. The old man: "I'm going in there and kill the bastard." Hugh
    said "Like hell you are." The old man said
"He got a dog." Hugh said "He'd get you too. You can't see past your face
    in that swither." Old Flodden,
His voice cracking falsetto with passion: "I've got a knife." Hugh said "Old
    fool: it's a boar in there?
You might as well stand on the railroad tracks at Monterey
And fight a freight-engine with a knife." Flodden answered, "When y' get
    old: you'll be old some day.
Look at me for God's sake." He was half dressed, naked from the waist up,
    wide sagging shoulders
Oily with rain-water, and pearls of rain on the pale hair in the groove
Between his big sagging breast-muscles; his belly sagged on the belt that
    had the sheath-knife. "Hm? Love of women?"
He said plaintively, "I get so damn' tired hearing your bed-springs creak in
    the evenings." Hugh said, "Where's Harry?"
"Up the hill on the other side, watching if he comes out." "Let me get the
    gun from him, I'll
Go in with you, father." He answered, "Got to have some fun," and rather
    delicately for one so thick-bodied
Slipped into the bushes, parting them with the barrel of his rifle, and
    disappeared. The dogs were silent.
Hugh called to Harry for the other rifle.

                                    However, it was not required.
    The old man searched and searched

Vainly all through the thicket; he found the two living dogs, meek and
  subdued, and the dead one
Trampled in a jelly of its own entrails, but the tall boar had vanished, like a
  piece of sea-fog
That blows up-canyon into warmer air and instantly vanishes.

                                                          It was now
broad daylight, and old Flodden
Returned out of the thicket, jeering at the cowardly dogs: that moment a
  heavy
Noise like distant cannon-fire roared at the mountain-top, the horses
  pasturing in the valley below
Raced up the opposite slope; then some great stones and a storm of
  fragments came bounding
Down the rock-face, felled an oak-tree or two, and cut several straight
  paths through the brush and chaparral.
The winter had been very rainy, a high blade of rock
Had settled and split away and rolled down; but it seemed as if the
  mountain had said something, some big word
That meant something, but no one could understand what it meant. Or the
  other mountains did.

III

June Flodden and Florrie Crawford were gathering mushrooms
In the green field, and Florrie found a thick-stemmed toad-stool with a
  close purplish cap,
She plucked it and giggled at it, showing it to June, who couldn't think
  what she meant; then Florrie formed
An oval doorway between the finger and thumb of her left hand, she forced
  the odd-looking fungus

Into the slot and made it play back and forth. When its head broke off
She screamed with pleasure, threw it on the ground and trampled it, her
    little white teeth grinning maliciously, "I'd love to
Do that to all of them." She looked at June
And June had laid down the sack of mushrooms and hid her face in her
    hands and wept. Florrie said "Oh
June! What's the matter?" "Nothing . . ." "Did a spider bite you?" June
    shook her head.
She had two-colored hair, cut at her shoulders, the outer locks were harvest
    yellow and the mass under them
Pale shadowy brown. Her hands covered her face and Florrie saw a bright
    tear trickle on the fingers.
She patted her twitching shoulder. "There, there. Hush dear. Are you
    going to have a baby, that's not so terrible."
June wept aloud and said "No. Now I never will." "Why, what's the
    matter?" "Hugh," she answered, and gasped "He's
Untrue to me." Florrie answered, "Good Lord. I thought
Something terrible had happened." June lowered her hands to look at her
    friend's face and saw the black hair
Through tear-filled eyes in the clear sunlight haloed with rainbows, and said
    solemnly, "Nothing
Worse could happen. If I knew who it was I'd shoot her." Florrie, eagerly:
    "Oh tell me dear,"
Laying her arm around her shoulder and her cheek
To the wet cheek; they made a beautiful picture on the green field starred
    with white stones and mushrooms
In rath sunlight of March, the dark head against the blond one, the soft
    young bodies touching each other;
Those long grave slopes and limestone precipices of Pico Blanco lifting
    beyond.

Florrie said,
"My Tom: you know how homely he is; you wouldn't think that a sick
    heifer would look at him. Well:
A dozen times. I always know what to do." June sobbed "Oh, Oh,
What do you do?" "No, I won't tell,
Until you tell me your story: how do you know Hugh's cheating you?
    Come up to the rock behind the oak-tree
And tell me everything; I'll teach you how to be happy, Tom and I are
    happy."

                The rock was a great lichen-grown
Fragment that must have fallen from the mountain centuries ago; chance
    and the weather had carved a rough
Bench in its base, where Florrie made June sit close to her and stilled her
    tears; from time to time a hard sob
Interrupted the story. June said that Hugh
Would sometimes ride away all the afternoon and into the evening. When
    he returned he always
Said he'd been looking for a strayed steer and she had believed him. But
    then she noticed . . . "I can't tell that.
Florrie I can't." "Darling you must tell all or how can I help you?" She
    looked away from her friend
And whispered in a ragged voice, "I noticed after those times when he'd
    been away, he never wanted to . . .
Oh . . . what we did every night when we went to bed. He turned away
    from me." Florrie compressed her lips
For fear of smiling, and said "That's bad." June said "At first I thought he
    was tired, riding so far.
But when I feared that he was unfaithful to me I prayed to die. I went down
    to the river
And dreamed of drowning myself; it was too cold, no hole was deep
    enough. Then Hugh rode by.

I scooched behind a bush and he didn't see me and I followed down
Clear to the sea." Florrie said "No, darling.
Don't tell me you kept up with the horse." She answered "You know that
    empty cabin at the river-mouth
With cypress trees around it: his horse was tied to
One of those trees." "Oh, Oh! What did you find?" "I didn't dare to go
    near. I went and sat
On the sand far away, and heard the wretched noise of the waves and
    watched his horse." Florrie said
"Did they come out?" June said "There was a bird on the beach, a great
    ugly pelican,
Starving to death, his feathers tarred with oil from a ship so he couldn't fly.
    He leaned on his wings
And they were like two crooked black fishing-poles. I guess that bird and I
    were the very wretchedest
Lives in the world. And the gray sea glittered, the river ran through the
    sand; after while they came out.
She seemed to be a little thing but I couldn't look. What shall I do?"
    Florrie said "Ha? Every time
That he does it, you do it. That's what I do wi' my Tom: that's the great
    secret." June said "I can't
Tell what you mean." She answered, "Take any pleasant young man, they
    are all willing. You'll find revenge
Is sweeter than love or honey." June said "I'd rather drown myself. I'd
    rather be like that wretched bird,
Ugly and alone and hopeless, waiting to die by the glittering sea." "Ah, Ah,
    never say die,"
Florrie answered quickly, "it's wicked for a married woman to talk like that,
    we must not be abject. Look, darling:
There's the first yellow violet, yellow outside and brown underneath, just
    like your hair."

NIGHT WITHOUT SLEEP

The world's as the world is; the nations rearm and prepare to change; the
   age of tyrants returns;
The greatest civilization that has ever existed builds itself higher towers on
   breaking foundations.
Recurrent episodes; they were determined when the ape's children first ran
   in packs, chipped flint to an edge.

I lie and hear dark rain beat the roof, and the blind wind.

                                                        In the morning
      perhaps I shall find strength again
To value the immense beauty of this time of the world, the flowers of decay
   their pitiful loveliness, the fever-dream
Tapestries that back the drama and are called the future. This ebb of
   vitality feels the ignoble and cruel
Incidents, not the vast abstract order.

                                 I lie and hear dark rain beat the
      roof, and the night-blind wind.

In the Ventana country darkness and rain and the roar of waters fill the
   deep mountain-throats.
The creekside shelf of sand where we lay last August under a slip of stars
And firelight played on the leaning gorge-walls, is drowned and lost. The
   deer of the country huddle on a ridge
In a close herd under madrone-trees; they tremble when a rock-slide goes
   down, they open great darkness-
Drinking eyes and press closer.

Cataracts of rock

Rain down the mountain from cliff to cliff and torment the stream-bed.
    The stream deals with them. The laurels are wounded,
Redwoods go down with their earth and lie thwart the gorge. I hear the
    torrent boulders battering each other,
I feel the flesh of the mountain move on its bones in the wet darkness.

Is this

    more beautiful
Than man's disasters? These wounds will heal in their time; so will
    humanity's. This is more beautiful. . . . at night. . . .

SELF-CRITICISM IN FEBRUARY

The bay is not blue but sombre yellow
With wrack from the battered valley, it is speckled with violent foam-heads
And tiger-striped with long lovely storm-shadows.
You love this better than the other mask; better eyes than yours
Would feel the equal beauty in the blue.
It is certain you have loved the beauty of storm disproportionately.
But the present time is not pastoral, but founded
On violence, pointed for more massive violence: perhaps it is not
Perversity but need that perceives the storm-beauty.
Well, bite on this: your poems are too full of ghosts and demons,
And people like phantoms — how often life's are —
And passion so strained that the clay mouths go praying for destruction—
Alas it is not unusual in life;
To every soul at some time. *But why insist on it? And now*
For the worst fault: you have never mistaken
Demon nor passion nor idealism for the real God.
Then what is most disliked in those verses
Remains most true. *Unfortunately. If only you could sing*
That God is love, or perhaps that social
Justice will soon prevail. I can tell lies in prose.

SHIVA

There is a hawk that is picking the birds out of our sky.
She killed the pigeons of peace and security,
She has taken honesty and confidence from nations and men,
She is hunting the lonely heron of liberty.
She loads the arts with nonsense, she is very cunning,
Science with dreams and the state with powers to catch them at last.
Nothing will escape her at last, flying nor running.
This is the hawk that picks out the stars' eyes.
This is the only hunter that will ever catch the wild swan;
The prey she will take last is the wild white swan of the beauty of things.
Then she will be alone, pure destruction, achieved and supreme,
Empty darkness under the death-tent wings.
She will build a nest of the swan's bones and hatch a new brood,
Hang new heavens with new birds, all be renewed.

NOW RETURNED HOME

Beyond the narrows of the Inner Hebrides
We sailed the cold angry sea toward Barra, where Heaval mountain
Lifts like a mast. There were few people on the steamer, it was late in the
    year; I noticed most an old shepherd,
Two wise-eyed dogs wove anxious circles around his feet, and a thin-armed
    girl
Who cherished what seemed a doll, wrapping it against the sea-wind. When
    it moved I said to my wife "She'll smother it."
And she to the girl: "Is your baby cold? You'd better run down out of the
    wind and uncover its face."
She raised the shawl and said "He is two weeks old. His mother died in
    Glasgow in the hospital
Where he was born. She was my sister." I looked ahead at the bleak island,
    gray stones, ruined castle,
A few gaunt houses under the high and comfortless mountain; my wife
    looked at the sickly babe,
And said "There's a good doctor in Barra? It will soon be winter." "Ah,"
    she answered, "Barra'd be heaven for him,
The poor wee thing, there's Heaval to break the wind. We live on a wee
    island yonder away,
Just the one house."

               The steamer moored, and a skiff — what they call a
    curragh, like a canvas canoe
Equipped with oars — came swiftly along the side. The dark-haired girl
    climbed down to it, with one arm holding
That doubtful slip of life to her breast; a tall young man with sea-pale eyes
    and an older man

Helped her; if a word was spoken I did not hear it. They stepped a mast
    and hoisted a henna-color
Bat's wing of sail.

                  Now, returned home
After so many thousands of miles of road and ocean, all the hulls sailed in,
    the houses visited,
I remember that slender skiff with dark henna sail
Bearing off across the stormy sunset to the distant island
Most clearly; and have rather forgotten the dragging whirlpools of London,
    the screaming haste of New York.

THEORY OF TRUTH

(Reference to Chapter II, The Women at Point Sur)

I stand near Soberanes Creek, on the knoll over the sea, west of the road. I remember

This is the very place where Arthur Barclay, a priest in revolt, proposed three questions to himself:

First, is there a God and of what nature? Second, whether there's anything after we die but worm's meat?

Third, how should men live? Large time-worn questions no doubt; yet he touched his answers, they are not unattainable;

But presently lost them again in the glimmer of insanity.

How many
minds have worn these questions; old coins
Rubbed faceless, dateless. The most have despaired and accepted doctrine; the greatest have achieved answers, but always
With aching strands of insanity in them.

I think of Lao-tze; and the dear beauty of the Jew whom they crucified but he lived, he was greater than Rome;
And godless Buddha under the boh-tree, straining through his mind the delusions and miseries of human life.

Why does insanity always twist the great answers?

Because only
tormented persons want truth.
Man is an animal like other animals, wants food and success and women, not truth. Only if the mind
Tortured by some interior tension has despaired of happiness: then it hates its life-cage and seeks further,

And finds, if it is powerful enough. But instantly the private agony that made the search
Muddles the finding.

Here was a man who envied the chiefs of the provinces of China their power and pride,
And envied Confucius his fame for wisdom. Tortured by hardly conscious envy he hunted the truth of things,
Caught it, and stained it through with his private impurity. He praised inaction, silence, vacancy: why?
Because the princes and officers were full of business, and wise Confucius of words.

Here was a man who was born a bastard, and among the people
That more than any in the world valued race-purity, chastity, the prophetic splendors of the race of David.
Oh intolerable wound, dimly perceived. Too loving to curse his mother, desert-driven, devil-haunted,
The beautiful young poet found truth in the desert, but found also
Fantastic solution of hopeless anguish. The carpenter was not his father? Because God was his father,
Not a man sinning, but the pure holiness and power of God. His personal anguish and insane solution
Have stained an age; nearly two thousand years are one vast poem drunk with the wine of his blood.

And here was another Savior, a prince in India,
A man who loved and pitied with such intense comprehension of pain that he was willing to annihilate
Nature and the earth and stars, life and mankind, to annul the suffering. He also sought and found truth,
And mixed it with his private impurity, the pity, the denials.

                                                Then search
for truth is foredoomed and frustrate?
Only stained fragments?

                          Until the mind has turned its love from itself
and man, from parts to the whole.

Be Angry at the Sun

1938-41

FAITH

Ants, or wise bees, or a gang of wolves,
Work together by instinct, but man needs lies,
Man his admired and more complex mind
Needs lies to bind the body of his people together,
Make peace in the state and maintain power.
These lies are called a faith and their formulation
We call a creed, and the faithful flourish,
They conquer nature and their enemies, they win security.
Then proud and secure they will go awhoring
With that impractical luxury the love of truth,
That tries all things: alas the poor lies,
The faith like a morning mist burnt by the sun:
Thus the great wave of a civilization
Loses its forming soul, falls apart and founders.
Yet I believe that truth is more beautiful
Than all the lies, and God than all the false Gods.
Then we must leave it to the humble and the ignorant
To invent the frame of faith that will form the future.
It was not for the Romans to produce Christ.
It was not for Lucretius to prophesy him, nor Pilate
To follow him. . . . Or could we change at last and choose truth?

COME LITTLE BIRDS

I paid the woman what she asked and followed her down to the water-side, and her two sons

Came down behind us; one of them brought a spade, the other led the black calf and tied him up short

To a sycamore trunk over the stream-bank. It was near the foot of the mountains, where the Sur River

Pours from its gorge, foaming among great stones; and evening had come

But the light was still clear. The old woman brought us to a tongue of grassed land under the stream-bank;

One of her boys gathered dry sticks for a fire, the other cleared and repaired a short shallow trench

That scored the earth there; then they heaped up the sticks and made yellow flame, about ten feet from the trench

On the north side, right against the water; the woman sat opposite the fire and facing it, gazing northward,

Her back against a big stone.

                                    She closed her eyes and hummed tuneless music, nodding her vulturine head

To the dull rhythm; through which one heard the fire snoring and the river flowing, and the surf on the shore

Over the hill. After some time she widened her eyes, and their sight was rolled up

Under her forehead, I saw the firelight

Flicker on the blank whites; she raised her arms and cried out

In a loud voice. Instantly her two boys went up and fetched the black calf though he plunged and struggled,

They tied his hind feet with a tight knot, and passed the bight of the rope over a sycamore bough

That hung above the stream and the head of the trench; they tugged his
    hind feet up to it, so that he fell
On the knees of his forelegs over the trench-head. Then one of the two
    young men sheared the calf's throat
With a sharp knife, holding him by one ear, the other by an ear and the
    nostrils, and the blood spouted
Into the furrow. The woman, her body twitching convulsively: "Come little
    birds,"
She screamed through her tightened throat like a strangling person,
"Put on the life, here is the blood, come you gray birds."

                                By this time
    deep night had come,
And the fire down to red coals; there was a murmur along the stream side
    as if a sea-wind were moving
Through the dark forest; then I saw dimly in the light of the coals the
    steam that climbed the cold air
From the hot blood and hung stagnant above the trench
Stirred, as if persons were stooping through it and stirring it; and distant
    whispers began to hiss in the trench
And gray shapes moved. One said, wiry-thin: "Out of my way, you dregs."
    Another answered "Stand back.
You've had your turn."

                These were no doubt the souls of the dead, that
    dark-eyed woman
Had promised would come and tell me what I had to know: they looked
    rather like starlight sheep,
That were driven through the dust all day and deep night has come, they
    huddle at a bend of the lane, scared by the dogs,
Gray and exhausted, and if one goes under the others trample him.

                                                           One of the old
        woman's boys
Gradually revived the spent fire with dry leaves and twigs, so that the light
        increased imperceptibly,
Yet many of that whispering flock were frightened away. Those that
        remained, several still greedy cowered
Over the blood-trench, others erect wavered like long pale water-weeds: I
        went near them,
They sighed and whispered, leaning away from me like rooted water-weeds.
        I said "If you are the souls of the dead,
And this old woman's trance and the warm blood make you able to
        answer —" And I was about to say:
"Then tell me what death is like: is it sleep or waking, captivity or
        freedom, dreams or reality?" — but they
Hearing my thought whispered "We know, we know, we know," wavering
        like water-weeds: then one leaned toward me
Saying "Tell my mother." "What?" I said. "Tell her I was well enough
Before that old buzzard waked me. I died in the base-hospital —" Another
        of the forms crossed him and said
"God curse every man that makes war or plans it." (This was in nineteen
        twenty, about two years
After the armistice.) "God curse every congressman that voted it, God
        curse Wilson," his face like an axe
Passed between my eyes and the fire and he entered the darkness beyond
        the light-rim. I asked the other
"What is your mother's name?" But he could not answer, but only stared at
        me. I said "Does she live on the Coast
Or in Monterey?" He stared at me and struck his forehead and stood aside.

                                                           Others
        came toward me, two of whom

Seemed to be women; but now I saw a known form, tall, gaunt, gray-haired, and the shoulders so stooped

They appeared like a hump; he leaned to the fire warming his gray old hands. I avoided the other

Shapes of the dead and went to him; my heart was shaking

And my eyes wet. "Father," I said. He answered clearly "Is that you, Robin?" I said "Father,

Forgive me. I dishonored and wasted all your hopes of me, one by one; yet I loved you well."

He smiled calmly and answered, "I suppose hope is a folly. We often learn that

Before we die. We learn," he said, "nothing afterwards." Then I was silent, and breathed and asked:

"Is it a sleep?" "With a dream sometimes. But far too bloodless to grieve," he said, "or gladden the dreamer;

And soon, I conjecture, even this pin's weight and echo of consciousness that makes me speak to you

Will dissolve in the stream." He smiled and rubbed his gray hands together and said "Amen. If you come

To Endor again I shall not be present." Then I wished to tell him

Our little news: that his name would continue in the world, for we had two sons now; and that my mother and my brother

Were well; and also the outcome of the great war, because he had died

In its fifth month. He was patient and let me speak, but clearly not cared at all.

Meanwhile the woman

Had been groaning in her trance; I noticed the shapes of the dead changed with her breathing: when she drew breath

They became stronger, when her breath was delayed they grew faint and vague. But now she became exhausted, her breathing

Was like a death-rattle, with terrifying pauses between the gasps. One of
    her boys ran to restore her;
The other heaped the fire high, and the pale dead
Were fleeing away; but a certain one of them came running toward me,
    slender and naked, I saw the firelight
Glitter on her bare thighs; she said "I am Tamar Cauldwell from Lobos:
    write my story. Tell them
I have my desire." She passed me and went like a lamp through the dark
    wood.

                This was all. The young men
Carried their mother up to the cabin; I was left alone and stayed by the fire
    all night, studying
What I had heard and seen, until yellow dawn stood over the mountain.

                                    This
    was all? I thought not.
I thought these decaying shadows and echoes of personality are only a
    by-play; they are not the spirit
That we see in one loved, or in saint or hero
Shining through flesh. And I have seen it shine from a mountain through
    rock, and even from an old tree
Through the tough bark. The spirit (to call it so: what else could I call it?)
    is not a personal quality, and not
Mortal; it comes and goes, never dies. It is not to be found in death: dredge
    not the shadow-world. The dead
Have no news for us. We have for them, but they do not care. Peace to
    them.

THE HOUSE-DOG'S GRAVE

(Haig, an English bulldog)

I've changed my ways a little: I cannot now
Run with you in the evenings along the shore,
Except in a kind of dream: and you, if you dream a moment,
You see me there.

So leave awhile the paw-marks on the front door
Where I used to scratch to go out or in,
And you'd soon open; leave on the kitchen floor
The marks of my drinking-pan.

I cannot lie by your fire as I used to do
On the warm stone,
Nor at the foot of your bed: no, all the nights through
I lie alone.

But your kind thought has laid me less than six feet
Outside your window where firelight so often plays,
And where you sit to read — and I fear often grieving for me —
Every night your lamplight lies on my place.

You, man and woman, live so long it is hard
To think of you ever dying.
A little dog would get tired living so long.
I hope that when you are lying

Under the ground like me your lives will appear
As good and joyful as mine.
No, dears, that's too much hope: you are not so well cared for
As I have been,

And never have known the passionate undivided
Fidelities that I knew.
Your minds are perhaps too active, too many-sided. . . .
But to me you were true.

You were never masters, but friends. I was your friend.
I loved you well, and was loved. Deep love endures
To the end and far past the end. If this is my end,
I am not lonely. I am not afraid. I am still yours.

PRESCRIPTION OF PAINFUL ENDS

Lucretius felt the change of the world in his time, the great republic riding to the height

Whence every road leads downward; Plato in his time watched Athens

Dance the down path. The future is a misted landscape, no man sees clearly, but at cyclic turns

There is a change felt in the rhythm of events, as when an exhausted horse

Falters and recovers, then the rhythm of the running hoof-beats is changed: he will run miles yet,

But he must fall: we have felt it again in our own life-time, slip, shift and speed-up

In the gallop of the world; and now perceive that, come peace or war, the progress of Europe and America

Becomes a long process of deterioration — starred with famous Byzantiums and Alexandrias,

Surely, — but downward. One desires at such times

To gather the insights of the age summit against future loss, against the narrowing mind and the tyrants,

The pedants, the mystagogues, the barbarians: one builds poems for treasuries, time-conscious poems: Lucretius

Sings his great theory of natural origins and of wise conduct; Plato smiling carves dreams, bright cells

Of incorruptible wax to hive the Greek honey.

                                     Our own time, much greater and far less fortunate,

Has acids for honey, and for fine dreams

The immense vulgarities of misapplied science and decaying Christianity: therefore one christens each poem, in dutiful

Hope of burning off at least the top layer of the time's uncleanness, from the acid-bottles.

THE DAY IS A POEM
(September 19, 1939)

This morning Hitler spoke in Danzig, we heard his voice.
A man of genius: that is, of amazing
Ability, courage, devotion, cored on a sick child's soul,
Heard clearly through the dog-wrath, a sick child
Wailing in Danzig; invoking destruction and wailing at it.
Here, the day was extremely hot; about noon
A south wind like a blast from hell's mouth spilled a slight rain
On the parched land, and at five a light earthquake
Danced the house, no harm done. To-night I have been amusing myself
Watching the blood-red moon droop slowly
Into black sea through bursts of dry lightning and distant thunder.
Well: the day is a poem: but too much
Like one of Jeffers's, crusted with blood and barbaric omens,
Painful to excess, inhuman as a hawk's cry.

THE BLOODY SIRE

It is not bad. Let them play.
Let the guns bark and the bombing-plane
Speak his prodigious blasphemies.
It is not bad, it is high time,
Stark violence is still the sire of all the world's values.

What but the wolf's tooth whittled so fine
The fleet limbs of the antelope?
What but fear winged the birds, and hunger
Jewelled with such eyes the great goshawk's head?
Violence has been the sire of all the world's values.

Who would remember Helen's face
Lacking the terrible halo of spears?
Who formed Christ but Herod and Caesar,
The cruel and bloody victories of Caesar?
Violence, the bloody sire of all the world's values.

Never weep, let them play,
Old violence is not too old to beget new values.

THE STARS GO OVER THE LONELY OCEAN

Unhappy about some far off things
That are not my affair, wandering
Along the coast and up the lean ridges,
I saw in the evening
The stars go over the lonely ocean,
And a black-maned wild boar
Plowing with his snout on Mal Paso Mountain.

The old monster snuffled "Here are sweet roots,
Fat grubs, slick beetles and sprouted acorns.
The best nation in Europe has fallen,
And that is Finland,
But the stars go over the lonely ocean,"
The old black-bristled boar,
Tearing the sod on Mal Paso Mountain.

"The world's in a bad way, my man,
And bound to be worse before it mends;
Better lie up in the mountains here
Four or five centuries,
While the stars go over the lonely ocean,"
Said the old father of wild pigs,
Plowing the fallow on Mal Paso Mountain.

"Keep clear of the dupes that talk democracy
And the dogs that talk revolution,
Drunk with talk, liars and believers.
I believe in my tusks.
Long live freedom and damn the ideologies,"
Said the gamey black-maned wild boar
Tusking the turf on Mal Paso Mountain.

FOR UNA

I

I built her a tower when I was young —
Sometime she will die —
I built it with my hands, I hung
Stones in the sky.

Old but still strong I climb the stone —
Sometime she will die —
Climb the steep rough steps alone,
And weep in the sky.

Never weep, never weep.

II

Never be astonished, dear.
Expect change,
Nothing is strange.

We have seen the human race
Capture all its dreams,
All except peace.

We have watched mankind like Christ
Toil up and up,
To be hanged at the top.

No longer envying the birds,
That ancient prayer for
Wings granted: therefore

The heavy sky over London
Stallion-hoofed
Falls on the roofs.

These are the falling years,
They will go deep,
Never weep, never weep.

With clear eyes explore the pit.
Watch the great fall
With religious awe.

III

It is not Europe alone that is falling
Into blood and fire.
Decline and fall have been dancing in all men's souls
For a long while.

Sometime at the last gasp comes peace
To every soul.
Never to mine until I find out and speak
The things that I know.

IV

To-morrow I will take up that heavy poem again
About Ferguson, deceived and jealous man

Who bawled for the truth, the truth, and failed to endure
Its first least gleam. That poem bores me, and I hope will bore
Any sweet soul that reads it, being some ways
My very self but mostly my antipodes;
But having waved the heavy artillery to fire
I must hammer on to an end.

                    To-night, dear,
Let's forget all that, that and the war,
And enisle ourselves a little beyond time,
You with this Irish whiskey, I with red wine
While the stars go over the sleepless ocean,
And sometime after midnight I'll pluck you a wreath
Of chosen ones; we'll talk about love and death,
Rock-solid themes, old and deep as the sea,
Admit nothing more timely, nothing less real
While the stars go over the timeless ocean,
And when they vanish we'll have spent the night well.

DRUNKEN CHARLIE
(A person in the poem called "Give Your Heart to the Hawks")

I

I am dancing on the silver beach,
The bright moon is in my reach,
Willing girl with skin of pearl,
But nobody knows the turns of the world,
I won't touch her, for the tides
Run along her tender sides
Like foaming hounds,
And Oh the long water might wash me under.

I am a fisherman by trade,
And a drunkard as they say.
I dance alone to my own song,
Doctor says I won't live long,
Bowels blench and kidneys fret,
Doctor, I'll live ten years yet,
Drinking and dancing,
Unless the long water should wash me under.

Life is short but I have seen
The bitter ends of better men,
I have seen Michael and Lance Fraser
And Bruce Ferguson swim to heaven,
Long naked ghosts gleaming like fishes,
Dead men walk on the hills like torches,
Why should we cry for them?
Some night or some morning we all wash under.

Once I cried and that's enough.
I drew a girl into my skiff,
A bright girl from the blue wave,
She had not been dead three days.
I combed her hair and kissed her feet,
She was so quiet and so sweet,
I cried my heart out,
And wished the long water would wash me under.

I am by trade a hunter of fishes,
And a drunkard by conviction.
I've a kettle hid in a rift
Under the great lifting cliff
That I think might trouble the wise
If they smelled its mysteries.
Holy King Solomon,
Here is a magic that puts yours under.

From potatoes or common corn
I can make a God be born.
I spent a year in the county jail
For making God enter a pail
Through a coil of copper tube:
Is that worse than a virgin's womb?
Fill me with God,
And the water may wash this old carcass under.

II

Where did that drowned girl voyage from?
Why did she die?
On the blue water and foam

Where did that girl voyage from?
I never think but I cry.

She had a lover I believe,
Why did she die?
He was false or else a thief,
She had a lover I believe.
It is better to drink than to cry.

She was too kind, they were too merry,
Why did she die?
She was too kind, they were too merry.
Or was it death that swelled her belly?
I never think but I cry.

She wavered up through the green water
Like a moth flying.
She came to my boat on the blue water
As if she had been my own daughter.
Drinking's better than crying
But Oh child, *why?*
Said pickled in whiskey to pickled in brine.

III

She answered me, or did I dream?
She lay so passive and so sweet
In the stern of the boat,
And her body sang like a lark:
April Oh April.

I had a lover I believe
And he was neither false nor a thief,
He was torn by sea-lions' teeth
In the bitter month of April.

I know a beach where sea-lions drag
Their boat-hull bodies up the strand,
No one comes there, dear lover,
And the great cliff hangs over.
April Oh April.

My brothers they have eyes like hawks,
They ride all day watching the calves;
Or their hounds would find your tracks
In the bitter month of April.

He came to me under the cliff
And I could never have enough.
He came to me in March
And my soul was parched
For April Oh April.

The long sea-lions lie on the strand,
I used to stroke them with my hand,
How could I know that they turn bad
In the bitter month of April?

There was one that I loved well,
I would have trusted him with all,
He watched once while my dear
And I did the secret thing.
But not in April.

In April they began to stir,
Their long sea-women came ashore,
I never cared how much they roared
In the bitter month of April.

If their loves came why should not mine?
I watched them crawl up from the brine,
I loved to watch them come
Out of the sea foam
In April Oh April.

They used to fight, I hated that.
Sometimes the blood ran on the sand,
Yet I could stroke them with my hand
Even in the month of April.

These northern sea-lions they are longer
Than the length of two men, and stronger
Than all but the killer whale:
I never knew that I cared.
April, Oh April.

My love came striding up the strand,
He touched the beast, it caught his hand,
How could we know that they turn bad
In the bitter month of April?

Oh red thing writhing on the sand
How could we know when they turn bad?
This was their breeding season,
Cruelty was out of prison.
April, Oh April.

IV

She lay in the stern of the boat,
And her body sang like a lark:

I curse the war-makers I curse
Those that run to the ends of the earth
To exalt a system or save
A foreign power or foreign trade.

My boy was killed by a sea-lion,
And that was cruel but it was clean.
There are men plotting to kill
A million boys for a dead dream.

Oh my dear there are some things
That are well worth fighting for.
Fight to save a sea-gull's wings:
That would be a sacred war.

The Double Axe

1942-47

PEARL HARBOR

I

Here are the fireworks. The men who conspired and labored
To embroil this republic in the wreck of Europe have got their bargain, —
And a bushel more. As for me, what can I do but fly the national flag from
    the top of the tower, —
America has neither race nor religion nor its own language: nation or
    nothing.

        Stare, little tower,
Confidently across the Pacific, the flag on your head. I built you at the other
    war's end,
And the sick peace; I based you on living rock, granite on granite; I said,
    "Look, you gray stones:
Civilization is sick: stand awhile and be quiet and drink the sea-wind, you
    will survive
Civilization."

        But now I am old, and Oh stones be modest. Look, little
tower:
This dust blowing is only the British Empire; these torn leaves flying
Are only Europe; the wind is the plane-propellers; the smoke is Tokyo. The
    child with the butchered throat
Was too young to be named. Look no farther ahead.

II

The war that we have carefully for years provoked
Catches us unprepared, amazed and indignant. Our warships are shot
Like sitting ducks and our planes like nest-birds, both our coasts
    ridiculously panicked,
And our leaders make orations. This is the people
That hopes to impose on the whole planetary world
An American peace.

                (Oh, we'll not lose our war: my money on amazed
    Gulliver
And his horse-pistols.)

                Meanwhile our prudent officers
Have cleared the coast-long ocean of ships and fishing-craft, the sky of
    planes, the windows of light: these clearings
Make a great beauty. Watch the wide sea; there is nothing human; its gulls
    have it. Watch the wide sky
All day clean of machines; only at dawn and dusk one military hawk passes
High on patrol. Walk at night in the black-out,
The firefly lights that used to line the long shore
Are all struck dumb; shut are the shops, mouse-dark the houses. Here the
    prehuman dignity of night
Stands, as it was before and will be again. Oh beautiful
Darkness and silence, the two eyes that see God; great staring eyes.

ADVICE TO PILGRIMS

That our senses lie and our minds trick us is true, but in general
They are honest rustics; trust them a little;
The senses more than the mind, and your own mind more than another
    man's.
As to the mind's pilot, intuition, —
Catch him clean and stark naked he is first of truth-tellers; dream-clothed,
    or dirty
With fears and wishes, he is prince of liars.
The first fear is of death: trust no immortalist. The first desire
Is to be loved: trust no mother's son.
Finally I say, let demagogues and world-redeemers babble their emptiness
To empty ears; twice duped is too much.
Walk on gaunt shores and avoid the people; rock and wave are good
    prophets;
Wise are the wings of the gull, pleasant her song.

CASSANDRA

The mad girl with the staring eyes and long white fingers
Hooked in the stones of the wall,
The storm-wrack hair and the screeching mouth: does it matter, Cassandra,
Whether the people believe
Your bitter fountain? Truly men hate the truth; they'd liefer
Meet a tiger on the road.
Therefore the poets honey their truth with lying; but religion-
Venders and political men
Pour from the barrel, new lies on the old, and are praised for kindly
Wisdom. Poor bitch, be wise.
No: you'll still mumble in a corner a crust of truth, to men
And gods disgusting. — You and I, Cassandra.

HISTORICAL CHOICE

(written in 1943)

Strong enough to be neutral — as is now proved, now American power
From Australia to the Aleutian fog-seas, and Hawaii to Africa, rides every
    wind — we were misguided
By fraud and fear, by our public fools and a loved leader's ambition,
To meddle in the fever-dreams of decaying Europe. We could have forced
    peace, even when France fell; we chose
To make alliance and feed war.

                                 Actum est. There is no returning now.
Two bloody summers from now (I suppose) we shall have to take up the
    corrupting burden and curse of victory.
We shall have to hold half the earth: we shall be sick with self-disgust,
And hated by friend and foe, and hold half the earth — or let it go, and go
    down with it. Here is a burden
We are not fit for. We are not like Romans and Britons — natural
    world-rulers,
Bullies by instinct — but we have to bear it. Who has kissed Fate on the
    mouth, and blown out the lamp — must lie with her.

CALM AND FULL THE OCEAN

Calm and full the ocean under the cool dark sky; quiet rocks and the
    birds fishing; the night-herons
Have flown home to their wood ... while east and west in Europe and
    Asia and the islands unimaginable agonies

Consume mankind. Not a few thousand but uncounted millions, not a day
    but years, pain, horror, sick hatred;
Famine that dries the children to little bones and huge eyes; high explosive
    that fountains dirt, flesh and bone-splinters.

Sane and intact the seasons pursue their course, autumn slopes to
    December, the rains will fall
And the grass flourish, with flowers in it: as if man's world were perfectly
    separate from nature's, private and mad.

But that's not true; even the P-38s and the Flying Fortresses are as natural
    as horse-flies;
It is only that man, his griefs and rages, are not what they seem to man, not
    great and shattering, but really

Too small to produce any disturbance. This is good. This is the sanity, the
    mercy. It is true that the murdered
Cities leave marks in the earth for a certain time, like fossil rain-prints in
    shale, equally beautiful.

THE BLOOD-GUILT

So long having foreseen these convulsions, forecast the hemorrhagic
Fevers of civilization past prime striving to die, and having through verse,
    image and fable
For more than twenty years tried to condition the mind to this bloody
    climate: — do you like it,
Justified prophet?

I would rather have died twenty years ago.

                                    "Sad sons of the
stormy fall,"
You said, "no escape; you have to inflict and endure . . . and the world is
    like a flight of swans."

I said, "No escape."

                            You knew also that your
own country, though ocean-guarded, nothing to gain, by its destined
fools
Would be lugged in.

I said, "No escape."

                            If you had not been beaten
beforehand, hopelessly fatalist,
You might have spoken louder and perhaps been heard, and prevented
    something.

I? Have you never heard
That who'd lead must not see?

                        You saw it, you despaired of preventing it, you
share the blood-guilt.

Yes.

INVASION
(written May 8, 1944)

Europe has run its course, and whether to fall by its own sickness or ours is not
Extremely important; it was a whittled forepeak and condensation of profuse Asia, which presently
Will absorb it again. (And if it had conquered eastward and owned the Urals, would yet be absorbing it.)
Freedom and the lamp have been handed west. Our business was to feed and defend them; it was not our business
To meddle in the feuds of ghosts and brigands in historical graveyards. We have blood enough, but not for this folly;
Let no one believe that children a hundred years from now in the future of America will not be sick
For what our fools and unconscious criminals are doing to-day.

                                                But also
      it is ghastly beautiful. Look:
The enormous weight is poised, primed and will slide. Enormous and doomed weight will reply. It is possible
That here are the very focus and violent peak of all human effort. (No doubt, alas, that more wasting
Wars will bleed the long future: the sky more crammed with death, the victims worse crushed: but perhaps never
Again the like weights and prepared clash.) Admire it then; you cannot prevent it; give it for emotion
The aesthetic emotion.

                  I know a narrow beach, a thin tide-line
Of fallen rocks under the foot of the coast-range; the mountain is always sliding; the mountain goes up

Steep as the face of a breaking wave, knuckles of rock, slide-scars, rock-ribs, brush-fur, blue height,
To the hood of cloud. You stand there at the base, perched like a gull on a tilted slab, and feel
The enormous opposed presences; the huge mass of the mountain high overhanging, and the immense
Mass of the deep and sombre Pacific. — That scene, stationary,
Is what our invasion will be in action. Then admire the vast battle. Observe and marvel. Give it the emotion
That you give to a landscape.

                                 And this is bitter counsel, but required and convenient; for, beyond the horror,
When the imbecility, betrayals and disappointments become apparent, — what will you have, but to have
Admired the beauty? I believe that the beauty and nothing else is what things are formed for. Certainly the world
Was not constructed for happiness nor love nor wisdom. No, nor for pain, hatred and folly. All these
Have their seasons; and in the long year they balance each other, they cancel out. But the beauty stands.

ORIGINAL SIN

The man-brained and man-handed ground-ape, physically
The most repulsive of all hot-blooded animals
Up to that time of the world: they had dug a pitfall
And caught a mammoth, but how could their sticks and stones
Reach the life in that hide? They danced around the pit, shrieking
With ape excitement, flinging sharp flints in vain, and the stench of their
  bodies
Stained the white air of dawn; but presently one of them
Remembered the yellow dancer, wood-eating fire
That guards the cave-mouth: he ran and fetched him, and others
Gathered sticks at the wood's edge; they made a blaze
And pushed it into the pit, and they fed it high, around the mired sides
Of their huge prey. They watched the long hairy trunk
Waver over the stifle trumpeting pain,
And they were happy.

                    Meanwhile the intense color and nobility of
  sunrise,
Rose and gold and amber, flowed up the sky. Wet rocks were shining, a
  little wind
Stirred the leaves of the forest and the marsh flag-flowers; the soft valley
  between the low hills
Became as beautiful as the sky; while in its midst, hour after hour, the
  happy hunters
Roasted their living meat slowly to death.

                         These are the people.
This is the human dawn. As for me, I would rather

Be a worm in a wild apple than a son of man.
But we are what we are, and we might remember
Not to hate any person, for all are vicious;
And not be astonished at any evil, all are deserved;
And not fear death; it is the only way to be cleansed.

ORCA

Sea-lions loafed in the swinging tide in the inlet, long fluent creatures
Bigger than horses, and at home in their element
As if the Pacific Ocean had been made for them. Farther off shore the
  island-rocks
Bristled with quiet birds, gulls, cormorants, pelicans, hundreds and
  thousands
Standing thick as grass on a cut of turf. Beyond these, blue, gray, green,
  wind-straked, the ocean
Looked vacant; but then I saw a little black sail
That left a foam-line; while I watched there were two of them, two black
  triangles, tacking and veering, converging
Toward the rocks and the shore. I knew well enough
What they were: the dorsal fins of two killer-whales: but how the sea-lions
Low-floating within the rock-throat knew it, I know not. Whether they
  heard or they smelled them, suddenly
They were in panic; and some swam for the islands, others
Blindly along the granite banks of the inlet; one of them, more pitiful,
  scrabbled the cliff
In hope to climb it: at that moment black death drove in,
Silently like a shadow into the sea-gorge. It had the shape, the size, and it
  seemed the speed
Of one of those flying vipers with which the Germans lashed London. The
  water boiled for a moment
And nothing seen; and at the same moment
The birds went up from the islands, the soaring gulls, laborious pelicans,
  arrowy cormorants, a screaming
And wheeling sky. Meanwhile, below me, brown blood and foam
Striped the water of the inlet.

Here was death, and with terror, yet it
looked clean and bright, it was beautiful.
Why? Because there was nothing human involved, suffering nor causing; no
lies, no smirk and no malice;
All strict and decent; the will of man had nothing to do here. The earth is a
star, its human element
Is what darkens it. War is evil, the peace will be evil, cruelty is evil; death is
not evil. But the breed of man
Has been queer from the start. It looks like a botched experiment that has
run wild and ought to be stopped.

THE INQUISITORS

Coming around a corner of the dark trail ... what was wrong with the
    valley?
Azevedo checked his horse and sat staring: it was all changed. It was
    occupied. There were three hills
Where none had been: and firelight flickered red on their knees between
    them: if they were hills:
They were more like Red Indians around a campfire, grave and dark,
    mountain-high, hams on heels
Squatting around a little fire of hundred-foot logs. Azevedo remembers he
    felt an ice-brook
Glide on his spine; he slipped down from the saddle and hid
In the brush by the trail, above the black redwood forest. This was the
    Little Sur South Fork,
Its forest valley; the man had come in at nightfall over Bowcher's Gap, and
    a high moon hunted
Through running clouds. He heard the rumble of a voice, heavy not loud,
    saying, "I gathered some,
You can inspect them." One of the hills moved a huge hand
And poured its contents on a table-topped rock that stood in the firelight;
    men and women fell out;
Some crawled and some lay quiet; the hills leaned to eye them. One said:
    "It seems hardly possible
Such fragile creatures could be so noxious." Another answered,
"True, but we've seen. But it is only recently they have the power." The
    third answered, "That bomb?"
"Oh," he said, " — and the rest." He reached across and picked up one of
    the mites from the rock, and held it
Close to his eyes, and very carefully with finger and thumb-nail peeled it:
    by chance a young female

With long black hair: it was too helpless even to scream. He held it by one
    white leg and stared at it:
"I can see nothing strange: only so fragile." The third hill answered, "We
    suppose it is something
Inside the head." Then the other split the skull with his thumb-nail,
    squinting his eyes and peering, and said,
"A drop of marrow. How could that spoil the earth?" "Nevertheless," he
    answered,
"They have that bomb. The blasts and the fires are nothing: freckles on the
    earth: the emanations
Might set the whole planet into a tricky fever
And destroy much." "Themselves," he answered. "Let them. Why not?"
    "No," he answered, "Life."

                                    Azevedo
Still watched in horror, and all three of the hills
Picked little animals from the rock, peeled them and cracked them, or
    toasted them
On the red coals, or split their bodies from the crotch upward
To stare inside. They said "It remains a mystery. However," they said,
"It is not likely they can destroy all life: the planet is capacious. Life would
    surely grow up again
From grubs in the soil, or the newt and toad level, and be beautiful again.
    And again perhaps break its legs
On its own cleverness: who can forecast the future?" The speaker yawned,
    and with his flat hand
Brushed the rock clean; the three slowly stood up
Taller than Pico Blanco into the sky, their Indian-beaked heads in the
    moon-cloud,
And trampled their watchfire out and went away southward, stepping across
    the Ventana mountains.

QUIA ABSURDUM

Guard yourself from the terrible empty light of space, the bottomless
Pool of the stars. (Expose yourself to it: you might learn something.)

Guard yourself from perceiving the inherent nastiness of man and woman.
(Expose your mind to it: you might learn something.)

Faith, as they now confess, is preposterous, an act of will. Choose the
    Christian sheep-cote
Or the Communist rat-fight: faith will cover your head from the
    man-devouring stars.

THE INHUMANIST (Part II of *The Double Axe*)

An old man with a double-bit axe
Is caretaker at the Gore place. The cattle, except a few wild horns, died in
    that fire; the horses
Graze high up the dark hill; nobody ever comes to the infamous house; the
    pain, the hate and the love
Have left no ghost. Old men and gray hawks need solitude,
Here it is deep and wide.

I

                    "Winter and summer," the old man says, "rain
    and the drought;
Peace creeps out of war, war out of peace; the stars rise and they set; the
    clouds go north
And again they go south. — Why does God hunt in circles? Has he lost
    something? Is it possible — himself?
In the darkness between the stars did he lose himself and become godless,
    and seeks — himself?"

II

"Does God exist? — No doubt of that," the old man says. "The cells of my
    old camel of a body,
Because they feel each other and are fitted together, — through nerves and
    blood feel each other, — all the little animals
Are the one man: there is not an atom in all the universes
But feels every other atom; gravitation, electromagnetism, light, heat, and
    the other
Flamings, the nerves in the night's black flesh, flow them together; the stars,
    the winds and the people: one energy,

One existence, one music, one organism, one life, one God: star-fire and
    rock-strength, the sea's cold flow
And man's dark soul."

III

       "Not a tribal nor an anthropoid God.
Not a ridiculous projection of human fears, needs, dreams, justice and
    love-lust."

IV

"A conscious God? — The question has no importance. But I am conscious:
    where else
Did this consciousness come from? Nobody that I know of ever poured
    grain from an empty sack.
And who, I would say, but God, and a conscious one,
Ended the chief war-makers with their war, so humorously, such accurate
    timing, and such
Appropriate ends? The man of vanity in vanity,
Having his portrait painted; the man of violence at violence most dire high
    tide, in the fire and frenzy
Of Berlin falling."

V

       "And nothing," he thought,
"Is not alive." He had been down to the sea and hooked a rock-cod and was
    riding home: the high still rocks
Stood in the canyon sea-mouth alert and patient, waiting a sign perhaps;
    the heavy dark stooping hills

Shouldered the cloud, bearing their woods and streams and great loads of
    time: "I see that all things have souls.
But only God's is immortal. The hills dissolve and are liquidated; the stars
    shine themselves dark."

VI

Cutting oak fence-posts, he stopped to whet his axe edges. He
considered the double-bladed axe: "In Crete it was a God, and they named
the labyrinth for it. That's long before the Greeks came: the lofty Greeks
were still bushmen. It was a symbol of generation: the two lobes and the
stiff helve: so was the Cross before they christened it. But this one can clip
heads too. Grimly, grimly. A blade for the flesh, a blade for the spirit; and
truth from lies."

VII

A sheet of newspaper
Blown from the road, the old man caught it and read at arm's length, and
    said, "No wilderness
But this babbler comes in. — What, will they have a long dusty trial
And hang the men, Goering and all his paladins: why? Why?
For losing the war.
That is a fact, and Julius Caesar or Genghiz Khan
Could be honest about it; not our gray hypocrites.
What judges, what prosecutors, what a panel!
Down, you apes, down. Down on your knee-caps, you talking villains, take
    off your eye-glasses
And beat your foreheads against the rubble ground and beseech God
Forgive America, the brutal meddler and senseless destroyer; forgive the old
    seamed and stinking blood-guilt of England;

Forgive the deliberate torture of millions, the obscene slave-camps, the
    endless treacheries, the cold dirty-clawed cruelty
Of the rulers of Russia. — By God," he laughed, "winners and losers too,
    what hellhounds.
What a nest this earth is." He groaned and said heavily,
"If it were mine to elect an animal to rule the earth
I'd choose tiger or cobra but nothing cruel, or skunk
But nothing foul."

VIII

"What does God want?"
The old man was leaning on the dusk edge of dawn, and the beauty of
    things
Smote him like a fierce wind: the heads of the mountains, the morning star
    over them, the gray clearness, the hawk-swoop
Fall of the hundred-folded ridges, night in their throats, the deep-coiled
    night dying
On the dark sea, — and all this hushed magnificence violently rushing
    eastward to meet the sunrise: "How earnest he is.
How naively in earnest; nothing reserved; heavy with destiny. Earnest as the
    grave eyes of a child
That doubts his mother.

I see he despises happiness; and as for goodness
    he says What is it? and of evil, What is it?
And of love and hate, They are equal; they are two spurs,
For the horse has two flanks. — What does God want? I see here what he
    wants: he wants what man's
Feeling for beauty wants: — if it were fierce as hunger or hate and deep as
    the grave.

The beauty of things —
Is in the beholder's brain — the human mind's translation of their transhuman
Intrinsic value. It is their color in our eyes: as we say blood is red and blood is the life:
It is the life. Which is *like* beauty. It is *like* nobility. It has no name — and that's lucky, for names
Foul in the mouthing. The human race is bound to defile, I've often noticed it.
Whatever they can reach or name. They'd shit on the morning star
If they could reach."

IX

"Or as mathematics, a human invention
That parallels but never touches reality, gives the astronomer
Metaphors through which he may comprehend
The powers and the flow of things: so the human sense
Of beauty is our metaphor of their excellence, their divine nature: — like dust in a whirlwind, making
The wild wind visible."

X

The heads of the high redwoods down the deep canyon
Rippled, instantly earthquake shook the granite-boned ridge like a rat
In a dog's teeth; the house danced and bobbled, lightning flashed from the ground, the deep earth roared, yellow dust
Was seen rising in divers places and rock-slides

Roared in the gorges; then all things were stilled again and the earth stood
   quiet. The old man coughed and said
"Is that all? You have forgotten how to be angry: look again, old woman.
   They were not half so disgusting
The time you split your tea-kettle at Krakatoa."

XI

"How quiet they are, the dead; humble and quiet; how careless; how quiet
   they are!
The most amazing and painful things
Have happened to them, they have no answer. They go aside and lie down
   in silence and shrink to nothing."
The old man had gone up-stairs in the house to trace a roof-leak
That stained the planks; he moved in the stale air and still rooms, among
   the little personal possessions
With dust on them. A man and his wife and their son had lived here;
   "Now I could take an axe and split all
To splinters; they would not lift one word nor one finger.

                                                             Time will
   come no doubt
When the sun too shall die; the planets will freeze, and the air on them;
   frozen gases, white flakes of air
Will be the dust: which no wind ever will stir: this very dust in dim
   starlight glistening
Is dead wind, the white corpse of wind.
Also the galaxy will die; the glitter of the Milky Way, our universe, all the
   stars that have names are dead.
Vast is the night. How you have grown, dear night, walking your empty
   halls, how tall!"

XII

A skeleton with hair and teeth, a black hound-bitch
Crawled from a bush and grovelled at the old man's feet: he was in the
    dooryard, admiring
The vast red ostentation of a December sundown, and when he looked, the
    dog's eyes
Were green with famine. He said "You have been betrayed by someone?
    But hungry freedom
Is better than a bad master." She moaned in her throat; he went in and
    fetched food, but the first bite
The long teeth pierced his hand, blood ran on the knuckles: then he
    laughed and said
"What? Are you human?" She erected all the hair on her back, snarling,
    and sprang; and was kicked down
And stood crying, far off. "Neither," he said, "am I: not entirely," —
    sopping the bread
In his own blood for savor and he tossed it to her.

                                           In the morning she
    was at the door; he fed her and said
"Go your ways," but she would not. He said "You are fed and free: go your
    ways," and flung stones at her, but she
Crawling returned. He said "Must you have security also? Stay, slave."

XIII

                                         Trespassers
From time to time crossed the place, then the dog yelled at them
And the man drove them off. One stayed to argue. "The land," he said,
    "belongs to the people; we make its value.

I am one of the people." The old man listened to his axe and said, "You are the people.
You are Caligula's dream: only one neck. Listen, fellow:
This land is clean, it is not public. Surely you've noticed that whatever is public, land, thoughts or women,
Is dull, dirty and debauched. And it is not *my* land: I have nothing
But an axe and a dog: I am the people-stopper. I tell you that exclusion and privilege
Are the last bleeding clawhold of the eagle, honor." Then the man thought "He is mad and he has an axe:
I will not vex him."

XIV

But a day of black wind and rain
Another transgressor came; he was trembling with cold and blue with terror: "Let me pass, I am hunted.
I am going to the hills to hide, I know a cave.
I killed my wife and her lover." "Two," the old man said, "out of two thousand million. Do you see those horns
Coming over the hill? That's the third world-war. It is not worth fearing and not worth welcoming,
Futile as you: it will not kill one in ten."

But after the man had passed he thought:
"Ah, can I never swallow that lump the people? I am old and deaf, but the huge music might miss
Their gnashing treble. — But two thousand million!"

XV

                                   In the morning soft,
   white and staring snow
Lay on the ridges above the wet black slopes; the distant mountain-summits
   glittered like wolf's teeth
In the gray sky; the old man rejoiced and said, "In this pure world . . . In
   this pure world. . . . Oh axe
You are not needed." The axe twitched and giggled in his hand, as if it
   were saying "You pure old innocence:
Because your hair is gone white; holy is whiteness." "No," he answered,
   "my eyes are snail-eyes, they are outside of me.
Man is no measure of anything. Truly it is yours to hack, snow's to be
   white, mine to admire;
Each cat mind her own kitten: that is our morals. But wait till the moon
   comes up the snow-tops,
And you'll sing Holy."

XVI

                 The old man heard
An angry screaming in heaven and squinted upward, where two black stars
Hunted each other in the high blue; they struck and passed,
Wheeled and attacked again, they had great hate of each other; they locked
   and fell downward and came apart
And spiralled upward, hacking with beaks and hooks and the heavy wings:
   they were two eagles;
He watched them drift overhead, fighting, to the east
And pass from view. Then the old man said: "To-day I shall meet someone
   I know." He considered and said:

"How do I know that? Because any omen or senseless miracle, any strange
   cry or sight
Stretches the mind: we feel the future through the strained fabric."

XVII

                                                        In the
   evening when he came home
There was a little fire in the dooryard and a tall girl
Stood up beside it. She had dark hair; doe eyes, and was minding a pot
That seethed on three stones over the coal-bed. The old man stood silent,
   gazing at her; his dog at his knee
Made a low throat of wrath. The girl answered and said, "Come.
Supper is ready." "Yea," he said, "for whom?" He saw the evening planet
Beside her shoulder in the deep-throated rose of the sea, and said more
   gently:
"Eat if you are hungry, but you cannot stay here. I am not stone yet." She
   answered, "Don't you
Remember me? I do you." "No," he said, "A gipsy?" "I am the Spanish
   woman's little girl.
You called me Gaviota, father." He sighed and answered:
"My eagles did not tell me that. I thought I could live alone and enjoy old
   age. First a dog: now a daughter:
And to-morrow a canary!" He looked attentively and said: "Your eyes,
   Sea-gull, have lamps in 'em. It's not for love
Of your father's old bones."

XVIII

                              For no apparent reason an army
   bombing-plane
Pitched from the sky, and exploded on the rock-ridge

Below the peak. The old man at that time was riding not far away; he
    followed the smoke-tree
To its hot yellow root. A spirit in the fire sang
"Oh Kittyhawk." The old man mocked it and said
"Oh Hiroshima." It sang "Oh San Francisco, Seattle, New York." He
    answered "Oh stony goat-pastures.
But not to-morrow nor o' Monday. But," he said, dismounting,
And kneeling on the sharp rock his old knotted shin-bones, "Oh holy fire,
    the cruel, the kind, the coarse feeder,
Oh cleansing fire."

XIX

                    That blown-over tower of smoke, a swollen black
    leech clinging
By its hot yellow teeth to the mountain's neck, was seen far off
Along the shores and ridges and by ships at sea. A woman named Dana
    Enfield saw it, and rode
With her brother Bill Stewart to see the crashed plane; they took the
    bushed-over short-cut not for years used
Up Llagas Ridge, and where it clears on the cliffhead they saw the white
    mane of a tied horse
In the green gorge below. Stewart looked, grinned and rode on; Dana
    checked and said:
"Is there any other palomino in these mountains?
What is he doing down there?" "Oh: after some cow," he said, " – or
    heifer." He saw her face
Grown sharp and sallow: she had a fox-pointed chin, pale lips, yellow-dusk
    hair
And yellow eyes: she said "I have never spied on him nor listened to you
When you snickered and hinted. Will you go down and see?" "Yea?" he
    said,

"To hell with that." She answered "What a coward you are when you are
  sober," wheeling her horse
On the precipice brink so blindly that stones fell: a bitter woman of forty
  seeing in her mind
A long white child like a peeled willow-fork: it was the panting mouth
That made her sick: but in the dark of her mind more dreadful presences,
  this war and this peace,
A monster leading a monster to the monster's house, proceed.

XX

                                                            The old
      man leaned on his axe and watched
Certain brown canvas bundles, the bodies of six young men lashed on three
  horses,
Come down the bend of the mountain to the air-force truck
Parked at the drivehead. It is curious how things repeat themselves, but
  always changed: it was thus Bull Gore's
And David Larson's were borne down the burnt mountain; their escort
  soldiers were negro and these were white;
That was in time of war, this of so-called peace: it made no difference;
The horses went foot by foot, the men who rode them were dead.

                                                            The
      old man's daughter
Led the first horse; when she came down he called to her and said:
"Listen Sea-gull: there was a yellow-eyed woman here asking for you. The
  truth is too precious
To be spent on such people: so I told her
That you'd gone back to town. I am not sure whose creek you are fishing
  in, little one:
Look out for snags."

XXI

                    Like the steep necks of a herd of horses
Lined on a river margin, athirst in summer, the mountain-ridges
Pitch to the sea, the lean granite-boned heads
Plunge nostril-under: on the rock shore between two great heads
Stands the Stewart ranch-house in its canyon-mouth,
Tall, cube-shaped and unadorned, painted dull yellow,
And the creek runs below. It is here that yellow-eyed woman lives
With her two brothers and her new husband,
And her daughter Vere Harnish.

                         Vere came up from the creek
Carrying a wet towel, her light-brown hair
Hung lank and wet; a narrow-hipped girl of sixteen or so, broad faced, and
    thick
Eyelids that made the eyes reticent slits: she drew backward into the
    gorge-bank bushes,
Hearing leather creak, wishing not to be seen, and watched a horseman
Go by; it was Clive Enfield her mother's husband riding his beautiful
    palomino,
A hawk-faced young man with a silvered bridle and a red neck-cloth,
His quick eyes could not miss her; he waved and passed and went up the
    canyon. Presently she heard the night-herons,
That roost all day in the canyon-throat wood, indignantly shouting. They
    hate every passer-by
Under their private forest; two or three flew up
Over the tree-tops, great birds with soft owly wings,
Wheeling and cawing.

                  Vere Harnish went on,
And met her mother by the side of the house, who said flat-voiced,

"Which way did he go?" "What?" she answered sullenly. "Clive," she
    answered, "Did he go by the road
Or up the canyon?" "Your husband," she answered, "that great lover, that
    slicked-up and perfumed tramp. Mother,
How you degrade yourself!" Who blazed at her
With her clear yellow eyes and said flat-voiced, "Did he go up the canyon?
    I thought I heard
The herons squawk." "You heard a crow or a gull. I liked you once,
    mother, I even respected you.
Now I will go and wash again." "Who," she answered,
"Made you my judge? Did I neglect you when you were little? Did I
    neglect your father when he lay dying
Month after month?" "And in six months another man. I wish you had.
    You are horrible, mother.
All twittering with love and jealousy . . . Ah, ah, ah," she moaned, "Ah,
Please yourself."

XXII

            A cold night of no moon and great stars, crystals in
    granite, and little foxes down the dark mountain
Singing from ridge to ridge, the distant ocean sighing in her sleep, the old
    man looked up
At a black eyelet in the white of the Milky Way, and he thought with
    wonder: "There — or thereabout —
Cloaked in thick darkness in his power's dust-cloud,
There is the hub and heavy nucleus, the ringmaster
Of all this million-shining whirlwind of dancers, the stars of this end of
    heaven. It is strange, truly,
That great and small, the atoms of a grain of sand and the suns with
    planets, and all the galactic universes

Are organized on one pattern, the eternal roundabout, the heavy nucleus
and whirling electrons, the leashed
And panting runners going nowhere; frustrated flight, unrelieved strain,
endless return — all — all —
The eternal firewheel."

             While he considered the matter, staring upward,
and the night's noises
Hushed, there came down from heaven a great virile cry, a voice hoarser
than thunder, heavily reverberated
Among the star-whorls and cliffs of darkness: "I am caught. I am in the
net." And then, intolerably patient:
"I see my doom."

            The old man trembled and laughed, gaping upward:
"My God: have they got Oedipus
Or Lear up there? Was it a cry of nature? Is it possible that man's passion is
only a reflex of
Much greater torment; and what was shouted among the stars comes
dwindling and tottering down
Into human jaws and a king's bursting heart — or a lynched black's: — very
likely: hates, loves and world-wars —
Hypnotized players: look at their vacant eyes:
Of obscure tragedies that being uncomprehended echoes of misheard
fragments are nonsense.
But the great voice was in earnest."

XXIII

The rain paused about dawn, the southeast wind raged like an axe, there
was no sleep

In the tumult of storm and the house trembling. Vere Harnish dressed and
    went down, she stood and stared
From a west window at the mud-yellow sky streaked with flying cloud, and
    black under foam-sheets
The beaten sea; she heard the south window hiss in the pelting
Of twigs and gravel, she thought it might burst presently. Her mother
    Dana Enfield came in half-dressed;
They had no eyes for each other and sat stiffly apart, staring
At the west window: branches of trees and formless rags of foam fled
Down the dark light, and streaks of yellow floodwater now became visible
    below the foam-drift
On the sea's beaten face: but all this rage of the air,
No air to breathe.

                    At that moment an undreamed-of thing like a flying
    cowhide
Came dark on the south window and smashed it; glass-fragments rained,
    chairs fell, Dana Enfield
Fled from the room; Vere sat frozen and saw a huge bird
Snared in its broken wing wrestling against the wall-foot; a pelican, the
    nine-foot-spread bird
With the great beak; it had been cropped from a sea-rock and the iron
    draught
On the cliffhead had caught it. Birds have their fates like men, and this one
Destined from the egg to die in a human house, — as the last Czar in a
    cellar, or Goering the luxurious
On a cast-iron jail-cot — had met its appointment. Vere stood up coldly in
    the whirlwind, she also
Under compulsion, she felt through two drawers and found a knife.

                                                            Sholto

    Stewart

Came into the room up the insane wind,

And Vere was on her knees in the room wreckage, mechanically pumping the penknife blade

Through the bird's bloody breast. Her mouth hung open like a dead clam-shell, she had no look of anything

But dull duty well done. She said, "It smells like fish-blood, it nearly mothers me."

XXIV

A gray-haired walker with an erect back-bone and benevolent spectacles

Paced up the hill to the Gore place; the old axeman watched him and went to meet him: "What do *you* want?" He answered:

"Advice, advice. I am a man much troubled about the future. I believed we were building peace,

And suddenly fantastic expressions of death and horror bob up like jumping-jacks

On all horizons. Our minds and our words go wrong, the peace has gone wrong, these years are deadly:

What can we do?" "*Me* you ask?" "Because they say you have a harsh wisdom, unperfumed, untuned, untaught,

Like Heraclitus's Sibyl." "Whose voice," the old man answered, "reaches over ten thousand years

Because of the God." "Well," he said, "more or less." "Who," the old man answered, "was Heraclitus? I have some wisdom—

In the head of my axe." "I am more humble than you," he answered,

"I am willing to be taught, and I am willing to teach, and the world wants wisdom. The axe

Is in its root." The old man sighed and smiled: "I have noticed that." "What can we do," he answered,

"To save the world? What has gone wrong with our peace? Why do we grin
   at the Russians and they at us?
All hangs on that." The old man counted his fingers: "France, England,
   Germany. Japan. You and the Russians.
There were six powers in the world, and peace was possible. You could have
   forced it and kept it, even when France fell,
But you preferred victory. Thence your two giants, alone in the rubble
   world, watching each other
For the weak moment." He groaned and said, "You are wrong. You are
   twice wrong. Why cannot two friends in victory.
Two friends be friends?" "Two bulls in one herd?" he answered. "But
   these," he said, "are people. We have minds." The old man
Laughed, and the other patiently: "Which side is evil then?
We or the others?" "Two stallions," the old man answered, "in a run of
   mares: which side is evil?" "Well," he said, "the Aggressor."
"I see you are superstitious," he answered, "you believe in words. But words
Are like women: they are made to lie with." "I understand at least," he
   answered, "that you utterly despair.
If nations have no morality, and words no meaning, and women
No other purpose." "Look down there," the old man answered, "on the
   green ridge, the second ridge.
Do you see the ivory-colored horse and the horseman — and the tall girl
Running to meet him?" "What?" he said: "Yes, I see." "Look," the old
   man said, "look how she leans
Her breast on the rider's thigh and his arm embraces her. Pretty, ah? It's
   even beautiful. Her name is Sea-gull.
She opens her little beak, she is gulping for love. She has no mind but an
   instinct. She will drop twins,
The race will live, though civilization burns like a straw-stack." "Does that
   please you?" He twitched his shoulder, saying "Me?
Had *I* a choice?

I think the whole human race ought to be scrapped and is on the way to it;
    ground like fish-meal for soil-food.
What does the vast and rushing drama of the universe, seas, rocks,
    condor-winged storms, ice-fiery galaxies,
The flaming and whirling universe like a handful of gems falling down a
    dark well,
Want clowns for? Hah?"

XXV

                          The old iron crowbar driven into the mountain
To mark a corner of the Gore place, had been forced and disrooted:
    whether by some intruder, or the sleepy rock
Moved underground, or a wild boar had moved it, rooting by moonlight.
    The old man hammered it home again,
And heaped a cairn of stones above it to guard it. There were fine stones
    on that ridge: the old man found himself
Taking an artist pleasure in his little pyramid, and said to himself:
"To whom this monument: Jesus or Caesar or Mother Eve?
No," he said, "to Copernicus: Nicky Kupernick: who first pushed man
Out of his insane self-importance and the world's navel, and taught him his
    place.

        And the next one to Darwin."

XXVI

Sholto Stewart was repairing the window
The bird had broken; he had putty and a pane of glass,
And was taking down the planks he had nailed for shelter
While the storm raged. His sister Dana Enfield came suddenly

Around the corner of the house; her face looked haggard green in the
  sea-shine, her drab-yellow
Hair was uncombed and her yellow eyes turbid: "He's gone again
Up the mountain to meet her. Sholto, Sholto," she caught his arm,
"Get me rid of that hill-crawler!" "Yea?" he said, "I told you
Before you married him." "I mean," she said, "the bitch. Clive loves me but
  he is soft.
It is the bitch." He answered: "A cunning morsel, mud, rags and all. I never
  liked him,
But I can see his point." "She is horrible," she answered; and stood and
  stared at the sea-glitter, her lips twitching
On silence: the way that lonely-hobbling old women, turbulent and
  undesired and remembering,
Talk to themselves. The man turned back to his work,
And drew with the claws of the hammer another nail; the wire shank
  screamed
In the wet wood. At the same moment a sea-gull mewed in the air. Dana
  breathed and said
"Lend me your hammer, Sholto." "What?" he said, detaching it
From another nailhead, and he gave it to her: she instantly
Swung it against the pane of glass at the wallfoot; the bright sheet flashed
In jags and fragments. "Well," he said: "What a woman." "I couldn't help
  it," she answered, "the handle
Slid in my hand." "So you say, Mrs. Fury." "Oh, it's my fault," she
  answered; "I'll have to send
Clive to town for more glass. While he's gone, Sholto,
We'll have a party. I have three or four quarts
Put away for New Year's: this will be New Year's
I hope and pray."

          Hope, as the old man said, is a great folly. It is often
  the wickedest

Hopes that prevail, as gardens liefer bear weeds than fruit, but good or evil, they are weighted
    they are weighted
With equal fear. It is far better therefore, the old man said, not to complicate
    complicate
Action with expectation, but go on by instinct. What comes will come.
The great bear and the sabre-tooth tiger, the powerful ones perish; an absurd ape drops from a tree
    absurd ape drops from a tree
And for a time rules the earth.

XXVII

                        Sea-gull: because a horse's hide is the color
    color
Of ancient ivory, and his mane and his tail white as a wave and a torrent: it does not prove
    does not prove
That his rider is with him. Be careful, Sea-gull. But she, when she looked down the mountain
    down the mountain
And saw the palomino on the green ridge in the winter sun-gleam tethered and beautiful,
    and beautiful,
Had no distrust; she ran on the side-hills and hastened
In the leaf-green barranca, she heard a trampling
In the bushes behind her: "Oh Clive where are you?" but it was Sholto Stewart
    Stewart
Grinning on a bay horse, whirling his rope, and the noose flew
But she escaped it. She fled and two men on foot pushed through the leaves; one was young and dark-skinned,
    leaves; one was young and dark-skinned,
A Spanish boy: she turned to him and smelled whiskey and said "Que hay amigo?" He in English
    amigo?" He in English
Giggled, "It is a peek-neek. You are invite," and caught her by the slim wrist. She strove against him,
    wrist. She strove against him,
But the older man, heavy and red with bloodshot blue eyes,

Lurched alongside her, Sholto rode hard behind, they ran her down to a
  clearance
Where two horses were tied and that yellow-eyed woman Dana Enfield
  came under a tan-oak tree,
Saying "Here you are. A long time I've tried to find you. Until my husband
  lent me his horse:
He said you'd come." "No," she said. "Oh, but he did," she answered, "Do
  you think he cares for you? You were his plaything,
His dirty dirty toy and he laughs at you. How could I know about you
Unless he told me!" The girl shook her head silently, writhing her arm in
  the hands that held it, beautiful
In the upward-beating soft golden sea-light, for the sun was clouded. A
  heavy wedge of dark hair fell forward
On her thin face; her worn shirt, torn at the throat, exposed
The thrust of the fine shoulder; and Sholto Stewart, now dismounted,
Stared at her, licking his hard thin lips, and the others held her. But Dana
  saw nothing beautiful in her,
But answered hoarsely: "He did though: he gave you to me. Men like to
  amuse themselves with little dirty ones,
Rags, bones and smell, but when it's in earnest, when it comes to the pinch,
  they choose a clean woman,
A person of some honor and importance. All right: he chose. He gave you
  to me. I'll tell you
What we are going to do." Her pale yellow eyes
Blazed hard and little, suddenly the reined-in wrath overcame her
And she shook like a flame: "You cast off rag-doll, you dirt-queen." Her
  hand flashed and she struck
The thin young face: "You soiled hill-crawler." Bill Stewart said heavily
"Easy, Sis, take it easy." Then Sea-gull with tears in the under-lids
Of her long eyes, and on her lip a small fleck of blood: "You needn't waste
  anger on me. Oh why?

I never harmed you, I never saw you before, I never spoke of you. I was happy to take the bits

Under your table." Suddenly the Spanish boy laughed like a fool; Dana Enfield glanced at him

And said to Sea-gull: "You're going to be whipped until you roar: bring the rope, Sholto.

You're going to go away and never come back — take your sore back

Out of these hills." Bill Stewart said heavily,

"You said that you would talk to her. To hell with whipping.

Whipping's for horses." "Until she's raw," she answered. "Until she falls,

And then awhile." The Spanish boy Louie Lopez said solemnly,

"You are dronk, Mrs. Enfiel'?" But Sholto, his meagre face twitching one side, from the right eye

To the corner of the mouth, came with his rope and stood swaying and said, "This is it, Frowline." Bill Stewart

Stood back from her; Lopez stood forward, saying "You are dronk. You will not do it." Sholto answered,

"Off," and his free hand suddenly striking forward took the girl's shirt, the neckband behind the shoulder

And tore it from her; she cried bitterly three times:

"Clive, help! Clive, help!" Dana answered, "He hears you:

He will not help you. Tie her up to the tree, Sholto: I wish the quirt

Were boiled in salt." The Spanish boy wildly laughed again,

Staring at the bared breasts: "I tell you. We take her

Into the bushes. Ah? Ah?" He was all at once as pale as his corpse would be; yellow gray. Sholto

Handling the rope said, "Hold out your hands, Frowline." Then Sea-gull turned and began to run, but Lopez

Tripped her first step and fell with her. She fought against him

On the ground in sharp silence. He tore open her blue-jeans

And was dragging them down; Dana cried fiercely, "You half-wit.

You drunken swine," and Sholto hooking his hands on the boy's throat subtracted him

From what he sought. "Wait your turn." He knelt by Sea-gull

And struck her throat with his fist. Dana gasped and said,

"When you're done with her, call me." She turned away a few steps, and stood

Looking down toward the sea. The sun hung in the cloud-bank a huge red disk, and across the water

A red causeway ran out to it; the mountainfoot shore

Was blue as dreams.

                    While up the slope that bestiality — I mean, that humanity —

Man and no other animal — performed itself. Louie Lopez

Stood leaning forward, gazing religiously

At the girl's sprawled white legs and her gasping face; Bill Stewart on the other side stood like an ox,

His little blue eyes staring at nothing, his red jowls ruminant, chewing his cud

Like an old ox that the butcher has forgotten: but after his brother and the Spanish boy finished

He took his turn. Then Lopez felt new desire and spent it. Sholto said, "Get up,"

But he would not, and Sholto with the whip flicked him; he stood up sullenly

And drew his clothing together. Sholto's breath hissed

As he striped the girl's flank: one stripe: and Lopez

Sprang at his throat. While they fought, clumsy with drunkenness,

Sea-gull fled naked into the brush to the north

And hid herself until night-fall; she went home wearily

And lay and slept. In the morning the old man her father

Said, "Why were you crying, Sea-gull? What happened to you?" "Oh no,"
    she answered.
He said "Was he unkind to you?" "Oh no," she answered,
Turning her face from him. "What bruised your face?" "I fell in a bush of
    trees
From a tall rock."

XXVIII

                    It rained all night and coyotes gathered, snapping and
    scritching
At the doors of the house; yet his black hound-bitch, the old man
In common kindness had brought in-doors, never rebuked them; and in the
    morning he said:
"Snapper you are too happy, you are too American. You need a little sleet
    on your hide,
And to taste hunger." She drooping her ears and tail trotted behind him,
    but at noon vanished. In the evening
Thunder from ridge to ridge leaped like a goat and bursts of hail
Whipped the hills white, Snapper had not come home; in the darkness the
    weather worsened; coyotes apparently
Fought a pitched battle, and complete with screams of the dying, right at
    the house-door; the old man went out
And all but the dark wind and sharp sleet was peace. But at dawn he looked
    out and saw
What darkness hid: the torn corpse of a dog in a cirque of bushes; gnawn,
    blood-smeared, the ears bitten off
And the teeth glaring. "This is strange. It is not Snapper. Do you know
    him, Sea-gull?" She on the doorstep,
Hooded with a blanket for the shrill air: "Where did he come from?
What happened to him?" "I think," he said, "he died for love,

Like a fellow in a play." "Look," she answered. Far away up the hill
    Snapper was seen
Coming down delicately between the black bushes in the gray light
From the dark dawn. She sniffed the carcass daintily and came to the house,
    ears lowered. The old man answered:
"How should I know that you were singing a love-song
In the throat under your tail, and with musk for music? But the wolves
    heard you, and that stark hero, wherever
He comes from, heard." She looked up and laughed doubtfully, as a dog
    does; and Sea-gull: "Oh she is hurt.
There is blood on her jaw." "Not hers," he said, "nor a wolf's either.
She has been a traitress, and in spring she'll drop wolf-cubs.
The world reverts. Dogs and men tire of a slow decline."

                                                    So he said.
    There was in fact a more merciless
And more life-weary beauty in the vast landscape, the dark gray light, the
    one dull streak of sulphur for dawn,
Dark headlong slopes, the black-fanged rocks and high grinning
    snow-teeth, the long row of the snow-struck mountain-tops
High up in heaven. The old man looked up: "Am I also a renegade? I
    prefer God to man.
But," he said grimly, "Snapper, I have not tasted
Any cannibal feasts. It is the people-lovers and nation-leaders, the
    human-centered,
Have bloody chops." He sighed and said, "In this pale light
All the little tricks are played out and finished. Retreat is no good,
    treachery no good, goodness no good.
But still remains the endless inhuman beauty of things; even of humanity
    and human history
The inhuman beauty; — and there is endurance, endurance, death's nobler
    cousin. Endurance."

XXIX

Sea-gull awoke to an angry noise of grinding in the deep night, and lay
    still,

Loving her own bare body warm in the bed, how clean and alive it was; nor
    man's brutality

Nor sky's hardship had numbed it; she thought that nothing could, —

But that's youth's dream, — and soon, the high angry noise continuing,

She stood up barefoot and wrapped the blanket around her and went to
    look. She found her old father

Working the treadle grindstone behind the house, grinding an axe, leaning
    the steel on the stone

So that it screamed, and a wild spray of sparks

Jetted on the black air. "What are you doing to your axe, father?" He
    would not hear her; she clutched

His hard shoulder and drove the finger-nails in. "Why are you grinding
    your axe, father,

In the deep night?" He turned a contorted face and said:

"It is not mine. Why should I ruin mine?

This is a rust-headed skull that the former people

Left in the shed." The steel screamed and she shouted "Why are you
    grinding it?" "I hate, and I want to kill."

"Whom are you going to kill?" "No one," he groaned, "Who is worth
    killing? I am sick to-night, I am human:

There is only one animal that hates himself. Truly the sweating toad and
    poison-gorged pit-viper

Are content with their natures. I'll be a stone at the bottom of the sea, or
    any bush on the mountain,

But not this ghost-ridden blood-and-bone-thing, civil war on two legs and
    the stars' contempt, this walking farce,

This ape, this — denatured ape, this — citizen —" He stooped over the
    stone, the steel screamed like a horse, and the spark-spray

Spouted from the high hill over land and sea. It was like the glittering night
    last October
When the earth swam through a comet's tail, and fiery serpents
Filled half of heaven. But in the morning Sea-gull said: "What was the
    matter with you, father, last night?"
"You are mistaken," the old man answered. "Possibly you saw my ghost: it
    may have gone out of me,
For I slept like a rock."

                    He looked up and down
At the cold peaks lining the lonely sky, and that opaque gray monster the
    ocean, incessantly
Gnawing his rocks. "Is it not enough? I see that the world is very beautiful,
    great and — in earnest.
It bred man and surrounds him and will reabsorb him: what more do I
    want? — It bred," he answered himself,
"Louse too: noble and ignoble, the eagle and her lice. What more I want is
    a little nobility in man
To match the world's." He looked again at the great landscape and laughed.
    "I am asking something.

                    Nevertheless —
Every tragic poet has believed it possible. And every Savior, Buddha down
    to Karl Marx,
Has preferred peace. Tragedy, shall we say, is a cult of pain, and salvation of
    happiness:
Choose and be sifted.

                    But I will be turned again to the outer
    magnificence, the all but inhuman God.
I will grind no more axes."

XXX

The tide ran out, leaving a forest of tumbled
rocks, wet fur and brown weed,
Where late ran the tall waves. Sholto Stewart and Clive Enfield came down
from the house
To gather shellfish, and soon Enfield came back with a sack of mussels,
along the slippery
And whale's-back reef. At the angle of the cliff by the creek sand-beach he
met Vere Harnish
His wife's daughter coming stiffly to meet him, her broad face greenish
white, her hands huddled up
Against her breast. Her mouth, with the white lips drawn on the teeth,
Moved like a fish's mouth. Clive dropped the briny-
Dripping sack from his shoulder and said, "My God —
What is the matter?" She moved her mouth like a fish two or three times
on silence, and moaned:
"It hurts me so. Kiss me, Clive, I am dying." She opened her hands at him
And they were full of blood from the slashed wrists; nothing arterial,
shallow razor-cuts
That would heal in a fortnight: and Enfield knew it: but he bawled for
Sholto;
And heard with dull contempt his own voice
Beating between the sea and the mountain like a mournful bird.

XXXI

Wildcat, coon and coyote, deer and wild pig, weasel and civet-cat, the
stalking puma and the dainty foxes
Travelled together, they all went the one way. On the other side of the rock
a dense-packed river

Of humanity, all races, brown, white, black, yellow, flowed along the wide ridge

In the opposite direction. The old man leaned on the rock, watching both ways. He heard the sad animals

In their innocence hum to each other "We are going into the past, into the past, we have no place

In the great age." Therefore he turned to the others and said:

"Where are you going?" "Into the future with the dawn on our faces. Come along with us." "No," he said.

They answered, "Will you go with the beasts then?" "Certainly not," he answered. "I would break both my legs

Liefer than go with beasts or men or angels *en masse*. What are you seeking?"

"The future, the human future." "You'll be surprised," he said.

                                                  "However,"
    he said, "time is a ring: what's future?

And when again you meet the beasts on this pleasant hill, the fox yaps in your faces, your harps are hushed, future is past, —

I shall be here."

XXXII

The palomino and his rider with a led horse, a gelding sorrel, came up the hill-drive

Toward the ranch-house. The old man did not see them; he saw his daughter staring, her hands at her throat;

He took his axe and stood beside her and saw the two horses: "Well, Sea-gull. I think your wings

Lift from this rock." She made no answer; he said "Are you happy?" She made no answer, her eyes

Pinned on the nearing rider. The old man said impatiently "Instinctive
    female: in all this magnificence
Of sea and mountain — one man." Her lover at the head of the drive let in
    the spurs; he ran the level, reined hard,
And said from the rearing saddle, "Come on, Gaviota." She ran to him, he
    leaned and kissed her and said,
"Get your stuff and we'll go." "Nothing," she said; "I had clean clothes but
    I lost them
The other day; they were torn all to pieces. Darling, if I had nothing at all
    I'd ride with you
Naked." "Yea," he said, "cold but beautiful." The old man said:
    "Remember, Sea-gull: if he turns bad,
Or goes to live in a city, you can come back here. Where are you going?"
    Clive answered him:
"We'll flip a nickel. All I know is, it's time.
I have been seduced by a chlorotic brat, and knocked my brother-in-law's
Teeth down his throat: — What did they do to you, Sea-gull, the other
    day?" "Oh," she said, "nothing.
I think they wanted to beat me; I got away." "Besides," he said, "I am very
    weary
Of that yellow-eyed woman every night draining me." The old man said:
"Be warned, Sea-mew: be moderate." She in her golden haze of joy
    overflowing gold
Suddenly flung herself on her father and embraced him, "Good-bye,
    good-bye," worming her body against him,
Crushing the fine grapes of her breasts
On his old ribs. He groaned across her dark hair to Enfield: "Look here,
    young man:
Give her a baby soon or she'll melt the rocks," — but she had already left
    him, and leaped
To the saddle of the sorrel, and they went their way.

The old man heard

A crying against his knee and looked down at the eyes

Of his black hound-bitch; he said "You are wrong, Snapper. It is no harm.
    We shall have less distraction now.

Death and departure are not evil things. I tell you sadly: every person that
    leaves

A place, improves it: the mourners at every funeral know that

In their shamed hearts: and when the sociable races of man and dog are
    done with, what a shining wonder

This world will be."

XXXIII

But the hound's eyes wavered from him, and
    suddenly

Grew fixed and wild; the black hair on her back stood like a hedge and her
    teeth like knives: the old man

Looked then, and saw himself, or an image of himself, tall, bony and
    repulsive to him, trough cheeks, gray beard-stubble,

And whitish gray eyes in sagging eye-slots: he like the hound flinched
    backward. "Did I say undistracted!

We send the living away: dummies and shadows

Pop up out of the ground. Can you talk?" "Yes," it said gravely. "What do
    you say then?" "That you are not honest.

If you in truth believed that man is a nuisance and life an evil — you'd act."
    "Act then," he answered.

"You know," it answered, "I cannot: I am a phantom." "You are a
    phantom," he said, "you will be gone

In five minutes: and the human race in a million years: and I in twenty: we
    phantoms.

But," he said, "as to action — truly the world is full of things the mind must
    know

And the hand must not do. Come, fool: be patient.
Life is not logic."

XXXIV

             Sholto's aching mouth kept him awake; light foot-steps
    and candle-flicker
Went up the passage; a bedroom conversation began; he lay and grinned
Painfully in the dark. A crazy cluster of screams got him up. One door-sill
    was light-lined,
His sister's room, he went and pushed wide the door and saw the candle on
    the dresser, and Vere Harnish
Kneeling against the bed beside her mother's half naked body, pumping a
    penknife into it,
As she had done to that storm-blown bird. There was a good deal of blood,
    and Sholto stood
In the room and howled. Then Vere stood up, saying "I loved my mother,
    but a certain thing happened,
She had to die. I have my reasons. She was a bad influence,
I have no respect for her." She passed him unhindered, and heard his
    brother Bill Stewart panting like a hill-climber
In the house darkness, and passed him.

XXXV

                 Rain-gray and dark the dawn, but
    for some reason
The old man's heart melted; he stood at gaze, his frost-gray eyes
Warm and hollow as a cow's. He leaned on his axe and slowly turned
    himself from the noble hill-tops

To the gray eye of the ocean, the gray rivers of mist in the branching
    gorges, the tall black rocks
Gray-based, and the still lakes of pale silver air, and slowly back again
To the nobility of the hill-tops. Suddenly he knelt, and tears ran down the
    gullied leather
Of his old cheeks. "Dear love. You are so beautiful.
Even this side the stars and below the moon. How can you be ... all this
        ... and me also?
Be Human also? The yellow puma, the flighty mourning-dove and flecked
    hawk, yes and the rattlesnake
Are in the nature of things; they are noble and beautiful
As the rocks and the grass: — not this grim ape
Although it loves you. — Yet two or three times in my life my walls have
    fallen — beyond love — no room for love —
I have been you."

                His dog Snapper
Pitied him and came and licked his loose hand. He pushed her off:
"I have been *you*, and you stink a little."

XXXVI

A small sharp light flashed on the black-green mountain
Opposite the morning sun: the old man looked attentively and rode down
    to it, and found a stranger
With glittering concave glasses on white-lashed eyes, who spoke from the
    back of his throat: "Is here not free either?
I do no harm here." The old man considered him and said "But plenty
    elsewhere: is that it?" "Ach no," he answered,

"I haf escaped. Is now with me clean science or nothing; I serve no more."
 "But you did serve," he said,
"Death, while it lasted." "While it lasted?" he answered, "It lasts, it lasts.
That you will see." "You are not telling me news," the old man answered,
 and listened to his axe
As one listens to a watch whether it ticks, and he held it toward him: "Do
 you hear it?" The foreigner heard it
Humming and yelping to itself, and stepped backward from it: "What for a
 thing is that?" "A hungry eagle-chick,"
The old man said, "yelping to itself." The foreigner's glasses flashed in the
 sun as he shook his head:
"It is not scientific." "No," the old man answered,
"It knows too much. It says that bitter wars and black ruin are necessary:
 but woe to those
That call them in." "I know," he said, "I have seen that.
I was a German." "And now," the old man said, "an American?" "No," he
 answered, "I serve no more.
I serve no more. I tell you: I was designing new weapons to save my people:
 it was not always shameful
To be a patriot: then all went into ruin and the Russians coming, we made
 a choice,
We will go with the West. I hired myself to the American army, my
 people's enemy,
A mercenary soldier, a man of science, and they gave me to work: and I
 knew well what war
I was preparing."

        He paused and wiped the sweat from his pink forehead
 and said, "But I found something.
It was to make a weapon, it is much more. It is a mathematische Formel,
 and I tell you

It solves, it solves. It brings under one rule atoms and galaxies, gravitation
and time,
Photons and light-waves." He fished his pocket and produced a black
note-book: "I let you see.
You will not understand." The page was lined with symbols like small dead
spiders; one brief equation
Stood pencil-circled. The stubby forefinger struck it and the man said,
"Your axe, it sings: but I tell you
This louder sings." The old man squinted down at it: "Not to me. And it
is likely
The lost war and much learning have turned you mad. But, if the thing
were proved, what will you do
With your equation?" "It is," he said, "proved.
Through work of some other men and three cheap experiments of my own.
So I will die and not publish.
I tell you why: — this little Gleichung, this bite of the mind, this little
music here,
It can make mortal weapons or immense power, an immense convenience to
man: these things I will not.
Science is not to serve but to know. Science is for itself its own value, it is
not for man,
His little good and big evil: it is a noble thing, which to use
Is to degrade." "I *see* you are not American," the old man answered, "nor
German either." And the other:
"Therefore astronomy is the most noble science: is the most useless." "You
are probably mad,"
He answered, "but you think nobly." "So I have cheated," he said, "the
American army and am run away.
Science is not a chambermaid-woman." "Brother," the old man said, "you
are right.

Science is an adoration; a kind of worship." "So?" he said,

"Worship?" His round blue eyes behind the bright glasses grew opaque and
    careful:

"What then is worship?" The old man considered him and said slowly: "A
    contemplation of God." "Das noch!" he answered,

"Das fehlte noch! I am a man who thought that even old peasants and
    leather cowboys after this war

Had learned something." "A coming nearer to God," the old man said
    slowly. "To learn his ways

And love his beauty." "Ja: so," he said, "Der uralte Bloedsinn. I hope the
    Russians

Destroy you and your God." Instantly the axe in the old man's hand

Began to scream like a hawk; he huddled it against his thigh, saying "Hush,
    be quiet. We and the Russians

Are," he said, "great destroyers: — and God will decide the issue. You have
    perhaps heard some false reports

On the subject of God. He is not dead; and he is not a fable. He is not
    mocked nor forgotten —

Successfully. God is a lion that comes in the night. God is a hawk gliding
    among the stars —

If all the stars and the earth, and the living flesh of the night that flows in
    between them, and whatever is beyond them

Were that one bird. He has a bloody beak and harsh talons, he pounces and
    tears —

And where is the German Reich? There also

Will be prodigious America and world-owning Russia. I say that all hopes
    and empires will die like yours;

Mankind will die, there will be no more fools; wisdom will die; the very
    stars will die;

One fierce life lasts."

While he spoke, his axe
Barked like a hunting eagle but incessantly; the old man lifted his voice to
    be heard above it;
The German, stunned by their double clamor, flung up his hands to his
    head and returned away from them
Down the dark silent hill. The gaunt old man on the little gray horse
Gazed after him, saying, "God does not care, why should I care?" He felt
    in his mind the vast boiling globes
Of the innumerable stars redden to a deadly starset; their ancient power and
    glory were darkened,
The serpent flesh of the night that flows in between them was not more
    cold. Nothing was perfectly cold,
Nothing was hot; no flow nor motion; lukewarm equality,
The final desert. The old man shuddered and hid his face and said,
"Well: God has died." He shook like an epileptic and saw the darkness
    glow again. Flash after flash,
And terrible midnight beyond midnight, endless succession, the shining
    towers of the universe
Were and were not; they leaped back and forth like goats
Between existence and annihilation. The old man laughed and said,
"Skin beyond skin, there is always something beyond: it comes in and stirs
    them. I think that poor fellow
Should have let in the mad old serpent infinity, the double zero that
    confounds reckoning,
In his equation."

            The axe was still fiercely yelling, the old man answered:
"What! After endless time?" He stripped his coat off
And huddled the axe-head in it, and rode down hastily
Behind the stranger. He came to him and said: "Brother:

Because you have chosen nobly between free science and servile science:
   come up with me —
If you are hungry, or have to hide from pursuers —
I know every crack of the mountain." But the man would not.

XXXVII

                              The old
   man heard rumors,
Of life and death, and heard that the power of Britain was falling in pieces
Like a raft on a reef. "I knew that," he answered,
"At the time of the Boer War.
I saw the most greedy empire gorged and disgorging.
It seems to me that all things happen in my mind
Before they happen."

             And again: "How beautiful," he said, "are these
   risings
And fallings: the waves of the sea, the Athenian empire,
The civilization of Europe, the might of America. A wave builds up
And it runs toward the shore, higher, higher, higher; nothing, you'd say, can
   resist it; it rakes the stars out of heaven;
It spouts a foam-head of empire and dirty wars and drives on, toppling and
   crashing, and it sighs its life out
At the foot of the rock. Slow was the rise,
Rapid the fall: God and the tragic poets
They love this pattern; it is like the beauty of a woman to them;
They cannot refrain from it. What goes high they bring down. And look —
   the race of man has become more numerous
Than the passenger pigeons, that flattened forests
With the weight of their hordes — but something has happened to them
   suddenly ..."

XXXVIII

Dark planets around a dead star, the vultures
Circled, and glided down. The old man came; they perched on rocks round
about, jutting their beaks
And bald red necks, huddling their scrawny bodies
In the broad wings. The carcass had little face and was eaten hollow, but
the hair on its head
And the hair below the belly were a nubile girl's. The old man dismounted
and stood
Looking down through the stench; the carcass mumbled with its black
tongue: "Have pity on me.
Pass your axe through my neck." The old man answered, "Surely you are
dead and decaying for many days.
Surely a stone is a stone and stone-dead is dead.
Why can you talk?" The black mouth worked and bubbled, it said "Vee
honsh," and cleared itself and said
"I am dead but I cannot sleep: I am Vere Harnish:
Choked by my mother's blood. Blub-lack, blood is black
By candleshine. I ran after her man
Because I loved her. When he unvirgined me
I was horrible to myself, but now I am
More horrible." The old man stood looking down through the awful
invisible cloud
Of the stench, and said nothing; and again the slime
Crackled and labored in the black throat: "Do you understand me?
I killed I killed." He answered, "There has been a war: the world is full of
people who have killed:
And I do think they sleep." It said: "My mother." "Well," he said, "she was
nearest.
It is a need, to kill." "The coyotes," she said, "have been, and the wild
swine have been, and the vultures have been,

And nothing sleeps me: but if you would hew the head
That dreamed it from the hands that did it." He groaned, and suddenly
Swung up the double axe, but as it flashed down
The carcass screamed: the man's heart failed, the blade
Hacked the gray earth. He stood gasping and looking down, the carcass mumbled
"Oh do it do it do it." "Not again," he said. It mumbled, "Have mercy on me.
I'll give you my mother's golden eyes." He was silent, and said "Was that
Yellow-eyed one your mother?" "Strike off my head, and look
Under my left arm-pit and you will find
Her golden eyes." "What do I want of gold?" "To buy a boat,"
It answered, "to buy a boat
When *your* need comes. Oh strike!" "There is not enough gold
In all the West." "But for pity," it said. It screamed again,
And he chopped the scream short.

                      He pried up the left shoulder
With his axe-head and found two lumps of speckled gold
On the stained soil. He said: "Perhaps the dead (when they talk!) are prophetic, *my* need is coming.
I will go buy a boat."

XXXIX

He was on the fish-wharf
Buying a boat: a man with white lips and the long eyes of terror tiptoed behind him whispering
"Are you going to escape?" The old man turned and made him a sign for silence and whispered
"I *have* escaped." "Oh," he said, "take me with you, take me with you."
   "But," the old man said, "it is likely

I have escaped the things you want, and am seeking
The things you fear. What do you fear?" "The war, the war," he said, "the
    death-rays, the fire-hail,
The horrible bombs." "Certainly," the old man said, "there will be a war —
After while. There will be a new ice-age —
After while." "Oh God," he answered, "more terror!"

                        It chanced that a
    load of ice for the fish-stalls
Had lately passed, and some lumps fallen lay melting: the man saw them
    and shouted, "Oh God, more terror.
An ice-age comes!" He ran and leaped from the wharf and cast himself
Into the sea's cold throat. The old man leaped after him,
And wrestled with him in the choking water,
And saved his life.

                "Why have I done so insanely?" the old man said. "It
    would be better
That twenty million should die than one be saved. One man in ten miles is
    more
Than the earth wants: and clearly this man's life's worthless, being full of
    fears. I have acted against reason
And against instinct." He laughed and said: "But that's the condition of
    being human: to betray reason
And deny instinct. Did I tell this poor fellow
I had escaped?"

             The man clung to him, as a pilot-fish
Clings to a shark. The old shark groaned and said, "The crime and the
    punishment: because I saved you
I must endure you." But when the boat was boughten and they sailed it
    south and were off Point Sur,

The man screamed "I fear shipwreck!" and flung himself
Over the side into the sea's cold throat. The old man watched him and said,
 "Who am I, that I should come
Between man and man's need?" But in a moment he kicked the tiller and
 swung back: "By God," he said,
"I have been in error again; I am full of errors. It is not death they desire,
 but the dear pleasure
Of being saved." He caught the drowner by the hair and dragged him
Inboard; who, after he had breathed and vomited,
"Beware," he gasped, "beware, old man, the dear pleasure
Of being Savior." "I am well warned," he answered.

XL

So he brought him home; but when they came up the hill to the house,
it was full of people. The old man said, "Who are you, and where is my
dog?" They answered, "We are refugees. The omens are coughing and
sputtering again —

Woe is the world and all tall cities fall — so we have fled from the cities,
and we found this house vacant." He said, "Where is my dog?" "There was
a black hound here," they answered, "she bit a child and ran away."

Then the old man said to his companion, the man of many terrors: "I
have made a bad bargain: I have got a man and lost a dog. Also I have got a
boat and lost a house: but that bargain's debatable. I shall debate it."

He said to the people in the house: "You are too many for me to drive
you out, even with an axe; and as for me, I can sleep on the hill. But my
friend here is sick, he is sick with many terrors. He is a refugee like you,
and you must take him into the house with you." So they did.

Then the old man went and sat on the hill, watching the house, and
presently his dog Snapper crept from a bush and joined him. He greeted
her, and he said:

"Let us sit here, Snapper, and watch the house. I have put an infection-carrier into it.

I have added fear to the fearful. When they smell his body, even unconsciously, their own fears will stand up and scream.

Terror is more contagious than typhoid, and fear than diphtheria."

So they sat and watched the house; and after three hours the doors burst open; the people fled and were scattered on the mountain, screaming like birds.

The old man said: "Did I call that fellow's life valueless! Nothing is valueless."

XLI

However, after he had considered the matter more fully, he said: "Nothing is valueless; but some things are obnoxious."

Then truly began the strain of thought. The old man paced back and forth on the hill, sweating and groaning, and at length he said humbly:

"To me."

But even so the matter was not concluded, for the old man's axe in his hand began to spit like a cat, and he stared at it and said proudly: "I agree with you. To *me*. Who has a better right to judge?

God does not judge: God *is*. Mine is the judgment."

XLII

It was rumored the old man had found gold,
Besides the bits that he had spent for the boat: therefore three robbers
    came up at moondown
Deep in the night; but the dog Snapper smelled them, the axe killed two of
    them, the old man wakened from sleep

And saved the third. He heard the man's teeth clacking, and the white dawn stole down the mountain,

He knew him and said, "My man of terrors — is it you? Why do you haunt me?" He chattered his teeth and said:

"I am your other self. The other half of yourself, white of your black. I am always with you."

"Therefore," the old man said, "you betrayed me

To these two thieves. Come," he said, "we must take them down to the water. Their bloody corpses here

Would make us trouble."

They tied them onto horses and led them down; and the old man said

"Now we must load the boat: here is that need

The damsel spoke of: and let these thieves not lack provision

Where they are going." So they laid stones in the boat for ballast, and wood for burning, and stretched the bodies

On the dry wood: then the old man looked at his companion, the man of terrors,

Whose hands had never ceased to tremble nor his teeth to chatter: "Thrice I have saved his life; now it seems

That he is I. — Lean forward," he said to him, "settle the log more decently

Under that dead thief's head." Then the man of terrors

Understood fate; and his teeth ceased from rattling, his face composed itself: "Sharp," he said, "is your mercy,"

And leaned forward over the loaded boat. The old man struck once, and fell

On the sand at the boat's tail and lay there senseless

Until the day's end.

His axe shook off the blood from its eyes and stood guard for him, and his dog Snapper

Licked his dead-seeming face. About sundown the old man groaned and
    came to himself, and said,
"It was not easy. Fortunate, Snapper, are all the beasts of the mountain:
    they live their natures: but man
Is outrageous. No man has ever known himself nor surpassed himself until
    he has killed
Half of himself." He leaned on the boat stern-strake and turned his dead
    man face upward, and the dead face
Was his own in his youth. He pulled him higher onto the firewood logs,
    and laid him straight
Between the others; then hoisted sail and struck fire, and pushed the
    boat-stern
Into the purple-shining sea from the sand, and the wind was east. The old
    man, the axe and the dog
Watched from the shore; the boat went softly out to sea, flaming
Into the crimson-flaming heart of the sunfall, and its long smoke
Mixed with the cloud. The old man laughed with gray lips. "There," he
    said, "goes myself, my self-murdered half-self
Between two thieves. It might be some tragic hero's death-voyage:
    Agamemnon's war's end, or world-hounded
Hitler's from the lost land he loved and misled
To stinking ruin: that mortal sea-star flaming away to the flaming cloud: it
    is no hero,
But how beautiful it is. Thank you, Vere Harnish."

XLIII

                            Rayed and
    tiger-straked, fire-hearted
Sundown went down; the world was misted, the afterglow made its vast
    rose; one tender color,

Solemn and high and luminous, terribly mournful. The old man stared, and
    muttered, "Is it possible America's
Bottomless luck has run out at last? We were foolish with happiness. We
    were a generous people
While we enjoyed it."

XLIV

                        A scattering pox of insurrections and civil war
Plagued the whole planet; even the patient Russians, a palace revolution
Was in the rumors again; even in North America
The pepper and salt of civilization, machine-guns and tear-gas, pickled the
    normal
Discontents of mankind and mistakes of government: and what they were
    doing in holy Asia
Made deserts there.

                        The old man was in a Monterey shop,
Fetching his monthly ration, meal, meat and beans, no Pythagorean. He
    heard a yell in the streets
And looked, and a headless riot was looting the stores. He observed them
    and said:
"Well, I was wrong. America has strained her luck: it has not run out yet. It
    is not the food-stores,
It is the liquor shops and the haberdasher's: Happy America: the luxuries
    and the vanities,
Whiskey and silk."

                        But certain people came to him and said: "What shall
    we do?
For civic order is dying, all men are law-breakers. They say you watch the
    world from your mountain — no doubt too high

To see it clearly — " So they mocked him and said,
"What's your advice?" "Mine?" he said, "It is not new: all the rulers know
    it.
If there's a flea in the water, swallow a toad. If you have trouble at home,
Try foreign war." "You are very foolish," they answered, "or very wicked."
    "Both," he said. "But look
How wealthy and how victorious you are. You will not labor to avert fate.
    Fate is your need."

XLV

When he went home to his mountain the summer cloud
Hid the high places. The old man rode in its fog and said:
"I am very foolish or very wicked. It is not little foxes crying in the gloom,
It is the children." He turned in the saddle and heard his own voice like a
    blind vulture
Beat through the canyon, bumping against the faces of rocks
In the smother of the air, while he said: "Come, little ones.
You are worth no more than the foxes and yellow wolfkins, yet I will give
    you wisdom.

                    Oh future children:
Trouble is coming; the world as of the present time
Sails on its rocks; but you will be born and live
Afterwards. Also a day will come when the earth
Will scratch herself and smile and rub off humanity:
But you will be born before that.

                    Oh future children:
When you are born do not cry; it is not for long.
And when your death-day comes do not weep; you are not going far.

You are going to your better nature, the noble elements, earth, air and
    water. That's the lost paradise
The poets remember: I wonder why we ever leave it: — Hm? What? —
    Experience.
What an experience."

                    He was silent, and heard the children crying, and he
    said: "Why?
It is not bad.
There is one God, and the earth is his prophet.
The beauty of things is the face of God: worship it;
Give your hearts to it; labor to be like it.
Oh future children:
Be reticent. Make no display. Let peafowl scream,
And red roses cry, Look at me: they are beautiful: but human minds
And bodies are not so pleasing. Therefore be reticent.
Make no display.

                    Oh future children:
Cruelty is dirt and ignorance, a muddy peasant
Beating his horse. Ambition and power-lust
Are for adolescents and defective persons. Moderate kindness
Is oil on a crying wheel: use it. Mutual help
Is necessary: use it when it is necessary.
And as to love: make love when need drives.
And as to love: love God. He is rock, earth and water, and the beasts and
    stars; and the night that contains them.
And as to love: whoever loves or hates man is fooled in a mirror." He
    grinned and said:
"From experience I speak. But truly, if you love man, swallow him in wine:
    love man in God.
Man and nothing but man is a sorry mouthful."

At this time a wind
came
And split the cloud. The old man stared up and down the enormous
    unpeopled nave of the gorge and laughed again:
"How strange that I cannot see them: but my voice carries
A long way off."

XLVI

                The sun blazed from the west; the old man saw his own
    shadow on his horse's shadow
Wending beside him along the cloud-wall. "Well, it is very curious," he
    said,
"That Worse always rides Better. I have seen in my lifetime many
    horsemen and some equestrian statues.
I have observed the people and their rulers; and a circus monkey on a great
    dane; and man on the earth."

XLVII

A youth came, and desired to be the old man's disciple. "But first tell me
your name, so that my friends may know it and listen, when I speak wisely."
"My name," the old man answered, "is Jones or McPherson or some other
word: and what does it matter? It is not true that the word was in the
beginning. Only in the long afternoon comes a little babble: and silence
forever.
    And those," he said, "to whom the word is God: their God is a word."
"Yet I will be your disciple," he answered.
    "My conditions," the old man said, "are not easy. My disciples must
never sleep, except the nights when a full moon sets at midnight."

The young man said, "When is that?" And he considered and said: "You do not *want* disciples!"

"But how," the old man answered, "did you ever guess it?"

XLVIII

The old axeman slept

In the house dooryard; a saddle — though he rode no more — served him for head-rest; he awoke, and the night

From the peaks to the sea was a standing pool of prodigious moonlight: he saw a white-legged woman

Lean over him, gazing at him; her jaw was crooked

And her mouth splotched with blood; and the white air

Smelled of geraniums. The old man stared upward at her,

And thought — having long ago inquired the story of the house — that she was Reine Gore, revisiting

Her scene and sorrow. He reached therefore his arm's length her narrow ankle, and felt his fingers

Through the skin and the bone close on mere nothing: as one feels the wind

And cannot see it: but here the sense of touch out of use,

The eyes went up the clear white legs to the female hair, and up the white belly and the sharp breasts,

To the dark dislocation and blood-splatch that were the face; — but that wried mouth

Labored to speak, not a murmur was heard: — therefore two senses

Were out of use. And two others active — the intense odor of geraniums! — The old man moistened his lips and said:

"You are not Reine Gore: that woman is gathered into the elements: You are a shell or a token.

Why are you sent?" She waved her long white hands toward the northeast,
    and passed him and glided away,
But he observed that she had a shadow.

                                He thought: "What a futile
    visitor! Why did my mind make that?
— Or be sensitive to that? — Trouble is coming."

XLIX

The horses were lame with age; as for the colts,
The old man was too old to catch them; therefore he went on foot
When he went up the mountain. He came to a place of dry rocks and wild
    sun, he saw three vultures
Perched on a crag; they looked as tall as old women, and their necks were
    yellow, their wings like the sails of ships
When they unfurled them; they were not common vultures but condors.
    The old man stared and said: "If *you* are coming back here,
Perhaps the race of man is withering away.
It is a thought; but unlikely."

L

                        "The unique ugliness of man and his
    works," the old man said,
"Seen astronomically, little and whole, in relation with time and vastness,
    the star-world,
And the bitter end waiting for modern man,
Disappears; it falls into pattern with the perpetual
Beauty of things. This is obvious, and this I have learned.

But the evil, the
    cruelties, the unbalanced
Excess of pain — that brutal survival-instinct
Tying the tooth to its ache and the man to his cancer —
These damn the race. I do not like the pyres of the martyrs.
I do not like barbed wire, squalor and terror. I do not like slave-sweat, I do
    not like torture.
Man invented these things.

        It is ignoble," he said, "and nearly senseless,
    to pray for anything.
But in so great and righteous a cause: — hear me, Lord God: Exterminate
The race of man. For man only in the world, except a few kinds of insect,
    is essentially cruel.
Therefore slay also these if you will: the driver ant,
And the slavemaker ant, and the slick wasp
That paralyzes living meat for her brood: but first
The human race. Cut it off, sear the stump."

        So he prayed, being old and
    childish, and the Lord answered him
Out of the driving storm: "I will; but not now."

        The old man looked at
    his axe,
For it was neighing like a stallion. "You wish to kill," he said,
"Every man that we meet. You two-faced violence," he said, "on the
    foresweep enemies,
And on the backsweep friends. But that is for God to do, not for you and
    me; and he has promised it. Meanwhile —
To cool your ardor: for I am sick and weary of the violences

That are done in the world": — He carried the double axe down to the sea, and whirled it, and flung it

From the high cliff; it flew a long flashing arc, dived gannetlike

And breached the wave: the old man rejoiced and said, "How quiet we shall be."

        But presently the sea boiled,

The water blackened and a broad corpse came up, it was one of those eight-armed monsters, beaked and carnivorous,

That crouch in the cold darkness in the deep sea-caves: its bulk was all hacked and mangled, and a fury of sharks

Fed on its wounds. But the axe floated clear among the shark-snouts,

And swam like a small gray dog in the whirling surf under the gull-sky, and came to the cliff and climbed it, and came

To the old man's hand.

                  Who gripped the hickory throat of the helve and answered: "Is it not enough

What they are doing in Europe and pitiless Asia, but you have to chivy

The deep sea also?"

LI

        After this his dog left him,

To den with her mate the wolf. He rejoiced and said, "At last

The delight of old age: I am alone. Neither dog nor woman,

Nor church nor state." But something jerked in his hand, he looked down at his axe: "You old gray gnawer,

Be quiet now. Bird with two beaks, two-petalled flower of steel, you rank blue flesh-fly

With the two biting wings: will you stop buzzing?

Though you are hungry to hack down heaven and earth, it is peace now.
    We are as old and alone
As the last mammoth in white Siberia
Mateless alone plodding the tundra snow. Here is our peace."

                                                              But the axe
    giggled in his hand,
And presently the great disasters began to fall. The sky flashed like a fish's
    belly, earth shuddered,
And black rain fell. "Perhaps I was wrong," the old man said, "I am not
    alone yet —
But soon to be." The sun's face came red through smoke,
A young man came up the hill in the dark red light, and his livid face
Looked green against it. The old man met him and said, "What are you, a
    mammoth-hunter?" "Are you laughing?" he said,
"No one else laughs." "No," he said, "it was my axe. She
Has the last laugh." "Death is hunting us," he answered, and suddenly
    screamed:
"The fire, the blast and the rays. The whiffs of poisoned smoke that were
    cities. Are you utterly merciless?" "No,"
He answered, "care-free. I did warn you." "I know you," he screamed,
"You have betrayed us, you have betrayed humanity. You are one of those
    that killed hope and faith,
And sneered at Progress; you have killed the lies that men live by, and the
    earth
Is one huge tomb." "A beautiful one," he answered. "Look. Only look.
    Even in this bad light
What a beautiful one." Then the youth flashed a knife and stabbed at him,
But failed through weakness. The old man laughed and said, "How they
    love to be comforted.
Yet," he said, "it is more than comfort: it is deep peace and final joy

To know that the great world lives, whether man dies or not. The beauty of
    things is not harnessed to human
Eyes and the little active minds: it is absolute.
It is not for human titillation, though it serves that. It is the life of things,
And the nature of God. But those unhappy creatures will have to shrug off
Their human God and their human godlessness
To endure this time."

LII

             The day like a burning brazen wheel heavily
    revolved, and in the evening
A tribe of panting fugitives ran through the place: the old man caught one
    of them,
Who was too sick to flee. He crouched and vomited some green bile and
    gasped, "God curse the army
That got us in, and the air-force that can't protect us. They've done it
    now." "Done," he said, "What?" "Rammed their bull-heads
Into the fire-death. This is the end of the world." "Yea?" he said, "Of yours
    perhaps.
The mountains appear to be on their feet still. And down there the dark
    ocean nosing his bays and tide-breaks
Like a bear in a pit. As for the human race, we could do without it; but it
    won't die.
Oh: slightly scorched. It will slough its skin, and crawl forth
Like a serpent in spring." He moaned and cried out and answered, "What
    is that to me?
I am dying." "Come to the house," he answered, "poor man, and rest. You
    will not certainly die." But the man
Coughed blood and died.

　　　　　　The old man sat down beside his body in the
　　blood-brown day's-end
On the dark mountain, and more deeply gave himself
To contemplation of men's fouled lives and miserable deaths. "There is," he
　　said, "no remedy. — There are *two* remedies.
This man has got his remedy, and I have one. There is no third."
About midnight he slept, and arose refreshed
In the red dawn.

Hungerfield

1948-53

ANIMALS

At dawn a knot of sea-lions lies off the shore
In the slow swell between the rock and the cliff,
Sharp flippers lifted, or great-eyed heads, as they roll in the sea,
Bigger than draft-horses, and barking like dogs
Their all-night song. It makes me wonder a little
That life near kin to human, intelligent, hot-blooded, idle and singing, can
    float at ease
In the ice-cold midwinter water. Then, yellow dawn
Colors the south, I think about the rapid and furious lives in the sun:
They have little to do with ours; they have nothing to do with oxygen and
    salted water; they would look monstrous
If we could see them: the beautiful passionate bodies of living flame, batlike
    flapping and screaming,
Tortured with burning lust and acute awareness, that ride the storm-tides
Of the great fire-globe. They are animals, as we are. There are many other
    chemistries of animal life
Besides the slow oxidation of carbohydrates and amino-acids.

THE BEAUTY OF THINGS

To feel and speak the astonishing beauty of things — earth, stone and
    water,
Beast, man and woman, sun, moon and stars —
The blood-shot beauty of human nature, its thoughts, frenzies and
    passions,
And unhuman nature its towering reality —
For man's half dream; man, you might say, is nature dreaming, but rock
And water and sky are constant — to feel
Greatly, and understand greatly, and express greatly, the natural
Beauty, is the sole business of poetry.
The rest's diversion: those holy or noble sentiments, the intricate ideas,
The love, lust, longing: reasons, but not the reason.

HUNGERFIELD

If time is only another dimension, then all that dies
Remains alive; not annulled, but removed
Out of our sight. Una is still alive.
A few years back we are making love, greedy as hawks,
A boy and a married girl. A few years back
We are still young, strong-shouldered, joyfully laboring
To make our house. Then she, in the wide sea-window,
Endlessly enduring but not very patient,
Teaches our sons to read. She is still there,
Her beautiful pale face, heavy hair, great eyes
Bent to the book. And a few years back
We sit with our grown sons in the pitching motor-boat
Off Horn Head in Donegal, watching the sea-parrots
Tumble like clowns along the thousand-foot cliff, and the gannets like
    falling stars
Hawk at the sea: her great blue eyes are brimmed
With the wild beauty. Or we walk in Orkney,
Under the mystery of huge stones that stand there,
Raised high in the world's dawn by unknown men to forgotten Gods,
And see dimly through the deep northern dusk
A great skein of wild swans drop from the cloud
To the gray lake. She weeps a little for joy of beauty. Only the
    home-coming
To our loved rock over the gray and ageless Pacific
Makes her such joy.

                    It is possible that all these conditions of us
Are fixed points on the returning orbit of time and exist eternally . . .
It is no good. Una has died, and I

Am left waiting for death, like a leafless tree
Waiting for the roots to rot and the trunk to fall.

I never thought you would leave me, dear love.
I knew you would die sometime, I should die first —
But you have died. It is quite natural:
Because you loved life you must die first, and I
Who never cared much live on. Life is cheap, these days;
We have to compete with Asia, we are cheap as dust,
And death is cheap, but not hers. It is a common thing:
We die, we cease to exist, and our dear lovers
Fulfil themselves with sorrow and drunkenness, the quart at midnight
And the cups in the morning — or they go seeking
A second love: but you and I are at least
Not ridiculous.

September again. The gray grass, the gray sea,
The ink-black trees with white-bellied night-herons in them,
Brawling on the boughs at dusk, barking like dogs —
And the awful loss. It is a year. She has died: and I
Have lived for a long year on soft rotten emotions,
Vain longing and drunken pity, grief and gray ashes —
Oh child of God!

It is not that I am lonely for you. I am lonely:
I am mutilated, for you were part of me:
But men endure that. I am growing old and my love is gone:
No doubt I can live without you, bitterly and well.
That's not the cry. My torment is memory.
My grief to have seen the banner and beauty of your brave life
Dragged in the dust down the dim road to death. To have seen you
    defeated,

You who never despaired, passing through weakness
And pain —

              to nothing. It is usual I believe. I stood by; I believe
I never failed you. The contemptible thought, —
Whether I failed or not! *I* am not the one.
I was not dying. Is death bitter my dearest? It is nothing.
It is a silence. But dying can be bitter.

                      In this black year
I have thought often of Hungerfield, the man at Horse Creek,
Who fought with Death — bodily, said the witnesses, throat for throat,
Fury against fury in the dark —
And conquered him. If I had had the courage and the hope —
Or the pure rage —
I should be now Death's captive no doubt, not conqueror.
I should be with my dearest, in the hollow darkness
Where nothing hurts.

              I should not remember
Your silver-backed hand-mirror you asked me for,
And sat up in bed to gaze in it, to see your face
A little changed. You were still beautiful,
But not — as you'd been — a falcon. You said nothing; you sighed and laid
   down the glass; and I
Made a dog smile over a tearing heart,
Saying that you looked well.

                  The lies — the faithless hopeless unbelieved
  lies
While you lay dying.

For these reasons
I wish to make verses again, to drug memory,
To make it sleep for a moment. Never fear: I shall not forget you—
Until I am with you. The dead indeed forget all things.
And when I speak to you it is only play-acting
And self-indulgence: you cannot hear me, you do not exist. Dearest . . .
The story:

Horse Creek drives blithely down its rock bed
High on the thin-turfed mountain as we have seen it, but at the sea-mouth
Turns dark and fierce; black lava cliffs oppress it and it bites through them,
    the redwood trees in the gorge-throat
Are tortured dwarfs deformed by centuries of storm, broad trunks ancient
    as Caesar, and tattered heads
Hardly higher than the house. There is an angry concentration of power
    here, rock, storm and ocean;
The skies are dark, and darkness comes up like smoke
Out of the ground.

It was here that Hungerfield sat by his mother's
    bedside
In the great room at the house-top, under the heavy slant of the rafters: she
    had chosen this loft to lie in
Because it was as wide as the house, one could see west and east, ocean and
    mountain, from the low-silled windows
Without lifting from bed. But now her eyes were closed, she lay under
    opiate, gasping and muttering;
A tall woman, big-boned and aquiline-faced, with thin gray hair
And thin gray lips. She had been on her bed helpless for half a year
Like a ship on a reef.

Hungerfield sat beside her, his great shoulders
hunched like a vulture's.
There was nothing to do, and he felt his strength
Turn sour, unused. He had been a man of violence, and formed for
violence, but what could violence do here?
He could not even breathe for her. She was in fact drowning, here on the
bed; metastases of cancer
Had found the lungs.

This is my wound. This is what never time nor
change nor whiskey will heal:
To have watched the bladed throat-muscles lifting the breast-bone, frail
strands of exhausted flesh, laboring, laboring
Only for a little air. The poets who sing of life without remembering its
agony
Are fools or liars.

Hungerfield watched the winter day's-end die in dark
fire
In the west windows. He lighted the little coal-oil lamp in its bracket and
sat down again,
Hunched, full of helpless fury. He had fought in two so-called world-wars,
he had killed men, he knew all the tricks,
But who kills cancer?

He remembered when he was young, after his first
battle,
He had met Death in a hospital. Dreamed it, no doubt, dizzy with ether,
having three machine-gun slugs through his belly
And killed some men, two of them with his hands after he was wounded:
he had seen Death come in for him,

Into the French barn which they called a hospital. Death walked in human
    form, handsome and arrogant
Among the camp-cots, a long dark and contemptuous face, emperor of all
    men, choosing the souls
That he would take. It was nothing horrible; it was only absolute power
Taking his own. He beckoned: the obedient soul
Flew into his hand. Hungerfield thought that Death was right to despise
    them, they came like slaves. He thought,
"The poor bastards are tired after a battle" — he thought in his own
    language — "and their wounds hurt,
They want relief" — but at that moment the towering dark power
    approached him and made a sign,
Such as one makes to a dog, trained but not liked,
"Come here to me." Hungerfield felt such a wave of rage
That his wounds closed their mouths; the leonine adrenal glands poured
    their blind fury
Into his blood, and the great nerves of the brain
Gave eyes to it; he was suddenly well and powerful, with burning eyes:
    "Come and try me. We'll see
Which one's the dog." Death amazed glared at him.

                                                        He was like the
    defeated Roman dictator in the ruins of Carthage,
Alone, when the two soldiers found him, unarmed and guardless, his head
    worth an ass's load of gold:
He lifted his indomitable head, scowling, and they
Fled from him, like boys who have chased a rabbit in the bushes and find a
    bear. So Death stared at Hungerfield,
Death himself, with his empty black eyes and sneering astonished face, at
    such a mask of fury

That he preferred to avoid it. The blue eyes and the black ones fought in
    the air: it was Death's that failed.
He shrugged his high heavy shoulders and turned aside.

                                                              "My senseless
        dream,"
Hungerfield thought, "The loss of blood and the dregs of ether made a fine
    dream.
How I wish it were true." He looked at his mother's face, gasping and
    drained, and the thin lips
Black in the half-light. She had enormous vitality, he hoped she was not
    conscious. He heard light footsteps
Mounting the stair, and the door opened. It was his young wife Arab, a girl
    so blonde that her hair
Shone like another lamp at the end of the room, in the dark doorway. She
    stood a moment,
And came quietly and kissed him. "Won't you come down to supper,
    dearest, I will stay here." "No" he said,
And twitched his thumb toward the dark door: she patiently
Went out and closed it.

                Hungerfield was waiting for his enemy,
And coiled to strike. The conscious upper layer of his mind did not one
    moment believe
That Death had a throat and one could reach it, but his blood did. What
    he had seen he had seen. It was dangerous
For any person to come into the room: he had only by force and will kept
    his hands
From his dear Arab.

                Meanwhile the gentle click of the door-latch and
        Arab's entrance

Had touched the ears of the old woman dying; and slowly from
      nerve-complex to nerve-complex
Through the oxygen-starved brain crawled into her mind. She rolled her
      head on the pillow: "Who is that? There! There!"
Her tremulous finger pointing at shapes and shadows in the room twilight,
      her terrified eyes peering,
Following phantoms. "Nothing, mother, nothing: there's no one. Arab was
      here,
But she has gone." "I'm dying now," she said, "Can't you see?"
She gasped rapidly awhile and whispered, "Not a nice death: no air." "You
      will not die, mother.
You are going to get well."

                              It is a common lie to the dying, and I too
      have told it; but Hungerfield—
While his mind lied his blood and body believed. He had seen Death and
      he would see him again.
He was waiting for his enemy.

                                 Night deepened around the house; the
      sea-waves came up into the stream
And the stream fought them; the cliffs and standing rocks black and
      bone-still
Stood in the dark. There were no stars, there were some little sparkles of
      glowworms on the wet ground,
If you looked closely, and shapes of things, and the shifting foam-line. The
      vast phantasmagoria of night
Proceeded around that central throat begging for breath, and Hungerfield
Sat beside it, rigid and motionless as the rocks but his fingers twitching,
      hunched like a cat
To spring and tear.

Then the throat clicked and ceased. Hungerfield
looked at it; when he looked back
The monster was in the room. It was a column of heavy darkness in the
dim lamplight, but the arrogant head
Was clear to see. That damned sneer on his face. Hungerfield felt his hair
rise like a dog's
And heard Death saying scornfully: "Quiet yourself, poor man, make no
disturbance; it is not for you.
I have come for the old woman Alcmena Hungerfield, to whom death
Will be more kind than life." Hungerfield saw his throat and sprang at it.
But he was like a man swimming
A lake of corpses, the newly harvested souls from all earth's fields, faint
shrieks and whispers, Death's company,
He smote their dim heads with his hands and their bowels with his feet
And swam on them. He reached Death's monstrous flesh and they cleared
away. It had looked like a shadow,
It was harder than iron. The throat was missed, they stood and hugged each
other like lovers; Hungerfield
Drove his knee to the groin, Death laughed and said,
"I am not a man," and the awful embrace tightened
On the man's loins, he began to be bent backward, writhing and sobbing;
he felt the years of his age
Bite at his heart like rats: he was not yet fifty: but it is known that little by
little God abandons men
When thirty's past. Experience and cunning may perhaps increase
But power departs. He struck short at the throat and was bent further
backward, and suddenly
Flung himself back and fell, dragging Death down with him, twisting in the
fall, and weasel-quick on the floor
Tore at the throat: then the horrible stench and hopelessness of dead bodies
filled the dim air, he thought

He had wounded Death. What? The iron force and frame of nature with
  his naked hands? It bubbled and gasped,
"You fool — what have you done!" The iron flesh in his grip melted like a
  summer corpse, and turning liquid
Slid from his hands. He stood up foaming and groped for it, there was
  nothing. He saw in the stair-door
Arab, and Ross his brother, and the hired cattle-hand
Staring with eyes like moons. They had heard a chair crash and seen the
  fury; Arab had screamed like a hawk,
But no one heard her; now she stood moaning, gazing at him. But Ross
  entered the room and walked
Carefully wide around him to their mother's bed. The old woman was
  sitting up and breathed easily, saying
"I saw it all. Listen: they are taking him away." A strain of mournful music
  was heard, from the house
Flitting up the black night. This was the time — it was near midnight
  here — for a quarter of an hour
Nobody died. Disease went on, and the little peripheral prophetic wars, the
  famines and betrayals,
Neither man nor beast died, though they might cry for him. Death, whom
  we hate and love, had met a worse monster
And could not come.

      Hungerfield writhed his mouth striving to speak,
  and failed. He stood swaying,
And spoke loud but not clearly: "To kill the swine. How did he get — " He
  lurched a step toward the bed
And righted the fallen chair and sat on it, vulture-hunched and gray-faced.
  Then Arab ran to him,
But stopped a man's length distant: "Dear are you hurt?" "No," he said,
  "Keep away from me." "Oh God I'm in terror of you.

What have you done?" "Nothing. Nothing at all. I wiped the damned sneer
     off his face but he got away from me."
She with her hands on her throat like a leaf shaking:
"Who was it, who?" "Uh," he said, "Death. Can't you smell him? But the
     swine tricked me,
And slip-slopped out." He worked his hard hands and stared at them:
     "Ross: is there any liquor in the house?" "Drunkard,"
The old woman answered, "as your father was." "Yea?" he said. "You're
     better, uh?
You'll be all right, mother."

                              In the morning she dressed herself without
     help, in the dim of dawn,
And came down-stairs. Then Hungerfield, who had watched all night
     beside her and dozed in the graying, awoke
And followed down. He made a fire in the stove, and washed his hands and
     sliced meat; the old woman fried it
And brought the coffee to boil. Arab came in with her little son, who ran
     to Hungerfield:
"What happened, Daddy?" "Your grandmother has got well," he answered.
     "Then why is Mahmie so scared?" "Uh? No.
Your Mahmie's glad.— Arab," he said, "I know there's a little whiskey
     hidden in the house.
By God I want it." She smiled, and brought a half bottle from the
     linen-closet behind the linen. He said
To his mother, "Don't look, mother," and filled a water-glass full and
     drained it; she watched him with sidelong hatred
Through her gray brows. "Take a little more," she said, "and go blind—
While Ross goes in to Arab and Death to me." "I had my hands in him,"
     he said— "Uh?— What?
What did you say?" "I said that one of my two sons is a drunken bully, and
     the other defiles

His brother's wife." He stared at her and said, "You're ... pretty sick,
    mother. Forget it, Arab.
Something has happened to her." "Something has happened to me," the
    old woman answered. "I was dying and you filled the room
With beastly violence. My beautiful dark angel, my lord and love, who like
    a bridegroom had come for me,
You took him by the throat and killed him. Will you like it, Arab,
When he kills Ross?" The girl suddenly knelt to her, where she was sitting,
    and laid her hands on her knees:
"Please tell the truth, mother." "I'm telling the truth. From my windows I
    watched you. He will surely kill him,
He kills horses and men."

                            Ross at that moment sleepily came in the
    room. The old woman said
"How do you dare?" "What?" he said. "How do you dare to come in
    where our handy killer whom you dishonored
Waits for your throat?" Then Arab, her face withered half size and as white
    as paper, leaped up from kneeling:
"Quit lying, mother!" and furiously turned on Hungerfield, who had not
    stirred, "Be quiet!" she said, "Stand still!
It is a dream from hell." "No," he said quietly, "from the morphine.
They get delusions." He looked over Arab's head at his brother: "It's all
    right, Ross." And to his mother:
"I have to think you're mistaken." "Tell that sulphur-haired harlot," she
    screamed, pointing, "that I always hated her —
And well she earns it, I watched their antics.
I kept it quiet while I died, not to cause trouble: but you force me to live
    in this horrible world,
I'll see it straight. Here's a knife, Hawl —
If you're tired from last night." Suddenly she hooded her face with her
    hands

And wept in them. "Don't you believe me, Hawl? You are as quiet as a
    great cold stone standing there,
Standing there blind —" "I think you're still sick, mother. You will get
    well." "What have you done to me?" she answered,
"What awful thing? All that I said was false and I knew it.
You are all good and faithful, so far as I know. I hate life.
I hate the world. Oh children, pray for me.
Forgive me: I might have managed a horror here —
If your minds had been quick —" "I think you're still troubled by the drug,
    mother," he answered; and Arab's child
Began to wail like a little dog that has lost his master. He is all alone by the
    bombed house,
And they never come home; he sits in the empty gate, his mouth small and
    rounded, turned straight to heaven,
Starving, and wails.

                        The old woman watched Arab trying to quiet him,
And spoke, but no one through the crying of the child
Could hear her words. She tottered up from her chair and reached her
    hands to him, but Arab
Turned her shoulder against her, hugging him from her; then little Norrie
    (they called him) ceased crying,
But only sobbed, and looked up dimly through tears and said
"Granma." She reached her hands to him: "He knows already, he knows
    what life is, it breaks his heart;
But we shall be so good to him . . . Oh little pearl, little wet frightened
    face, flower in the rain,
Forgive me dear, I forgot
That I have someone to live for and love and pray for. Come to me dear."
    Hungerfield watched her carefully,
And said, "Let her have him, Arab." "No," she said, "I will not." His eyes
    darkened toward wrath. The old woman said,

"You know that I'd never hurt him, are you jealous of me? Will you come
   to Granma dearest?" He smiled at her
Over Arab's arm. "See now, he's not afraid of me" — "*I* am afraid of you,"
   Arab answered,
And took the child in her arms out of the room.

                                                    All that day
The old woman wandered about the house unreconciled, wringing her
   hands, peering at the household things,
Jealous of changes. Hungerfield remained near her, fearing that his great
   enemy might yet return —
Not hoping now — for his wrath was spent and his blood stilled,
Like the black ebb of the sea, cold, flat and still: deep-lying rocks, furred
   with dark weed and slime,
Rise from the slack. Suddenly she turned on him, crying wildly, "Let me
   alone! You've done enough to me.
D' y' have to follow me like a monstrous poodle all through the house?"
   He patiently answered, "Well, mother —
You nearly died . . ." "I died," she said, "and you dragged me back, to
   gloat on my misery.
Oh you are very brave with your strangler hands: your murderous hands
   tearing the holy angel of God —
God will punish you for it." "God-if-there-is-a-God," he answered wearily,
   "is neutral, it is nothing to him.
He has the stars." He made a thin smile on his mouth and said " — as
   America
Ought to have been." "He is punishing *me*," she said, "I know for what
   crime: life is the crime. I gave you
The horrible gift, I was ignorant and gave it.
I forced out that great head of yours between my thighs, bleeding and
   screaming, tearing myself to pieces:

I am now punished for it — and the monstrous plant that grew up out of
  my body is the stick to beat me:
That's you, that's you!" "You've had a bad time, mother," he answered
  patiently, "you'll soon be better I think.
Will you go up to town to the doctor with me? Or the young doctor
Can come down here." "I had one friend in the world," she answered,
  "loving and faithful: when he came you killed him.
I hate your hangdog face and your horrible hands: I cannot bear you: have
  mercy on me,
Get out of my sight." He felt a sharp gust of wrath returning: "I didn't kill
  him:
By God I *will*." "I am so homesick for him, his peace and love, it is pitiful,"
  she answered.
But she came more into control of herself
As the days passed. She stared at the sea a great deal; she watched the
  sunsets burn fierce and low, or the cormorants
Roosting on the offshore rock, their sharp black wings half spread, and
  black snaky throats; and the restless gulls
Riding the air-streams. She watched coldly the great south storms,
  tiger-striped, mud-yellow on purple black,
Rage in the offing. She seemed to find consolation in them. There is no
  consolation in humanity —
Though Arab sometimes allowed her (carefully in her presence) to hold
Little Norrie in her arms — only the acts and glory of unhuman nature or
  immortal God
Can ever give our hurts peace.

                    But Alcmena Hungerfield
Was not for peace; she had become Death's little dog, stolen from him
By the strong hand, yelping all night for her dear master. She stared at the
  sea a great deal, and her son

Came in from Monterey, stinking of whiskey but not altered by it: "Here's
    the paper, mother,"
He said, and laid it carefully on her knees, the Monterey newspaper
With headlines about the outflash of war in Asia. "We've got our nose
    caught in the door again.
We always do." "Well . . . what?" she answered, staring at him
As she stared at the sea. "I thought you might be int'rested," he answered,
    "Ross and I are too old
To go to it." She turned to an inner page and read,
Squinting her eyes to pull the print into shape, in the manner of old age
In lack of glasses. Suddenly she began to tremble and said "Thank God!
Why did you lie to me, Hawl? People still die." "So do the calves," he
    answered,
"Three or four every night and no reason known." "Why did you lie about
    it then? Look here" —
She thrust the paper at him, trembling and pointing — "Satella Venner died
    yesterday, my old friend.
I never liked the old woman but I'd like to go." "Uh," he said, "the
    funeral? Sure.
I'll take you there." "I want to see her dead face," she answered.

                                                                  In the
        night Arab sat up
Gasping with fear. "Wake up!" she whispered. He lay inert, softly
    breathing; she dug her finger-ends
Into his great shoulder and the softer flesh over the gullet: "Wake up for
    God's sake, Hawl.
He has come in!" Hungerfield brushed the little hand from his throat like a
    biting fly and said
Quietly "What?" "Something came in," she whispered through clicking
    teeth, "I can hear it padding

Inside the house." "Ah hell," he said impatiently; but slid from bed and
    went about the house naked,
Flashing the little electric torch into doors and corners, for the night was
    black. He went up-stairs
To the loft where his mother lay, and heard her on the bed quietly
    breathing. He drew the torchlight across,
And her eyes were wide open. "Are you all right, mother? It's Hawl." She
    made no answer. He stood awhile,
And said, "Good-night, mother." He went back to bed, and Arab
Sat huddled on it, small as a frightened child, hugging her knees to her
    throat. "Every night I hear it
Hulking around the house, pawing at the walls —
But to-night it came in." "Lie down," he said, "and be quiet." "Let her die,
    Hawl, she is so unhappy.
Oh let her die!" "Little fool," he said, "there was nobody. I'm sorry for
    her. Unhappy — what's that?
We win or *they* do." "I pray you, Hawl," she answered, "as if you were God:
    when *my* time comes
Oh let me die!"

                In the morning Hungerfield took his mother to
        Monterey, to her friend's funeral. They drove home
Late in the afternoon in the amber afterglow. The day had been like a
    festival. Hungerfield
Accepted his mother's mood and was patient with her, and had supper with
    her
On the Monterey fish-pier, they alone together. He thought that she
    seemed at last perhaps
Not quite unhappy. She was even willing to taste wine, in the bright wind
    on the platform
Over the gentle sea, and made no objection to him

That what he drank was more violent than wine. She had even urged him
    to it, saying that the day
Was a holiday; he failed to observe the calculation
In her old eyes.

                  They were driving the coast-road
Where it loops into Torres Canyon over great precipices in the heavy
    half-light. She said, "De Angulo
Went down here, he lay all night in the butt of the gorge, broken to bits
    but conscious,
Lying crushed on his dead son, under the engine of the car — let's try, let's
    try!" — she leaped at the steering-wheel,
Trying to slew it to the right, to the blue chasm: it was firm as rock. She
    like a mountain-cat
Fought with her finger-nails her son's hands; he said indulgently, "Don't be
    afraid, mother. *I'm* driving.
You are quite safe." "Safe in hell," she panted. "Oh — child —
What have I done to your hands!" They rounded the great headlands and
    came to Granite Point and drove down
Into the heavy fog clotted on Horse Creek.

                             The front of the house was
    empty and blind
When they came near; only at the side two dim-lit rectangles
Faintly reddened the fog-stream. The front door stood wide open, the steps
    were wet. Hungerfield
Helped his mother out of the car and they climbed them. A wavering light
Walked in the room: Ross came slow to the door, the smoke-blackened
    glass lamp skew in his hand;
He moved a chair with the other and said,
"Sit down, mother." "We've had supper," she said, "I'll go straight to bed."
    Hungerfield said fiercely:

"What's the matter? Where's Arab?" "Gone . . . gone," he answered. His
    face was like a skull, stripped and hollow, and the lamp
Rolled in his hand, so that his brother took it and said
"Are you drunk, Ross?" He mumbled, "Unq-uh," shaking his head. "Four
    more calves and your bay horse
Are — *dead*" — he screamed the word — "He comes behind you, Hawl,
He works 'n the dark" — his head still shaking, apparently he could not stop
    it; his hair and his shirt hung
As if they were soaked with water. Hungerfield said "You fool: talk sense.
Where has she gone?" "Oh, wait," he said, "for God's sake," pointing at the
    inner doorway; and gulped and shivered:
"In there." Hungerfield set the lamp down and strode to the door: it was
    pitch dark within: he said, "Arab?
Are you there, Arab?" Ross echoed him for no reason, saying loudly,
"Arab." His brother entered the room and they heard him fumbling in it,
    and his voice: "Where are you?" The old woman,
Leaning against the chairback said coolly: "Well, Ross,
What has happened?" "Mother," he said. He stood moving his lips without
    further words, and they heard Hungerfield
Move blind in the black room, and croak
In a strange voice, "Light, light!" They stood and stared at each other; then
    Ross opened his mouth and sucked
His lungs full, as if he were going to dive into deep water; he took the
    lamp from the table and carried it
To the dark room. The old woman followed him; and in the room quickly
    found matches, and lighted
A second lamp.

        Arab and little Norrie lay without life together on the
    narrow bed,
Phantoms of what they had been. Hungerfield stood above them, gaunt,
    straight, and staring

At Arab's discolored hair: their clothes and their yellow hair soaked with
    water and foam. Hungerfield said,
"I knew in the dark well enough." A frond of sea-weed stuck beside the
    child's nostrils, but Arab's face
Was clean pale marble; except her eyes were open, blue and suffused, and
    her half open mouth
Had foam inside. Hungerfield said heavily "How did they drown?" Ross
    answered:
"I dived and pulled them out. I pumped her ribs with my hands for an hour
    I think,
And she grew cold." Hungerfield heavily turned and said:
"Why did they go in water?" Ross answered, "He comes behind you, you
    know. I heard her screaming" — The old woman
Went around the bed and dropped by the child, her knees loud on the
    floor, her shaking gray head
On the child's breast. Ross said, "I was at the stable you know, unsaddling.
    I ran down and saw her
Running out on the rocks carrying the baby, crying and running. She
    thought someone was after her.
She either jumped or fell in." "So that's your help," Hungerfield said. He
    felt his arm swell and strike —
One blow, but the neck broke. They heard the head strike the floor and the
    body shuddering, and Hungerfield
Did not look down. The old woman lifted up her desert-dry eyes from the
    child's breast and said:
"You've done it *now.*" He stood considering the matter, hearing the rub of
    Ross's boots on the floor
As he twitched and was dying. "Ah," Hungerfield said, "I did it. Yes. My
    monstrous fault." "Oh," she answered,
"Now me, now me!" "The fool had to interfere," he answered. He
    knuckled his eyes and said heavily,

"I have another son in Alaska. I have no other brother, and no other love. Arab.

Arab alone." "You've had many," she answered eagerly. "Look," he said.

"Oh, she was beautiful, mother. She was always sweet, patient and cheerful; she loved Norrie — and now

She has death in her mouth."

As if his name had called him, Death

Stood in the room. Alcmena Hungerfield well remembered him,

The towering stature, the high thick shoulders and the arrogance, the long dark narrow face and deep eyes

Set close together. "Oh dear dark God," she said, "I am here. Gently I pray." But Hungerfield

Gazing at Arab's face did not hear her, and did not see

What came behind him and with a slight motion of the hand beckoned

To Ross to come. The old woman saw the unfleshed soul

Blind and erratic as a beetle flying rise from the body; it jigged and darted in the air, and swam

Into Death's hand, which crushed it. Hungerfield turned and said, "Is it you, horse-face? I haven't called you yet.

Come again in ten minutes." He turned away, saying "Arab is dead. My dear Arab is dead.

And Ross, who was quick and loyal, skillful with cattle and a great rider, is dead. My brave little man

Norrie is dead. — Hell, he gets three for one, and now the whole game, he has tricked me witless.

But I'll make a good sunset — We'll dance in fire, horse-face,

And go up yelling."

He went in the dark to the kitchen store-room and fetched the big can of coal-oil,

Going heavily like a rock walking, violent and certain; but in the darkness returning
He walked into a half open door, and with one hand
Tore it down from the hinges. He poured the coal-oil onto the floor and the bed and the wooden walls,
And turned a lamp to flaring and flung it
Into the oil-pool. Bright flame stood up. The old woman said, "Hawl...
Kill me before I burn." He said, "I've done enough and too much, mother.
Find a knife for yourself." She, thinly laughing: "You're not much help, are you? But I've lived with pain
As fish live with the sea. Or if it's tough I can drink smoke." But her courage after a time
Failed, and she fled from the house before the bright flame embraced her.

                                             Horse
   Creek sea-mouth at last for once
Was full of light; the fire drove away the fog, there was light everywhere. Black rock shone bright as blood;
The stream and the deep-throated waves of the ocean glittered with crimson lightnings, and the low cloud
Gaped like a lion's mouth, swallowing the flights of flame and the soul of a man. It is thus (and will be) that violence
Turns on itself, and builds on the wreck of violence its violent beauty, the spiring fire-fountain
And final peace: grim in the desert in the lion's carcass the hive of honey. But Alcmena Hungerfield
Hating both life and death fled from the place. She lived two years yet, Death remembering her son, and died
As others do.

      Here is the poem, dearest; you will never read it nor hear it. You were more beautiful

Than a hawk flying; you were faithful and a lion heart like this rough hero
  Hungerfield. But the ashes have fallen
And the flame has gone up; nothing human remains. You are earth and air;
  you are in the beauty of the ocean
And the great streaming triumphs of sundown; you are alive and well in the
  tender young grass rejoicing
When soft rain falls all night, and little rosy-fleeced clouds float on the
  dawn. — I shall be with you presently.

CARMEL POINT

The extraordinary patience of things!
This beautiful place defaced with a crop of suburban houses —
How beautiful when we first beheld it,
Unbroken field of poppy and lupin walled with clean cliffs;
No intrusion but two or three horses pasturing,
Or a few milch cows rubbing their flanks on the outcrop rock-heads —
Now the spoiler has come: does it care?
Not faintly. It has all time. It knows the people are a tide
That swells and in time will ebb, and all
Their works dissolve. Meanwhile the image of the pristine beauty
Lives in the very grain of the granite,
Safe as the endless ocean that climbs our cliff. — As for us:
We must uncenter our minds from ourselves;
We must unhumanize our views a little, and become confident
As the rock and ocean that we were made from.

DE RERUM VIRTUTE

I

Here is the skull of a man: a man's thoughts and emotions
Have moved under the thin bone vault like clouds
Under the blue one: love and desire and pain,
Thunderclouds of wrath and white gales of fear
Have hung inside here: and sometimes the curious desire of knowing
Values and purpose and the causes of things
Has coasted like a little observer air-plane over the images
That filled this mind: it never discovered much,
And now all's empty, a bone bubble, a blown-out eggshell.

II

That's what it's like: for the egg too has a mind,
Doing what our able chemists will never do,
Building the body of a hatchling, choosing among the proteins:
These for the young wing-muscles, these for the great
Crystalline eyes, these for the flighty nerves and brain:
Choosing and forming: a limited but superhuman intelligence,
Prophetic of the future and aware of the past:
The hawk's egg will make a hawk, and the serpent's
A gliding serpent: but each with a little difference
From its ancestors — and slowly, if it works, the race
Forms a new race: that also is a part of the plan
Within the egg. I believe the first living cell
Had echoes of the future in it, and felt
Direction and the great animals, the deep green forest
And whale's-track sea; I believe this globed earth
Not all by chance and fortune brings forth her broods,

But feels and chooses. And the Galaxy, the firewheel
On which we are pinned, the whirlwind of stars in which our sun is one
    dust-grain, one electron, this giant atom of the universe
Is not blind force, but fulfils its life and intends its courses. "All things are
    full of God.
Winter and summer, day and night, war and peace are God."

III

Thus the thing stands; the labor and the games go on —
What for? What for? — Am I a God that I should know?
Men live in peace and happiness; men live in horror
And die howling. Do you think the blithe sun
Is ignorant that black waste and beggarly blindness trail him like hounds,
And will have him at last? He will be strangled
Among his dead satellites, remembering magnificence.

IV

I stand on the cliff at Sovranes creek-mouth.
Westward beyond the raging water and the bent shoulder of the world
The bitter futile war in Korea proceeds, like an idiot
Prophesying. It is too hot in mind
For anyone, except God perhaps, to see beauty in it. Indeed it is hard to see
    beauty
In any of the acts of man: but that means the acts of a sick microbe
On a satellite of a dust-grain twirled in a whirlwind
In the world of stars. . . .
Something perhaps may come of him; in any event
He can't last long. — Well: I am short of patience
Since my wife died . . . and this era of spite and hate-filled half-worlds
Gets to the bone. I believe that man too is beautiful,

But it is hard to see, and wrapped up in falsehoods. Michael Angelo and the
    Greek sculptors —
How they flattered the race! Homer and Shakespeare —
How they flattered the race!

V

One light is left us: the beauty of things, not men;
The immense beauty of the world, not the human world.
Look — and without imagination, desire nor dream — directly
At the mountains and sea. Are they not beautiful?
These plunging promontories and flame-shaped peaks
Stopping the sombre stupendous glory, the storm-fed ocean? Look at the
    Lobos Rocks off the shore,
With foam flying at their flanks, and the long sea-lions
Couching on them. Look at the gulls on the cliff-wind,
And the soaring hawk under the cloud-stream —
But in the sage-brush desert, all one sun-stricken
Color of dust, or in the reeking tropical rain-forest,
Or in the intolerant north and high thrones of ice — is the earth not
    beautiful?
Nor the great skies over the earth?
The beauty of things means virtue and value in them.
It is in the beholder's eye, not the world? Certainly.
It is the human mind's translation of the transhuman
Intrinsic glory. It means that the world is sound,
Whatever the sick microbe does. But he too is part of it.

THE DEER LAY DOWN THEIR BONES

I followed the narrow cliffside trail half way up the mountain
Above the deep river-canyon. There was a little cataract crossed the path, flinging itself
Over tree roots and rocks, shaking the jewelled fern-fronds, bright bubbling water
Pure from the mountain, but a bad smell came up. Wondering at it I clambered down the steep stream
Some forty feet, and found in the midst of bush-oak and laurel,
Hung like a bird's nest on the precipice brink a small hidden clearing,
Grass and a shallow pool. But all about there were bones lying in the grass, clean bones and stinking bones,
Antlers and bones: I understood that the place was a refuge for wounded deer; there are so many
Hurt ones escape the hunters and limp away to lie hidden; here they have water for the awful thirst
And peace to die in; dense green laurel and grim cliff
Make sanctuary, and a sweet wind blows upward from the deep gorge. — I wish my bones were with theirs.

But that's a foolish thing to confess, and a little cowardly. We know that life
Is on the whole quite equally good and bad, mostly gray neutral, and can be endured
To the dim end, no matter what magic of grass, water and precipice, and pain of wounds,
Makes death look dear. We have been given life and have used it — not a great gift perhaps — but in honesty
Should use it all. Mine's empty since my love died — Empty? The flame-haired grandchild with great blue eyes
That look like hers? — What can I do for the child? I gaze at her and wonder what sort of man

In the fall of the world . . . I am growing old, that is the trouble. My
   children and little grandchildren
Will find their way, and why should I wait ten years yet, having lived
   sixty-seven, ten years more or less,
Before I crawl out on a ledge of rock and die snapping, like a wolf
Who has lost his mate? — I am bound by my own thirty-year-old decision:
   who drinks the wine
Should take the dregs; even in the bitter lees and sediment
New discovery may lie. The deer in that beautiful place lay down their
   bones: I must wear mine.

Last Poems

1953-62

THE SHEARS

A great dawn-color rose widening the petals around her gold eye
Peers day and night in the window. She watches us
Lighting lamps, talking, reading, and the children playing, and the dogs by
    the fire,
She watches earnestly, uncomprehending,
As we stare into the world of trees and roses uncomprehending,
There is a great gulf fixed. But even while
I gaze, and the rose at me, my little flower-greedy daughter-in-law
Walks with shears, very blonde and housewifely,
Through the small garden, and suddenly the rose finds herself rootless
    in-doors.
Now she is part of the life she watched.
So we: death comes and plucks us: we become part of the living earth
And wind and water we so loved. We are they.

PATRONYMIC

What ancestor of mine in wet Wales or wild Scotland
Was named Godfrey? — from which by the Anglo-French erosion
Geoffrey, Jeffry's son, Jeffries, Jeffers in Ireland —
A totally undistinguished man; the whirlwinds of history
Passed him and passed him by. They marked him no doubt,
Hurt him or helped him, they rolled over his head
And he I suppose fought back, but entirely unnoticed;
Nothing of him remains.

                    I should like to meet him,
And sit beside him, drinking his muddy beer,
Talking about the Norman nobles and parish politics
And the damned foreigners: I think his tales of woe
Would be as queer as ours, and even farther
From reality. His mind was as quick as ours
But perhaps even more credulous.

                     He was a Christian
No doubt — I am not dreaming back into prehistory —
And christened Godfrey, which means the peace of God.
He never in his life found it, when he died it found him.
He has been dead six or eight centuries,
Mouldering in some forgotten British graveyard, nettles and rain-slime.

Nettlebed: I remember a place in Oxfordshire,
That prickly name. I have twisted and turned on a bed of nettles
All my life long: an apt name for life: nettlebed.
Deep under it swim the dead, down the dark tides and bloodshot eras of
    time, bathed in God's peace.

BIRDS AND FISHES

Every October millions of little fish come along the shore,
Coasting this granite edge of the continent
On their lawful occasions: but what a festival for the sea-fowl.
What a witches' sabbath of wings
Hides the dark water. The heavy pelicans shout "Haw!" like Job's warhorse
And dive from the high air, the cormorants
Slip their long black bodies under the water and hunt like wolves
Through the green half-light. Screaming the gulls watch,
Wild with envy and malice, cursing and snatching. What hysterical greed!
What a filling of pouches! the mob-
Hysteria is nearly human — these decent birds! — as if they were finding
Gold in the street. It is better than gold,
It can be eaten: and which one in all this fury of wildfowl pities the fish?
No one certainly. Justice and mercy
Are human dreams, they do not concern the birds nor the fish nor eternal
    God.
However — look again before you go.
The wings and the wild hungers, the wave-worn skerries, the bright quick
    minnows
Living in terror to die in torment —
Man's fate and theirs — and the island rocks and immense ocean beyond,
    and Lobos
Darkening above the bay: they are beautiful?
That is their quality: not mercy, not mind, not goodness, but the beauty of
    God.

LET THEM ALONE

If God has been good enough to give you a poet
Then listen to him. But for God's sake let him alone until he is dead; no
  prizes, no ceremony,
They kill the man. A poet is one who listens
To nature and his own heart; and if the noise of the world grows up around
  him, and if he is tough enough,
He can shake off his enemies but not his friends.
That is what withered Wordsworth and muffled Tennyson, and would have
  killed Keats. That is what makes
Hemingway play the fool and Faulkner forget his art.

The unformed volcanic earth, a female thing,
Furiously following with the other planets
Their lord the sun: her body is molten metal pressed rigid
By its own mass; her beautiful skin, basalt and granite and the lighter
    elements,
Swam to the top. She was like a mare in her heat eyeing the stallion,
Screaming for life in the womb; her atmosphere
Was the breath of her passion: not the blithe air
Men breathe and live, but marsh-gas, ammonia, sulphured hydrogen,
Such poison as our remembering bodies return to
When they die and decay and the end of life
Meets its beginning. The sun heard her and stirred
Her thick air with fierce lightnings and flagellations
Of germinal power, building impossible molecules, amino-acids
And flashy unstable proteins: thence life was born,
Its nitrogen from ammonia, carbon from methane,
Water from the cloud and salts from the young seas,
It dribbled down into the primal ocean like a babe's urine
Soaking the cloth: heavily built protein molecules
Chemically growing, bursting apart as the tensions
In the inordinate molecule become unbearable —
That is to say, growing and reproducing themselves, a virus
On the warm ocean.

                    Time and the world changed,
The proteins were no longer created, the ammoniac atmosphere
And the great storms no more. This virus now
Must labor to maintain itself. It clung together
Into bundles of life, which we call cells,
With microscopic walls enclosing themselves

Against the world. But why would life maintain itself,
Being nothing but a dirty scum on the sea
Dropped from foul air? Could it perhaps perceive
Glories to come? Could it foresee that cellular life
Would make the mountain forest and the eagle dawning,
Monstrously beautiful, wings, eyes and claws, dawning
Over the rock-ridge? And the passionate human intelligence
Straining its limits, striving to understand itself and the universe to the last
    galaxy—
Flammantia moenia mundi, Lucretius wrote,
Alliterating like a Saxon—all those Ms mean majesty—
The flaming world-walls, far-flung fortifications of being
Against not-being.

                 For after a time the cells of life
Bound themselves into clans, a multitude of cells
To make one being—as the molecules before
Had made of many one cell. Meanwhile they had invented
Chlorophyll and ate sunlight, cradled in peace
On the warm waves; but certain assassins among them
Discovered that it was easier to eat flesh
Than feed on lean air and sunlight: thence the animals,
Greedy mouths and guts, life robbing life,
Grew from the plants; and as the ocean ebbed and flowed many plants and
    animals
Were stranded in the great marshes along the shore,
Where many died and some lived. From these grew all land-life,
Plants, beasts and men; the mountain forest and the mind of Aeschylus
And the mouse in the wall.

What is this thing called life?—But I believe

That the earth and stars too, and the whole glittering universe, and rocks
    on the mountain have life,
Only we do not call it so — I speak of the life
That oxydizes fats and proteins and carbo-
Hydrates to live on, and from that chemical energy
Makes pleasure and pain, wonder, love, adoration, hatred and terror: how
    do these things grow
From a chemical reaction?

                            I think they were here already. I think the
    rocks
And the earth and the other planets, and the stars and galaxies
Have their various consciousness, all things are conscious;
But the nerves of an animal, the nerves and brain
Bring it to focus; the nerves and brain are like a burning-glass
To concentrate the heat and make it catch fire:
It seems to us martyrs hotter than the blazing hearth
From which it came. So we scream and laugh, clamorous animals
Born howling to die groaning: the old stones in the dooryard
Prefer silence: but those and all things have their own awareness,
As the cells of a man have; they feel and feed and influence each other, each
    unto all,
Like the cells of a man's body making one being,
They make one being, one consciousness, one life, one God.

But whence came the race of man? I will make a guess.
A change of climate killed the great northern forests,
Forcing the manlike apes down from their trees,
They starved up there. They had been secure up there,
But famine is no security: among the withered branches blue famine:
They had to go down to the earth, where green still grew
And small meats might be gleaned. But there the great flesh-eaters,

Tiger and panther and the horrible fumbling bear and endless wolf-packs made life
A dream of death. Therefore man has those dreams,
And kills out of pure terror. Therefore man walks erect,
Forever alerted: as the bear rises to fight
So man does always. Therefore he invented fire and flint weapons
In his desperate need. Therefore he is cruel and bloody-handed and quick-witted, having survived
Against all odds. Never blame the man: his hard-pressed
Ancestors formed him: the other anthropoid apes were safe
In the great southern rain-forest and hardly changed
In a million years: but the race of man was made
By shock and agony. Therefore they invented the song called language
To celebrate their survival and record their deeds. And therefore the deeds they celebrate —
Achilles raging in the flame of the south, Baltic Beowulf like a fog-blinded sea-bear
Prowling the blasted fenland in the bleak twilight to the black water —
Are cruel and bloody. Epic, drama and history,
Jesus and Judas, Jenghiz, Julius Caesar, no great poem
Without the blood-splash. They are a little lower than the angels, as someone said. — Blood-snuffing rats:
But never blame them: a wound was made in the brain
When life became too hard, and has never healed.
It is there that they learned trembling religion and blood-sacrifice,
It is there that they learned to butcher beasts and to slaughter men,
And hate the world: the great religions of love and kindness
May conceal that, not change it. They are not primary but reactions
Against the hate: as the eye after feeding on a red sunfall
Will see green suns.

The human race is one of God's sense-organs,
Immoderately alerted to feel good and evil
And pain and pleasure. It is a nerve-ending,
Like eye, ear, taste-buds (hardly able to endure
The nauseous draught) it is a sensory organ of God's.
As Titan-mooded Lear or Prometheus reveal to their audience
Extremes of pain and passion they will never find
In their own lives but through the poems as sense-organs
They feel and know them: so the exultations and agonies of beasts and men
Are sense-organs of God: and on other globes
Throughout the universe much greater nerve-endings
Enrich the consciousness of the one being
Who is all that exists. This is man's mission:
To find and feel; all animal experience
Is a part of God's life. He would be balanced and neutral
As a rock on the shore, but the red sunset-waves
Of life's passions fling over him.
Slowly, perhaps, man may grow into it —
Do you think so? This villainous king of beasts, this deformed ape? — He
    has mind
And imagination, he might go far
And end in honor. The hawks are more heroic but man has a steeper mind,
Huge pits of darkness, high peaks of light,
You may calculate a comet's orbit or the dive of a hawk, not a man's mind.

THE OCEAN'S TRIBUTE

Yesterday's sundown was very beautiful — I know it is out of fashion to
say so, I think we are fools
To turn from the superhuman beauty of the world and dredge our own
minds — it built itself up with ceremony
From the ocean horizon, smoked amber and tender green, pink and purple
and vermilion, great ranks
Of purple cloud, and the pink rose-petals over all and through all; but the
ocean itself, cold slate-color,
Refused the glory. Then I saw a pink fountain come up from it,
A whale-spout; there were ten or twelve whales quite near the deep shore,
playing together, nuzzling each other,
Plunging and rising, lifting luminous pink pillars from the flat ocean to the
flaming sky.

ON AN ANTHOLOGY OF CHINESE POEMS

Beautiful the hanging cliff and the wind-thrown cedars, but they have no
   weight.
Beautiful the fantastically
Small farmhouse and ribbon of rice-fields a mile below; and billows of mist
Blow through the gorge. These men were better
Artists than any of ours, and far better observers. They loved landscape
And put man in his place. But why
Do their rocks have no weight? They loved rice-wine and peace and
   friendship,
Above all they loved landscape and solitude.
— Like Wordsworth. But Wordsworth's mountains have weight and mass,
   dull though the song be.
It is a moral difference perhaps?

The mathematicians and physics men
Have their mythology; they work alongside the truth,
Never touching it; their equations are false
But the things *work*. Or, when gross error appears,
They invent new ones; they drop the theory of waves
In universal ether and imagine curved space.
Nevertheless their equations bombed Hiroshima.
The terrible thing *worked*.

                    The poet also
Has his mythology. He tells you the moon arose
Out of the Pacific basin. He tells you that Troy was burnt for a vagrant
Beautiful woman, her face launched a thousand ships.
It is unlikely: it might be true: but church and state
Depend on more peculiarly impossible myths:
That all men are born free and equal: consider that!
And that a wandering Hebrew poet named Jesus
Is the God of the universe. Consider that!

VULTURE

I had walked since dawn and lay down to rest on a bare hillside
Above the ocean. I saw through half-shut eyelids a vulture wheeling high up
   in heaven,
And presently it passed again, but lower and nearer, its orbit narrowing, I
   understood then
That I was under inspection. I lay death-still and heard the flight-feathers
Whistle above me and make their circle and come nearer. I could see the
   naked red head between the great wings
Beak downward staring. I said "My dear bird we are wasting time here.
These old bones will still work; they are not for you." But how beautiful
   he'd looked, gliding down
On those great sails; how beautiful he looked, veering away in the sea-light
   over the precipice. I tell you solemnly
That I was sorry to have disappointed him. To be eaten by that beak and
   become part of him, to share those wings and those eyes —
What a sublime end of one's body, what an enskyment; what a life after
   death.

GRANDDAUGHTER

And here's a portrait of my granddaughter Una
When she was two years old: a remarkable painter,
A perfect likeness; nothing tricky nor modernist,
Nothing of the artist fudging his art into the picture,
But simple and true. She stands in a glade of trees with a still inlet
Of blue ocean behind her. Thus exactly she looked then,
A forgotten flower in her hand, those great blue eyes
Asking and wondering.

                Now she is five years old
And found herself; she does not ask any more but commands,
Sweet and fierce-tempered; that light red hair of hers
Is the fuse for explosions. When she is eighteen
I'll not be here. I hope she will find her natural elements,
Laughter and violence; and in her quiet times
The beauty of things — the beauty of transhuman things,
Without which we are all lost. I hope she will find
Powerful protection and a man like a hawk to cover her.

THE EPIC STARS

The heroic stars spending themselves,
Coining their very flesh into bullets for the lost battle,
They must burn out at length like used candles;
And Mother Night will weep in her triumph, taking home her heroes.
There is the stuff for an epic poem —
This magnificent raid at the heart of darkness, this lost battle —
We don't know enough, we'll never know.
Oh happy Homer, taking the stars and the Gods for granted.

Goethe, they say, was a great poet, Pindar, perhaps, was a great poet,
   Shakespeare and Sophocles
Stand beyond question. I am thinking of the few, the fortunate,
Who died fulfilled.

                     I think of Christopher Marlowe, stabbed through the
   eye in a tavern brawl by a bawdy serving-man,
Spilling his youth and brains on the greasy planks. I think of young Keats,
Wild with his work unfinished, sobbing for air, dying in Rome. I think of
   Edgar Poe
And Robert Burns. I think of Lucretius leaving his poem unfinished to go
   and kill himself. I think of Archilochus
Grinning with crazy bitterness. I think of Virgil
In despair of his life-work, begging his friends to destroy it, coughing his
   lungs out.

                Yet the young men
Still come to me with their books and manuscripts,
Eager to be poets, eager to be praised, eager as Keats. They are mad I
   think.

HAND

Fallen in between the tendons and bones
It looks like a dead hand. Poor hand a little longer
Write, and see what comes forth from a dead hand.

OYSTERS

On the wide Texan and New Mexican ranches
They call them prairie oysters, but here on the Pacific coast-range,
Mountain oysters. The spring round-up was finished,
The calves had been cut and branded and their ears notched,
And staggered with their pain up the mountain. A vast rose and gold
    sunset, very beautiful, made in April,
Moved overhead. The men had gone down to the ranch-house,
But three old men remained by the dying branding-fire
At the corral gate, Lew Clark and Gilchrist
And Onofrio the Indian; they searched the trampled
Earth by the fire, gathering the testicles of gelded bull-calves
Out of the bloody dust; they peeled and toasted them
Over the dying branding-fire and chewed them down,
Grinning at each other, believing that the masculine glands
Would renew youth.

               The unhappy calves bawled in their pain and their
    mothers answered them.
The vast sunset, all colored, all earnest, all golden, withdrew a little higher
    but made a fierce heart
Against the sea-line, spouting a sudden red glare like the eye of God. The
    old men
Chewed at their meat.

               I do not believe the testicles of bull-calves
Will make an old man young again, but if they could —
What fools those old men are. Age brings hard burdens,
But at worst cools hot blood and sets men free

From the sexual compulsions that madden youth.
Why would they dip their aging bodies again
Into that fire? For old men death's the fire.
Let them dream beautiful death, not women's loins.

It nearly cancels my fear of death, my dearest said,
When I think of cremation. To rot in the earth
Is a loathsome end, but to roar up in flame — besides, I am used to it,
I have flamed with love or fury so often in my life,
No wonder my body is tired, no wonder it is dying.
We had great joy of my body. Scatter the ashes.

Prose

PREFACE, *Tamar*
[1923]

Poetry has been regarded as a refuge from life, where dreams may heal the wounds of reality; and as an ornament of life; and as a diversion, mere troubadour amusement; and poetry has been in fact refuge and ornament and diversion, but poetry in its higher condition is none of these; not a refuge but an intensification, not an ornament but essential, not a diversion but an incitement. As presenting the universal beauty poetry is an incitement to life; an incitement to action, because our actions are a part of that beauty; an incitement to contemplation, because it serves to open our intelligence and senses to that beauty.

The poetry that means to be amusing, or ornamental, or a refuge, has its own licenses; it may play the clown or the dreamer, it may chatter like a fashionable person, or mince out bits of life for its enjoyment, like a dilettante. Its one condition is to be what it sets out to be, amusing, or ornamental, or a refuge. But the higher form of poetry has laws, many of them too basic to be conscious; there are three to be spoken of because they are so much ignored: this poetry must be rhythmic, and must deal with permanent things, and must avoid affectation.

The superfluousness of imitative poetry is quite clearly recognized nowadays (in principle) by everyone who thinks on the subject; and this is a gain; but a second-rate mind is sure to confuse eccentricity with originality; its one way of saying something new is to deform what it has to say; like the bobbed fox it sets a fashion for third-rate minds; and these are inevitably imitative, only now they follow a bad model instead of a good one. Here, I believe, is the origin of those extraordinary affectations which distinguish so much of what is called modern poetry. But this is not a disease of adults; and all to say further on the subject is that one's clearest thinking is not certain enough, nor one's most natural choice of words appropriate enough, for the passionate presentment of beauty which is poetry's function. If we alter thought or expression for any of the hundred reasons: in order to seem original, or to seem sophisticated, or to conform to a fashion, or to startle the citizenry, or because we fancy ourselves decadent, or merely to avoid commonplace: for whatever reason we alter them, for that reason they are made false. They have fled from reality.

As to the necessity of dealing with permanent things I have spoken in the verses called "Point Joe," in this volume; and need but add that permanence is only another aspect of reality; a railroad, for example, is not real as a mountain is; it is actual, in its fantastic way, for a century or two; but it is not real; in most of the human past and most of the human future it is not existent. (Novelty is in itself no bar to poetic quality; permanence is the condition. An airplane is as poetic as a plow or a ship; it is not existent in the human past except as a most ancient of dreams, but it is existent, in some form or other, in all the human future. It is a real thing, not a temporary expedient, but the incarnation in metal and tissue of a permanent human faculty.) Most of our inventions are mere expedients, or the possible essential in them remains hidden; and here is what makes the life of modern cities barren of poetry; it is not a lasting life; and it is lived among unrealities. A life immensely fantastic; often highly romantic; but what is fantastic is not poetic; and what is romantic is not usually poetic, though people think it is.

This poetry must be rhythmic. By rhythm I do not mean the dissolved and unequal cadences of good prose, nor the capricious divisions of what is called free verse, (both these being sometimes figuratively spoken of as rhythmic), but a movement as regular as meter, or as the tides. A tidal recurrence, whether of quantity or accent, or of both, or of syllables and rhyme as in French verse, or of syllables and rhyme and tone as in Chinese verse, or of phrase and thought as in old Hebrew verse, has always been the simplest and inevitable one of the qualities of poetry. A reason is not far to seek. Recurrence, regular enough to be rhythmic, is the inevitable quality of life, and of life's environment. Prose belongs rather to that indoor world where lamplight abolishes the returns of day and night, and we forget the seasons. Human caprice, the volatile and superficial part of us, can only live sheltered. Poetry does not live in that world but in all the larger, and poetry cannot speak without remembering the turns of the sun and moon, and the rhythm of the ocean, and the recurrence of human generations, the returning waves of life and death. Our daily talk is prose; we do not often talk about real things, even when we live with them; but about factitious things; expedients, manners, pastimes, and aspects of personality that are not real because they are superficial or exceptional.

So we are brought a third time to the question of reality. It is the distinction of all the higher sort of poetry that it deals in the manner of reality with real things; not with abstract qualities; but not either with fantasies nor pretences, nor with things actual indeed, but so temporary and exceptional that they are not to be counted among realities.

The two earliest of the longer poems in this volume were written six years ago; the manner and versification of the story about Myrtle Cartwright, and the Theocritan echoes of "Fauna," do not much please me now; but the latter is retained for a geographical sort of richness that closes it, and the other because it is part of a series and seems useful to the purpose of the series: to make apparent the essential beauty in conditions and events of life that from the ordinary point of view appear merely painful, or wicked, or comical.

TOR HOUSE, CARMEL, CALIFORNIA
AUGUST, 1923.

INTRODUCTION, *Roan Stallion, Tamar and Other Poems*
[1935]

My publisher wrote that if I wanted to revise anything, here was my chance, for new plates would have to be made. I thought in a kind of panic, "Of course I ought to revise, but how terrible!" for it is a pleasure to write, but after a thing has been written I hate to see it again; poems are the sort of children that it is delightful to beget, dreary to educate. Yet it seemed clearly a duty. So I made terms with my conscience and my publisher: "If you'll let me off the revising I'll write an introduction instead; that will only take a few hours, the other would take weeks." This is the introduction, a mere conscience-penny.

It might be entitled "Meditation by a Water-main." We used to walk in the Del Monte Forest in the days when it was uninhabited. Near the place where we climbed a fence to enter the woods there was a deep ravine, bridged by the water-main that ran from the dam up the Carmel Valley to the reservoir lake back of Monterey. A wooden trestle supported the big pipe where it crossed the gorge, and this was our bridge into the farther woods; but we had to scramble carefully, for wild bees hived half way over, in the timbers against the pipe. And it was harder coming back; I had to make two crossings then, one to carry the dog, and one with the firewood that we brought home from the forest.

This was twenty-one years ago, and I am thinking of a bitter meditation that worked in my head one day while I returned from the woods and was making my two crossings by the pipe-line. It had occurred to me that I was already a year older than Keats when he died, and I too had written many verses, but they were all worthless. I had imitated and imitated, and that was all.

I have never been ambitious, but it seemed unpleasant just the same to have accomplished nothing, but exactly nothing, along the only course that permanently interested me. There are times when one forgets for a moment that life's value is life, any further accomplishment is of very little importance comparatively. This was one of those times and I can still taste its special bitterness; I was still quite young at twenty-seven.

When I had set down the dog and went back over our bridge for the bundle of firewood my thoughts began to be more practical, not more pleasant. This originality, without which a writer of verses is only a verse-writer, is there any way to attain it? The more advanced contemporary poets were attaining it by going farther and farther along the way that perhaps Mallarmé's aging dream had shown them, divorcing poetry from reason and ideas, bringing it nearer to music, finally to astonish the world with what would look like pure nonsense and would be pure poetry. No doubt these lucky writers were imitating each other, instead of imitating Shelley and Milton as I had done, . . . but no, not all of them, someone must be setting the pace, going farther than anyone had dared to go before. Ezra Pound perhaps? Whoever it was, was *original*.

Perhaps this was the means to attain originality: to make a guess which way literature is going, and go there first. Read carefully your contemporaries, chart their line of advance, then hurry and do what they are going to do next year. And if they drew their inspiration from France, I could read French as well as any of them.

(This was not all quite seriously thought, partly I was just tormenting myself. But a young man is such a fool in his meditations, at least I was, let me say for shame's sake that I have not considered "trends" since turning thirty, nor been competitive either.)

But now, as I smelled the wild honey midway the trestle and meditated the direction of modern poetry, my discouragement blackened. It seemed to me that Mallarmé and his followers, renouncing intelligibility in order to concentrate the music of poetry, had turned off the road into a narrowing lane. Their successors could only make further renunciations; ideas had gone, now meter had gone, imagery would have to go; then recognizable emotions would have to go; perhaps at last even words might have to go or give up their meaning, nothing be left but musical syllables. Every advance required the elimination of some aspect of reality, and what could it profit me to know the direction of modern poetry if I did not like the direction? It was too much like putting out your eyes to cultivate the sense of hearing, or cutting off the right hand to develop the left. These austerities were not for me; originality by amputation was too painful for me.

But — I thought — everything has been said already; there seems to be only this way to go on. Unless one should do like the Chinese with their heavy past: eliminate one's own words from the poem, use quotations from books as the elder poets used imagery from life and nature, make something new by putting together a mosaic of the old. A more promising kind of amputation; one or two noble things might be done that way, but not more, for the trick would pall on western ears; and not by me, who never could bear the atmosphere of libraries since I escaped from my studious father's control.

I laid down the bundle of sticks and stood sadly by our bridge-head. The sea-fog was coming up the ravine, fingering through the pines, the air smelled of the sea and pine-resin and yerba buena, my girl and my dog were with me ... and I was standing there like a poor God-forsaken man-of-letters, making my final decision not to become a "modern." I did not want to become slight and fantastic, abstract and unintelligible. I was doomed to go on imitating dead men, unless some impossible wind should blow me emotions or ideas, or a point of view, or even mere rhythms, that had not occurred to them. There was nothing to do about it.

We climbed the fence and went home through the evening-lighted trees. I must have been a charming companion that afternoon.

This book began to be written three or four years later. I was past my green-sickness by that time, and did not stop to think whether the verses were original or followed a tendency, or would find a reader. Nor have I ever considered whether they deserved to find one.

FOREWORD, *The Selected Poetry of Robinson Jeffers*
[1938]

This book presents in one volume about half of my published work. In making the selection it was easy to eliminate the poems published in 1912 and 1916, which were only preparatory exercises, to say the best for them; and it was easy to omit a number of shorter poems from later volumes. After that the selection became more or less arbitrary. Several of the longer poems had to be omitted, for I have no desire to publish a "collected works" at this time, but there appears little reason to choose among them. "The Women at Point Sur" seems to me — in spite of grave faults — the most inclusive, and poetically the most intense, of any of my poems; it is omitted from this selection because it is the least understood and least liked; and because it is the longest. "Dear Judas" also was not liked and is therefore omitted, though I think it has value if any of these poems has. "Such Counsels You Gave to Me" is omitted in order to make room for a number of shorter pieces from the same volume. The omission of "Cawdor" is purely arbitrary and accidental; I had finally to choose between this and "Thurso's Landing"; and there was no ground for choice; I simply drew lots in my mind.

The arrangement of the book is merely chronological; the long poems are presented in the order of their writing, the short ones in groups as they were first published. The earliest of the long poems was written I think in 1921 and 1922; the earliest of the short ones in 1917. This is "The Songs of the Dead Men to the Three Dancers" — choruses from a wartime play — reprinted here only as a sample of the metrical experiments that occupied my mind for awhile.

A good friend of mine, who is also my publisher, wants me to turn this foreword to some account; he says that a number of people have written pro and con about my verses, and it is high time for the author himself to say something. Very likely. But I do not wish to commend or defend them, though sufficiently attacked; and it seems to me that their meaning is not obscure. Perhaps a few notes about their origins may be of interest, to anyone who is interested in the verses themselves.

Long ago, before anything included here was written, it became evident to me that poetry — if it was to survive at all — must reclaim some of the power and reality that it was so hastily surrendering to prose. The modern French poetry of that time, and the most "modern" of the English poetry, seemed to me thoroughly defeatist, as if poetry were in terror of prose, and desperately trying to save its soul from the victor by giving up its body. It was becoming slight and fantastic, abstract, unreal, eccentric; and was not even saving its soul, for these are generally anti-poetic qualities. It must reclaim substance and sense, and physical and psychological reality. This feeling has been basic in my mind since then. It led me to write narrative poetry, and to draw subjects from contemporary life; to present aspects of life that modern poetry had generally avoided; and to attempt the expression of philosophic and scientific ideas in verse. It was not in my mind to open new fields for poetry, but only to reclaim old freedom.

Still it was obvious that poetry and prose are different things; their provinces overlap, but must not be confused. Prose, of course, is free of all fields; it seemed to me, reading poetry and trying to write it, that poetry is bound to concern itself chiefly with permanent things and the permanent aspects of life. That was perhaps the great distinction between them, as regards subject and material. Prose can discuss matters of the moment; poetry must deal with things that a reader two thousand years away could understand and be moved by. This excludes much of the circumstance of modern life, especially in the cities. Fashions, forms of machinery, the more complex social, financial, political adjustments, and so forth, are all ephemeral, exceptional; they exist but will never exist again. Poetry must concern itself with (relatively) permanent things. These have poetic value; the ephemeral have only news-value.

Another formative principle came to me from a phrase of Nietzsche's: "The poets? The poets lie too much." I was nineteen when the phrase stuck in my mind; a dozen years passed before it worked effectively, and I decided not to tell lies in verse. Not to feign any emotion that I did not feel; not to pretend to believe in "optimism" or "pessimism," or unreversible "progress"; not to say anything because it was popular, or generally accepted, or fashionable in intellectual circles, unless I myself believed it; and not to believe easily. These negatives limit the field; I am not recommending them but for my own occasions.

Here are three principles that conditioned the verse in this book before it was written; but it would not have been written at all except for certain accidents that changed and directed my life. (Some kind of verse I should have written, of course, but not this kind.) The first of these accidents was my meeting with the woman to whom this book is dedicated, and her influence, constant since that time. My nature is cold and undiscriminating; she excited and focussed it, gave it eyes and nerves and sympathies. She never saw any of my poems until it was finished and typed, yet by her presence and conversation she has co-authored every one of them. Sometimes I think there must be some value in them, if only for that reason. She is more like a woman in a Scotch ballad, passionate, untamed and rather heroic, — or like a falcon — than like any ordinary person.

A second piece of pure accident brought us to the Monterey coast mountains, where for the first time in my life I could see people living — amid magnificent unspoiled scenery — essentially as they did in the Idyls or the Sagas, or in Homer's Ithaca. Here was life purged of its ephemeral accretions. Men were riding after cattle, or plowing the headland, hovered by white sea-gulls, as they have done for thousands of years, and will for thousands of years to come. Here was contemporary life that was also permanent life; and not shut from the modern world but conscious of it and related to it; capable of expressing its spirit, but unencumbered by the mass of poetically irrelevant details and complexities that make a civilization.

By this time I was nearing thirty, and still a whole series of accidents was required to stir my lazy energies to the point of writing verse that seemed to be — whether good or bad — at least my own voice.

So much for the book as a whole: a few notes may be added as to the origins of particular poems.

"Tamar" grew up from the biblical story, mixed with a reminiscence of Shelley's "Cenci," and from the strange, introverted and storm-twisted beauty of Point Lobos. "Roan Stallion" originated from an abandoned cabin that we discovered in a roadless hollow of the hills. When later we asked about its history no one was able to tell us anything except that the place had been abandoned ever since its owner was killed by a stallion.

This is the only one of my poems of which I can remember clearly the moment of conception. I had just finished "The Tower Beyond Tragedy" and was looking about for another subject — which was to be contemporary, because I repented of using a Greek story when there were so many new ones at hand. I was quarrying granite under the sea-cliff to build our house with, and slacking on the job sat down on a wet rock to look at the sunset and think about my next poem. The stallion and the desolate cabin came to mind; then immediately, for persons of the drama, came the Indian woman and her white husband, real persons whom I had often seen driving through our village in a ramshackle buggy. The episode of the woman swimming her horse through a storm-swollen ford at night came also; it was part of her actual history. . . . So that when I stood up and began to handle stones again, the poem had already made itself in my mind.

"The Tower Beyond Tragedy" was suggested to me by the imposing personality of a Jewish actress who was our guest for a day or two. She was less than successful on the stage, being too tall, and tragic in the old-fashioned manner; but when she stood up in our little room under the low ceiling and recited a tragic ballad — "Edward, Edward" — for a few people gathered there, the experience made me want to build a heroic poem to match her formidable voice and rather colossal beauty. I thought these would be absurdly out of place in any contemporary story, so I looked back toward the feet of Aeschylus, and cast this woman for the part of Cassandra in my poem.

"Apology for Bad Dreams" originated from the episode of the woman and her sons torturing a horse, a thing which happened on our coast. Cruelty is a part of nature, at least of human nature, but it is the one thing that seems unnatural to us; the tension of the mind trying to recognize cruelty and evil as part of the sum of things is what made the poem. (This woman a few years later was killed by another horse: an unusual piece of justice.)

The story of "The Loving Shepherdess" was suggested by a foot-note in one of the novels of Walter Scott, which I was reading aloud to our sons. I cannot remember which novel it was. The note tells about a half-insane girl who wandered up and down through Scotland with a dwindling flock of sheep, that perished one by one.

The story of "Thurso's Landing" was suggested entirely, I think, by the savage beauty of the canyon and sea-cliff that are its scene, and by the long-abandoned lime-works there. I cannot remember planning the story at all. When we first saw this place, in 1914, the heavy steel cable was hanging across the sky of the canyon, still supporting a rusted skip. During the war it was taken down for scrap-iron.

The phrase "Give Your Heart to the Hawks" swam about in my mind for several years as a good title for a poem; then one day I noticed the scene and farmhouse that seemed to fit the title, in Sycamore Canyon, just south of Big Sur; and between the title and the scene the poem unrolled itself.

"At the Birth of an Age" had a more calculated origin. I was considering the main sources of our civilization, and listed them roughly as Hebrew-Christian, Roman, Greek, Teutonic. Then it occurred to me that I had written something about the Hebrew-Christian source in "Dear Judas"; and that "The Tower Beyond Tragedy" might pass for a recognition of the Greek source. About the Roman source I should probably never write anything, for it is less sympathetic to me. Recognition of the Teutonic source might be an interesting theme for a new poem, I thought; . . . and the Volsung Saga might serve for fable. Only as the poem progressed did the Teutonic element begin to warp and groan under the tension of Christian influence. The symbol of the self-tortured God, that closes the poem, had appeared to me long before in "Apology for Bad Dreams" and in "The Women at Point Sur" — Heautontimoroumenos, the self-tormentor — but it stands most clearly in the self-hanged Odin of Norse mythology.

PREFACE, *The Double Axe and Other Poems*
[original version, 1947]

The first part of "The Double Axe" was written during the war, and finished a year before the war ended. The earliest of the shorter poems were written before America officially entered the war; but it had long been evident that our government was promoting war — not with threats, like the Germans, but with suggestion and pressure and personal promises — and would take part in it. Yet it was equally evident that America's intervention in the European war of 1914 had been bad for America and really fatal for Europe; as it will be clear a few years from now that our intervention in the war of 1939 has been even terribly worse in effect.

But this book is not mainly concerned with the war, and perhaps it ought to be called "The Inhumanist" rather than "The Double Axe." It presents, more explicitly than previous poems of mine, a new attitude, a new manner of thought and feeling, which came to me at the end of the war of 1914, and has since been tested in the confusions of peace and a second world-war, and the hateful approach of a third; and I believe it has truth and value. It is based on a recognition of the astonishing beauty of things and their living wholeness, and on a rational acceptance of the fact that mankind is neither central nor important in the universe; our vices and blazing crimes are as insignificant as our happiness. We know this, of course, but it does not appear that any previous one of the ten thousand religions and philosophies has realized it. An infant feels himself to be central and of primary importance; an adult knows better; it seems time that the human race attained to an adult habit of thought in this regard. The attitude is neither misanthropic nor pessimist nor irreligious, though two or three people have said so, and may again; but it involves a certain detachment.

A man whose mental processes continually distort and prevent each other, so that his energy is devoted to introversion and the civil wars of the mind, is an insane man, and we pity him. But the human race is similarly insane. More than half its energy, and at the present civilized level nine-tenths of its energy, are devoted to self-interference, self-frustration, self-incitement, self-tickling, self-worship. The waste is enormous; we are able to commit and endure it because we are so firmly established on the planet; life is actually so easy, that it requires only a slight fraction of our common energies. The rest we discharge onto each other — in conflict and charity, love, jealousy, hatred, competition, government, vanity and cruelty, and that puerile passion the will to power, — or for amusement. Certainly human relationships are necessary and desirable; but not to this extent. This is a kind of collective onanism, pathetic and ridiculous, or at noblest a tragic incest, and so I have represented it.

But we have all this excess energy: what should we do with it? We could take a walk, for instance, and admire landscape: that is better than killing one's brother in war or trying to be superior to one's neighbor in time of peace. We could dig our gardens; the occupation that seemed to Voltaire's man, after he had surveyed the world, least foolish. We could, according to our abilities, give ourselves to science or art; not to impress somebody, but for love of the beauty that each discloses. We could even be quiet occasionally.

> Better than such discourse doth silence long,
> Long barren silence square with my desire.

We must always be prepared to resist intrusion; we might be quiet in the intervals.

Well: do I really believe that people will be content to take a walk and admire the beauty of things? Certainly not. I am speaking of a racial disease; it was in the monkey blood we derive from, and no doubt it is incurable; but whoever will can minimize it in his own life. Thoreau's life was not a bad one; nor Lao-tsze's. The influential thoughts and books were produced by men meditating alone; and they were not produced in order to be influential, nor "to serve humanity," nor for praise or pay, but because the mind drove. The great work in science was done by men working alone: — Copernicus, Leeuwenhoek, Darwin; Newton and Einstein, in youth, when they did their work. The great theorists of atomic structure worked as individuals; only when their work was to be used for mass murder a tight association became necessary.

To sum up the matter: — "Love one another" is a high commandment, but it polarizes the mind; love on the surface implies hate in the depth, — (Dante who hated well because he loved) — as the history of Christendom bitterly proves. "Love one another" ought to be balanced, at least, by a colder saying, — this too a counsel of perfection, i.e. a direction-giver, a guide though it cannot be a rule, — "Turn away from each other," — to that great presence of which humanity is only a squirming particle. To persons of Christian faith, if any should read this, I would point out that Jesus himself, intuitive master of psychology, invoked this balance. "Love your neighbor as yourself" — that is, not excessively, if you are adult and normal — but "God with all your heart, mind and soul." Turn outward from each other, so far as need and kindness permit, to the vast life and inexhaustible beauty beyond humanity. This is not a slight matter, but an essential condition of freedom, and of moral and vital sanity.

It is understood that this attitude is peculiarly unacceptable at present, being opposed not only by tradition, but by all the currents of the time. We are now completely trapped in the nets of envy, intrigue, corruption, compulsion, eventual murder, that are called international politics. We have always been expansive, predatory and missionary; and we love to lie to ourselves. We have entered the period of civil struggles and emerging Caesarism that binds republics with brittle iron; civilization everywhere is in its age of decline and abnormal violence. Men are going to be frightened and herded, increasingly, into lumps and masses. A frightened man cannot think; and the mass mind does not want truth, — only "democratic" or "Aryan" or "Marxian" or other-colored "truth," — it wants its own voices. However, the truth will not die; and persons who have lost everything, in the culmination of these evils, and stand beyond hope and almost beyond fear, may find it again.

But if in some future civilization the dreams of Utopia should incredibly be realized, and men were actually freed from want and fear, then all the more they would need this sanctuary, against the deadly emptiness and insignificance of their lives, at leisure fully appreciated. Man, much more than baboon or wolf, is an animal formed for conflict; his life seems to him meaningless without it. Only a clear shift of meaning and emphasis, from man to what is not man, nor a man-dreamed God, a projection of man, can enable him in the long run to endure peace.

"But I having told you" — to quote from the tag of an old poem — have once again and beyond obligation "paid my birth-dues."

POETRY, GONGORISM,
AND A THOUSAND YEARS
[1948]

It used to be argued, and I think it is still accepted by many people, that poetry is a flower of racial childhood, and must wither away as civilization advances. For civilization is based on reason and restraint, poetry on imagination and passion; poetry (they say) is dreams, and civilization the daylight that disperses them. This would be an interesting theory if it were true, but there is no truth in it. The greatest Greek poetry, after Homer, was written at the clear and rational summit of Greek civilization, by the Athenian tragic poets in the fifth century B.C.; and then, as civilization declined, Greek poetry declined. It had its revivals, in Sicily, in Alexandria, and these coincided with revivals of civilization. Latin poetry also, though less typical, because the Romans were not originators but cultivators, has a similar history. It flowered at the peak of Roman civilization, in the late republic and early empire, and declined with it. These are but two examples out of many that could be cited, but they are enough to scuttle the supposed rule. They do not reverse it, for actually there is no rule at all; or at least none is discernible. Poetry is less bound by time and circumstance than any other of the arts; it does not need tangible materials; good poetry comes almost directly from a man's mind and senses and blood-stream, and no one can predict the man. It does not need a school nor an immediate tradition; and it does not need, though Whitman said so, "great audiences too." How much of an audience did Keats have in his lifetime?

The present is a time of high civilization rapidly declining; it is not a propitious period for any of the arts; men's minds are a little discouraged, and are too much occupied with meeting each day's distractions or catastrophe. Yet there is no final reason why great poetry should not be written by someone, even to-day. Whether its greatness would be recognized is another question, for greatness is strange, unexpected, and sometimes repellent; but probably it would, in time. What seems to me certain is that this hypothetical great poet would break sharply away from the directions that are fashionable in contemporary poetic literature. He would understand that Rimbaud was a young man of startling genius but not to be imitated; and that *The Waste Land*, though one of the finest poems of this century and surely the most influential, marks the close of a literary dynasty, not the beginning. He would think of Gerard Hopkins as a talented eccentric, whose verse is so overloaded with self-conscious ornament and improbable emotion that it is hardly readable, except by enthusiasts, and certainly not a model to found one's work on, but a shrill note of warning.

Aside from these instances, and to put the matter more fundamentally, I believe that our man would turn away from the self-conscious and naive learnedness, the undergraduate irony, unnatural metaphors, hiatuses and labored obscurity, that are too prevalent in contemporary verse. His poetry would be natural and direct. He would have something new and important to say, and just for that reason he would wish to say it clearly. He would be seeking to express the spirit of his time (as well as all times), but it is not necessary, because an epoch is confused, that its poet should share its confusions. On the contrary, detachment is necessary to understanding. I do not think that Shakespeare mixed Hamlet or Lear into his life, as Byron did Childe Harold; the greater poet saw his creatures objectively, all the way through, but also all the way around; and thus our supposed poet, being distinctly separate from his time, would be able to see it, and to see around it. And I do not think he would give much attention to its merely superficial aspects, the neon lights and tooth-paste advertising of this urban civilization, and the momentary popular imbecilities; these things change every year and presently change out of recognition, but great poetry is pointed at the future. Its author, whether consciously or not, intends to be understood a thousand years from now; therefore he chooses the more permanent aspects of things, and subjects that will remain valid. And therefore he would distrust the fashionable poetic dialect of his time; but the more so if it is studiously quaint and difficult; for if a poem has to be explained and diagrammed even for contemporary readers, what will the future make of it?

There was a seventeenth century Spanish poet named Góngora, a man of remarkable talent, but he invented a strange poetic idiom, a jargon of dislocated constructions and far-fetched metaphors, self-conscious singularity, studious obscurity. It is now only grotesque, but for its moment it was admired in the best circles, and it stimulated many imitators. Then fashion changed, Gongorism was named, and ridiculed, and its poet is now remembered because his name was given to one of the diseases of literature. Euphuism in England had a similar vogue and a similar catastrophe. It seems to me that the more extreme tendencies of modernist verse — and shall I say also of painting and sculpture? — are diseases of like nature, later forms of Gongorism; doctrinaire corruptions of instinct. It is not generally a failure of execution but a collapse of taste — of critical and creative instinct — that brings an art to eclipse. The error in the artist, which perhaps was only momentary and experimental, is echoed with approval by his admirers and a shoal of imitators, so they mislead each other, and gregariousness and snobbery complete the corruption. ("We understand this art, which the ordinary person can only gape at: we are distinguished people.") So the flock gathers sheep. But poetry has never fallen so deep into this bog as painting and sculpture have, and I believe is now pulling out of it. Poetry must use language, which has a resistant vitality of its own; while sculpture (for instance) may sink to fiddling with bits of wire and tin trinkets.

On the other hand, let it be far from me to propose the average educated man as arbiter of poetry or any other art. He has his own perversions of taste or complete nullity, duller than Gongorism. Usually he does not care for poetry — and no harm in that — but alas that he has a deep uneasy respect for it; — he associates it vaguely with "ideals" and a better world, and may quote Longfellow on solemn occasions. This piety without instinct or judgment is a source of boredom, insincerity and false reputations; it is as bad as the delusions of the little groups; it is worse, because more constant. I write verses myself, but I have no sympathy with the notion that the world owes a duty to poetry, or any other art. Poetry is not a civilizer, rather the reverse, for great poetry appeals to the most primitive instincts. It is not necessarily a moralizer; it does not necessarily improve one's character; it does not even teach good manners. It is a beautiful work of nature, like an eagle or a high sunrise. You owe it no duty. If you like it, listen to it; if not, let it alone.

Lately I had occasion to read more attentively the *Medea* of Euripides, and, considering the reverence that cultivated people feel toward Greek tragedy, I was a little shocked by what I read. Tragedy has been regarded, ever since Aristotle, as a moral agent, a purifier of the mind and emotions. But the story of "Medea" is about a criminal adventurer and his gun-moll; it is no more moral than the story of "Frankie and Johnny"; only more ferocious. And so with the yet higher summits of Greek tragedy, the Agamemnon series and the Oedipus Rex; they all tell primitive horror-stories, and the conventional pious sentiments of the chorus are more than balanced by the bad temper and wickedness, or folly, of the principal characters. What makes them noble is the poetry; the poetry, and the beautiful shapes of the plays, and the extreme violence born of extreme passion. That is to say, three times, the poetry: — the poetry of words, the poetry of structure, and the poetry of action. These are stories of disaster and death, and it is not in order to purge the mind of passions, but because death and disaster are exciting. People love disaster, if it does not touch them too nearly — as we run to see a burning house or a motor-crash — and also it gives occasion for passionate speech; it is a vehicle for the poetry.

To return now to the great poet whom we have imagined arising among us at this time. He would certainly avoid the specialists, the Gongorist groups, and he would hardly expect response from the average, the average educated person: then whom should he speak to? For poetry is not a monologue in a vacuum: it is written in solitude, but it needs to have some sort of audience in mind. Well: there has been a great poet in our time, — must I say comparatively great? — an Irishman named Yeats, and he met this problem, but his luck solved it for him. The first half of his life belonged mostly to the specialists, the Celtic Twilight people, the Decadents, even the Gongorists; he was the best among them but not a great poet, and he resented it. He had will and ambition, while Dowson and the others dropped by the wayside. Yeats went home to Ireland and sought in the theater his liberation from mediocrity; and he might possibly have found it there, if he had been as good a playwright as he was a poet. For the theater — unless it is a very little one — cannot belong wholly to a group; it has to be filled if possible; and it does not inevitably belong to the average. When many people together see and hear the thing — if it is fierce enough, and the actors and author can make it beautiful, — it cuts deep. It cuts through many layers. The average person may even forget his education and delight in it, though it is poetry.

But Yeats found in another way his immortality. He was not a first-rate playwright but he had an insuperable will; and when his Ireland changed, he was ready. Suddenly, in that magic time when a country becomes a nation, it was Ireland's good fortune that there was a great poet in Ireland. Her unique need, and his will, had produced him.

But the great poet whom we have imagined would not expect all that luck. He might not have a fighting will, as Yeats did, to push on with time and abide its turnings; or his time might never come. If he should write a great poetic play he would probably never see it staged; for that is a matter of luck, and against the odds. And it is not likely that his country will ever feel the need of a great national poet, as Ireland did; or as Germany did in her stormy awakening, and produced Goethe. Yet our poet must feel (in his own mind I mean) the stimulation of some worthy audience. He will look, of course, to the future. "What do I care about the present," Charles Lamb exclaimed, "I write for antiquity!" But our man will reverse that. It may seem unlikely that he will have readers a thousand years from now, but it is not impossible, if he is really a great poet; and these are the audience whom he will habitually address. If the present time overhears him, and listens too — all the better. But let him not be distracted by the present; his business is with the future. This is not pleasantry; it is practical advice. For thus his work will be sifted of what is transient and crumbling, the chaff of time and the stuff that requires foot-notes. Permanent things, or things forever renewed, like the grass and human passions, are the material for poetry; and whoever speaks across the gap of a thousand years will understand that he has to speak of permanent things, and rather clearly too, or who would hear him?

"But," a young man cries, "what good will it do me to imagine myself remembered after death? If I am to have fame and an audience I want them now, while I can feel them." — It seems to me that the young man speaks in ignorance. To be peered at and interviewed, to be pursued by autograph hunters and inquiring admirers, would surely be a sad nuisance. And it is destructive too, if you take it seriously; it wastes your energy into self-consciousness; it destroys spontaneity and soils the springs of the mind. Whereas posthumous reputation could do you no harm at all, and is really the only kind worth considering.

Unpublished Poems

AESTHETICS

Why will you cry and not be satisfied,
Crying always after impossible hopeless things,
A wonder born with wings, and too high up
For any man's achievement, and too dim
For any beauty? — This at least I know,
That that which is not is not beautiful;
And mystic is another name for fool.

If you would seek for beauty — and what more
Is worth the seeking? — seek it in the flesh.
For there we have seen it and we know it there;
But whether it be otherwhere who knows?
— Nay, ask your father Plato: he is wise,
Doubtless, and doubtless he will answer you.

I have seen a youth's broad shoulder brown with the sun
Tug on the broad sweep of a bending oar;
And that was beauty; while his close-curled head
Drew forward on the strong columnar neck.
I have seen my Elytra rise against the dawn
From the tossed bed as Venus from her waves
Pure in an alabaster nakedness.
She stood and thought me sleeping: I beheld
The lyric curve above those marvellous flanks
More clear than Phidian marble, and the deep

White magic of the moulding of her breasts
Under a shadow unbound of heavy hair.
— Was not that beauty? Is the simple flesh
Not beautiful, not only beautiful?

I at the least want nothing more than that,
No higher beauty than the simple flesh
Loved for its own sake. — Put the trance away
And see and learn by seeing. — Or if yet
Your eyes grown purblind with long abstinence
Cannot endure undazzled the strong light
Of simple carnal human loveliness,
The passion and the fervent purity, —
Why, look to art, and what the painters make
And what the sculptors. Study a little while
The armless Melian Goddess, or that youth
Apollo the destroyer, whose curled lip
Of calm contempt may teach you to see clear.
Or, less than these, but very beautiful,
Behold with open and contented eyes
King Alexander's profile on a coin,
A tetradrachma of Lysimachus.

(1910)

THE PALACE

Let us reenter the ruined palace again.
   Let us clean the weeds from the walls;
And raise up the fallen columns, and roof against rain
   The large and beautiful halls.

This palace was builded of old; it is comely and great;
   No coward nor slave in the world
Had a hand in the work, nor has entered the outermost gate,
   Nor has seen the high banner unfurled.

Is the throne-room spacious and wonderful? Shakespeare made it.
   He adorned it with statues of kings.
And the firm foundation takes root where Wordsworth laid it
   In the permanence of natural things.

The shafts of the columns were carved by no other than Milton,
   Of clear marble from quarries afar;
And golden at top is the tower Shelley fashioned, and built on,
   Spiring its tip to a star.

But smaller men came; and men are so easily tired;
   And great good is so heavy to hold;
And, Well for our fathers, they said; but the good they desired
   Was good in its time, but is old.

Let us go forth from the palace; the stair is too long,
   Too steep; and the courts are too broad;
And our feet grow tired in the hallways, where strengthened with song
   Our fathers of old time trod.

They called in the curlew to cry in the empty rooms;
    The dock and the thistle to dance
In clefts of the wall; they quarried the marble for tombs;
    They despoiled their inheritance.

Is it not better? they said. The wind in the weeds
    Is a better harp than a harp.
And too obvious a beauty is common, and the soul needs
    Savors more strange, more sharp.

We find the great beauty grows wearisome. Also a crowd
    Is gathered to praise it. We get
Small joy out of music too shining and sunlight too loud,
    We lovers of twilight.

                    And yet?

For surely the palace is comely. And marble is polished
    Though covered with moss or with dirt,
And life — has that died? Or the beauty of life been abolished?
    Or the girdle of Orion been ungirt?

We have lived in the palace and loved it. We love not in vain.
    Let us stand on the strength of the walls
To make firm the fine shafts of the columns and roof against rain
    The large and beautiful halls.
                (MAY 22, 1914)

MAY 5, 1915
To U.J.

To-day a year ago you went
Into the tangible shadow of death;
And though upon your flamelike breath
He had no power, yet suffering did.
I waited on the steep descent
Like one cast off, useless, forbid,
Incapable of even prayer,
That visionary opiate lent
To other men in like despair.

Death could not touch you; anguish could.
But O much crueller anguish yet
To come! For death laid desolate
That late-born loveliness your pain
Should have redeemed; your motherhood
Was violated and made vain.
I was so glad at having you
Back from that fearful solitude
I grieved not then as now I do.

Our little daughter would have been
Perhaps beyond humanity
Divinely beautiful and free,
Being yours. I know not: but I know
A region stormless, all-serene,
Far from this dark, beholds her so.
We need not follow the vain road
Of creeds that men walk lampless in
To her imperishable abode.

My dearest, over the small urn
That holds but ashes and our loss
We, reaching hands and loves across,
More intimately now renew
The tears we have wept, the vow we have sworn.
We need no comfort, I and you.
We gazing earnestly ahead
Behold the dawning of that morn
Whose star is our most holy dead.

OBLATION

No. If that youth were dead would I feel deeply?
Because with youth well lost there's room to live.
The days shall not be sold as of old cheaply.
Daughter of God I will not sell but give.
I will not sell for wine nor any woman
My nature now it's sacred in your keeping,
A gift, a soiled vain gift and very human,
Of base esteem and stained with wine and weeping.
Not stained with blood yet though a little in honor,
Not blindfolded you see though often blind;
You dearest count the gift clean and the donor
Guiltless toward you, poor sinner of Christ, and find
Some fountains of vexed blood yet faithful there
To flush your triumph or flow in your despair.

TESTAMENT

Youth dead and wasted does one still love deeply?
Because once youth's well lost there's room to live.
The years shall not be sold as of old cheaply,
Spirit of God I will not sell but give.
Not sell for wine nor future wars nor woman
My nature now it's sacred in your keeping,
A gift, a soiled vain gift and very human,
Of base esteem, stained through with wine and weeping.
Not stained with blood yet though a little in honor,
Not blindfolded you see though often blind;
You dearest call the gift clean, find the donor
Guiltless toward you, this fault of God. The rind
Nibbled by living and guilt, the good fruit's yours,
The bitter core you'll give the earth-grubbing wars.

THE SHORE OF DREAMS

This is a strange shore, and misty with many dreams of beauty and of
    wonder;
The great gray wind that comes out of the west brings them in flocks: he
    is the shepherd of them all.
They wander over the wide wild waste of the worn waters; and in the
    muffled thunder
Of the mounting surf, and in the mist, they call.

They call and they sing; and even the fire of noon-day is not fierce enough
    to melt them.
For even at noon, in the shadows under the hills, and in the shadows
    under the sea,
They call and they sing, with beautiful beckonings: do I not know it who
    have felt them,
Heard them, seen them, gathered them to me?

Ah — they are very lovely here! I think that under the evening star the
    sparkles of the dew are
Their raiment; and faint fair mists are their white feet; and their souls are
    the evening star's most delicate fire.
But even here I am lonely for you — crying for you — there is none of the
    dreams so beautiful as you are,
O flame-white bird, Una, little bird of my desire!

THE HILLS BEYOND THE RIVER

Coast-range creeks, veins of the body of mine that will not die
When this spirit is nothing and this flesh new dirt and the eager eye
Sucked its last and is drunk with darkness — I am content I think to cease,
I rejoice no death will drag you peaks and slopes down to that peace.
Neither failure of the blood will make you faint nor its fevers choke,
Canyon creeks that are my arteries, hair of forest and body of rock.
If long hence and after a thousand long millenniums you go down
I will go, the last of me then, and the endless dance of suns go on.
Therefore I turned from the high lamps and limited to low hills my love.
Sweet you are immortality enough, identity enough.
..... As while life lasts I am content with the stone belts of my own
    house,
Windows opening west over salt water and south to the coast-range
    brows,
Walls on a rock above the sea, and granite ecstasy kept clean
By its very narrowness from much that troubles luckier men.

DOORS TO PEACE

Sphere beyond sphere
Of blazing crystal . . . .
I see the half moon rise at midday
Over the rocks in the air's clearness.
The spirit of the moon with blazing wings,
The arms uplifted, the eyes in ecstasy,
Stands on that crystal round, as the others
On the pale hills . . . and the ocean
Rounds like a dew-drop, the huge dome
Hangs inconceivably above,
The spirit spiring from it,
The arms uplifted, the eyes in ecstasy,
And though the sun's not to be borne
I see the spirit of the sun standing
On the unendurable dome of crystal,
Not looking down at his adorers,
The arms uplifted, the eyes in ecstasy
. . . Toward whom? Sphere beyond sphere,
Dome above dome the stars
Tower with winged figures
And the eyes of ecstasy . . .

I think they admire the silence
Outside the stars, what should light love
But that which having in itself
Enough, needs not to shine nor move?
Love, motion, light, and change, imply
Inward insufficiency;

God's other shore knows none; they die
And all the suns will die to see.

I think ... I think says the brain ...
But the little spire with the eyes of ecstasy
On the brain's dome is the life,
Not thinking anything,
But flaming ... little fool you will cease
Flaming when you flame up to peace.

FORECAST

Whose life is like a tree's or more like a stone's
Must not make haste; there are decades yet in the pitcher.
I shall be thirty-nine next month, and live yet
Ten years to fifty, and on that peak perhaps
Be ready to write the poem to be remembered.
Who flames in season has a better flaming
No doubt, hardly a luckier; it is sad to look back
On the ashes of fire; who's done nothing in season
May come to an edge when the half century's counted
And frost in the brown hair.

                    Mere attempts meanwhile,
Experiments: nor by sports of casual praise
Ever be drawn to try the same theme twice.

NOT A LAUREL ON THE PLACE

Did I ever desire what they call recognition? But, having it,
Now I want fame: fame's coinable: fame coined,
To ring the place with a ten-foot wall, splintered glass on top,
And keep a man at the gate to meet visitors,
Saying "Jeffers is not at home. Jeffers has gone to Lhasa.
Jeffers is buying camels in Urga.
He hopes to meet the living Buddha in the Gobi Desert. No, sir, he
  cannot
Answer letters, he has writer's cramp" —
Whilst I walk here at peace under my planted trees, not a laurel on the
  place.

NINTH ANNIVERSARY

Only a fortnight out of nine years has found me afield
From the ocean-cliff where I perched my house,
And long before that I lived in hearing of the long voice
And thunder of the shore: yet to this hour
I never look west but shaken with a joyful shock of astonishment,
By dark nor by day: there the most glorious
Creature on earth shines in the nights or glitters in the suns,
Or feels of its stone in the blind fog,
Or shakes its hair in the storms: I never wake in my bed
But surprised with pleasure to hear it speaking.
An east wind brings me the smell of the river, all the others carry
The sea-fragrances, the salt and the sea-wings.
— What, did my blood before me live inland always? — Admire
One's next neighbor after nine years?

OCT. 27 Lunar Eclipse–98%   (On the Calendar)

The moon went naked to-night, she thought she was hid
In the earth shadow,
Shy and so trustful
She drew off the shining veil, slowly, slowly,
From the dove breasts
To the white feet,
All her pearly body
(There was light enough)
Breathing and bare
Stood undefended,
One saw again how much more beautiful is beauty
When the jewels and shining
Clothes are laid down.

TRAGEDY HAS OBLIGATIONS

If you had thrown a little more boldly in the flood of fortune
You'd have had England; or in the slackening
Less boldly, you'd not have sunk your right hand in Russia: these
Are the two ghosts; they stand by the bed
And make a man tear his flesh. The rest is fatal; each day
A new disaster, and at last Vae Victis.
It means Weh den Gesiegten. This is the essence of tragedy,
To have meant well and made woe, and watch Fate
All stone, approach.

                      But tragedy has obligations. A choice
Comes to each man when his days darken:
To be tragic or to be pitiful. You must do nothing pitiful.
Suicide, which no doubt you contemplate,
Is not enough; suicide is for bankrupt shopkeepers.
You should be Samson, blind Samson, crushing
All his foes, that's Europe, America, half Asia, in his fall.
But you are not able; and the tale is Hebrew.

I have seen a wing-broken hawk, standing in her own dirt,
Helpless: a caged captive, with cold
Indomitable eyes and disdain meet death. There was nothing pitiful,
No degradation, but eternal defiance.
Or a sheepfold harrier, a grim, gray wolf, hunted all day,
Wounded, struck down at the turn of twilight,
How grandly he dies. The pack whines in a ring and not closes,
The head lifts, the great fangs grin, the hunters
Admire their victim. That is how you should end — for they prophesied
You would die like a dog — like a wolf, war-loser.

                      (JUNE '43.)

RHYTHM AND RHYME

The tide-flow of passionate speech, breath, blood-pulse, the sea's waves
   and time's return,
They make the metre; but rhyme seems a child's game.
Let the low-Latin languages, the lines lacking strong accents, lean on it;
Our north-sea English needs no such ornament.
Born free, and searaid-fed from far shores, why should it taggle its head
With tinkling sheep-bells, like Rome's slaves' daughters?

INDEX OF TITLES

Advice to Pilgrims   579

Aesthetics   731

All the Little Hoof-Prints   524

Animals   651

Answer, The   522

Apology for Bad Dreams   141

Artist, An   168

At the Birth of an Age (vision of
the self-hanged God)   506

Autumn Evening   110

Beaks of Eagles, The   523

Beauty of Things, The   652

Bed by the Window, The   376

Birds   103

Birds and Fishes   687

Birth-Dues   159

Bixby's Landing   167

Blood-Guilt, The   582

Bloody Sire, The   563

Boats in a Fog   105

Broadstone, The   365

Broken Balance, The   160

Calm and Full the Ocean   581

Carmel Point   676

Cassandra   579

Cawdor   182

Clouds at Evening   139

Come Little Birds   554

Contemplation of the Sword   527

Continent's End   24

Credo   147

Cruel Falcon, The   501

Cycle, The   22

Day Is a Poem, The   562

Deer Lay Down Their Bones,
The   680

De Rerum Virtute   677

Descent to the Dead   361

Distant Rainfall   501

Divinely Superfluous Beauty   17

Doors to Peace   740

Drunken Charlie   568

Epic Stars, The   699

Evening Ebb   298

Excesses of God, The   17

Faith   553

Fire on the Hills   394

Flight of Swans   505

Fog   104

Forecast   742

Foreword, *The Selected Poetry of
Robinson Jeffers*   713

For Una   565

Gale in April   99

Ghosts in England   370
Give Your Heart to the
   Hawks   400
"Goethe, they say, was a great
   poet"   700
Granddaughter   698
Gray Weather   508
Hand   701
Hands   298
Hills Beyond the River, The   739
Historical Choice   580
Hooded Night   297
House-Dog's Grave, The   559
Hungerfield   653
Hurt Hawks   165
Inhumanist, The (Part II of *The
   Double Axe*)   582
Inquisitors, The   589
Inscription for a Gravestone   372
In the Hill at Newgrange   366
Introduction, *Roan Stallion, Tamar and
   Other Poems*   710
Invasion   583
"It nearly cancels my fear of
   death"   704
Joy   110
Let Them Alone   688
Little Scraping, A   397
Love-Children   145
Love the Wild Swan   500
Loving Shepherdess, The   299
Machine, The   171

Margrave   382
May 5, 1915   735
Meditation on Saviors   172
Memoir   518
Natural Music   19
New Mexican Mountain   380
Night   107
Night Without Sleep   541
Ninth Anniversary   744
Not a Laurel on the Place   743
Notes to "Descent to the
   Dead"   375
Nova   520
November Surf   381
Now Returned Home   545
Oblation   737
Ocean's Tribute, The   694
Oct. 27 Lunar Eclipse — 98% (On
   the Calendar)   745
October Week-End   531
Oh Lovely Rock   529
On an Anthology of Chinese
   Poems   695
Orca   587
Original Sin   585
Ossian's Grave   362
Oysters   702
Palace, The   733
Patronymic   686
Pearl Harbor   577
Pelicans   140
People and a Heron   106

Phenomena   111
Place for No Story, The   379
Poetry, Gongorism, and a Thousand
    Years   723
Point Joe   98
Post Mortem   137
Preface, *The Double Axe and Other
    Poems*   719
Preface, *Tamar*   707
Prelude   148
Prescription of Painful Ends   561
Purse-Seine, The   514
Quia Absurdum   591
Rearmament   513
Redeemer, A   178
Red Mountain   509
Return   499
Rhythm and Rhyme   747
Roan Stallion   115
Rock and Hawk   502
Salmon Fishing   19
Self-Criticism in February   543
Shane O'Neill's Cairn   361
Shears, The   685
Shine, Perishing Republic   23
Shine, Republic   503
Shiva   544
Shore of Dreams, The   738

Sign-Post   504
Stars Go Over the Lonely Ocean,
    The   564
Steelhead, Wild Pig, the
    Fungus   532
Still the Mind Smiles   399
Subjected Earth   373
Suicide's Stone   16
Tamar   26
Testament   737
Theory of Truth   547
"The unformed volcanic
    earth"   689
To His Father   15
Tor House   181
To the House   18
To the Rock That Will Be a
    Cornerstone of the House   21
To the Stone-Cutters   18
Tower Beyond Tragedy, The (final
    scene)   112
Tragedy Has Obligations   746
Treasure, The   100
Triad   398
Vulture   697
Wind-Struck Music, The   516
Winged Rock   376
Wise Men in Their Bad Hours   20

INDEX OF FIRST LINES

A desert of weed and water-darkened stone under my western windows
106

A great dawn-color rose widening the petals around her gold eye   685

A little too abstract, a little too wise,   499

And here's a portrait of my granddaughter Una   698

An eagle's nest on the head of an old redwood on one of the precipice-
footed ridges   523

A night the half-moon was like a dancing-girl,   26

An old man with a double-bit axe   582

Ants, or wise bees, or a gang of wolves,   553

At dawn a knot of sea-lions lies off the shore   651

At East Lulworth the dead were friendly and pitiful, I saw them peek from
their ancient earth-works on the coast hills   370

At night, toward dawn, all the lights of the shore have died,   297

At the equinox when the earth was veiled in a late rain, wreathed with wet
poppies, waiting spring,   24

Beautiful the hanging cliff and the wind-thrown cedars, but they have no
weight.   695

Beyond the narrows of the Inner Hebrides   545

Beyond the Sierras, and sage-brush Nevada ranges, and vast   509

Calm and full the ocean under the cool dark sky; quiet rocks and the birds
fishing; the night-herons   581

Christ was your lord and captain all your life,   15

Civilized, crying how to be human again: this will tell you how.   504

Coast-range creeks, veins of the body of mine that will not die   739

Coming around a corner of the dark trail ... what was wrong with the
valley?   589

Contemplation would make a good life, keep it strict, only   501

Did I ever desire what they call recognition? But, having it,   743

Ed Stiles and old Tom Birnam went up to their cattle on the bare hills   516

Enormous cloud-mountains that form over Point Lobos and into the sunset,   139

Europe has run its course, and whether to fall by its own sickness or ours is not   583

Every October millions of little fish come along the shore,   687

Fallen in between the tendons and bones   701

Farther up the gorge the sea's voice fainted and ceased.   524

Four pelicans went over the house,   140

Goethe, they say, was a great poet, Pindar, perhaps, was a great poet, Shakespeare and Sophocles   700

Great-enough both accepts and subdues; the great frame takes all creatures;   III

Guard yourself from the terrible empty light of space, the bottomless   591

Happy people die whole, they are all dissolved in a moment, they have had what they wanted,   137

Here are the fireworks. The men who conspired and labored   577

Here is a symbol in which   502

Here is the skull of a man: a man's thoughts and emotions   677

I am dancing on the silver beach,   568

I am heaping the bones of the old mother   18

I am not dead, I have only become inhuman: 372

I built her a tower when I was young —   565

I chose the bed down-stairs by the sea-window for a good death-bed   376

I drew solitude over me, on the lone shore,   148

I followed the narrow cliffside trail half way up the mountain   680

If God has been good enough to give you a poet   688

If time is only another dimension, then all that dies   653

If you had thrown a little more boldly in the flood of fortune   746

If you should look for this place after a handful of lifetimes: 181
I had walked since dawn and lay down to rest on a bare hillside   697
"I hate my verses, every line, every word.   500
I left the madness of the house,   112
In nineteen-nine a fire swept our coast hills,   182
Inside a cave in a narrow canyon near Tassajara   298
Intense and terrible beauty, how has our race with the frail naked nerves,
   99
In the purple light, heavy with redwood, the slopes drop seaward,   141
Invisible gulls with human voices cry in the sea-cloud   104
I paid the woman what she asked and followed her down to the water-side,
   and her two sons   554
I saw the laboratory animals: throat-bandaged dogs cowering in cages, still
   obsessed with the pitiful   518
Is it not by his high superfluousness we know   17
I stand near Soberanes Creek, on the knoll over the sea, west of the road. I
   remember   547
It is autumn still, but at three in the morning   531
It is not bad. Let them play.   563
It is true that, older than man and ages to outlast him, the Pacific surf   508
It nearly cancels my fear of death, my dearest said,   704
It seems hardly necessary to stipulate that the elegiac tone   375
It used to be argued, and I think it is still accepted by many people, that
   723
I've changed my ways a little: I cannot now   559
I watch the Indians dancing to help the young corn at Taos pueblo. The
   old men squat in a ring   380
Joy is a trick in the air; pleasure is merely contemptible, the dangled   159
Let us reenter the ruined palace again.   733
Like mourning women veiled to the feet   501
Lucretius felt the change of the world in his time, the great republic riding
   to the height   561

Mountains, a moment's earth-waves rising and hollowing; the earth too's an
    ephemerid; the stars —   100
My friend from Asia has powers and magic, he plucks a blue leaf from the
    young blue-gum   147
My publisher wrote that if I wanted to revise anything, here was my   710
No. If that youth were dead would I feel deeply?   737
Old garden of grayish and ochre lichen,   21
One who sees giant Orion, the torches of winter midnight,   505
Only a fortnight out of nine years has found me afield   744
On the small marble-paved platform   382
On the wide Texan and New Mexican ranches   702
Our sardine fishermen work at night in the dark of the moon; daylight or
    moonlight   514
Pain and their endless cries. How they cry to me: but they are I: let them
    ask themselves.   506
Peace is the heir of dead desire,   16
Poetry has been regarded as a refuge from life, where dreams may heal
    707
Point Joe has teeth and has torn ships; it has fierce and solitary beauty;   98
Reason will not decide at last; the sword will decide.   527
Science, that makes wheels turn, cities grow,   398
Sea-lions loafed in the swinging tide in the inlet, long fluent creatures   587
So long having foreseen these convulsions, forecast the hemorrhagic   582
Some lucky day each November great waves awake and are drawn   381
Sphere beyond sphere   740
Sports and gallantries, the stage, the arts, the antics of dancers,   105
Still the mind smiles at its own rebellions,   399
Steep up in Lubitavish townland stands   362
Stone-cutters fighting time with marble, you foredefeated   18
Strong enough to be neutral — as is now proved, now American power   580
That Nova was a moderate star like our good sun; it stored no doubt a little
    more than it spent   520

That our senses lie and our minds trick us is true, but in general   579
That sculptor we knew, the passionate-eyed son of a quarryman,   168
The apples hung until a wind at the equinox,   400
The bay is not blue but sombre yellow   543
The broken pillar of the wing jags from the clotted shoulder,   165
The clapping blackness of the wings of pointed cormorants, the great
    indolent planes   22
The coast hills at Sovranes Creek;   379
The days shorten, the south blows wide for showers now,   19
The deer were bounding like blown leaves   394
The dog barked; then the woman stood in the doorway, and hearing iron
    strike stone down the steep road   115
The ebb slips from the rock, the sunken   107
The extraordinary patience of things!   676
The fierce musical cries of a couple of sparrowhawks hunting on the
    headland,   103
The first part of "The Double Axe" was written during the war, and   719
The flesh of the house is heavy sea-orphaned stone, the imagination of the
    house   376
The heroic stars spending themselves,   699
The little biplane that has the river-meadow for landing-field   171
The little one-room schoolhouse among the redwoods   299
The mad girl with the staring eyes and long white fingers   579
The man-brained and man-handed ground-ape, physically   585
The mathematicians and physics men   696
The moon went naked to-night, she thought she was hid   745
Then what is the answer? — Not to be deluded by dreams.   522
The ocean has not been so quiet for a long while; five night-herons   298
The old voice of the ocean, the bird-chatter of little rivers,   19
The people buying and selling, consuming pleasures, talking in the
    archways,   160

The quality of these trees, green height; of the sky, shining; of water, a clear
    flow; of the rock, hardness   503
There is a hawk that is picking the birds out of our sky.   544
The road had steepened and the sun sharpened on the high ridges; the
    stream probably was dry,   178
These grand and fatal movements toward death: the grandeur of the mass
    513
The sky was cold December blue with great tumbling clouds, and the little
    river   532
The storm-dances of gulls, the barking game of seals,   17
The tide-flow of passionate speech, breath, blood-pulse, the sea's waves and
    time's return,   747
The trail's high up on the ridge, no one goes down   145
The unformed volcanic earth, a female thing,   689
The world's as the world is; the nations rearm and prepare to change; the
    age of tyrants returns;   541
They burned lime on the hill and dropped it down here in an iron car   167
This book presents in one volume about half of my published work. In
    713
This is a strange shore, and misty with many dreams of beauty and of
    wonder;   738
This morning Hitler spoke in Danzig, we heard his voice.   562
Though joy is better than sorrow joy is not great;   110
Though the little clouds ran southward still, the quiet autumnal   110
To-day a year ago you went   735
To feel and speak the astonishing beauty of things — earth, stone and water,
    652
True, the time, to one who does not love farce,   397
Unhappy about some far off things   564
Walking in the flat Oxfordshire fields   373
We climbed by the old quarries to the wide highland of heath,   365

We stayed the night in the pathless gorge of Ventana Creek, up the east
  fork.   529
What ancestor of mine in wet Wales or wild Scotland   686
When I considered it too closely, when I wore it like an element and smelt
  it like water,   172
When you and I on the Palos Verdes cliff   361
While this America settles in the mould of its vulgarity, heavily thickening
  to empire,   23
"Who is it beside me, who is here beside me, in the hollow hill?"   366
Whose life is like a tree's or more like a stone's   742
Why will you cry and not be satisfied,   731
Wise men in their bad hours have envied   20
Yesterday's sundown was very beautiful — I know it is out of fashion to say
  so, I think we are fools   694
Youth dead and wasted does one still love deeply?   737